The development of the vertebrate limb

Frontispiece
  Two of the greatest adaptive triumphs of the pentadactyl limb: (a) flight in birds and (b) the horse at speed. ((a) Courtesy of B. L. Sage, Ardea, London; (b) courtesy of R. Moore.)

THE DEVELOPMENT OF THE VERTEBRATE LIMB

An approach through experiment, genetics, and evolution

J. R. HINCHLIFFE
and
D. R. JOHNSON

CLARENDON PRESS · OXFORD
1980

Oxford University Press, Walton Street, Oxford OX2 6DP

OXFORD LONDON GLASGOW
NEW YORK TORONTO MELBOURNE WELLINGTON
KUALA LUMPUR SINGAPORE JAKARTA HONG KONG TOKYO
DELHI BOMBAY CALCUTTA MADRAS KARACHI
NAIROBI DAR ES SALAAM CAPE TOWN

© J. R. Hinchliffe and D. R. Johnson 1980

Published in the United States by Oxford University Press, New York

British Library Cataloguing in Publication Data

Hinchliffe, J R
    The development of the vertebrate limb.
    1. Embryology — Vertebrates
    2. Extremities (Anatomy)
    I. Title   II. Johnson, D R
    596'.03'3   QL959   79-41387
    ISBN 0-19-857552-1

*Typeset by Hope Services, Abingdon
Printed in Great Britain by
Morrison & Gibb, Edinburgh*

What can be more curious than that
the hand of a man, formed for grasping,
that of a mole for digging, the leg of a
horse, the paddle of the porpoise, and
the wing of the bat should all be
constructed on the same pattern and
should include similar bones, and in
the same relative positions?

Charles Darwin
On the Origin of Species

Preface

Analysis of limb morphogenesis has today come to play a central part in the study of developmental biology. While there are excellent reviews which examine this topic from various standpoints, there is no one book which attempts to survey all the varied aspects — topographical, experimental, pattern, genetic and evolutionary. A reference book which is also an account of the current 'state of the art' is clearly needed. We have attempted to provide it.

The first two chapters sketch the origin and evolution of the limb and its adaptive radiation within the vertebrates. Experimental workers on the chick wing are perhaps inclined to forget, as they put forward unified models of vertebrate-limb development, how specialized is the system they study. Chapter 3 covers the descriptive embryology of the limb, while Chapter 4 describes its experimental analysis, and is dominated by consideration of ectoderm–mesoderm interaction. In Chapter 5 we consider amphibian-limb regeneration: a topic not only of great practical interest to mammals such as ourselves who have lost this power, but one which also raises fundamental questions about the stability of the differentiated state. Chapter 6 considers the genesis of pattern and current explanations in terms of 'standing wave' hypotheses or of the fashionable 'positional information' models. We conclude with a consideration of the evidence provided by mutations of genetic control of pattern, and whether this explains at a developmental level the diversity of the vertebrate limb. Thus we return to the evolutionary issues with which we started.

Our book reflects the two main phases of experimental analysis of the limb. The first phase was initiated by Zwilling's analysis in the 1950s of ectoderm-mesoderm interaction. This interpretation, and in particular its emphasis on the role of the apical ectodermal ridge in inducing outgrowth, is today widely accepted. The second and contemporary phase emphasizes the importance of cell lines and pattern. Chick-limb-bud mesenchyme was for long believed to be homogeneous and of somatopleural origin, but Christ's recent work demonstrates that — at least in chimaeras — the limb muscle is of somitic origin. The generation of pattern in the limb has aroused particular attention, since the discovery by Saunders that the posterior 'zone of polarizing activity' (ZPA) is able to initiate an antero-posterior axis in experimental limb duplication. But the idea that the ZPA controls the normal axis is still controversial, since its properties are apparently widespread in mesenchyme outside the limb bud, and since some claim that normal limb development will still take place after its removal. Sophisticated mathematical models present the ZPA as a morphogen source, but, alas, the physical morphogen still eludes us, its metaphysical powers appearing to some eyes as extensive as were once those of the elusive Galenic spirits. Equally, we may be on the brink of a major advance in understanding pattern generation.

It is this hope which has placed the ZPA at the centre of current debate on the generation of developmental patterns.

We are grateful for the helpful discussions of several of these topics we have had with our friends, and especially with Madeleine Gumpel, Martin Hicks, Tim Horder, Oliver Flint, and Peter Thorogood. We also thank Drs D. S. Dawd, Paul Goetinck, Juan Hurlé, J. M. Slack, and Cheryl Tickle for kindly providing photographs, Dr Iolo ap Gwynn for greatly assisting one of us (JRH) with the SEM, the University of Leeds for financial assistance with the frontispiece, and Celia Peters and Susan Gwynne for their cheerful typing of the many drafts of the book.

Aberystwyth and Leeds   J.R.H.
July 1979   D.R.J.

Contents

List of plates

1 The origins of the vertebrate limb or how the tetrapods got their legs

1.1. Introduction

The limbs of vertebrates provide one of the best examples of the relationships between form and function in nature. At first glance there is little resemblance between the leg of a horse and the wing of a bat, or between the massive pillars which support an elephant and the slender limbs of a shrew. But closer investigation reveals that these structures, in fact, have remarkable similarities. We believe that these similarities arise from the possession of a common ancestor, because the number of main elements in each of these limbs is the same, as is their arrangement (Fig. 1.1).

Overlying this basic similarity is another layer of sameness: limbs which have evolved from the need to fulfil a similar role resemble each other closely. For example, terrestrial vertebrates have secondarily taken to the water on a large number of occasions and, on each occasion, a terrestrial limb has been modified into a paddle. Because the structure of the paddle is governed by its efficiency, and because the shape of an efficient paddle is fairly circumscribed, paddle-like limbs tend to resemble each other closely. The same logic governs limbs adapted for other purposes: for running, jumping, flying, or weight-bearing.

Most vertebrates possess, or have possessed, four limbs. The skeleton within these limbs, the muscles which operate them, and the nerves which control the muscles always show basic similarities. Before we consider functional modifications, we must ask ourselves: why four limbs, and how did the basic pattern of skeletal and muscular elements come into existence?

The four limbs possessed by most land vertebrates correspond well to two pairs of fins possessed by most fishes, and it seems certain that the ancestors of the first terrestrial vertebrates were fishes of some kind. We must, therefore, extend our horizons even further and look for the ancestors of fishes. To find these ancestors, we must leave the vertebrates altogether and look at some near-vertebrate relatives.

1.2. Vertebrate ancestors

Although the vertebrates are a widespread and important group of animals, they do not by themselves constitute a major division or phylum of the animal kingdom: in fact, they are a sub-phylum of the phylum Chordata, which also includes two other sub-phyla: the Cephalochordata and the Tunicata. Features which are common to two or more of these sub-phyla may well be ancestral, and from such similarities we may be able to make informed guesses about the vertebrate ancestor.

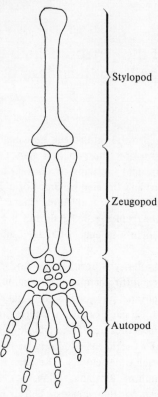

FIG. 1.1. Basic configuration of the vertebrate limb. Limbs may be divided into a proximal segment or stylopod (one bone, humerus in the forelimb, femur in the hind), followed by one containing two bones, the zeugopod (radius and ulna or tibia and fibula), then a complex of small elements, the autopod = carpus or wrist, tarsus or ankle, and a series of up to 5 digits (fingers, toes).

Adult cephalochordates are small (5–100 mm), fish-like, marine organisms. Probably the best known is *Branchiostoma lanceolatum,* the Amphioxus (Fig. 1.2). They are poor swimmers and spend most of their life buried in mud or sand with only their anterior ends exposed. They lack paired fins, but have a dorsal fin supported by cartilage-like material, paired ventro-lateral folds of skin (metapleural folds) (Fig. 1.2(b)) and a fish-like tail fin. Body musculature consists of a segmentally arranged series of myotomes, <-shaped blocks whose apices are directed anteriorly. Alternate contraction of these myotomes throws the body into S-shaped curves and produces a swimming motion. The paired gills have a rather different function to that seen in vertebrates: respiration is mainly through the one-cell-thick skin of the body surface, and the gills are a mechanism of food capture.

Amphioxus is clearly a chordate and also has many vertebrate-like features,

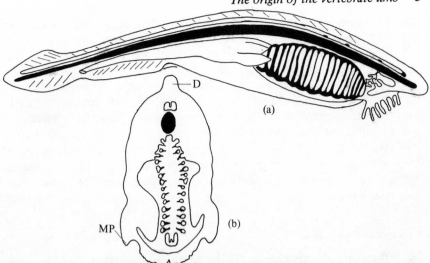

FIG. 1.2. The Amphioxus (*Branchiostoma lanceolatum*), a cephalochordate thought to resemble the hypothetical vertebrate ancestor. Note in transverse section (b) the dorsal (D) and metapleural (MP) fin folds.

but the exact relationship of the cephalochordates and vertebrates is contentious. The majority of investigations suggest that vertebrates arose from an ancestor similar to the cephalochordates, a minority that the cephalochordates represent 'degenerate' vertebrates. We can easily imagine an Amphioxus-like ancestor with the potential for vertebrate evolution. Our special interest lies in the presence of segmented musculature for swimming and in the presence of ventro-lateral metapleural folds.

The second division of the non-vertebrate chordates, the Tunicata, looks at first sight to be very unvertebrate-like. They comprise solitary or colonial animals with a wide variety of shapes, sizes, colony structure and life histories. They range from solitary sessile or free-floating individuals to large sedentary colonies enclosed in a common tunic. Despite this variety of form, they have a series of features in common, which, once again, places them firmly within the Chordata.

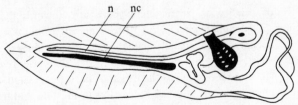

FIG. 1.3. Free-swimming larva of a tunicate. n = nerve cord, nc = notochord.

The sessile adult form, like Amphioxus, is a filter feeder, but the real resemblance between the tunicates and other chordates is best seen in the free-swimming larval form (Fig. 1.3). This has a muscular tail, a hollow dorsal nerve cord, which widens into a brain-like vesicle anteriorly, and a notochord. The tail is used as a propulsive organ, dispersing the larvae before they settle down on the sea bed and metamorphose into adult form. During this metamorphosis, the tail is resorbed, the 'brain' vesicle becomes reduced, and the associated sensory apparatus appears to be lost completely.

The Tunicata can be split into three groups, in which the relative importance of the larval form varies greatly. In the Thaliacea (where adults are usually barrel-shaped and free-swimming) the larva may or may not be present; the Ascidiacea have a motile larval form and a sessile adult, while in the Larvacea the original larval stage seems to have become able to reproduce, and metamorphosis into a sessile adult form does not take place. Such a process of a larval form acquiring potential for sexual reproduction (neoteny) could have given rise to our vertebrate ancestor.

1.3. Jawless vertebrates

The first recognizable vertebrates, the jawless Agnatha, are Ordovician–Devonian (480–350 million years ago) fossils, known as ostracoderms: a few related forms, the lampreys and hagfish, have survived to modern times.

Superficially, ostracoderms (Fig. 1.4) are unlike lampreys and hagfish, but morphological similarities suggest that they are closely related. The ostracoderms appear to be descendants of a stock which must have been close to the stem vertebrates, although much variation in body shape and habit is already present.

Modern Agnatha (Fig. 1.5) are specialists: the petromyzontoids or lampreys are small to moderately large eel-like fish and active predators. The myxinoids or hagfish are marine scavengers burrowing into the flesh of dead or dying fish. Both forms have paired gill openings, but lack paired fins. The marine hagfish lay eggs, which develop into miniature adults, but, interestingly, the freshwater lamprey's eggs hatch into a larval form, often known as an ammocoete, which is filter-feeding, remains embedded in the mud and gravel of stream beds for several years, and is, therefore, in many ways similar to Amphioxus.

1.4. Jawed vertebrates

At the height of the jawless ostracoderm radiation, towards the end of the Silurian period (370 million years ago) further groups of rather peculiar fish fossils start to appear. These are all characterized by the presence of bone in their skeletal system, some form of paired fins and by the presence of jaws. This is not the place to consider in detail the origin of jaws, but it should be appreciated that their presence allowed greater variation in lifestyle and the possibility of greater efficiency and increase in size. Thus, amongst these rather specialized jawed fishes are to be found highly mobile predators of shark-like form (but un-shark-like anatomy) and flattened bottom-dwelling species, with a size range of a few centimetres to over 9 metres in length.

Amongst this rather heterogeneous collection of jawed fishes is one particularly

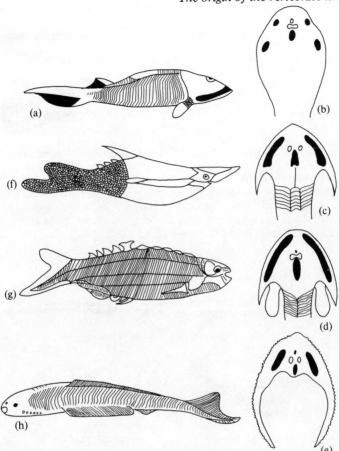

FIG. 1.4. Representatives of the four known orders of jawless fossil ostracoderms. The Osteostraci (*Cephalaspis* (a)) were small with a solid bone head shield variously shaped (b–e), often with evidence of scale-covered flaps equivalent to pectoral fins. The Heterostraci (*Pteraspis* (f)) also had a head shield which lacked bone cells and resembles fragments of even older bony plates from the Ordovician. The Anaspida (*Birkenia* (g)) were armoured by a series of small plates: the tail tilts down – a feature found elsewhere only in the larva of Amphioxus. The Coelolepida (*Jamoytius* (h)) are poorly known.

interesting group, the acanthodians or spiny sharks (so called because of their general resemblance to true sharks, rather than because of any close relationship), which clearly show a series of paired lateral appendages. In more recent fishes these appendages, unless secondarily lost or modified, consist of two pairs of fins, the pectorals in the 'shoulder' region and the pelvics just anterior to the anus: usually, the pectorals are the more prominent of the two. In the acanthodians, however, this uniformity has not been reached. The number of pairs of fins and their structure is variable and clearly experimental (Figs 1.6 and 1.9(b)).

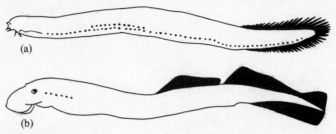

FIG. 1.5. Modern jawless vertebrates. The hagfishes (*Bdellostoma* (a)) are marine scavengers, burrowing into the flesh of dead or moribund fishes. The adult lamprey (*Petromyzon* (b)) has a rounded sucker with which it attaches to fishes upon which it preys, removing flesh with its rasping tongue. Both types lack bone, jaws and paired fins. The marine lamprey has a fresh-water larval stage: the ammocoete larva, which is a filter feeder lying buried in the gravel of brooks and streams, very reminiscent of Amphioxus.

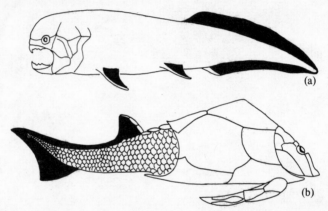

FIG. 1.6. The first jawed fishes contained the acanthodians (*Dinichthys* (a)) with paired fins based upon a dermal spine and membrane, and the antiarchs (*Pterichthyodes* (b)) which had freely movable appendages in the shoulder region with both proximal internal skeletal elements and an exoskeleton reminding one of the jointed arthropod limb. ((b) after Parker and Haswell 1940.)

1.5. Locomotion in stem vertebrates and chordates – why did they need paired fins?

At this point it might be instructive to consider just why lateral appendages in general, and paired fins in particular, are necessary or, at any rate, desirable. Locomotion in the cephalochordates, the larval tunicates, the modern Agnatha and their ammocoete larvae and, by inference, the ostracoderms and acanthodians is by axial flexion of the body from side to side in the manner of modern fish. As we see in Amphioxus, this flexion is brought about by serial contraction of paired muscle blocks or myotomes.

In order to understand the problems involved in this kind of locomotion, we must briefly consider the hydrodynamic aspects. A solid body moving through a fluid will experience resistance. This varies according to the shape of the body, its speed, and the properties of the fluid through which it moves.

From these properties we can calculate the drag: the ideal shape is that which minimizes drag. In practice, the ideal shape is found to be that of a torpedo, rounded at the nose and tapering gently towards the tail. It is no coincidence that this is the shape of a shark minus its fins.

When a body is moving along its axis of symmetry, drag is the only force acting upon it. But, as soon as we deflect the tail from this axis by contracting muscles, another force (lift) arises, acting at right angles to drag (not, confusingly, always upwards). Aerofoils (in air) and hydrofoils (in water) are bodies designed to produce maximum lift with minimum drag. The wings of aeroplanes are perhaps the most familiar example (Fig. 1.7(a)). The tail fin of fishes is a hydrofoil, arranged vertically. In the simplest cases, like sharks, the tail follows a wavy path. In one complete cycle (left–right) of the tail, the components of force acting to right and left cancel out, leaving only the forward component. As this is larger than the drag, the fish moves forwards.

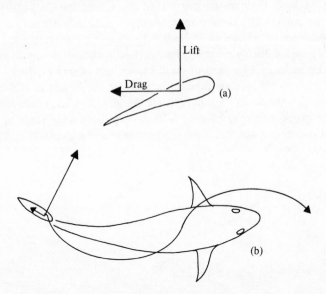

FIG. 1.7. The fish tail acts as an aerofoil. (a) shows the forces of lift and drag exerted when an aerofoil moves through a fluid. (b) shows the same forces exerted by the vertical aerofoil tail of a shark-like fish.

Although this is a good description of the swimming of a shark or tunny (Fig. 1.7(b)), it is a poor description of a cephalochordate, hagfish or eel, where the tail is not hydrofoil-like, and the swimming action is very unlike a side-to-side wagging of the tail. In fact, in such fish the body is thrown into waves travelling backward, which propel the fish forward. It can be shown (Alexander 1975) that the efficiency of such swimming depends on the amplitude of the wave when it reaches the posterior end of the body, and on the size of the tail. In practice, there is no clear distinction between these two extreme kinds of swimming: many fishes are intermediate.

The density of modern sharks is in the region of 1.08, and they live in sea water which has a density of 1.03. Consequently, if no correction is made, the fish will slowly sink. Correction is made by the tail, which exerts a net upwards push, tending to counteract the excess weight of the fish, and by paired fins. Paired fins will also produce upthrust: the argument here is similar to that applied to the tail. Consider the fin as an aerofoil (but this time horizontal). Lift in this case acts upwards and tends to lift the fish.

But paired fins are much more than devices for imparting lift, especially if they can be made flexible. In most modern bony fishes (teleosts) the fins consist only of widely-spaced mobile rays, united by thin webs of tissue. A shark's fin is extended permanently, that of a teleost can be folded and unfolded like a fan. Because of the structure of this fin, it can be thrown into waves, which, like the waves in the body of an eel, could exert propulsive force. When swimming fast, most teleosts keep their paired fins folded flat against the body: they are not necessary to provide lift, as they are in sharks, because teleosts have an air-filled swim bladder which adjusts their density to close to that of the sea or fresh water. They spread their fins as efficient brakes: a stationary teleost adjusts its position continuously by means of small movements of its fins; these will maintain it at a set depth and counteract the slow jet propulsion caused by taking in water via the mouth and expelling it via the gills. As well as stabilizing movements, the paired fins may be used to make possible a wide range of leisurely movement, swimming upwards, downwards, and even backwards (Fig. 1.8).

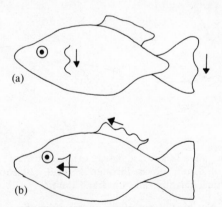

FIG. 1.8. Teleost fishes can use their mobile-based fins to execute all manner of movements, including maintaining a given depth in the water (a) and swimming backwards (b).

The advantages of fins, both propulsive midline fins and paired fins, to combat roll, pitch, and yaw, and as an aid to steering, are thus obvious. Let us return to primitive vertebrates and see to what extent they were developed.

The tail and dorsal fins are seen in nearly all types: the cephalochordates, tunicate larvae, and Agnatha all have specializations of this kind. Paired fin-like developments are seen in the metapleural folds of Amphioxus (Fig. 1.2), in the similar ventral folds of the fossil *Endeiolepis* (Fig. 1.9(a)), in the pectoral fins of osteostracans (Fig. 1.4), and in the pectoral spines of some anaspids. Similar essays into the provision of stabilizing fins are seen in the acanthodians and antiarchs (Figs 1.6 and 1.9(b)).

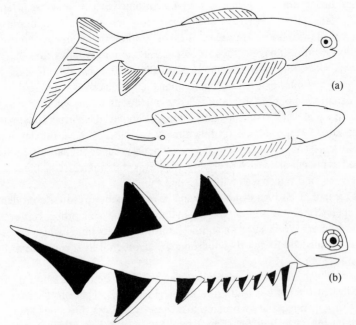

FIG. 1.9. Two possible ancestral types, which may have been on the line giving rise to paired fins: (a) the jawless Anaspid, *Endeiolepis,* with ventro-lateral fin folds; (b) the acanthodian, *Climatius,* with paired fins (seven in this case) supported by dermal spines.

1.6. The origin of fins

Because of the utility of such structures, it is probable that paired fins evolved not once, but several times in various early vertebrates. Possible modes of origin of paired fins have been suggested by many authorities; the three best authenticated are discussed here (Goodrich 1930):

(1) The gill-arch theory. Gegenbaur suggested that paired fins were derived from the most posterior pair of serial gills together with their supporting skeletal tissue. This theory is not now widely accepted, because of evidence from embryos. The gill arch skeleton is now known to be derived from the neural crest: that of the paired fins and their girdles is not.

(2) Body-spine theory. A series of ventro-lateral spines, as seen in acantho-

dians (Figs 1.6(a) and 1.9(b)), are interpreted as fin skeletons when equipped with an overlying covering of skin. These later migrated into the positions presently occupied by pectoral and pelvic paired fins. Again, there is an embryological objection, that the spines would be made of dermal bone derived from the bony covering of early armoured vertebrates, whilst the present-day limb skeleton is not.

(3) The fin-fold theory Dean (1896). This supposes that the lateral fins arose from folds of the body wall similar to those thought to have given rise to the dorsal fin: a stage like this is seen in Amphioxus and may be inferred in *Endeiolepis* (Fig. 1.9(a)). This theory presupposes a *de novo* origin of the appendicular skeleton. However, as cartilage-like supporting rays are found in the dorsal fin of the cephalochordates, there seem no grounds for objecting to a similar development in the morphologically similar lateral fin folds.

It seems possible, or even probable, that the various essays at paired fins contained attempts along all these lines. The objections to the gill-arch and body-spine theories are based on the embryology of present-day vertebrates: although it seems most likely that the fin-fold theory accounts best for the development of the fins present in our ancestors, there are no grounds for supposing that fish equipped with gill-arch or body-spine type fins did not exist – indeed, some fossils correspond rather well with this idea.

It is clear that all types of jawless and jawed vertebrates so far considered are highly specialized: the search for a generalized type will probably never bear fruit. As Romer (1966) said: 'An animal cannot spend its time being a generalized ancestor; it must be fit for the environment in which it lives and constantly and variably adapted for it.'

This constant and varied adaptation can be illustrated by a study of the fins and girdles of the earliest shark-like fishes (Fig. 1.10). These had stabilized the number of appendages at two pairs, but there is still considerable variety in the form taken by the paired fins. One type, the fin fold (Fig. 1.10(a)), has a broad base, and a skeleton consisting of numerous parallel bars articulating with a basal series of elements. Another (Figs 1.10(b) and (e)), characteristic of modern sharks, has greater flexibility bestowed by virtue of a narrower base achieved by attaching only the most anterior part of the fin to the body. A third (Fig. 1.10(c)) is leaf-shaped, with a long jointed central axis carrying marginal elements on each side. Any of these types may be modified to some special purpose (Fig. 1.10(d)), and the skeleton of each may not represent the full extent of the soft tissue fin. *Tristychius* (Fig. 1.10(f)) even had a fin bearing a remarkable superficial resemblance to the tetrapod limb.

1.7. Conquest of the land

Adaptability to a changing environment paved the way for the next important modification of paired fins, which was one factor allowing the eventual colonization of land. Two parallel adaptations made this possible: the ability to respire

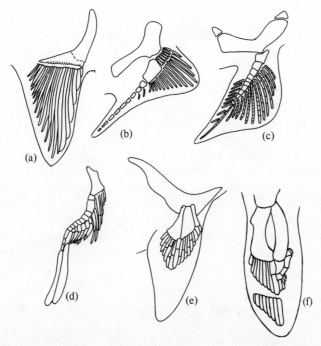

FIG. 1.10. Fins and girdles of shark-like fishes. These include the fin-fold type (*Cladoselache* (a)); types with a narrow base giving greater flexibility (*Cladodus* (b)) and a pleurocanth shark (c) with a central axis and marginal elements; and *Hybodus* (e), a possible Mesozoic descendant; specialized forms concerned with reproduction (pelvic-clasping fins (d)); and at least one pectoral fin with a remarkable superficial similarity to the vertebrate limb (*Tristychius* (f)).

by using lungs, efficient in air rather than in water, and the development of appendages capable of dragging the organism over dry ground.

The probable ancestors of land-dwelling forms are fairly clearly recognized, and were by no means generalized. They are known from a large variety of fossil forms, the living fossil coelacanth (crossopterygians), and as rather altered lung-fishes (Fig. 1.11). The fossil crossopterygians combined an ability to use their lungs (structures found intermittently from the first jawed fishes onwards) with the possession of rather mobile narrow-based fins. The latter we can see directly; the former we may infer from the types of deposits in which crossopterygians are found. Although some specialized types (like the coelacanth) became marine, crossopterygians are only found in abundance in freshwater continental deposits, areas subject to drought or choked with lush coal-swamp vegetation. We may imagine our fish ancestors living in the marginal areas of inland lakes fed by rivers amid dense, swamp-like vegetation. In the wet season, this location no doubt provided ample food and oxygen, and a good environment for breeding. In the dry season, however, the pools would have partially dried out, and, with stagnant water and rotting vegetation, dissolved oxygen in the water would have

FIG. 1.11. The coelacanth (*Latimeria* (a)) is a deep-sea crossopterygian known from the sea off Africa; the lungfishes (*Epiceratodus* (b)) are found in Australia, Africa, and South America, where they survive periods of drought by air-breathing or burrowing. The African form is so dependent on air-breathing that it will drown if forced to remain under water.

been low and carbon dioxide concentration high. Mobile-based fins enabled the head to be raised clear of the water to take a gulp of air, and possibly also allowed the body to be dragged from pool to pool over a substratum of rotting vegetation. *En route,* it may have been possible to take advantage of a prolific new source of food – the abundant terrestrial insects which flourished at this time.

It is important to emphasize that the modern Amphibia are still not entirely free from the aquatic habitat: they still have a slimy fish-like skin and return to the water to reproduce.

1.8. Paired fins and limbs

As mentioned earlier, the paired fins characteristic of modern fish were arrived at only after a period of evolutionary experimentation. There is clearly a relationship between the paired fish fins and the paired limbs of the ancestral amphibians. We shall consider next the way in which the fish paired fins, and in particular their skeleton, might have become transformed into the first tetrapod limbs. Discussion is focused on the pectoral fins and limbs, but the same principles apply to the pelvic region.

   Goodrich (1930) has put forward a plausible scheme consistent with palaeonto-
logical and embryological data for the evolution of the paired fins of fishes. But
it should be borne in mind that the evolutionary relationships of the various
major fish groups are problematic, and no primitive, generalized form can be
identified with certainty. As Moy-Thomas and Miles (1971) put it: 'Fossil and
living fishes . . . fall readily, unfortunately too readily, into . . . sub-divisions, for
in no case have convincing intermediate types been described. . . . the phylogeny
of fishes as a whole can only be reconstructed in its broadest outlines.'
   Goodrich (1930), following the fin-fold theory of Balfour (1881) (see section
1.6), considers that, in the ancestral broad-based fish fin, the endoskeleton consisted of segmentally arranged radials, as in the primitive shark, *Cladoselache*
(Fig. 1.10(a)). There is then a tendency along almost all evolutionary lines to
narrow the fin base forming a posterior notch (Fig. 1.12). The originally
segmental radials could have been compressed and fused at their base, this
tendency towards concrescence being greater at the anterior end of the fin as
illustrated by the elasmobranch, *Cladodus* (Figs 1.10(b) and 1.12(a)). The fused
basal parts then extended internally and became the limb girdle. Supporting
embryological evidence is provided by Sewertzoff (1924), who showed that in
Acipenser the masses of cartilage at the fin base (Fig. 1.12(e)) are formed by
fusion of originally separate segmental elements.

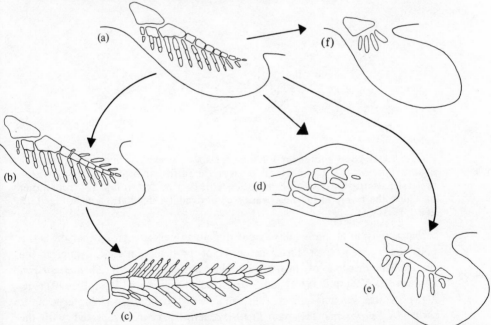

FIG. 1.12. Diagrammatic representation of possible evolution of the fish fin from
a broad-based ancestral form (a) via (b) to an archipterygium (*Ceratodus* (c)), to
a *Eusthenopteron*-type fin (d), to an *Acipenser*-type (e), and to the teleost-type
(f). (After Goodrich 1930).

From the primitive form, with its axis parallel to the body-wall, it is plausible to derive the other fin forms through the freeing of the posterior end of the axis, so that this, hinging on the girdle element, projects outwards to a greater or lesser extent (Fig. 1.12). Once the posterior tip is formed, postaxial radials appear (Fig. 1.12(b)). In this way, as in the Dipnoan, *Ceratodus*, by a major shift in the axis a leaf-like biserial mesorachic fin (or archipterygium) would result (Fig. 1.12(c)). A more minor shift would give the form of the sturgeon, *Acipenser*, while in teleosts, with their fins composed principally of dermal rays, the endoskeletal component is reduced to a small number of preaxial radials, e.g. four in the trout pectoral fin (Fig. 1.12(f)).

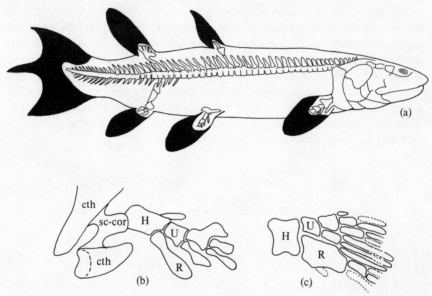

FIG. 1.13. A good contender for land tetrapod ancestry – the crossopterygian *Eusthenopteron* (a). The pectoral fin was a modified archipterygium (b), whose skeletal pattern shows some similarities with that of *Sauripterus* (c) from either of which the tetrapod limb can easily be derived. (Abbreviations as in Figs 1.15 and 1.16.)

Since it is, in all probability, from the crossopterygian group that the tetrapods are derived, their fin skeleton is of particular interest. Amongst the rhipidistian division of this group, the endoskeletons of *Eusthenopteron* (Andrews and Westoll 1968) and *Sauripterus* (Andrews and Westoll 1970) (Fig. 1.13) are well known, and in both the axis of the modified archipterygium is short. In *Sauripterus*, the main *Eusthenopteron* pattern is repeated, with the modification that each preaxial radial is continued distally by two elements. In both there is a single 'humerus' articulating with the limb girdle and two more distal elements ('radius' and 'ulna'). This is clearly a fin skeleton from which the limb skeleton of the first tetrapod could be derived, but in making the comparison with tetrapods it is unwise to go beyond the point of proposing that the three proximal elements, humerus, radius, and ulna, are homologous. The humerus of *Eusthenopteron* in particular has a striking similarity, including foramina and muscle attachment areas, to that of early tetrapods.

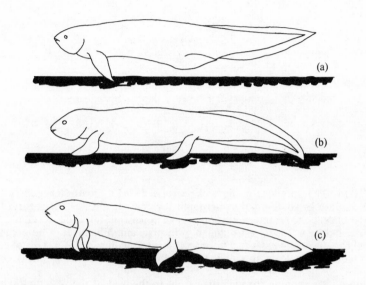

FIG. 1.14. The lungfish *Neoceratodus* walking on the bottom (a) forwards, (b) backwards and (c) resting. (After Young 1962.)

The lobe fins of the crossopterygians presumably allowed them to 'walk' on the bottom, as do the related modern lungfish to this day (Fig. 1.14). As we have just discussed (section 1.7), selection was likely to have favoured fish able to escape from one drying-up pool to search for larger ones. Once the capacity for terrestrial locomotion, however transitory, had been acquired it is easy to see how a new ecological niche could be exploited by air breathers able to improve the efficiency of their walking. Initially, the limb paddle may have carried little weight, and moved mainly up and down, but, to work effectively, the paddle must first be turned under the body, raising it off the ground, and then must bend at the elbow and turn outwards at the wrist, so that the digits are firmly applied to the ground.

The question of the homology of the crossopterygian paddle and primitive amphibian limb skeleton has inevitably given rise to much speculation. The scheme of Gregory (Gregory, Miner, and Noble 1923; Gregory and Raven 1941), using the *Sauripterus* fin (Fig. 1.15), has been widely accepted. Starting with the well-established homology of the three proximal elements, this assumes that the ulna became relatively lengthened to equal the radius. This scheme then attempts to identify the main axis, clear in *Eusthenopteron,* but less so in

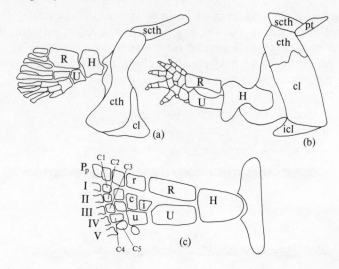

FIG. 1.15. The shoulder girdle and pectoral fin of a crossopterygian (a) and a fossil amphibian (b) similarly orientated for comparison. (c) is Gregory, Miner, and Noble's (1923) interpretation of an ancestral tetrapod forelimb, intermediate between *Sauripterus* and a primitive amphibian. H = humerus, R = radius, U = ulna, r = radiale, u = ulnare, i = intermedium, C1–C5 = distal carpals, I–V = metacarpals, Pp = prepollex. (Other abbreviations as in Fig. 1.19.)

Sauripterus, as running through the carpus to the base of the fifth digit. Gregory regards five of the eleven *Sauripterus* rays as surviving as axes of the tetrapod carpus, while the digits with their metacarpals and phalanges are regarded as neomorphic, i.e. newly evolved structures. Thus, the essential radial structure of the fish fin is still seen in the bony arrangement of the tetrapod carpus, even though he does not claim that individual fin bones are still present as carpal bones. Holmgren's (1933) scheme is essentially similar but that of Steiner (1922) differs considerably. Almost every investigation, however, comes to a different conclusion about homology, especially in the difficult carpus region. This is a sure sign that the evidence is equivocal. Holmgren regards the urodele limb as being constructed differently from those of other tetrapods, a view contradicted by Thomson (1968). Jarvik (1960) supports Holmgren, deriving the urodele limb from *Sauripterus,* and the limb of the other tetrapods from *Eusthenopteron.* It is perhaps wise to stress some of the difficulties involved. The two fish paddles, which are used so frequently in these interpretations, show important pattern differences from each other and represent only a randomly preserved sample of their group. It would be a colossal stroke of luck if either pattern was a direct tetrapod limb precursor. The embryological basis of many of the schemes of homology is equivocal (see section 3.22). We know nothing about the embryonic mechanisms by which the apparently simple crossopterygian adult fin skeleton was achieved, but we do know from *Acipenser* that parts of the fin skeleton are formed by embryological fusion of originally separate cartilage elements (Sewertzoff 1924). This means that, even if the developing chondrogenic pattern of the tetrapod limb skeleton was precisely known (which it is not), comparison with the bony fin skeletons of fossil fish would be a dubious exercise. On the other hand, while the precise details of the transition remain doubtful and disputed, no-one challenges the central assumption that the tetrapod limb arose by transformation of the crossopterygian fin paddle.

1.9. Increased efficiency of the limbs − locomotion on land

Because of the relationship between form and function, it is possible to work out quite a lot about the way of life of an animal known only as a handful of fossil bones. An anatomist or zoologist familiar with the skeleton of modern animals will quickly be able to see the most likely relationships of fossil bones and hence the posture of the long-dead creature from which they came.

If we apply this kind of expertise to the earliest land-dwelling vertebrates, the early Amphibia (Fig. 1.15(b)), we can see that their limbs must have been arranged well to the side of the body with the humerus and femur horizontal. In early forms, the foot probably pointed outwards (Fig. 1.17(a)). In fact, tracks preserved in Palaeozoic rocks, made by early amphibians or reptiles walking on mud, confirm this newt-like gait. One particularly exciting track even shows the toes pointing laterally.

Walking on legs arranged like this is an exhausting business: the tracks show few marks which could have been caused by the body dragging along the ground so presumably it was held clear by muscular effort, in a pose exactly equivalent to a press-up. The stride must have been short to avoid limbs fouling the body sides. But, if we look at modern newts and many lizards, we see that it is a viable proposition (Fig. 1.18). The muscular effort involved is reduced by limiting running to short periods, and the stride is considerably lengthened by the flexibility of the backbone, which moves the hip and shoulder joint backwards and forwards.

Although amphibians have four legs, they are stable with only three of them in contact with the ground. Stability, in this context, means that the centre of gravity of the animal must lie within the triangle formed by the three feet in contact with the ground (Fig. 1.16). This, in turn, means that in stable progression the order of moving the feet is circumscribed. This order − RF, LH, LF, RH − is common to all slow-moving tetrapods. With a slight increase in speed, however, small liberties can be taken and the next foot in order raised before the last is set down. This is halfway to the trot, with diagonally opposite limbs moving in unison, and which is seen in toads at speed, many reptiles, and mammals.

Modifications to improve the efficiency of walking seem to have taken place at least three times in tetrapod history, in dinosaurs, birds, and mammals. The proximal segment of the limb is first rotated, so that the humerus or femur, while still horizontal, points along the same axis as the backbone (Fig. 1.17(b)).

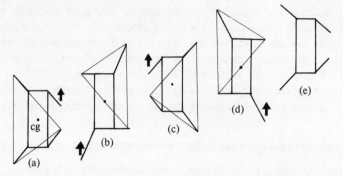

FIG. 1.16. Locomotion on land demands that the centre of gravity (cg) of an animal remains within the triangle whose points are formed by the contact with the ground of three feet when a fourth is raised.

This brings the knee forward and the elbow back, a manoeuvre which would cause the forefoot to point backwards were it not for rotation or pronation of the forearm (Fig. 1.17(c)), which causes the bones to cross. A further refinement is to change the orientation of the humerus and femur yet again, so that their long axes are vertical and the legs are tucked beneath the body. This gives an un-restricted stride and means that the body-weight is supported by the bones of the legs rather than by muscles.

1.10. Changes in the limb girdles

The regular use of fins as terrestrial limbs demanded that they were able to support at least part of the body-weight in air. As weight-bearing organs, the limbs have to transmit forces to the midline girder formed by the vertebral column. This is achieved by means of the limb girdles.

The pectoral girdle, which supports the anterior pair of limbs, is derived from those elements which lie adjacent to the original fish fin. These in turn are derived either from the internal skeleton (preformed in cartilage) or from the dermal bony armour which clothed many early vertebrates. In primitive bony fishes and many fossil amphibians, the latter predominate and the two types of element form a pattern from which all other vertebrate types may be derived (Fig. 1.19(a)). The dermal bones are arranged in a dorso-ventral band behind the gill opening: attached posteriorly is the smaller endoskeletal component. The main dermal element is a vertical cleithrum: below it is the clavicle which runs downwards and forwards beneath the gill chamber to fuse with its neighbour on the opposite side. Above the cleithrum is a series of other elements which attach it to the rear of the skull. This basic pattern is seen in many forms, both extinct and extant. We can trace the development of the shoulder girdle in comparing typical girdles from the various classes of vertebrates.

In its most primitive form, the glenoid region forms an articulation with several fin elements: attachment points for muscles are provided above by the

Anterior

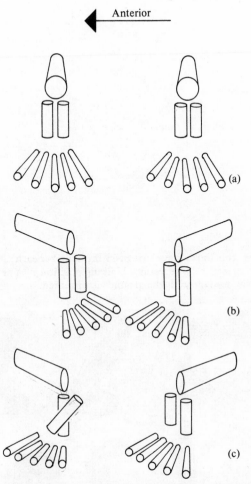

FIG. 1.17. Modification of limb posture in tetrapods. The sprawling posture presumed to be the original (a) is modified by rotation at shoulder and hip (b) and rotation (pronation) of the forelimb at the elbow (c).

scapular blade, and below by the coracoid plate (Fig. 1.19). These areas are small in fishes and frequently poorly ossified. In fossil amphibians and early reptiles, however, they are much larger. The mammal-like reptiles (ancestors of the mammals) added a further element, the true coracoid, behind the coracoid plate. This tended to grow as the coracoid plate diminished: a situation seen in early fossil mammals and in present day monotremes (Figs 1.19(b) and (f)). Modern marsupials and placental mammals, however, have undergone a rather drastic re-arrangement. The coracoid and the remains of the coracoid plate have almost vanished, represented only by the coracoid process of the scapula (Fig. 1.19(g)). The scapula itself has enlarged and developed a scapular spine, which divides it into supraspinous and infraspinous regions.

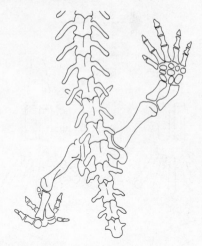

FIG. 1.18. When the limbs have not been brought beneath the body, rotation at the elbow or knee is still necessary. Walking position of a newt, showing how the left hindleg (in contact with the ground) is pronated.

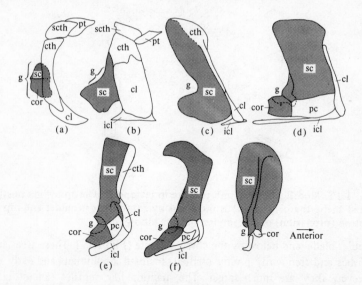

FIG. 1.19. Modifications of the pectoral girdle in the vertebrates: (a) schematic view of the pectoral girdle of a bony fish, (b) '*Eogyrinus*', now believed to be a crossopterygian and (c) *Eryops*, a fossil amphibian, the latter with no connection between pectoral girdle and skull, (d) *Ophiacodon*, a primitive synapsid reptile, (e) *Kannemeyeria*, a mammal-like reptile, (f) *Ornithorhynchus*, the duck-billed platypus and (g) *Didelphys*, the opossum. cl = clavicle, cth = cleithrum, cor = coracoid, g = glenoid fossa, icl = interclavicle, pt = post-temporal, sc = scapula, scth = supracleithrum. Note the increase in bone formed in cartilage (shaded) at the expense of dermal bone.

In contrast to the pectoral girdle, the pelvic girdle is entirely endochondral. In fishes each half of the girdle is a small triangular plate embedded in the abdominal musculature, just in front of the anus. The two half girdles are often in contact ventrally at the pelvic symphysis, where they may fuse. There is no connection with the backbone (Fig. 1.20).

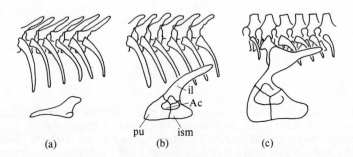

FIG. 1.20. The development of the pelvic girdle during the transition from fishes to tetrapods. In the fish (a) the pelvic girdle consists of a small plate embedded in the body with no connection with the backbone. In some early fossil amphibians (b) the pelvis has expanded into the three typical elements – pubis (= pu), ilium (=il), and ischium (= ism) – and has a central articular facet, the acetabulum (= Ac). Although the ilium is expanded, it is connected to the spine only by ligaments. In later types (c) the ilium is firmly attached to the column via an enlarged sacral rib.

The use of the hindlimbs for terrestrial locomotion and weight-bearing demanded elaboration of the pelvic region. The original element expanded both anteriorly and posteriorly as the pubo-ischiadic plate, offering a greater surface for muscle attachment. Above the centre of this plate a third element (the ilium) developed, making contact with an enlarged sacral rib, and thus uniting girdle and vertebral column. Articulation with the limb was at the acetabulum, a depression formed at the point of junction of the three bony elements.

This is the type of pelvis found in the Amphibia, although in some fossil forms and many modern representatives of the group the pelvis fails to ossify (Fig. 1.21).

In the reptiles (Fig. 1.22) the ilium is even broader, and forms the attachment for even more musculature; it also tends to be associated with two sacral ribs, rather than one. Primitively, the pubo-ischiadic plate is covered by a large muscle mass: perhaps as a weight-saving device a large foramen, the obturator foramen, pierces the plate and tends to divide pubis and ischium. This condition is still seen in turtles and lizards. In the archosaurs and their descendants, the birds, this separation has been extended. The rotation of the femur beneath the body, which makes bipedalism possible, is facilitated by the modification of pubis and ischium into long, rod-like bones running antero-laterally and postero-laterally

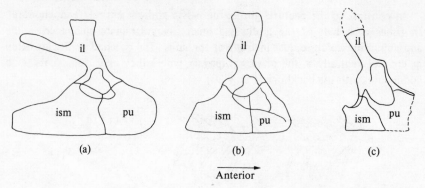

Anterior

FIG. 1.21. The pelvis in amphibians resembles that shown in Fig. 1.20: (a) *Archeria*, a primitive fossil amphibian, (b) *Eryops*, a later form, (c) a modern urodele, *Salamandra*. The primitive posterior prong of the *Archeria* ilium is retained by many reptiles, but is lost by many fossil Amphibia. In many modern types the pelvis ossifies only partially (cartilaginous areas bordered by dotted lines in (c)). For abbreviations, see Fig. 1.20.

Anterior

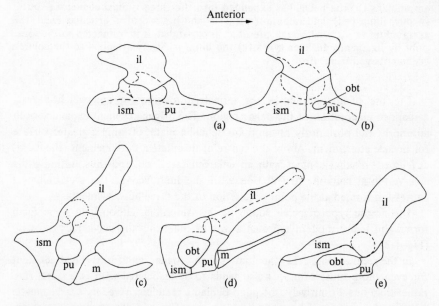

FIG. 1.22. Evolution of the pelvis in reptiles and primitive mammals: (a) primitive reptilian type, *Dimetrodon*, (b) *Lycaenops*, (c) *Ornithorhynchus*, a monotreme, (d) *Didelphys*, a marsupial. In monotremes and marsupials the function of the anterior prong of the pubis is taken over by the 'marsupial bone', a specialization not found in early mammals such as *Daphoenodon* (e). m = marsupial bone. Other abbreviations as in Fig. 1.20.

respectively. The acetabulum tends to become incomplete ventrally and the ilium makes contact with even more vertebrae.

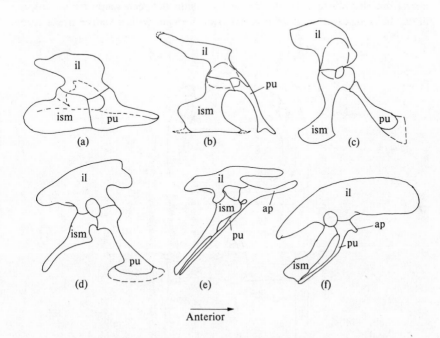

FIG. 1.23. Modifications of the reptilian pelvis: (a) primitive type, *Dimetrodon*; (b) a lizard, *Iguana*; (c) a crocodile, *Alligator*; (d) a saurischian dinosaur, *Tyrannosaurus*; (e) an ornithischian dinosaur, *Thesecelosaurus*; (f) a kiwi, *Apteryx*. Note the progressive separation of pubis and ischium in (b)–(d), the way the pubis swings posteriorly in (e) and (f), and its replacement (especially in (e)) by an anteriorly directed process (= ap). For abbreviations, see Fig. 1.20.

In fact, in the ornithischian dinosaurs and in birds (Fig. 1.23), the story is even more complicated. For some poorly understood reason, the main part of the pubis runs downwards and backwards with the ischium: the original function of the pubis is taken over by a new, stout, anterior process of the bone. This may ossify, or remain cartilaginous. In birds this process is poorly developed, as the abdominal contents are supported by the enormously developed sternum.

In mammal-like reptiles and mammals, which have also undergone a change in limb posture, the pelvis is also modified. The whole of the pelvis seems to have rotated about the acetabulum: the ilium, which primitively lies postero-dorsally, is now antero-dorsal, and pubis and ischium have moved in the other direction, so that they lie mainly behind the acetabulum. In marsupials a pair of 'marsupial bones' of unknown origin help to support the body wall.

We have seen, therefore, the progressive modification of pectoral and pelvic girdles: in the amphibian or primitive reptile the essential point is that the girdles have become firmly attached to the axial skeleton (Fig. 1.24), although by rather different means, the pectoral girdle being supported by musculature running from scapula to ribs, the pelvic by fusion between sacral rib or ribs and ilium. In both cases a sturdy box has been formed, with a ventral brace across the body.

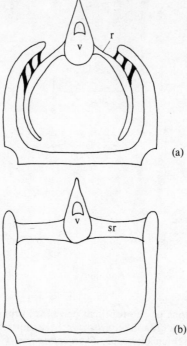

FIG. 1.24. Diagrammatic transverse section through (a) pectoral and (b) pelvic girdles showing how they form a strong cross-braced structure attached to ribs (= r) or sacral ribs (= sr) respectively. v = vertebra.

It must not be forgotten that the stresses transferred by these girdles to the vertebral column also changed with the transition from swimming to walking. It is important that the vertebral column of a terrestrial vertebrate does not sag between the box girders of the girdles, or the abdomen will drag along the ground. As the body is supported by only two limbs at diagonally opposite corners during walking, it is also necessary that the vertebral column resists twisting. Sagging and twisting were opposed in early Amphibia by the development of strong ligaments running between vertebrae and by the formation of articular facets between them. The development of ribs and rib musculature will also prevent sagging and twisting of the vertebral column.

1.11. Changes in the limb bones

Just as the limb girdles were subject to constant evolutionary modification, so were the more distal bones in the limb. These changes are also correlated with the need to support weight in air, the need to provide greater surfaces of attachment for muscles, and, in forms where the limbs were brought beneath the body for increase in stride, this is also reflected in bone structure. We also see a gradual reduction in the many small bones in the wrist and ankle regions, and often modifications in the numbers of digits, usually by reduction.

Proximal

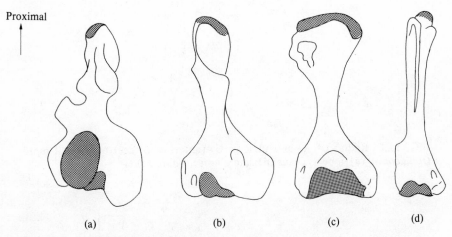

(a) (b) (c) (d)

FIG. 1.25. The progressive refinement of the humerus in tetrapods: (a) *Eryops*, a fossil amphibian; (b) *Edaphosaurus*, a primitive fossile reptile; (c) *Varanus*, a lizard; (d) *Didelphys*, an opossum. Shaded areas indicate articular surfaces. In (a) and (b) the humerus is twisted through 90°, so that the full extent of the proximal articulation cannot be seen.

Forelimb. The primitive humerus (Fig. 1.25) was greatly expanded at either end for the attachment of muscles, acting between pectoral girdle and humerus proximally, and humerus, and radius ulna distally. In addition, it carried articulations and these and the expansions for musculature occupy almost all the bone. In more advanced forms we see a more refined, rounded articulation capable of greater movement, and the appearance of a distinct, narrower shaft between proximal and distal expansions.

The radius (Fig. 1.26) tends to be columnar, to support body weight, and to vary little in shape. The ulna, which carries little weight, is more important as a site of muscle attachment. Especially important is the olecranon process (the funny bone) of the ulna, to which is attached the main extensor muscle of the forearm. We sometimes see in mammals a condition in which the shaft of the ulna is lost or partially fused with the radius (Fig. 1.26(c)), but the olecranon always persists.

The wrist region was primitively made up of a maximum of twelve elements arranged as follows (Fig. 1.27(a)): proximally a row of three elements, radiale, intermedium, and ulnare; centrally a series of four centralia; and distally a row of distal carpals, one opposite the base of each digit.

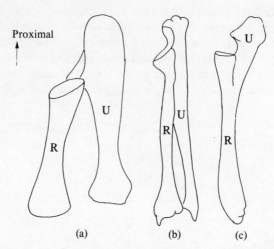

FIG. 1.26. Radius (= R) and ulna (= U) (anterior surface) of a fossil reptile, *Ophiacodon* (a); a bear, *Ursus* (b); and a horse, *Equus* (c).

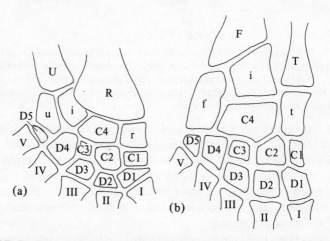

FIG. 1.27. Probable primitive arrangements of the small bones of the wrist (a) and ankle (b). R = radius, U = ulna, r = radiale, u = ulnare, i = intermedium, F = fibula, T = tibia, f = fibulare, t = tibiale, I-V = digits, C1-C4 = central carpals or tarsals, D1-D5 = distal carpals or tarsals.

This arrangement has undergone extensive reduction and modification (Fig. 1.28). Although the proximal carpals tend to persist, the centralia are reduced in almost all forms (there are never more than two even in primitive reptiles, and mammals have but one), and the fifth distal carpal tends to be lost, even when the fifth digit is retained. When digits are lost, even more reduction follows. In reptiles, birds, and mammals an additional postaxial bone, the pisiform, ossifies in

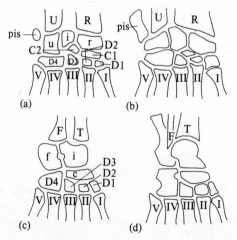

FIG. 1.28. Modifications of the carpus and tarsus in a generalized reptile (a) and (c), and in a generalized mammal (b) and (d). The general reduction in elements is evident: carpals and tarsals in mammals and man are generally known by two sets of nomenclature, each differing from that used here, and have accordingly not been labelled. pis = pisiform. Other labelling as in Fig. 1.27.

the tendons of the muscles of the ulnar margin of the limb.

The structure of the rest of the manus is highly dependent on the number of digits. It is probable that early tetrapods had a varied number of fingers, but the fossil record is poor. The primitive number of fingers seems to have been five, although many fossil and modern urodele amphibians have only four. Five fingers are also found in mammalian ancestors.

The number of phalanges per finger, the phalangeal formula, is also subject to variation: it is highest in the primitive reptile at 2.3.4.5.3. As with the number of digits, the Amphibia seem to have a lower phalangeal number, and even in fossil forms the formula does not exceed 2.3.3.3.3.

Hindlimb. The changes seen in the evolving hindlimb mirror those of the fore-limb. The femur (Fig. 1.29), initially stout with broad proximal and distal expansions for muscle attachments, articular surfaces and not much else, is gradually refined, becoming slimmer and often longer. The major change, however, is in the positioning of the head, where femur and pelvis articulate. Original-ly, this articulation was on the proximal end of the bone. As the hindlimbs were brought below the body, it gradually became a sub-spherical structure carried on a neck offset from the shaft.

The tibia (Fig. 1.30), like the radius, is a weight-bearing bone, and like the radius, has not been much modified. Proximally it carries the main attachment of the extensor muscles of the knee: in mammals this attachment has been modified by the presence of a sesamoid bone, the patella, in the tendon of these muscles. The fibula resembles the ulna in bearing little weight, but in being important for muscle attachment. Like the ulna, it is often reduced or fused

Proximal

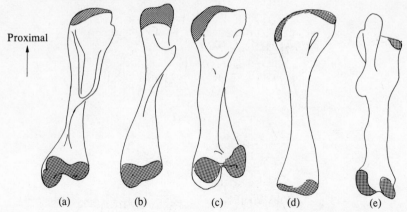

FIG. 1.29. Evolution of the femur in tetrapods: ventral views of (a) a fossil primitive amphibian, *Eryops*; (b) a urodele, *Salamandra*; (c) a primitive reptile, *Dimetrodon*; (d) a mammal-like reptile, *Cynognathus*; (e) the horse, *Equus*.

Proximal

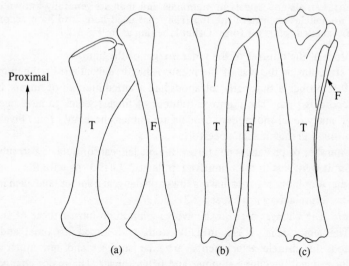

FIG. 1.30. Left tibia (T) and fibula (F) (posterior view) in (a) *Dimetrodon*, a primitive reptile; (b) *Sus*, a pig; (c) *Equus*, a horse.

with the shaft of the tibia. In some species it has been dispensed with entirely (Fig. 1.30).

The primitive tarsus resembled the primitive carpus closely (Fig. 1.27(b)), and corresponding reductions are found amongst the centralia and in the loss of the fifth distal element (Figs 1.28(c) and (d)). Here, the process has been extended to the proximal row as well. Although there are three elements in the proximal part of the carpus of reptiles, there are only two in the proximal tarsus, the calcaneum (= fibulare) and the astragalus, which seems to represent the fused radiale + intermedium.

In bipedal archosaurs the lengthening of the hindlimb has led to further modification. The joint between the astragalus and calcaneum, and tibia and fibula, and that between the distal tarsals and metatarsals have been immobilized. In birds the process has gone even further and the bones have fused to form a proximal tibiotarsus and tarsometatarsus.

In mammals the astragalus is modified to form a pulley: this restricts the lateral movement of the ankle and makes it a hinge only, but increases the amount of movement possible in flexion and extension. The calcaneum carries a posterior projection into which are inserted the powerful calf muscles via the 'Achilles' tendon (Fig. 1.31).

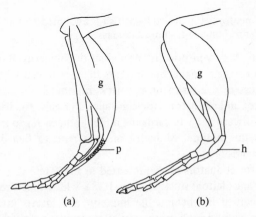

(a)   (b)

FIG. 1.31. Lateral views of the hindlimb of (a) a lizard, (b) a mammal to show the presence of plantar aponeurosis (p) in the former and heel (h) in the latter; g = gastrocnemius muscle.

Phalangeal formula for the pes often corresponds to that of the manus, except that in reptiles there is frequently a fourth phalanx to the fifth toe.

1.12. The prime movers − limb musculature

As the limb developed from the fish fin, we may look for similarities in fin and limb musculature as well as in skeletal elements.

Fin musculature (Fig. 1.32) is derived from part of the segmental musculature which produces axial locomotion in fishes. It consists of two groups of muscles, one above and one below the fin, which raise and lower or abduct and adduct it. In narrow-based fins, these muscles may also rotate the fin about its major axis. In transition from fin to limb, these muscle blocks, and the bones from which they take origin, have increased in size: with the increase in size a modification of function has occurred. Consider the muscles which primitively lifted or

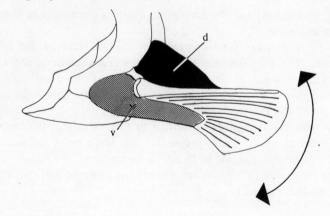

FIG. 1.32. The pectoral fin of a teleost fish is abducted and adducted by dorsal (black, d) and ventral (shaded, v) muscle masses.

abducted the fin: they will now lift or abduct the humerus. But, because of the increased width of their origin, the anterior fibres will also tend to move it forward, and the posterior fibres to move it back. In general, though, the distinction between abductor and adductor muscle groups still holds: the former will tend to draw the limb forwards and towards the midline, the latter to move it backward and away from the midline. Abductor muscles tend to flex distal joints, and adductors to extend them.

Forelimb. The fin abductors are represented in the forelimb by the fan-shaped latissimus dorsi and deltoid muscles (Fig. 1.33), which link girdle and humerus, by the triceps which lies behind the humerus and inserts into the olecranon process of the ulna, and by a group of flexor muscles on the back of the forearm which extend the wrist and joints of the hand.

On the ventral side, the adductors include the large and important pectoralis muscle, which runs from the chest wall to the humerus, pulling the humerus downwards and backwards. This is of obvious importance in locomotion. The brachialis and biceps flex the elbow, and a series of powerful flexors operate on the wrist and joints of the hand, providing an important backward push in locomotion.

In primitive tetrapods, where the stance was with the humerus extended horizontally, another important muscle, the supracoracoideus, ran from the coracoid plate to the underside of the humerus. This, in effect, prevented the body from sagging down between the limbs. When the limbs are moved to lie below th.. body, this muscle, and indeed the coracoid plate, is dispensed with.

Hindlimb. Running between the pelvis and the proximal end of the femur, and holding the latter into the acetabulum, is a large muscle, the puboischiofemoralis, which is divided in mammals into psoas and iliacus. The iliofemoralis runs from ilium to femur, as do the gluteal muscles of mammals. However, with the change in posture brought about by tucking the hindlegs beneath the body has come a

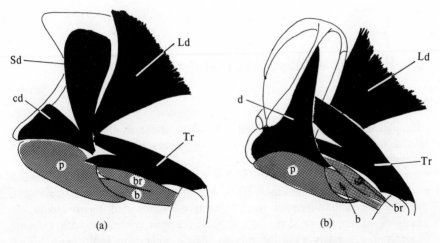

FIG. 1.33. In the lizard (a) and the opossum (b), dorsal and ventral muscle masses are split into discrete muscles: the black ones represent the original dorsal abductor group; the shaded, the ventral adductors. b = biceps, br = brachialis, cd = clavicular deltoid, d = deltoid, Ld = latissimus dorsi, p = pectoralis, Tr = triceps, Sd = scapular deltoid.

change in direction: gluteal muscles run backwards and downwards, and move the femur back in a vertical plane whilst the iliofemoralis runs backwards and outwards and moves the femur back horizontally. A series of extensor muscles, collectively known as quadriceps femoris, runs from the girdle, over the front of the thigh to the proximal end of the tibia, via the patella in mammals. Beyond the knee is a series of small extensors of the ankle and foot resembling those in the forelimb.

On the ventral side runs a group of muscles especially important in propulsion as they adduct the femur and flex the knee, or, with the foot in contact with the ground, lift the body and push it forwards. They comprise a group of muscles running from pelvis to the back of the femur and, superficial to these, a group of flexors of the knee, running to the tibia. In the sprawling gait, an important muscle, the caudiofemoralis, ran from the sides of the vertebrae to the midpoint of the femur, pulling it powerfully back. With postural change this became much less important.

Below the knee is a group of calf muscles which insert under the foot. This necessitates turning the corner at the ankle, achieved variously in different groups of vertebrates. For instance, in reptiles the tendons of these muscles are cushioned by a pad of soft tissue, whilst in mammals the problem is side-stepped: the tendons insert into the enlarged calcaneum (Fig. 1.31).

2   Functional adaptation and diversity

2.1. Introduction

Although the changes in limb skeletons, which allow an observer to assign an animal to the Amphibia, Reptilia, Aves, or Mammalia, are of interest to the taxonomist, and allow a palaeontologist confronted with a novel fossil to determine whether he is dealing with fish or fowl, of more immediate interest and much wider scope are the varied functional adaptations which have occurred in the tetrapod limb, often on many separate occasions in different groups. As examples of these, we shall look at modifications concerned with running, bipedalism, secondary axial locomotion, flying, swimming and digging, for we have to remember that limbs have functions other than locomotion.

2.2. Speed and power

The principles of limb mechanics were set out clearly by Gregory (1912). Speed in a running animal depends on two factors: length of stride and rapidity of step. Increases in stride are, in practice, brought about by increases in the distal part of the limb (Fig. 2.1). Keeping the humerus or femur short means that the muscles moving these bones with respect to the limb girdles act over a short distance. The dynamics of muscle are such that a given mass of muscle may contract powerfully over a short distance or less powerfully over a greater one (Fig. 2.2). The short humerus or femur can thus be moved with great power, and its muscles used to swing the rest of the elongated limb. The concentration of power in proximal muscles also means that distal muscles can be smaller; this, in turn, decreases the weight of the distal part of the limb, and hence the pendulum effect (which has to be overcome when the foot is slowed, stopped, and accelerated in the opposite direction, as it must be at each end of each stride). A limb built for speed will, therefore, have a short proximal segment with a long slim distal part. Gregory realized this and suggested that the ratio of femur : tibia was a good measure of attainable speed. This ratio is 0.6 in the elephant, 0.92 in the racehorse, and 1.25 in the gazelle.

Heavy animals are often slow-moving: here, weight support is of more importance than speed, and the distal part of the limb is not a light, slim, elongated rod, but a heavy, supporting pillar. The shorter limb is also more powerful in terms of the force that can be exerted at the fingers or toes. This is important, for instance, in digging animals.

(a)   (b)   (c)

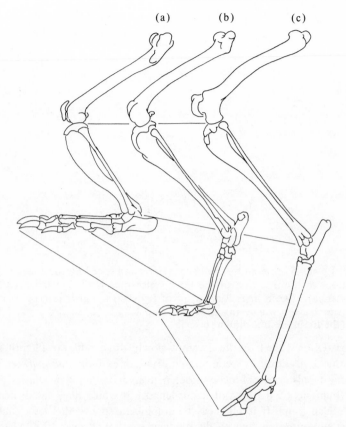

FIG. 2.1. Changes in limb proportion in animals adapted for fast running: (a) badger, (b) dog, and (c) deer. Femora all drawn to same scale. Note the elongation of distal segments in dog and deer, and change of posture at the ankle joint.

2.3. Bipedalism

Two main approaches towards increased efficiency can be seen in the tetrapods once the limbs have been re-arranged beneath the body. In the first, the centre of gravity of the animal is kept well forward and all four legs retain contact with the ground; in the second, the centre of gravity moves posteriorly and the hind-legs only are involved in locomotion, often steadied by stout tail; the front legs are freed for other purposes.

Bipedalism is very old. Although it was never a feature of the amphibia (perhaps because the necessary preliminary step of tucking the limbs beneath the body had never been mastered), it is seen as long ago as the lower Triassic (210 million years ago) in the early reptiles (Archosauria). Let us look at a small pseudosuchian thecodont reptile, *Euparkeria*, from South Africa. *Euparkeria*'s immediate ancestors were swamp-dwellers (Reig 1970) and had probably developed strong hindlimbs and a muscular tail to help in propelling them through

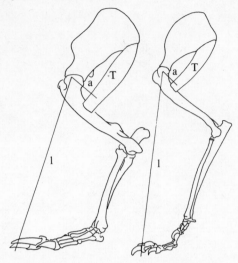

FIG. 2.2. Power is achieved by the badger (*left*) and speed by the cheetah (*right*) by variations in the insertion of the teres major muscle (T). In the cheetah the small distance between insertion and pivot (a) gives a higher rate of oscillation than in the badger where (a) is larger. Leg length (1) is also greater in the cheetah (the limbs are not drawn to scale).

the water (Olson 1971). As the swamps slowly dried out, these reptiles were faced with the necessity of locomotion on land, or extinction. *Euparkeria* seems to have mastered terrestrial locomotion. With its inheritance of relatively short forelegs (humerus 65 per cent of femur length), it would have had difficulty in walking on all fours. If it retained the amphibian sprawl, the body could not have been supported on land by the hindlegs and tail (Romer 1966). There are obvious grounds for suggesting that *Euparkeria* (a) was able to bring its hindlegs beneath its body and (b) was bipedal. Ewer (1965) suggests that it was capable of short bursts of bipedal locomotion with hindlegs beneath the body, but reverted to a quadrupedal amphibian sprawl for more leisurely progress.

Euparkeria and her kind evidently prospered. By the mid-Triassic, small rabbit-like thecodonts with stilt-like hindlegs tucked below the body were living in Argentina (Romer, 1971).

The archosaurs show a series of functional adaptations of the hindlimb and hindlimb girdle, which we see again and again in other bipedal types. With the weight carried on the hindlimbs, the forepart of the body is counterbalanced by a massive tail. The pelvic girdle is elongated with extensive bracing from ilium to the backbone. The ischium and pubis are massive and strong, in more advanced types losing their characteristic plate-like structure. Since the legs are beneath the body and the acetabulum looks outwards, the femur develops a medial articulating head: this pushes against the upper part of the acetabulum, which may become incomplete ventrally. The femur and tibia are long, and the fibula tends to be reduced. The length of the limb, and hence the length of stride, is increased by elongation of the metatarsals. The many small tarsals, a weak link in this type of limb, tend to be reduced, proximal ones fusing with tibia and fibula, distal ones with the heads of the metatarsals, leaving only a single movable joint in the middle of the tarsus. The foot has the central toes better developed than the lateral ones, with the third toe longest, and the second and fourth somewhat shorter. The fifth toe tends to be reduced to the point of extinction, and the first to be turned rearwards to act as a kind of prop.

The front legs in archosaurs became less important with the development of bipedal gait. They are thus usually shorter and weaker than the hindlegs, and fingers tend to be lost until only two or three of the inner (preaxial) ones remain. In the shoulder girdle the cleithrum is lost, and the scapula is long and slim.

These clearly functional adaptations are repeated again and again in bipedal tetrapods. In the saurischian dinosaurs (descendants of a group of archosaurs known as the thecodonts) bipedalism was developed *par excellence*. These were dinosaurs who retained the triradiate pelvis of the archosaurs, and improved it further. Some were herbivorous, some carnivorous with the terminal phalanges of their digits compressed and curved, indicating the presence of powerful claws. The bipedal saurischians can be classified into several groups. The small Coelurosauria were rather lightly built, with a two-pronged pelvis with an elongated rod, the pubis, somewhat dilated distally, and a similar ischium. The acetabulum is widely perforated, and the legs very slim. The limb bones were often hollow, a weight-saving device seen also in birds. The femur is rather shorter than the tibia, and the lateral toes are again reduced, as is the forelimb. More advanced coelurosaurs (e.g. *Struthiomimius*) were the size of an ostrich with a three-toed, bird-like foot, no teeth and hence presumably a bird-like beak and fairly well-developed forelimbs with an opposable thumb. The mode of life of the animal, which showed this rather bizarre combination of specialities, has aroused considerable speculation: one idea is that it was an egg-eater — no teeth would have been necessary; the opposibility of the thumb helped in handling eggs, and speed guaranteed escape from irate parents!

Many bipedal saurischians grew to a large size. In these, our familiar bipedal specializations are present, together with a partial fusion of the remaining three metatarsals, a condition also seen in birds. The large carnivorous bipedal dinosaurs (such as the legendary *Tyrannosaurus*) were colossal (14 metres long, 5.7 metres to the shoulder): the hindlimbs here showed obviously necessary strengthening. As Galileo first pointed out, the weight of an animal depends on the cube of its linear dimension whilst the strength of its legs varies as the square. Thus, an animal doubling its length increases the weight 8-fold, but increases the strength of its limbs only by a factor of 4. In a heavy animal, the bulk of the legs, therefore, must increase out of all proportion to the rest of the body. Perhaps an inevitable consequence of increase in size was that the largest descendants of the archosaurs, the herbivorous sauropods, should have a quadrupedal stance. Although they were considered in the last century to have reverted to quadrupedalism as a result of their huge size, it now seems that the features thought to betoken a bipedal ancestry (short forelimbs, long hindlimbs) are simply ancestral.

The extent to which dinosaurs were truly bipedal is a matter of contention. It has been traditional to reconstruct bipedal dinosaurs resting upon their tail as a prop in the manner of the kangaroo, perhaps because this was the only large tailed biped with which the nineteenth century reconstructors were familiar. However, the trend in recent years has been to restore dinosaurs with the tail outstretched, poker-straight. This reconstruction is based upon the remains of *Deinonychus,* a carnivore about 2½ m long, equipped with stout hindlegs, the first digit of which bears a 12-cm sickle-shaped claw. The most remarkable feature of *Deinonychus,* however, is its tail, apparently carried ramrod-straight (Ostrom 1969), and held in this position by very long (46 cm), slender (3.5 mm diameter), ossified vertebral processes. This led to the reconstruction of the animal as a disemboweller of its prey, standing on one leg the while, and balancing with its tail in the manner of a 'tightrope walker's balancing pole' (Desmond 1975). This reconstruction set a fashion: browsing through Desmond's book, we see the ramrod tail extrapolated into dinosaurs which had no ossified processes, Galton's reconstruction of *Anatosaurus* 'in a hurry' (Galton 1970), Bakker's *Cynidiognathus* (a sprawling therapsid – not even a dinosaur) and even *Barosaurus,* a brontosaur (Bakker 1971). Desmond even suggests that *Brontosaurus* itself held its tail in this manner, 'for fear of following members of the herd trampling on [it]'.

Pause for consideration makes all this seem most unlikely. The kangaroo may hold its tail straight during bipedal hopping, but it is not fixed in this position: to do this would take a great deal of energy. It seems likely that the reconstructors have run amok. There is little or no evidence of, or justification for, the stiff tail in any beast but *Deinonychus.* In *Deinonychus* itself, Ostrom (1969) is a little at a loss to explain his peculiar bony rods: he points out that this position is occupied in vertebrates by tendons. He is a little puzzled at the mode of ossification of the rods. Could it not be that the rods are, in fact, tendons impregnated *post mortem* and that the rigid tail reconstructors are basing their opinion on a misinterpretation?

The idea of dinosaurs as obligate bipeds also raises other problems. First, the limb skeletons: some forms, applying Gregory's criterion of femur:tibia ratio, were obviously very fast indeed. This has led to speculation (summarized by Desmond 1975) that these creatures were warm-blooded, this being necessary to sustain long periods of activity, such as running at speed. The introduction of homoiothermy to the dinosaurs led Bakker (Bakker and Galton 1974) to reconstruct the classification of much of the vertebrates, setting up a new (homoiothermic) group, the Dinosauria, which includes the birds. Secondly, known obligate bipedal types (primates, birds) have a very well-developed brain, with excellent sense of balance. Did the dinosaurs? Bakker would argue yes – as bird ancestors, dinosaurs would naturally have well-developed brains.

The well-developed bipedal limb is seen again and again: in birds; in the jerboas, jumping mice, and kangaroo rats, which have a remarkably bird-like hindlimb with three toes and fused metatarsals; and in the kangaroos and wallabies, where increased leverage is gained by extension of digit 4, digits 2 and 3 being small and syndactylous (i.e. united with digit 4 by soft tissue).

The biped with which we are most familiar is, of course, man. It is worth pausing for a moment, before thinking about human bipedalism, to consider that most of the bipeds so far described are no such thing. With the exception of man and birds, they are, in fact, tripods relying heavily on the support of their tails for stability, at least when at rest. True bipedalism, with the ability to stand erect on two feet, is limited to groups which have at some point spent a considerable period of the evolutionary history freed from the ground, either in flight or aerial locomotion through the branches of trees. The development of excellent vision, which is also shared by birds and primates, is another consequence. This may be coincidental, but, on the other hand, there is a case for suggesting that true bipedalism, besides structural modification to the limb, requires an excellent sense of proprioception and balance, which is developed as a consequence of flight or near-flight through the forest canopy.

2.4. Bipedalism in man

Bipedalism in man is worth considering separately, both because of its intrinsic interest and because the modifications seen in the human skeleton are in some respects different from those seen in the types already considered. Most of our primate relatives can stand on their hindlimbs, and many may occasionally walk for a few paces, but this is far from habitual. Napier (1967) has classified extant and fossil primates according to the proportions of their limbs: he found that a hitherto neglected group of lemurs and the earliest fossil primates had long hindlimbs and short forelimbs, a situation which contrasts markedly with living apes, usually considered to be our closest extant relatives. This category was supposed to have exhibited 'vertical clinging and leaping' as a mode of progress from tree to tree. This may even have been the basic locomotor pattern which made arboreal life possible. However, it seems from the fossil evidence that an intermediate quadrupedal stage must have occurred between this group and man.

Modern quadrupedal primates (the closest thing we have to the hypothetical intermediate quadrupedal stage) are so constructed that, when a bipedal stance is adopted, the hip has to be bent (Fig. 2.3). This moves the centre of gravity forwards, requiring a compensatory bending of the knees. In order to avoid this rather ungainly and inefficient bent-knee stance, a number of anatomical changes are required. The hindlimbs need to be lengthened relative to the forelimbs (a familiar bipedal/tripedal modification). The pelvis needs to be modified, but in the opposite direction to that seen in dinosaurs and birds, because of the change in the major axes. In bipedal reptiles, the tail was used to counterbalance the weight of the forepart of the body. The backbone was, therefore, held within a

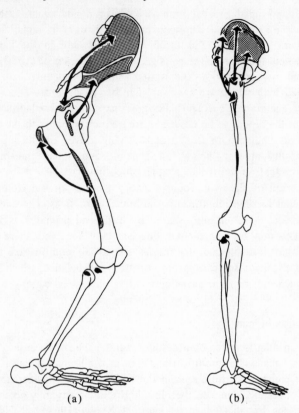

(a) (b)

FIG. 2.3. In the gorilla (a) an upright stance can only be achieved at the expense of bent hip and knee. In man (b) bones and muscles are modified so that an upright stance is possible with hip and knee extended.

few degrees of parallel to the ground. The same condition is seen in the truly bipedal flightless birds, such as the emus and ostriches: although the tail is reduced, the spine is almost horizontal at pelvic level. In man, a reverse condition has been established, and the axis of the vertebral column is vertical. The pelvis has accordingly become tilted backwards so that the formerly anterior ilium is now superior. To achieve stability in the reptiles and birds the pelvis was lengthened: to achieve stability in man it is shortened and broadened. The hip and knee joints are also modified, as is the design of the foot. The femora slope inwards, because of the width of the pelvis, which allows the knees to be placed close together in the midline.

These modifications allowed, or were a consequence of, the development of the striding gait of modern man, which permits long distances to be covered at considerable speed and with relative ease. The striding gait involves retraction of the leg to a position behind the axis of the vertebral column. This can be done only if the ischium is short. Amongst possible human ancestral fossils, *Austra-*

lopithecus had a long ischium almost the size of that of a modern ape, and stabilization of the pelvis by the strong gluteus medius and minimus muscles was incomplete: it may be pictured as moving at something of a jog trot. *Homo habilis*, a more advanced hominid of 1.75 million years ago, was almost certainly a strider. The foot here was almost identical to that of modern man, with the very human, robust, great toe aligned with its fellows.

2.5. Quadrupedal running

Efficient quadrupedal locomotion dates from the modifications which allowed the limbs to be brought below the body, and has been brought to perfection in mammals. Again and again in the Reptilia we see the shortened front legs of archosaurian ancestors, but the line leading to mammals (which diverged from a common stock very early on, before archosaurian specialities had developed) showed no bipedal tendencies; indeed, they still had the sprawling amphibian gait. Amongst the primitive, mammal-like reptiles, the pelycosaurs, we can find *Varanosaurus,* a smallish animal measuring about 1 metre overall, including a very long tail, with legs a little longer and slimmer than those of its ancestral cotylosaurs, but resembling them in being aquatic. Other groups of pelycosaurs were herbivorous (implied by rather bulky proportions consistent with large volume of food intake) or carnivorous (implied by tooth structure). The limbs in those types are again slim, suggesting a rapid gait.

In the more advanced mammal-like reptiles, we see further modification. Associated with the more efficient positioning of the limbs are changes in the structure of the limbs themselves and of their girdles. The shoulder girdle still contains both dermal and cartilaginous elements, although the cleithrum has disappeared. The front edge of the scapula is turned out, a foretaste of the mammalian scapular spine. In the pelvis the ilium extends forwards rather than back (as primitively) and is more firmly attached to the backbone by an increased number of sacral ribs. The pubis and ischium have also moved posteriorly. All these changes can be explained by variations in the pectoral and pelvic musculature associated with the new limb positioning. The femur now lies vertically rather than horizontally and has, therefore, developed an articulation at the side of the bone rather than at the proximal end. Humerus and femur alike have become slimmer and more nearly circular in cross-section. The phalangeal formula is the mammalian 2.3.3.3.3.

The basis of the mammalian skeleton was already laid down in mammal-like reptiles: almost the only losses in elements seen in mammals are due to locomotory adaptations. Two advances which characterize the Mammalia are involved with locomotory efficiency. The first of these is homoiothermy, the ability to control body temperature and to maintain it at a constant high level; the second is the development of the epiphysis. The locomotor advantages of the first of these developments is obvious: it allowed controlled expenditure of energy over long periods and independence over climatic variations in both mammals and birds. The epiphysis allowed greater skeletal efficiency. In reptiles, the articular ends of a bone are frequently covered by cartilage. Replacement of this by bone is a slow process and leads to relatively inefficient joint surfaces. In mammals, this difficulty is overcome by moving the growth point away from the articular surface: the articular surface is thus completed early in life and the bone can grow without disturbance of the joint surface (see Chapter 3). On the attainment of adult size, the epiphysis is replaced by bone and growth ceases, in contrast to the reptilian condition where slow growth continues throughout life.

Many groups of mammals have taken advantage of homoiothermy and skeletal efficiency, and developed rapid quadrupedal locomotion. We may trace the process from the stage seen in unspecialized mammals through the intermediate condition seen in the dog, for example, to the advanced condition seen in the horse or antelope. Locomotion in unspecialized mammals seems to be similar in the opossums, tree-shrews, rats, and ferrets, where studies have been made, and we may take the way in which these species move as typical. Small mammals stand with the forefoot vertically below the shoulder joint. The foot is lifted and set down more anteriorly, and during the course of the stride the body moves laterally, so that the foot lies below its centre line. The shoulders thus sway from side to side, bringing the centre line of the chest over whichever foot is resting on the ground. On the recovery stroke the forelimb is moved laterally, so as to clear the leg on the other side. The movement of the body from side to side involves rotation of the humerus.

This is very different from the movement described in newts and in reptiles where the forefeet are well lateral to the shoulder joints, and which needs strong pectoral and supracoracoid muscles. These muscles are not required in the modified gait of mammals, nor is the strut-like connection formed by the coracoid between shoulder and sternum. In fact, in mammals the scapula is loosely attached to the body wall by muscles, and tends to rotate as a unit with the humerus in walking, so that the pivot point is not at the shoulder joint but somewhere on the upper margin of the scapula: this will increase the length of stride a little.

The hindfoot is usually anterior and lateral to the hip joint when standing; again the body sways over the particular foot which is in contact with the ground.

The repositioning of the limbs in this way obviously gives a longer stride for a given limb length: the effective length of the limbs can be further increased by holding them straighter (Fig. 2.1). We may chart an increase in stride length as we progress from the plantigrade foot of the opossum, rat or badger, to the digitigrade stance of the dog. The opossum stands on the soles of its feet, the dog on its toes with metacarpals and metatarsals almost vertical, and wrist and ankle clear of the ground.

We saw that, in the newt, the stable configuration of three feet on the ground at once could be amended into two diagonally opposite feet on the ground in the trot; this is common in mammals, but the backbone is not bent from side to side to increase the stride. A faster method of progression adopted by many mammals is the gallop. Here, the two forefeet and two hindfeet move more or less together, the animal progressing in a series of bounds, landing on its two forefeet and kicking off with its two hindfeet. The back is bent in the gallop, but in the dorso-ventral plane, not from side to side. A galloping dog can achieve four times the speed of a trotting one: for part of the cycle all feet are clear of the ground. In advanced gallopers, such as the greyhound and cheetah, this period may represent 40–50 per cent of the cycle.

When speed is of no importance, mammals may progress at a slow walk, or they may amble, that is to say both left legs are advanced, followed by both right legs. This is seen especially in long-legged species like the giraffe and camel. Probably the amble involves less risk of legs becoming entangled than would the trot.

Other mammals have progressed further by reduction in the number of toes and the adoption of the hoof. The ungulates, or hoofed mammals, are of two main types: the odd-toed perissodactyls (e.g. horse) and even-toed artiodactyls (sheep, cow). However, with respect to locomotor adaptations, these can be considered together (Figs 2.4 and 2.5).

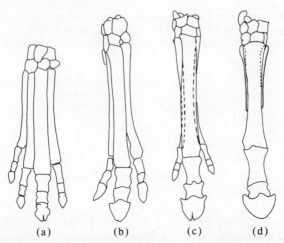

FIG. 2.4. Manus of various perissodactyls: (a) *Eohippus,* (b) *Miohippus,* (c) *Merychippus,* (d) the modern horse, *Equus.* These fossils provide an excellent series demonstrating the increasing specialization of the pentadactyl limb in evolution of the form seen in the modern horse.

We see again in these groups the familiar fast-running adaptations noted previously in bipedal forms: the proximal segment of the limb (humerus or femur) remains short, allowing the thigh musculature to work over a short distance whilst the rest of the limb is elongated to produce a long stride. Weight is usually carried on the radius or tibia, the companion bones being retained simply as convenient points of muscle attachment. The carpus and tarsus are supported by surviving toes. The astragalus develops a deep, rounded groove over which the tibia glides. Only the tips of the toes touch the ground (cf. the position in the dog) and they develop hooves: the terminal phalanx of the toe broadens and becomes surrounded by a thick, nail-like derivative of the claw, with the surface in contact with the ground protected by a horny layer with elastic connective tissue.

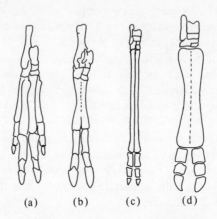

(a)   (b)   (c)   (d)

FIG. 2.5. Pes of various fossil artiodactyls: (a) *Bothoiodon,* with the primitive 4-toed arrangement, (b) *Mylohyus,* an advanced type of peccary, (c) *Oxydactylus,* a fossil camel, and (d) the cow, with a cannon bone formed from two metatarsals.

As the middle toes were the longest in primitive mammals, it is clear that adoption of the ungulate tip-toe position would leave the radial and lateral digits clear of the ground (remember that the hallux and pollex are already reduced in the dog). At this point, a division seems to have occurred as to which of the remaining digits were retained. In one group of fossil ungulates toes 1 and 5 were lost, leaving a three-toed condition evolving into the one-toed foot; in the other, the third and fourth toes were equally long and were both retained. These lines lead to the familiar division between horses on one hand, and the cloven-hoofed sheep and cows on the other.

With the loss of lateral digits went the loss of, or reduction in, the corresponding elongated metapodals. These are often represented, as in the horse, by splints of bone or, in other forms, by reduced but complete digits bearing dew claws. In the even-toed ungulates, the two main remaining metapodals have fused as the canon bone.

In ungulate running the initial spring comes from the powerful hindquarters whilst the animal lands on its forefeet. The loss of the clavicle allows the forelimb to 'float' a little on its muscular attachments providing a shock-absorbing effect.

2.6. The primate forelimb

The primates provide a clear example of the way in which a limb can be extensively modified without loss of digits. Irrespective of variations in the habitual patterns of use, the basic primitive pentadactyl pattern is retained. Furthermore, the ability to rotate the forearm − radio-ulnar rotation − is retained in some measure by all genera.

The degree of retention of radio-ulnar rotation can be neatly correlated with the patterns of primate locomotion. In quadrupedal primates the arm forms a supporting strut, and rotation is sacrificed for stability; in more acrobatic apes and monkeys, and in man extensive pronation and supination are retained.

The basic limb structure is, therefore, modified to take compression forces as a strut or to take tensile forces: in the latter case mobility of the forearm is retained, and is allied to a great deal of mobility at the shoulder.

We cannot, of course, separate all primates into quadrupeds or brachiators: intermediate types occur, and this has led to further subdivisions of the classification. Some monkeys are equally at home on all fours, hanging from a branch or pulling themselves up by their arms. As primate behaviour is studied more closely, finer and finer subdivisions continue to arise. But can we, in a simplified way, look at differences between quadrupedal and brachiating primates?

We have already mentioned stability: the other striking difference is one of proportion. Brachiating types have very long arms. If we are a little more refined in our analysis, we can specify that the forelimb and hand are relatively long, and that the thumb is relatively short, enabling the hand to form an efficient hook. In quadrupeds proportions are not so modified: incidentally, although man and monkey can extend their fingers and place palm and fingers flat on the ground, the great apes cannot. Extension of their wrists produces flexion of the fingers and thus the characteristic 'knuckle-walking' posture.

More detailed analysis demands a sophisticated technique. Recent studies (Ashton, Flinn, Oxnard, and Spence 1976) have used multivariate analysis to investigate the possible relationships between bony and muscular differences between species and behaviour. In general, these studies enable biomechanically significant 'locomotor' divisions to be defined, and these vary according to the force pattern to which the limb is subjected. These studies show, for example, that in the most mobile brachiators the articular cartilage on the trochlea of the humerus is smallest, producing a mobile elbow joint, and that the insertion of triceps gives the best mechanical advantage in quadrupedal forms, where the arm forms a propulsive strut. The scapula is also modified (Fig. 2.6), both in shape and position. It lies on the back as in man, rather than on the side of the rib-cage, and the glenoid points more laterally so that the arm may be extended in a wider range of directions: an extended rib-cage helps in this arrangement.

Man does not fit neatly into this pattern: in some respects he resembles the brachiators, in some the quadrupeds. In general, correlation is closest with the more acrobatic types, a feature perhaps best explained by his retention of the high degree of pronation–supination characteristic of these athletes.

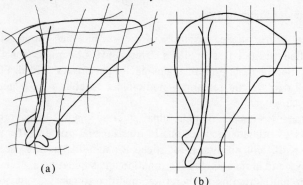

(a)

(b)

FIG. 2.6. The scapula of a brachiating primate (a) and that of man (b) to show the changes in shape associated with man's ultra-mobile forelimb. Grid lines show that the changes in shape are associated with localized growth in some regions.

2.7. Flight

The problems associated with flight have been solved with varying success by different groups of vertebrates. Most of these are gliders of varying efficiency, including flying fish, flying frogs, flying snakes and lizards, flying phalangers, flying squirrels, and flying lemurs. Gliding animals may be classified roughly into two categories: those which rely on immediate muscular effort to achieve take-off, and those which store potential energy by climbing to a high place. The flying fishes belong to the former group. Here the pectoral fins are much enlarged and, when in flight, held at right angles to the body, the initial impulse to lift the fish clear of the water having been imparted by the tail. Flight lasts only a second or two on average. Flying frogs have unusually long fingers and toes: when they jump from branch to branch, they spread these out, and the web between them forms an aerofoil. Flying lizards (such as *Draco*) have lateral skin folds which, when extended, form a fair-sized wing; these are supported by extending the ribs. The Indian flying snake also uses expanded ribs, but, in this case, they are spread wide and the ventral body wall muscles are contracted to form a concave undersurface: the alarmed flying snake makes a rigid-bodied parachute descent to the safety of the ground.

The flying lemur (*Galeopithecus*) of the East Indies is a tree-living herbivore with a fold of skin (patagium) on each side of the body which extends from neck to tail, including the hands and feet. When spread by extending the legs, this allows glides of 60 m to be made.

The problem of powered flight has been successfully tackled three times: by the birds, the pterosaurian reptiles, and the bats (Fig. 2.7). Of these three groups the birds are best known; let us look at their locomotory adaptations. A little consideration will show that the first impression conjured up by the word 'bird', an impression of vast variety of shape, size, colour and plumage, is, in fact, false. Birds are consistent in many things. The size range between ostrich and

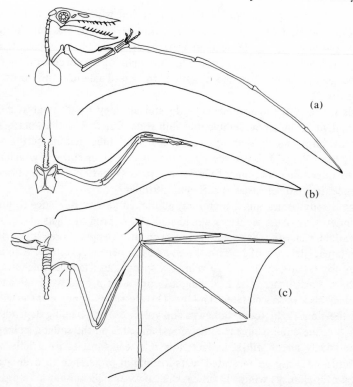

FIG. 2.7. Modifications of the pectoral limb for flight in (a) a pterosaur; (b) a modern bird; (c) *Palaeochiropteryx*, an Eocene bat.

humming-bird is far less than between whale and shrew. Powered flight has applied constraints to bird anatomy and physiology. These constraints may be reduced to the requirements of any flying machine – high power and low weight. Low weight is achieved with great subtlety. Bird bones contain cavities full of air: the skeleton of a frigate bird with a wingspan of 2 metres weighs just over 100 g – less than the weight of its feathers. Strength has not been sacrificed: there is considerable fusion of elements to provide a strong, light sacrum for bipedal locomotion, and in the proportionately light heads (achieved by the loss of teeth, heavy jaws, and jaw muscles, the function of jaws and teeth being taken over by the gizzard, located near the centre of gravity). The long, reptilian tail has been reduced to a stump and the overlapping, elegant, jointed ribs have the resilience and strength of a wicker basket. The female has only one ovary (weight-saving again?) and the gonads of both sexes atrophy outside the breeding season, to weigh only 1/1500 of their peak weight.

Perhaps the most distinctive adaptation of the bird is the feather. Feathers are ultra-light, ultra-strong and excellent insulation. Their flexibility allows the broad, trailing edge of each feather to bend on the downstroke, producing a pro-peller-shaped aerofoil, so that each contributes lift and forward motion. The principle of bird-flight is exactly the same as that which moves a fish through water (see section 1.5); an aerofoil moving through a fluid. The fluid in this case (air) is considerably less dense than water, but the same aerodynamic factors apply — lift and drag are proportional to the square of the speed, and enough lift must be generated to equal the weight. If the speed falls too low to do this, a stall results.

Birds, in fact, fly in several ways. In still air they must progress either by flapping flight or by an inexorable downhill glide. But air is seldom perfectly still and many birds can be seen to soar for many minutes, gaining height without flapping their wings. This is achieved by making use of air currents which may be thermals (ascending columns of warm air), gusts (variation of wind velocity), or differences in wind velocities at different altitudes.

Wing aerodynamics must, therefore, be looked at with reference to function; the slender wing of an albatross would stall at the speed of flight of a crow. The main variables in wing-shape are area, aspect ratio (length : breadth), wing outline or taper, presence of holes or slots, and camber or curvature. A small wing suffices for fast flight since drag $\propto$ area $\times$ speed^2, and fast aeroplanes and fast birds have small wings. The bird-wing also produces propulsive force and small wings can also be accelerated rapidly. On the other hand, a large wing area allows the slow flight found in hawks and vultures. Wing-loading depends on the weight (i.e. the cube of linear dimensions) and area on the square, so large birds need relatively larger wings; in fact, this rule seems not to be strictly applied, large birds suffering an increased wing-loading in preference to over-large (and perhaps over-clumsy) wings. In all cases a safety margin is built in: a pigeon can still fly if 45 per cent of its wing surface is removed, and hawks and owls can carry prey almost as heavy as themselves.

Despite the advantages of small wing area for fast flight, we find that many fast birds have a large wingspan in order to take advantage of the fast rate of glide which this makes possible; the albatross has an aspect ratio of 25:1, but its wing will stall at a relatively high speed. The vulture has a low aspect ratio (6:1) to allow for slow, soaring flight. Slow flight can also lead to turbulence (break-up of the smooth progress of air over the wing) which can be counteracted by separation of wing-tip feathers, producing slots which allow air to escape through the wing.

Take-off and landing in flapping flight involve a complex movement of the wing forwards and downwards with a more rapid upwards and backwards recovery. The downstroke produces lift and is powered by the pectoralis major. On the upstroke, the wing is adducted, folded and flexed, then supinated at the wrist by the pectoralis minor, supracoracoideus and other muscles. A rapid backward flick follows, produced by upward and forward rotation of the humerus, extension of the wing and pronation of the manus. These movements (largely produced by the triceps) provide a forward component. Take-off is often aided by running (to increase the forward component) or even kicking off with the legs in small birds. Landing is also fraught with peril, especially as it often involves an accurate rendez-vous with a small branch. In this case the tail is used as an air-brake, the legs are lowered, the power stroke is directed forwards rather than downwards, and one final flap gives the bird momentum to drop onto the branch.

The take-off and landing cycle is evidently very tiring, and can be maintained only for a few seconds. In sustained flight the upstroke is much simplified, being mainly passive under the influence of air pressure below the wing. The wing is flexible, and the upper arm is usually descending before the tip has reached its highest point; this contributes stability to the line of flight.

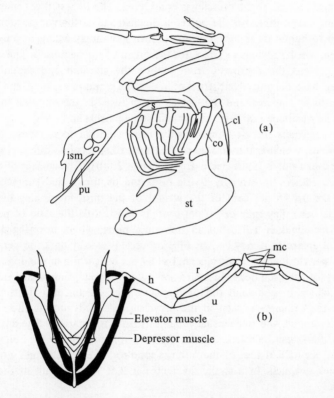

FIG. 2.8. (a) The skeletal modifications of a modern bird. cl = clavicle, co = coracoid, ism = ischium, pu = pubis, s = scapula, st = sternum. (b) The pectoral flight muscles (white meat of a chicken or turkey breast) are oganized into two layers: the wing depressors are superficial and the elevators deeper. h = humerus, mc = metacarpals, r = radius, u = ulna.

The anatomy of the bird wing is highly specialized (Fig. 2.8). The part which corresponds to the forefoot is most modified, comprising a carpometacarpus made up of two of the metacarpals and the distal carpal fused into a single element, on which the primary feathers are carried. The remaining metacarpals are usually regarded by embryologists as being those of the second, third, and fourth digits. These digits have few phalanges (2.2.1 in the chick), those of the anterior digit forming the bastard wing while the others are partly fused into a single unit.

Radius and ulna are strong, the latter larger since it carries important flight feathers, and are not capable of pronation and supination. Indeed, if they were, muscles to prevent this action in flight would be required. The wrist and elbow joints are so constructed that when the latter is bent, the former automatically bends also: this occurs when the wings are folded.

The pectoral girdle and sternum are also highly modified, but make sense if the attachment of flight muscles is considered. The largest flight muscle is the pectoralis, responsible for the powered downstroke of the wings, running from sternum to humerus, and the sternum is correspondingly enlarged to form a keel or carina, which provides a surface for the origin of the pectoralis. The coracoids, which prevent the pectoralis from pulling the sternum and shoulder region together, have become stout struts of bone. The scapulae are long, and anchored to the ribs by muscles, and the clavicles have fused in the mid-line to form the furcula or wishbone (although separate in some parrots and owls).

The pectoralis muscle runs directly from sternum to humerus; the supra-coracoideus, which is responsible for the upstroke, acts less directly, its tendon passing over a notch in the pectoral girdle (Fig. 2.8(b)). The surface of this notch is cartilage-lined. In strongly flying birds the pectoralis and supracoracoideus may make up 25 per cent of the weight of the bird; in running birds (coot, domestic hen) they may be 10 per cent. In most birds the ratio of pectoralis : supracoracoideus is 10:1, but in humming birds, where hovering demands a powerful upstroke, it may be 2:1. Flight muscle is usually dark (86 per cent dark and 14 per cent white in the pigeon, but 67 per cent white in the domestic hen).

Many of the limb bones of a bird are hollow. A wide, thin-walled tube will be much lighter than a solid rod of the same section, and not significantly less strong: the principle is seen in the bicycle frame. This modification is seen in many tetrapods, the bone usually being filled with marrow. The advantage of tubular bones can be calculated: for the human femur, where the inner diameter is about one-half of that of the outer, a solid rod of equal strength would weigh 1.3 times as much. In a swan, the factor is 2.5, for the walls of the tube are thinner.

Flapping flight is obviously expensive in terms of energy, but soaring or gliding, using naturally occurring updrafts or thermals, is very economical. Vultures, crows and some gulls keep airborne for long periods in this way. The albatross applies a different technique: over the sea, windspeed is lower near the surface than higher in the air. The albatross glides down gaining speed, then faces into the wind and rises.

Legs. Because of the highly modified forelimb, birds are bipeds. Bipedal lizards and dinosaurs relied on a long balancing tail, and many modern birds replace this with a group of long tail feathers (think of a magpie in flight). Nevertheless, if they stood with feet directly below their hip joints, they would almost certainly fall over: in practice, the femur is kept nearly horizontal, so that their knees are lateral to the centre of gravity, and their feet almost directly below their knees. The femur is usually short, and three of the metatarsals are fused into a single bone of the same order of length as the femur. The tibia and some tarsals fuse into a single tibiotarsal element; metatarsals fuse with other tarsals to form the tarsometatarsus.

Birds have large feet: this is a necessity for bipeds. They often have four rather long toes, with one pointing backwards, for grasping and perching. The muscles that bend these toes lie beside the tibiotarsus, and their tendons pass behind the ankle joint. Bending the ankle under the weight of the body thus tends to 'lock' the toes around a branch or perch.

The legs are variously adapted according to habitat. Waders, like the heron, have long legs, whilst the swift, which remains on the wing practically the whole time, has very short legs. The Sussex martlet, a legendary member of the swallow family, was said to be legless, and appears so on the sweaters of Sussex cricketers! Birds of prey have strong legs with large muscles, and sharp claws which help to seize their prey. Swimming birds usually have webbed feet or flaps of skin on either side of each toe.

2.7.1. *The evolution of flight*

Ancestral birds are not well known in the fossil record, but a few individuals have been preserved. The earliest and most famous of these is *Archaeopteryx* from the Jurassic (80 million years ago).

It is probably worthwhile at this point to consider the implications of flight. We believe that the wing must have evolved according to natural selection, an accumulation of favourable mutations each conferring a rather small selective advantage. If we follow this line of argument, the feather must have developed from a less efficient proto-feather, the wing from a less efficient proto-wing. A variant is the idea of pre-adaptation: that the feather and the wing developed for some purpose other than flight, but proved well suited to flight at a later stage. This may sound far-fetched, but we have already seen a similar process in the crossopterygian fishes, which developed a limb suitable for locomotion on land whilst still living in the water. Might not a similar transition have occurred in the ancestors of birds?

For want of other evidence we must rely rather heavily on *Archaeopteryx*. This is a very reptilian creature: the type specimen was found in lithographic limestone of very fine grain, which had clearly preserved the outlines of feathers. But for these feathers it would undoubtedly have been classified as a small coelurosaurian dinosaur, with coelurosaurian features such as light, hollow bones, long hindlimbs with extended metatarsals and reversed 'hindtoe', long neck and tail, and large orbits. The detailed similarity of dinosaur and *Archaeopteryx* forelimb skeleton is particularly striking, and includes the presence of three digits, carpus structure, and the phalangeal formula (Fig. 2.9).

These similarities would suggest a dinosaurian ancestry for birds, but there

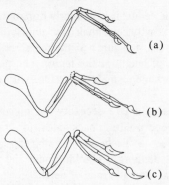

FIG. 2.9. The similarities of the limb skeleton of *Archaeopteryx* (possible bird ancestor) (a), *Ornitholestes* (b), and *Deinonychus* (c) (coelurosaurian dinosaurs) are brought out by these sketches of right forelimbs with all humeri drawn to the same size. (After Ostrom 1976.)

was a snag: birds have a clavicle which coelurosaurs appear to have lacked. This became a major obstacle to dinosaurs as the ancestors of birds (Heilmann 1926), which was not removed until the recent discovery of further species of dinosaurs complete with clavicles.

Archaeopteryx is thus belatedly restored as a child of the dinosaurs: but how good was it as a flying machine? The main flight musculature of birds runs from the extensive keel of the sterum to well-defined insertions on the humerus (Fig. 2.8(b)). *Archaeopteryx* lacked both the keel and the insertions, and presumably the muscles as well. Powered flapping flight thus seems unlikely. Also, the wing of *Archaeopteryx* was flexible, as opposed to the rigid girder of modern birds, and the pelvis was typically dinosaurian, without the modifications seen in birds to allow landing without damage. Heptonstall (1970) was able to estimate the weight of *Archaeopteryx* and also, from the size and density of the wing bones, the weight it could sustain in flight. The wings, it would seem, would just cope with gliding, but not with flapping flight.

So *Archaeopteryx* must have been a glider. But, if it habitually climbed trees and launched itself from their branches, as was commonly supposed, the feathered forelimb must have made climbing difficult, and the dinosaurian pelvis landing hazardous.

An alternative view is that *Archaeopteryx*, like the other coelurosaurs, was a runner, whose feathers served some other purpose (Nopsca 1907; Ostrom 1974). One school of thought maintains that the feathers served to retain heat, for the coelurosaurs were already homoiothermic. This implies a feathering of at least the coelurosaurian dinosaurs. Traces of these feathers have presumably not been found, because of the less than perfect conditions of fossilization which usually occur.

Feathers as heat insulation are all well and good if we accept the premise of the warm-blooded dinosaur and the idea that feathers are rarely fossilized. But *Archaeopteryx* also sported long feathers which trailed behind the arm, and which could not have provided insulation. At least two explanations have been put forward. First, that if *Archaeopteryx* did not glide from tree to tree, it must have leapt from bump to bump, gaining some lift from its 'flight' feathers (Nopsca 1907). Secondly, that *Archaeopteryx* was insectivorous, and that the feathers acted as a butterfly net (Ostrom 1974). This feat of capture demanded good coordination, which is reflected by the rather large brain of the beast.

So, we may take our pick: intrepid bird–reptile, launching itself from a tree, climbed with difficulty, to a potentially hazardous landing; fast runner becoming airborne for short periods like an early aviator caught by the new-fangled cinematograph; or serendipitous, warm-blooded, well-coordinated, feathered insectivore ready to take to the air at a moment determined by a changing environment. Of these possibilities, the arboreal glider seems to present fewest difficulties. Perhaps one day more fossils will emerge to clarify the picture.

The next group of known fossil birds is much later, and comprises specialized sea-birds: of these *Ichthyornis* was tern-like, with very well-developed modern-looking wings, whilst the six-foot *Hesperornis* was a swimmer and almost wing-less. All we can say from these two fortunate finds is that Cretaceous bird-life must have been varied. *Hesperornis* set a precedent followed by several other birds: flight was probably lost in the ostrich, cassowary, rhea, emu, and kiwi, which all became cursorial bipeds.

Pterosaurs. Archaeopteryx was clearly a descendant of the archosaurian reptile stock. The archosaurs made another sortie into the air in the unlovely shape of the Pterosauria. Again, the known types are fish eaters from marine deposits: this is probably a sampling effect, as the pterosaurs were a successful group during the Jurassic and Cretaceous periods. In the pterosaur, we find the features already described in birds, but the structure of the wing is rather different. The bones of the forelimb were hollow and airfilled, as in birds. The dermal shoulder elements were absent, but, again as in birds, the scapula and coracoid were well-developed, and the ventral sternum was large and shield-shaped to provide attachment for flight muscles (Fig. 2.10). The shoulder girdle was braced to the body by the coracoid (which was propped against the sternum) and by a lateral notch in a series of fused vertebrae into which fitted, in some forms, the upper edge of the scapula. The humerus was short and stout, with a large process for the attachment of flight muscles, and the radius and ulna were long and placed close together as a structural unit. The carpus was reduced and probably im-mobile: it carried a small backwardly directed pteroid bone of doubtful antecedence, which is thought to have supported a web of skin running to the neck region. The fifth digit is absent, the other four metacarpals running together to the base of the fingers. Three of these were of normal length, but the fourth was enormously elongated with four long phalanges forming the whole support of the skin-like membrane which formed the main part of the wing.

The pterosaurs, though widespread, could never have been very efficient in flight. The mechanical efficiency of the wings, with their limited support and soft, one-piece membrane, must have been low; partial movements, as found in

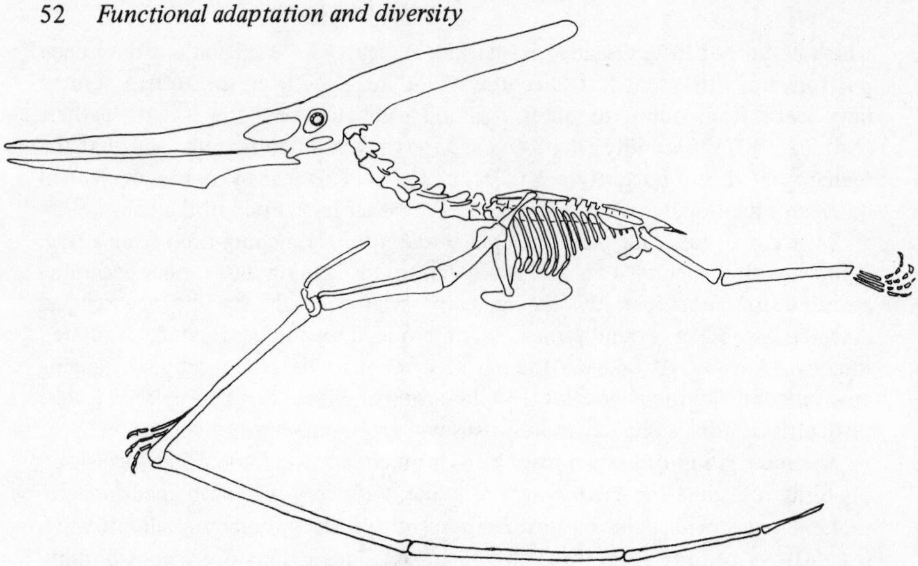

FIG. 2.10. Skeleton of a giant pterosaur, *Pteranodon*.

birds, would not have been efficient, and the large membrane must have been vulnerable to damage which would render the whole wing useless. In contrast, the loss of a few feathers has little effect on the flight of birds. Some authorities (Seeley 1901) have argued that the pterosaurs were warm-blooded with an efficient four-chambered heart, and were protected against heat loss by a coating of hair: indeed, the presence of hair is certain in at least one Russian species, *Sordes pilosus* (filthy fur, or hairy devil) (Sharov 1971). If we allow these speculations as valid, then the smaller pterosaurs, which range in size from sparrow to fruit bat, could have used flapping flight. However, these arguments are irrelevant when we consider the giant *Pteranodon* (Fig. 2.10): this could only have been a glider. On land it must have had all the easy grace of a partially furled umbrella. The long digits supporting the wing can only have pointed skywards as the animal attempted to crawl. The modified hindlegs resemble those of bats: this has led to the supposition that the resting position was hanging. But the seas over which *Pteranodon* soared were not bordered by cliffs or trees: perhaps the hooked rear limbs were used in fishing.

If we can just accept the soaring *Pteranodon* as an albatross-like wanderer, then the Texan 'Jumbo' pterosaurs, which are currently being described (Lawson 1975), must surely stretch our imagination to breaking point. The wingspan of these beasts is estimated at 15 m, and they are not marine, being found 250 miles inland. With a toothless beak, they must presumably have been carrion feeders, restricted to soft internal organs. However, this argument has its drawbacks: the pterosaurs must either have landed frequently, with great risk to life and limb, and eaten small amounts, or they must have minimized the risk by landing infrequently and gorging themselves. A gorged pterosaur must have had enormous difficulty in regaining the air, and the presence of dead dinosaurs (its food) implies the presence also of live dinosaurs (its predators), which would not encourage lengthy digestive torpor on the ground.

Bats. Bats are the only mammals which have developed powered flight, but are very numerous in terms of both number of species and number of individuals. They range in size from 3 g to 1 kg as adults. They fly by means of a wing membrane stretched between limbs and body. The second to fifth digits are very long with the membrane stretched between them. Elbow and wrist joints are simple hinges and can bend only in the plane of the wings: this means that, as in birds, the wing cannot twist in flight.

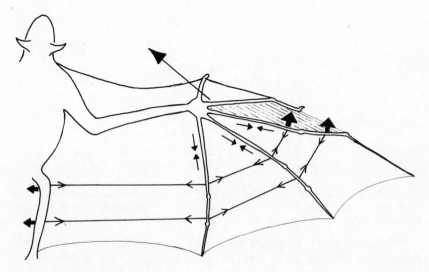

FIG. 2.11. The skin of a bat's wing is kept taut during flight by muscle action. For fuller explanation, see text.

In flight the wing is kept taut (Fig. 2.11) by means of the extensor carpi radialis longus muscle, which inserts into the second metacarpal and tends to swing it forwards. A ligament running from the top of the second digit to the base of the terminal phalanx of the third ensures that this digit is also kept extended. Other muscles act in the opposite direction, pulling the hindlimb medially towards the tail. The direction of the tension exerted on the membrane changes at each digit, so that the bones of the fingers are kept in compression. Elastic fibres in the wing membrane run in the same direction as these forces, and the wing contains some small muscles. That part of the wing anterior to the arm, for example, is kept taut by the occipitopollicalis muscle (Fig. 2.12).

The main flight muscle, as in birds, is the pectoralis, but this is aided by the serratus anterior and subscapularis. Between them, these muscles total 10-12 per cent of body weight, less than in most birds. The sternum, although enlarged, is not as large as in birds, reflecting the importance in flight of other muscles which originate elsewhere. Small bats can fly rapidly upwind, but seem to fly slowly in strong tailwinds. The large fruit bats glide almost as well as falcons or vultures.

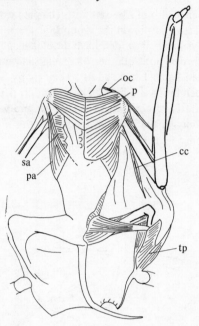

FIG. 2.12. Many muscles of both fore- and hind-limb are concerned in bat flight. cc = coracocutaneus, oc = ocipitopollicalis, p = pectoralis, pa = pectoralis abdominalis, sa = serratus anterior, tp = tensor plagiopatagii.

Perhaps one of the most remarkable aspects of bat flight is manoeuvrability. This seems to be due to the structure of the wing, the flexibility of the membrane due to the presence of individual digits combining with the small wing muscles already mentioned to provide a wing susceptible to very fine control of shape, and presumably aerodynamic efficiency.

2.8. Return to the water – adaptations to swimming

The continued changes in climate and flora and fauna, which the earth under-goes periodically, mean that alternative habitats are continually becoming available. It is perhaps ironic that the descendants of land-living tetrapods should so often return to the aquatic habitat of their ancestors, but this recolonization of water has occurred again and again during tetrapod history.

The evolution of appendicular locomotion and the virtual loss of segmental musculature has continually posed problems for the animal attempting to return to an existence based upon swimming. Yet the turtles, the ichthyosaurs and pleiosaurs, many birds, the seals and sea-lions, the sea-cows, dolphins, porpoises, and whales among others have successfully re-adapted. The degree of this adapta-tion varies, as does the method of swimming. Some groups have modified limbs into rowing oars, others have relegated them to their former role of aerofoils and redeveloped axial propulsion; in yet others, a compromise has been reached.

The turtles are a good example of 'paddlers'. In fact, they had very little choice in the matter. The presence of the familiar bony carapace, developed as terrestrial armour, meant that axial locomotion was impossible. Marine turtles have limbs adapted for efficient paddling: the proximal elements short and stout, the distal ones elongated and broadened to form large, webbed flippers. The return to an aquatic environment meant that large, heavy turtles were possible because of the uplift of the water, and, in the absence of many predators, the armoured shell could be reduced to a minimum, probably as a weight-saving device.

Although by no means a phylogenetic classification, we may arrange the various extinct marine reptiles in order of completeness of the aquatic modifications (Figs 2.13 and 2.14).

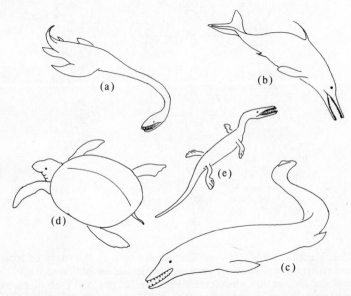

FIG. 2.13. Various types of aquatic reptiles: (a) *Elasmosaurus,* a plesiosaur, (b) ichthyosaur, (c) mososaur, (d) turtle, (e) mesosaur.

The mesosaurs were a group of secondarily aquatic reptiles of rather crocodilian appearance: unhampered by a shell, they were able to use their considerable tail for swimming, aided by powerful hindfeet. The smaller front limbs were perhaps used in steering.

The nothosaurs were clearly aquatic, with a short tail, a longer neck than that of mesosaurs, but with rather unspecialized limbs which were probably webbed. The mososaurs, an early group of marine lizards, form a similar, but unrelated, group.

The plesiosaurs were also long-necked and had developed the limb paddle (with which they rowed through the water) to a much higher degree. In the plesiosaurs, the body was broad and flat, the tail of reduced importance. The head was again set on a flexible neck. In the shoulder region the dorsal part of the scapula was small, but ventrally it and the coracoid formed a huge, long plate for the attachment of the powerful muscles needed for a downward and backward paddling action. The pubis and ischium had developed similarly. The rowing paddles had elongated proximal elements, but distally the large number of elements is difficult to homologize with certainty.

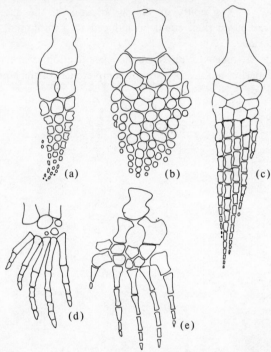

FIG. 2.14. Various degress of modification are seen in the limbs of secondarily aquatic vertebrates: (a) pectoral limb of *Merriamia*, an ichthyosaur, (b) pectoral limb of *Ophthalmosaurus*, another ichthyosaur, (c) pectoral limb of a plesiosaur, *Elasmosaurus*, (d) pelvic limb of a nothosaur, *Lariosaurus*, (e) pectoral limb of a mososaur, *Clidastes*.

If the plesiosaurs represent the ultimate in the paddling aquatic reptile, then the ichthyosaurs represent the ultimate 'pseudo-fish', occupying the position of the present-day dolphins and porpoises. Ichthyosaurs had a fish-like caudal fin, with the vertebral column bending downwards into its lower part, and a rather fusiform, laterally compressed body. Preserved outlines of body contours show a large dorsal fin, which had no bony skeletal support. The limbs are reduced, especially the pelvic ones, to steering paddles. The main method of locomotion must have been axial, aided by the large fish-like tail. Although all elements of the limb girdles were present, they were small and poorly ossified: the pelvis had lost its connection with the vertebral column. The humerus and femur were much shortened, and all other elements tended to become hexagonal or rounded discs. There was always hyperphalangy, and the number of digits was variable: in some forms a reduction to three, in others an increase to seven or eight, which seems to have been accomplished by the division of single toes into two at some point in the paddle.

Many different orders of birds have exploited the abundant food supply of the aquatic habitat. The degree of modification here depends on how complete the adaptation has become. We mentioned *Hesperornis,* one of the few known Cretaceous birds, which had already abandoned flight in favour of an almost totally marine existence and had, in consequence, almost totally lost its wings (marine birds must come ashore to breed: the ichthyosaurs were better adapted and were probably viviparous, giving birth at sea). More common is a combination of flight and swimming ability, the most obvious concession to the latter being webbing of the digits, or, in some cases, a pseudo-webbing of broad flaps of skin on each toe which allows the foot to function as a paddle in water, but is less hampering on land (Fig. 2.15). This type of adaptation is seen again and again in the divers, the grebes, the pelican family, ducks and geese, auks, and gulls. A few types have followed the *Hesperornis* in abandoning flight; of these, the now extinct great auk and the penguins are best known. In penguins, flight is impossible: the wing bones have flattened and fused to become a powerful fin (Fig. 2.15(f)). The foot, too, is modified. It is, of course, webbed and the metatarsals are only partially fused, giving a wider paddle.

Many mammals have also taken to the water again (Fig. 2.16). The degree of adaptation shown by aquatic animals is very variable, and this point is best brought out by listing the types of mammals, many of which are familiar to us, which spend at least some of their time in water. One might like to speculate whether future generations of these types will be more or less aquatic and ask which way evolution is progressing in each group.

When one speaks of aquatic mammals, one thinks first of the Cetaceans (whales, dolphins, porpoises) and pinnipeds (seals), but a longish list can be compiled (Table 2.1).

Those mammals which spend most, as opposed to some, of their time in water have much greater modifications. The pinnipeds – seals and walruses – are exclusively paddlers. We must assume that the seals' ancestors had a tail reduced to such an extent that salvage was impossible. The hindlimbs have been turned back as a substitute horizontal tail, whilst the front ones are steering organs (Fig. 2.17). The upper parts of the fore- and hind-limbs lie within the trunk, and the hand and foot are long, although the number of phalanges is not increased. All five toes are retained and webbed, the anterior digit being the longest. The scaphoid, lunare and centrale are fused in the hand: this is probably an ancestrally inherited feature rather than a structural modification. Ashore, seals can barely drag themselves along. The eared seals, which include the sea-lions, are probably more primitive, as the hindlimbs are still flexible enough to be brought forward for locomotion on land.

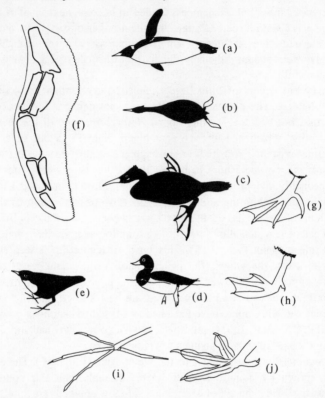

FIG. 2.15. Modifications in aquatic birds: the penguins (a) 'fly' under water using wings modified as paddles (f), grebes (b) and cormorants (c) swim under water using powerful webbed feet. Ducks and other waterfowl (d) paddle on the surface while the dipper (e) runs along the bottom of swift-flowing streams using no morphological adaptations. Modifications in the hindlimbs of birds: (g) shag, (h) duck, (i) jacana, suited to walking on floating plants, (j) coot.

The other order of marine mammals, the Cetacea, which includes the whales, dolphins, and porpoises, are pseudo-fish rather than paddlers, having regained the torpedo-like, streamlined shape, and reverted to axial locomotion via a pair of horizontal flukes and an up-and-down rather than a side-to-side propulsive force. The hindlimbs are lost completely, although they may be represented by a vestigial femur and sometimes also a tibia. The forelimbs are transformed into broad, short, steering flippers, which are usually pentadactyl (though in rorquals the digital number is reduced to four), and may have around a dozen phalanges in the elongated central digits (Fig. 2.17). The humerus, radius, and ulna are short and flattened, and the mobility of the elbow and other joints is much reduced.

Secondary modifications of the limbs for swimming in these diverse groups demonstrate clearly the principle of convergent evolution. Tendencies for short

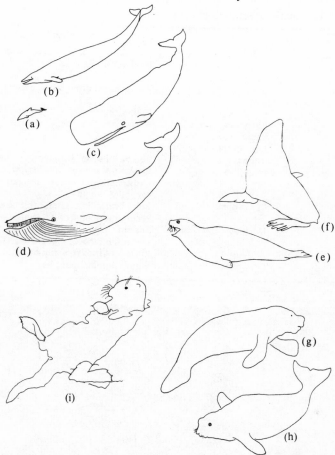

FIG. 2.16. Modifications seen in secondary aquatic mammals: dolphins and porpoises (a). Whales (b), (c), and (d) are pseudo-fish. Seals and sea-lions, (e) and (f), are also streamlined, but have retained external hindlimbs as a means of propulsion. Dugongs and manatees, (g) and (h), are slow-moving vegetarians, which paddle through the water using their forelimbs. The otters (i) swim using a combination of webbed feet and broad tail.

proximal bones, loss of joint mobility, hyperphalangy, and webbing appear repeatedly.

One remarkable feature of the cetaceans is that, although the hindlimbs were lost 40 million years ago, there are a number of reports of rare cases of external pelvic limbs (Lande 1978). Thus, in the sperm whale, six cases are known of external hindlimbs, including the presence of some phalanges (Yablokov 1974), while Andrews (1921) described a humpback whale with hindlimbs which, although poorly developed, protruded 127 cm. Dolphins also, in rare cases, possess external pelvic limbs. According to Dollo's law, characters once lost in evolution can never be regained, but these examples indicate clearly that the

TABLE 2.1. Aquatic adaptation in mammals

Group	Order	Members spending significant periods of time in the water
Monotremes	–	Duck-billed platypus
Marsupials	–	–
Placentals	Insectivores	Water-shrew, otter-shrew, desman
	Bats	–
	Primates	Crab-eating macaque, proboscis monkey
	Edentates	–
	Pholidotes	–
	Lagomorphs	–
	Rodents	Sewellel, beaver, fishing-rat, water-vole, muskrat, water-rat (Florida), water-rat (Australia), water-rat (New Guinea), capybara, coypu
	Carnivores	Polar bear, mink, otter, otter civet, water-genet, marsh mongoose, jaguar, seal
	Ungulates	Sea-cow, tapir, hippopotamus, water-chevrotain, mouse elk, buffalo (Indian), buffalo (African), water-buck, marsh-buck
	Cetaceans	Whale, dolphin, porpoise

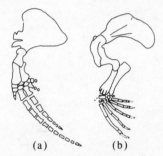

(a)   (b)

FIG. 2.17. Skeleton of the flippers of a pilot whale (a) and a seal (b).

capacity to develop atavistic structures may be retained through a lengthy period. Presumably the genes controlling hindlimb development are still present, but their expression is repressed, probably through the selection of other modifying genes.

In addition to these major modifications, consider the many minor adaptations seen in the partially aquatic mammals. The European water-shrew lives in streams and ponds, and subsists on a diet of freshwater crustaceans and insects and occasional small fish. It dives and swims well, its toes being fringed with hairs which form a semi-web. Desmans, closer to moles than shrews, have webbed feet.

Fringing or partial webbing of the toes is also seen in fishing-rats, muskrats, the New Guinea and Australian water-rats (the former with small front feet and large webbed hind ones), and the duck-billed platypus. But many mammals, though lacking special adaptations, can put up a good performance in the water: few mammals, in fact, cannot swim if compelled.

2.9. Loss of limbs

One further locomotory group, again phylogenetically heterogeneous, is those
vertebrates which have renounced appendicular locomotion and gone back to
axial S-curves (Fig. 2.18). This type of adaptation is seen in fossil Amphibia, in
the snake-like *Ophiderpeton* and *Sauropleura,* in the living forms such as the
burrowing Apoda, in fossil and modern reptilian forms, including the burrowing
skinks and Amphisbaenia, anguimorphs, and, of course, the snakes.

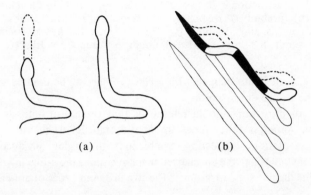

FIG. 2.18. Locomotion in snakes and limbless lizards has reverted to S-curve,
using axial musculature (a). This is exceptionally efficient, and side-winding
snakes (b) may achieve great speeds.

It seems that in long, slimly built amphibians and reptiles some degree of
axial locomotion has always been retained (as in the modern lizards). The
development of a freely movable rib system allied to horny scales allowed
snakes to prevent backslip without the aid of limbs. The burrowing habit, so
common in other limbless forms, must also have rendered limbs superfluous.

The lizards are the best group in which to study the evolution of limblessness,
since they have a large number of forms at intermediate stages of limb reduction.
Gans (1975) argues that the process begins with body elongation which precedes
the reduction of the limbs. Lande (1978) has analysed all the species of the
skinks, which exhibit all varieties of limb reduction, to show that there is close
association between relative body elongation and relative limb reduction
including loss of digits. Lizards may be arranged in a series according to their
degree of limb reduction (Underwood 1976). Loss of elements begins distally,
with digital and phalangeal number being reduced, and proceeds to the proximal
level (Fig. 2.19). Severely reduced limbs may consist of stylopod and zeugopod
capped by a single fused digit (*Tetradactylus africanus*) or of reduced stylopod
alone (e.g. the femur of *Pygopus lepidopus*). While most snakes have lost all
traces of both fore- and hind-limbs and their girdles, in *Python* and other boids

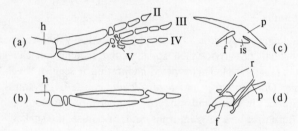

FIG. 2.19. Limb reduction in lizards and a snake: (a) forelimb, *Chalcides sepoides* (a skink), (b) forelimb, *Tetradactylus africanus*, (c) pelvis and hindlimb, *Lialis burtoni*, (d) pelvis and hindlimb (within the ribs), *Trachyboa gularis* (a boid snake). f = femur, h = humerus, is = ischium, p = pubis, r = ribs. (After Underwood 1976.)

there is a reduced femur capped with a claw, thought to be used by the male to stimulate the female during coitus.

Mention of burrowing should remind us that the use of limbs is not solely locomotory. Amongst other functions of the limb, let us mention briefly an associated adaptation. Burrowing, combined with digging, produces its own specializations: consider the specialized hand in various mole-like mammals (Fig. 2.20) and the digging specialization of the five different types of ant-eaters.

2.10. Homology and the pentadactyl limb pattern

The common plan which lies behind the vertebrate limb, however specialized, has always intrigued and puzzled biologists. Aristotle, the founder of comparative anatomy, remarked on the structural similarities between fish fin, bird wing and quadruped leg. Richard Owen (1849), the mid-nineteenth century opponent of evolution and the greatest comparative anatomist of his day, was sufficiently impressed by the agreement between the fundamental plans of many organ systems, such as the limb in its variety of form in different species, that he introduced the concept of 'homology' (1843). Homologous structures are those which show such fundamental similarity. But, believing as he did in special creation, Owen was unable to explain homology since he admitted that there is no reason why structures serving such different functions as paddles, wings and legs should be constructed according to a similar pattern.

The solution emerged when Charles Darwin's concept of evolution by natural selection revolutionized biological thought. When evolution is taken into consideration, homology ceases to be an inexplicable similiarity of certain organ systems of different animals; instead, it is a consequence of these animals' descent from a common ancestor (Lovejoy 1959). Homology as illustrated by the similarity in skeletal structure of vertebrate limbs is one of the set-pieces in *The Origin of Species*. 'What can be more curious', Darwin (1872) asks, 'than that the hand of a man, formed for grasping, that of a mole for digging, the leg

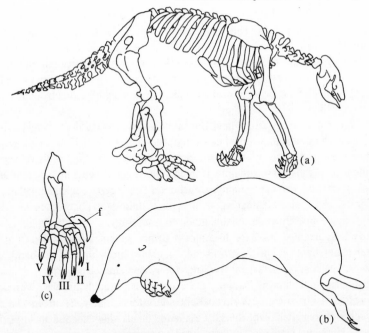

FIG. 2.20. Graviportal (weight-bearing) adaptations are evident in the pillar-like hindlimbs of the ground sloth. The forelimbs are modified for digging, as are those of the mole (b). Note that the broad foot of the mole *Talpa* (c) has a well-developed falciform bone (f), forming in effect a sixth pre-axial digit.

of the horse, the paddle of the porpoise, and the wing of the bat, should all be constructed on the same pattern, and should include similar bones, and in the same relative positions?' He concludes, quoting Flower, that 'this conformity to type . . . is powerfully suggestive of inheritance from a common ancestor.' Homology is explained by evolution. Let Darwin conclude the argument in his own words:

> The explanation is to a large extent simple on the theory of the selection of successive slight modification . . . In changes of this nature, there will be little or no tendency to alter the original pattern, or to transpose the parts. The bones of a limb might be shortened and flattened to any extent, becoming at the same time enveloped in thick membrane, so as to serve as a fin; or a webbed hand might have all its bones, or certain bones, lengthened to any extent, with the membrane connecting them increased, so as to serve as a wing; yet all these modifications would not tend to alter the framework of the bones or the relative connexion of the parts. If we suppose that an early progenitor – the archetype as it may be called – of all mammals, birds, and reptiles, had its limbs constructed on the existing general pattern, for whatever purpose they served, we can at once perceive the plain signification of the homologous construction of the limbs throughout the class.

It thus appears that the concept of homology is soundly based and is satisfactorily explained in terms of inheritance from a common ancestor, whose 'archetypal' limb plan has undergone adaptive radiation and has been modified for different functions in different tetrapods. But, as de Beer (1971) has recently pointed out, homology still raises many unsolved problems.

Since organs arise through embryonic development, evidence as to homology was eagerly sought from this field of biology as well as from comparative anatomy. Darwin, in his glossary to the sixth edition of *The origin of species* prepared by Dallas, defined homology as 'that relation between parts which results from their development from corresponding parts, either in different animals, as in the case of the arm of man, the foreleg of a quadruped, and the wing of a bird . . .'

In fact, embryology in its post-Darwinian phase provides equivocal evidence concerning the determination of homology (de Beer 1958, 1971). The arguments are complex and cannot be considered in detail here. Suffice it to say that homologous organs may originate from different germ layers in different animal groups, while, on the other hand, a particular tissue type, such as cartilage, may be formed by cells originating from either mesoderm or ectoderm. Hence, embryology is not always a reliable guide to homology.

Darwin's attempt to base homology firmly in embryology led him to a further generalization which is no longer tenable, and which, in the hands of his follower, Haeckel, diverted embryology for a time along the barren pathways of phylogenetic speculation. Darwin, great naturalist though he was, was not an embryologist: but the embryological considerations briefly set out in *The origin of species* represented evolutionary evidence in his view 'second in importance to none'. His views were greatly influenced by those of the German embryologist, von Baer (1828), who had pointed out that, in development, general characters appeared before the special characters of the particular species, and that, during its development, an embryo gradually diverges from the form of other embryos. But von Baer emphasized that embryos of one species are not like adult stages of animals lower in the scale, but resemble their younger stages. Darwin assimilated the first principles of von Baer but rejected the last (Oppenheimer 1959). Instead, he considered that embryos passed through stages which resembled the adult forms of animals lower in the evolutionary scale. 'The embryos of the existing vertebrata will shadow forth the full grown structure of some of the forms . . . which existed at the earlier period of the earth's history' (Darwin 1909), and again, 'the embryonic state of each species and group of species partially shows us the structure of their less modified ancient progenitors' (Darwin 1872).

It is clear that Darwin was thinking in particular of limb development as an example of this generalization.

The forelimbs, which once served as legs to a remote progenitor, may have become, through a long course of modification, adapted in one descendant to act as hands, in another as paddles, in another as wings: but . . . the forelimbs will not have been much modified in the embryo of these several forms; although in each form the forelimb will differ greatly in the adult stage. It is probable from what we know of the embryos of mammals, birds, fishes, and reptiles, that these animals are the modified descendants of some ancient progenitor, which was furnished in its adult state with . . . four fin-like limbs . . . fitted for aquatic life.

From this generalization of Darwin, mistaken though we now believe it to be, two important attitudes emerged which coloured later interpretations of limb structure and development. The first was that developing limbs at early stages were essentially similar, irrespective of species, and secondly, that the developing limbs of higher vertebrates would show structural similarities to the adult limbs of their ancestors, the primitive Amphibia.

Haeckel's famous doctrine of recapitulation formulates Darwin's generalization in a much 'harder' form. Ontogeny (individual development) repeats phylogeny (the evolutionary history of the race), he asserted, while phylogeny is the mechanical cause of ontogeny. Thus, as far as limb development is concerned, the limb buds of amniote ambryos represent the fin or limb paddles of their lungfish or primitive amphibian ancestors. Recapitulation is by now widely discredited: the contrary evidence has been emphasized by de Beer (1958). But the echoes of recapitulation still haunt embryology. Even relatively recent accounts (Holmgren 1933, 1955; Romanoff 1960) of the transition of the limb skeletal pattern from condensation through cartilage 'model' to bony element have as their basis the assumption that the skeleton of specialized limbs passes through a prechondrogenic stage at which the pattern of the ancestral adult amphibian limb skeleton is repeated. The assumption may not be as explicit as this; it may take the form of interpreting the development of a specialized limb skeleton, such as that of the bird wing, as taking place through modification of the fundamental archetypal pentadactyl limb pattern discernible at the prechondrogenic phase (Montagna 1945). This interpretation can no longer be accepted since recent studies (Hinchliffe 1976, 1977; Dalgleish 1964) (discussed at greater lengths in Chapter 3) suggest that the prechondrogenic condensation pattern is essentially the same as that of the cartilage 'models' and the final bony skeleton, and that the overall pattern is quite different (especially in wrist and ankle) in widely separated species, such as the chick and the mouse. It is straining the evidence to suggest that the resemblances between the varied forms of adult pentadactyl limbs, which make us consider them homologous, arise due to their development from a common pentadactyl archetype at the condensation phase.

Darwin's attempt to base homology firmly on embryology also fails when it is realized that limbs, despite their undoubted homology, do not occupy the same position in different tetrapod species (de Beer 1971). Somites contribute to the limb bud material which forms the limb musculature, and, since the ventral motor nerve roots remain 'faithful' to the muscle plates of their own segment, it is possible in the adult to determine which trunk segments have contributed to the limb. In man, the forelimb is formed at the level of somites 13-18, in the chick 15-20 (Chevalier, Kieny, Mauger, and Sengel 1977), in the lizard, *Lacerta,* 6-13 (Raynaud 1977), and in the newt 2-5. Thus, the position of the limb – and indeed the paired fish fins – may become shifted up or down the body in evolution.

What, then, remains of the concept of homology with reference to the limb? Certain features are repeated time and again: the stylopod with its single element, the zeugopod with its double element, the elbow and wrist joints, the autopod with metatarsals or metacarpals and phalanges organized as five digits. But even these fixed points sometimes disappear: in the secondarily aquatic reptiles even the stylopod/zeugopod/autopod distinctions have been lost. A reduction in the digital number from five is fairly common, although an increase, such as that in ichthyosaurs, is much rarer. On the other hand, features such as the number of elements and their arrangement in carpus or tarsus, and the number of phalanges, are much more subject to evolutionary change. In addition, as we have just seen, the limb is a pattern which has been transposed over the long axis of the verte-brate body, like a tune which can be transposed over the keys. The pentadactyl limb should be viewed, not as a fixed definable pattern, but as one with some relatively consistent features and with certain plastic areas, ever subject to change. But it is nonetheless clear that the primitive amphibian pentadactyl limb represented a pattern with remarkable evolutionary potential.

3 Descriptive embryology

3.1. The development of paired fins

Just as a discussion of the phylogeny of paired limbs must start with a discussion of paired fins, a consideration of the development of the limb must also embrace the development of the fin. Indeed, an understanding of the process of formation of the relatively uncomplicated fish fin may help to gain an understanding of the more complex limb of tetrapods.

The development of paired fins in fishes resembles that of the median fins whose adult structure is also very similar. In the midline of the developing fish embryo an epidermal fold develops which runs along the dorsum of the trunk to the tip of the tail, where it meets a similar fold which runs forward ventrally to end just posterior to the cloaca. This fold is invaded by mesoderm to produce an extensive 'provisional' embryonic fin. The provisional fin is later modified in shape, growing in regions where the definitive fin is to be, regressing elsewhere. On either side of the median plate of mesoderm, from which the skeleton will develop, the fin is invaded by a series of dorsal muscle buds, one from each myotome. The body at this stage is growing faster than the fin: this results in the strict relationship between myotome and bud being preserved only in the centre of the fin; at either end the buds appear to migrate into the fin, backwards from anterior segments and forwards from posterior ones. Buds at the ends may also be smaller than those contributed by central myotomes, and may ultimately fuse with one another.

Paired fins are also first seen as long narrow ridges of folded epidermis which are invaded by mesoderm and by muscle buds, though in this case from the ventral part of each myotome. This primitive embryonic ridge, or Wolffian ridge, may run almost the length of the body, and has been tentatively equated with the archetypal 'fin fold'.

In elasmobranchs and some other fishes, the paired fins also develop over an area larger than that which they will ultimately occupy, the relative narrowing of the base producing the characteristic posterior notch of the shark fin (Fig. 3.1). Muscle buds may develop along the whole length of the embryonic fold (Fig. 3.2) and indeed beyond it, gradually becoming vestigial and ultimately disappearing outside fin areas. In sharks two buds per myotome are found, except near the ends of the series where there may be only one. A large number of these reach the base of the fin, separate from their myotome and divide into an upper (dorsal) and a lower (ventral) portion, which spread out to form the abductor and adductor muscles of the adult fin. In bony fishes, there may be one or two myotomal buds per myotome according to species.

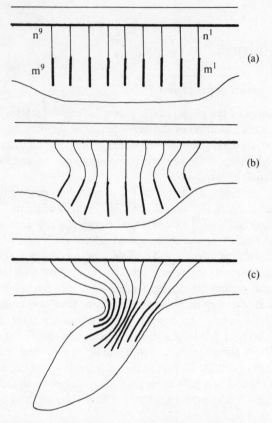

FIG. 3.1. The result of constriction of the fin base on its nerve supply and musculature. In (a), a fin fold, the nerve cord sends nine branches, n^1–n^9, to nine muscle blocks, m^1–m^9. In (b) and (c) we see the effects of progressive narrowing of the fin base on the course and disposition of these elements. (After Goodrich 1930.)

In the trout there are four somites contributing to the pelvic fins, and it is reported that the somitic cells contribute the muscle and also the endoskeleton, while the somatopleural cells contribute the dermal rays (Geraudie and François 1973).

As the skeletal elements of the fin develop from the mesoderm between the two halves of segmental muscle buds, the muscles which will ultimately operate on any one element will have the same segmental nerve supply. Owing to the narrowing of the base of the fin, however, the segmental nerves must converge anteriorly and posteriorly they may be gathered together to form a 'collector nerve' (Fig. 3.3).

The skeletal elements in the central mesodermal plate of sharks differentiate distally as separate elements, but proximally as a more or less continuous mass which contains the rudiments of both proximal elements and girdle. Some of the

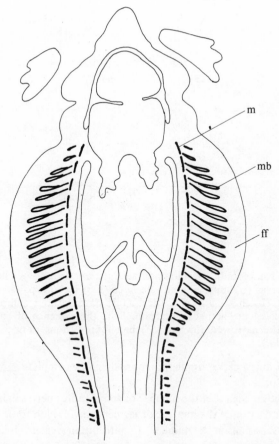

FIG. 3.2. Embryonic stage of the dogfish *Scyllium*. Note that in the extensive fin fold (ff) each myotome (m) contributes muscle buds (mb). (After Goodrich 1930.)

segmental nerve supply passes anterior or posterior to the girdle, while the rest pierces it.

It seems likely, from what we have said, that the nerve supply to each myotomal contribution, and hence to the muscles derived from it, is fixed and is established early over a short, direct route. Yet if we dissect the nerve supply of a fin or a limb, we see that the nerves enter via an apparently inextricably mixed nerve plexus. In fact, the apparent confusion is largely due to the spread of sensory nerves. Motor nerves usually correspond in number to the number of segments making myotomal contribution to the limb, often with little or no overlap. Experimental stimulation of the segmental nerves of selachians (Goodrich 1906) shows that radial muscles are often supplied in segmental order. In some cases there is overlap, thought to be due to the previously mentioned fusion of myotomal buds near the ends of a fin series. Where overlap does occur, it is

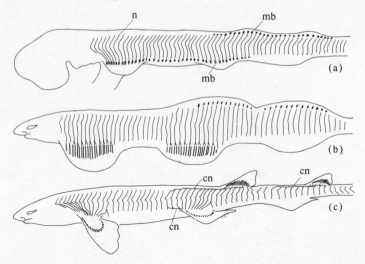

FIG. 3.3. Later stages in the development of *Scyllium*. (a) shows a late embryonic stage with nerves (n) supplying muscle buds (mb) in both paired and unpaired fin rudiments. (b) shows a hypothetical adult stage without compression of the fin bases, and (c) the actual adult form. Note the presence of collector nerves (cn) serving the narrowed fin bases. Other abbreviations as in Fig. 3.2. (After Goodrich 1906.)

usually found that a nerve supplies no more than one complete and two adjacent half-muscle blocks.

If we adopt the idea that the number of spinal motor nerves contributing to a plexus is an indicator of the number of segments involved in fin formation, then we find large variations in the number of contributing segments between species: every trunk element seems capable of forming fin elements, but not all are chosen. In various selachians the segments involved in the formation of paired fins are: *Scyllium*, 2–13 (pectoral), 25–35 (pelvic); *Heptanchus*, 2–19, 29–50; and *Torpedo*, 4–30, 31–42. In the embryos of these species all these myotomes contribute muscle buds.

Because of this variation in the extent and positioning of fins, it need come as no surprise to learn that fins and limbs are rarely derived from the same segments or the same number of segments in closely related species. Indeed, this segmental contribution may vary slightly in individuals of the same species, in some cases even varying from side to side within the same individual.

The mechanism of this variation has attracted some interest, and several putative explanations. The theory of intercalation and excalation (von Jhering 1878) suggested that the apparent differences are due to segments being lost or added by division of pre-existing segments. This explanation seems plausible and works in some instances. The shrew, *Sorex*, normally has 13 thoracic vertebrae, but some individuals have 14: the extra element may have arisen by subdivision. But in the rabbit the hindlimb plexus may include segmental nerves 25–30 or

24-30, whilst the last presacral vertebra is number 27 in each case. Here the theory clearly breaks down as a nerve has been intercalated whilst a vertebra has not.

The theory of redivision (Welker 1878) simply suggests that, if an organ is sometimes made up of 10 segments, sometimes of 9 or 11, then available material has just been sliced thicker or thinner. This, of course, is no explanation of the problem of relative movement of limbs, but simply a restatement of it.

Third, and last, the theory of transposition (Rosenberg 1875) suggests that the moving limb plexus simply accompanies the moving limb. This cannot be a physical movement: what must happen is that the plexus assimilates or drops nerves from either end so that the contribution made to the limb by a given nerve may wax and wane during the process of evolution.

With the recent interest in the apical ectodermal ridge (AER) and its role in tetrapod limb development (see Chapter 4, section 4.5), the fish fin has been examined for the presence of a similar structure. In fish generally there is no

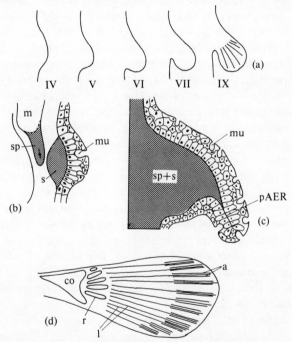

FIG. 3.4. Development of the pectoral fin of the trout, *Salmo trutta*. (a) Outline drawing of fin rudiment. Note development of posterior notch. Stages of Geraudie and François (1973): IV is at hatching, IX 3 weeks post-hatching, at 12°C. (b) and (c) transverse sections of stages IV and V. Note (b) somitic process (sp) leaving myotome (m) and migrating towards somatopleural thickening (s). In (c), note the pseudo-apical ectodermal ridge (pAER), formed by a fold of ectoderm (mu = mucous cell). (d) The completed fin. Endoskeleton comprises coracoid (co) and rays (r). Dermal skeleton comprises lepidotrichs (l) and the bony actinotrichs (a).

apical ridge corresponding precisely to that of amniotes and composed of pseudo-stratified epithelium. Instead, there is a fold of epithelium together with its basement membrane distal to the mesenchymal tip of the fin bud (Fig. 3.4). This fold, described as a pseudo-AER in the trout, persists for a much shorter period relatively than the amniote AER (Geraudie and François 1973). It is suggested that the supposed period of inductive pseudo-AER activity is short since only a single proximal row of endoskeletal elements is formed, which contrasts with the many rows of the amniotes. Eventually the pseudo-AER elongates into an apical fold within which form the rays of the dermal skeleton (Bouvet 1968, 1978).

3.2. Limb development in tetrapods

The early stages of limb development in tetrapods are essentially similar to those of paired fins. Again we see in many cases the development of an embryonic ridge extending over much of the length of the embryo. The central part of the ectoderm overlying this ridge becomes thickened in the region of the developing limb. While fish have only a simple, short-lived fold in the ectoderm, an apical ectodermal ridge (AER) has been demonstrated in *Xenopus,* an amphibian (Tarin and Sturdee 1971, 1973) and in many species of reptiles, birds, and mammals (Zwilling 1961). In the chick (Saunders 1948) and in reptiles (Milaire 1957), the cells of the ridge form a nipple-like extension of the simple epidermis (when seen in cross-section) and appear to be pseudostratified columnar epithelium. In other forms (e.g. in amphibians), there may be a thickened cap on the conical outgrowth of the limb bud or an apparently multi-layered ridge. The ridge is very easy to see in amniotes: in Amphibia, however, it is less easily recognized and may not appear as a morphological specialization at all in urodeles (Lauthier 1977). Shortly after the appearance of the ridge, a number of asymmetries become apparent: the dorsal surface of the bud is more rounded and the ridge located more ventrally, giving the ventral surface a flatter appearance. Cephalocaudal asymmetries are also detectable in both ectodermal and mesodermal components of the limb bud. The amount of basophilic mesoderm is greater postaxially and cytochemical markers of the AER gradually decrease in a caudocephalic direction, possibly due to degenerative changes in the pre-axial half of the structure.

The mesoderm of the bud consists at this stage of a compact, poorly vascularized outer shell, and an inner spongy core, rich in blood sinuses. There has been some controversy as to the contributions made by the somites to limb musculature in tetrapods. Many authorities have suggested that the somite contributes nothing, and that the muscle masses of the limb arise from mesoderm non-somitic condensations (Warwick 1973). This is based on experimental evidence that limbs can develop in situations where somitic contribution is not possible. Despite this, there are several good descriptions of somites sending tongues of tissue into the developing limb bud in both mammals (Milaire 1976) and reptiles (Rahmani 1974; Raynaud 1977). In birds, these contributions seem to be less well-defined, but have recently been elegantly demonstrated in the chick using a quail nucleolar marker (Gumpel-Pinot 1974; Christ, Jacob, and Jacob 1977).

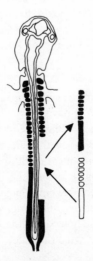

FIG. 3.5. Diagrammatic representation of the substitution of quail somites (white) in place of those excised (black) from a developing chick embryo. (After Christ, Jacob, and Jacob 1977.)

The nuclei of quail cells contain a large body of heterochromatin, which is absent in the chick, so that, in a mixture of quail and chick cells, the former can easily be identified after suitable staining. Christ *et al.* (1977) were able to remove somites from the presumptive area of a chick embryo and replace them with the equivalent quail tissue (Fig. 3.5). After incubation, they found that quail cells were present in the myogenic blastemata, but not in the precartilaginous ones. After further incubation, it could be seen that the quail cells (equivalent to somite cells) formed the developing muscle spindles and that the connective tissue cells within the muscle blastemata were from (chick) lateral plate mesoderm. Furthermore, pieces of limb lateral plate mesoderm grown as a graft in the coelomic cavity or on the chorio-allantoic membrane formed well-differentiated skeletal tissue but no muscle.

Histochemical studies of the early limb bud have shown that the various substances studied are not uniformly distributed throughout the limb bud (reviewed, Milaire 1962). The AER in some reptiles (Milaire 1957), several mammals (Milaire 1956, 1963), and in man (McKay, Adams, Hertig, and Danziger 1956) is richer than the rest of the limb in RNA. Glycogen is also found in some quantity in reptiles (Saunders 1948), the mole (Milaire 1963), and in man (McKay *et al.* 1956), as is alkaline phosphatase (Milarie 1956, 1963; McKay *et al.* 1956; McAlpine 1956). But Tarin and Sturdee (1973) point out that the significance of these findings is equivocal: besides similarities, there are marked differences between species in the distribution of these substances. For instance, the *Xenopus* AER had no detectable concentration of RNA, and glycogen, although present, was found in the outer layer of the ridge rather than the inner (as in reptiles and the mole). *Xenopus* lacks alkaline phosphatase in the AER as does *Ambystoma* and the green lizard (*Lacerta viridis*), while the slow-worm (*Anguis fragilis*) has no more in the AER than elsewhere in the limb bud.

3.2.1. *Changes in external appearance – reshaping of the bud*

The limb bud does not retain its original appearance as a low swelling, but increases in the amount by which it protrudes, while at the same time its base narrows, so that the bud becomes almost semicircular in outline. This outgrowth is, in chick, due to a decrease in the rate of mitosis in the non-limb bud area, rather than to an increase in mitosis within the bud (Janners and Searls 1970). Further growth produces a subcircular footplate on the end of a recognizable leg. The footplate then becomes angulated, with as many angles as digits. Between the digits, a little later, indentations form which may retain their initial webbed appearance or partially separate their digits. Flexures also develop in the region of elbow or knee, and wrist or ankle.

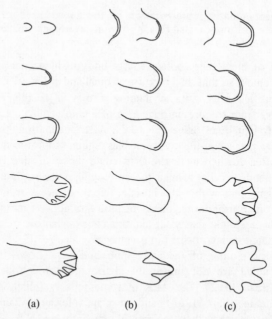

(a)   (b)   (c)

FIG. 3.6. Outline drawings of limb development in various tetrapods. (a) *Xenopus* hindlimb, stages 50–5, 15–32 days at 22–4°C. (b) chick forelimb, stages 22, 24, 26, 28, 30 and 32, 3.5–7.5 days' incubation. (c) mouse forelimb at 9.5, 10, 11, 12, 13 and 14 days' development. See also Figs 3.19 and 3.20, Plates 1–5, and Table 3.1.

The detailed timing of these events obviously depends on the species under consideration, as well as on external conditions such as temperature. For popular laboratory species, such as mouse (Grüneberg 1963), rat, chick (Hamburger and Hamilton 1951), *Xenopus* (Niewkoop and Faber 1956), and for man (Streeter 1948, 1951), tables of normal development have been compiled. The changes in external form and the relative rates of development of these species can be appreciated by reference to Fig. 3.6, Plates 1–4, and Table 3.1.

TABLE 3.1. Comparative developmental stages in various vertebrates

Stage (Witschi 1956)	Stage (Shumway 1942)	Stage (Hamburger and Hamilton 1951)	Age	Size (mm)	
Salmonid fishes					
22			50 d	6	Pectoral limb buds
23			60 d	10	Pectoral fins fairly large and well-differentiated
24			70 d	15	Hatching, pelvic limb bud
25			80 d	20+	Pelvic fins differentiated
Frog (*Rana pipiens*) (at 20 °C)					
20	20		140 h	6	Hatches
25b	I		3 d	13	Hindlimb appears
26b	V		23 d	39	Limb bud twice as wide as long
26c	VI		26 d	43	Flattened paddle
27a	VII		31 d	50	Paddle indented between toes 4 and 5
27c	IX		36 d	56	Spontaneous limb twitches
27d	X		40 d	58	Indentations delimit toe margins
40	XV		62 d	72	Hind limbs take part in swimming
45	XX		74 d	70	Forelimbs emerge
Chick					
18		16	51–6 h	—	Wing represented by thickened ridge: somite numbers 30–36
19		17	52–64 h	—	Wing and leg buds first defined: somite numbers 37–40
26		24	4.5 d	—	Digital plate defined in leg bud
27		25	4.5–5 d	—	Elbow and knee joints
28		26	5 d	—	First three toes defined
30		28	5.5–6 d	—	Three wing digits, four toes
31		29	6–6.5 d	—	Middle wing digit distinctly longest
33a		31	7–7.5 d	—	Web between digits 1 and 2
34a		33	7.5–8 d	—	Regression of inter-toe webbing
34c		35	8.5–9 d	—	Phalanges of toes distinct
34d		36	10 d	—	Third toe 5.4mm long; basic adult limb form now achieved

Stage (Witschi 1956)	Stage (Streeter 1951)	Age	Size (mm)	
Rat				
16		10.5 d	2.4	Appendicular folds
17		11 d	3.3	Arm and leg buds recognizable
18		11.5 d	3.8	Arm buds differ from leg
25		12.5 d	6.2	Arm buds opposite somites 8–14; leg buds opposite somites 28–31
26		12.75 d	7	Hand plate defined, arm bud vascularized
27		13 d	8	Rounded hand and foot plates
28		13.5 d	8.5	Pre-cartilaginous condensations in hand plates
Pig				
18		16.5–18.5 d	4.5	Anterior limb bud
19		16.5–17.5 d	3.6	Posterior limb bud
28		22 d	11.6–14.4	Handplate
29		22 d	16.4–18.6	Pentadactyl rudiments
32		32.5 d	26.5–29.5	Phalanges of toes 3 and 4 present
Man				
19	XII	30 d	4	Appendicular ridges
20	XIII	31 d	4.3	Arm and leg buds
25	XIV	33–37 d	6	Arm and leg buds fully formed
	XV	38 d	8	Differentiation of handplate
26	XVII	42 d	12	Pentadactyl rudiments
28	XVIII	46 d	15.6	Hands and feet lateral to body wall
31				
32	XIX	50 d	17	Phalanges, hand bending over heart
33	XX–XXII	56 d	22–25	First ossification of clavicle, fingers touch nose

There are marked differences in the rate of limb development between different species. Perhaps the most familiar example concerns the Amphibia. The anuran tadpole (larva) differs profoundly from the adult frog in both morphology and physiology. Forelimbs are developed in frogs beneath the opercular membrane and break through to the exterior. Every child knows that the hindlimbs of tadpoles of frogs and toads develop first, but, in contrast, in newt larvae, the forelimbs appear first. Also the limbs of newts are used almost as soon as they appear, whilst those of frogs are not seen to move until quite late in metamorphosis.

3.2.2. *The development of mesodermal condensations*

Within the changing limb bud, organizational changes occur, which result in the formation of condensations or blastemata of mesoderm cells within the initially

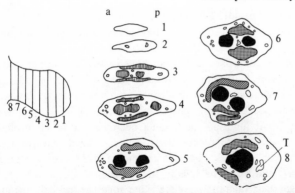

FIG. 3.7. Stage-26 chick hindlimb bud, showing a diagrammatic limb profile with levels of transection corresponding numerically with the accompanying sequence of transverse sections selected at 250 μm intervals. a = anterior, p = posterior. Blood vessels are depicted in outline only. Areas of increased mesenchymal cell number (3 and 4) are in outline with vertical hatching. Myogenic condensations (5–8) are in outline with stippling. Chondrogenic condensations are in black. The outlined area labelled T is a tendon: the dotted line represents the point of attachment to the flank. (After Thorogood and Hinchliffe 1975.)

spongy central core of mesenchyme (Fig. 3.7). Embryonic mesoderm contains a good deal of intercellular space, and it seems that these condensations are formed by the filling in of this space rather than by an increase in rate of cell division. The latter situation has been reported in some blastemata (Hale 1956; Jacobson and Fell 1941) outside the limb bud, but autoradiographic experiments involving the incorporation of radioactive precursors have failed to demonstrate such a burst of mitosis in chick limb buds (Janners and Searls 1970; Thorogood 1972). In fact, the mitotic rate in blastemata, which will ultimately give rise to either cartilage or muscle, gradually falls with time, presumably due to the formation of an increasing number of more specialized cells which do not divide frequently (Abbott and Holtzer 1966; Flickinger 1974).

The prechondrogenic condensations of 'closely packed cells in which the nuclei are almost in contact with each other' (Grüneberg 1963) have been described on numerous occasions in many species, usually in sections prepared for light microscopy (Zwilling 1961; Montagna 1945; Ham 1969). Some electron microscopic studies (Gould, Day, and Wolpert 1972; Searls, Hilfer, and Mirow 1972; Gould, Selwood, Day, and Wolpert 1974) have failed to demonstrate this stage, although other authors (Godman and Porter 1960; Schmidt 1968; Minor 1973; Thorogood and Hinchliffe 1975) have described the ultrastructural appearance of the condensation. Thorogood and Hinchliffe (1975) made a study of chick hindlimb blastemata, using quantitative, light and electron microscopic techniques. They were able to estimate the density of cell packing in chick·hindlimb by counting the number of nuclei per unit area, both centrally (in the region where the condensation would appear) and peripherally. In peripheral areas this figure remained constant, but centrally it increased sharply by more than 60 per cent at the time at which the condensations became visible in light microscope sections. Both scanning and transmission electron microscopy showed that un-condensed areas comprised a loosely constructed cellular network with large intercellular spaces, featureless but for an occasional bunch of immature collagen fibres. The cells were stellate, with a considerable number of filopodia (Plates 6B, 7B and 8A) and cells were in contact where their filopodia met, such junctions being of the 'tight junction' or 'zonula occludens' type (Farquhar and Palade 1963). The earliest type of condensation recognized featured exactly similar cells, with similar contacts, but with a decrease in the size of intercellular spaces (Plates 6D, 7C and 8B). The cells in these areas tended to have fewer filopodia, but, although their membranes were close together, no cell fusion was seen in those blastemata destined to become cartilage. In blastemata destined to become muscle, cell fusion (to form myotubes) had already begun (Hilfer, Searls, and Fonte 1973).

The next event in precartilage formation is the appearance of matrix com-ponents, abundant banded collagen fibres, and granular or amorphous deposits thought to represent the mucopolysaccharide component of the matrix. Pre-cartilage cells are characteristically oriented at right angles to the long axis of the blastema, and are gradually separated by the accumulating matrix (Plates 7D, 8C, F, and 6E, F). In transverse section characteristic whorling of cartilage cells is reported in the amphibian limb (Anikin 1929), and this is also present, though less pronounced, in the chick blastema (Ede 1976*b*) (Plates 6C, D and 8D, E).

There is general agreement that mesodermal condensations appear in a fixed order in a given limb: proximal parts tend to appear earlier than distal parts, and within a given condensation the proximal end is more differentiated than the distal. In the stage 22 chick leg bud, proximal condensations are easily dis-tinguished. Two of these lie beneath, but are separate from, the dorsal ecto-dermal surface and are destined to become dorsal and ventral muscle blocks. Between them lies a third, less distinct condensation, which represents the proximal limb skeleton. Distally, the muscle condensations merge with the dense mesenchyme below the ectoderm. By stage 24, the myogenic condensations are more marked, and the chondrogenic tissue has assumed its characteristic Y shape. Proximally, there is a single element, the presumptive femur, whilst distally, the two arms of the Y will form tibia and fibula. By stage 26, the myogenic blastemata have subdivided proximally to form the complex musculature of the limb, whilst distally, they extend in a less differentiated state as far as the ankle region (Fig. 3.7). Beyond the forked distal end of the Y-blastema are other con-densations which represent ankle elements and the digits.

In the mouse (Forsthoefel 1963*a*), a similar proximo-distal sequence can be determined, but in addition there is a tendency for posterior elements to con-dense first. At the 4.5 mm stage, before the footplate of the hindlimb is recognizable, a central condensation can be seen, which probably represents the girdle and femur. A little later, when the footplate can be recognized, a common condensation for tibia and fibula can be seen distal to the first and continuous with it. The fibular part of this common blastema becomes more marked, and distally the condensation for digit IV is formed by a thinning of tissue first pre-axially, then on the postaxial side. Later, the condensation of digit V can be made out, although its postaxial side remains continuous with the dense sub-ectodermal mesoderm. At this stage, the tibia condensation becomes more marked, then that of digit III, again formed by a thinning of mesoderm preaxial to it. The picture is completed by condensations for digits II and I, and then for the tarsal elements.

A similar sequence of condensations, digits V, IV, III and later II and I, has been demonstrated in human embryos (Yasuda 1975), and a sequence of IV, III, V, II, I in *Xenopus* (Tschumi 1954). In contrast to this, the Axolotl has a fore-limb bud which forms only digits I and II within the initial footplate, digits III and then IV appearing substantially later (Plate 1).

It is, of course, of great interest to see what happens to mesodermal con-densations in animals which have less than the full complement of five digits and indeed in those which have less than the primitive number of carpals or tarsals. Does the number of blastemata formed correspond to the number of digits eventually present, or is a full set present with later regression? And, if so, at what stage does the regression occur?

The chick wing has been most fully investigated; here the number of carpals eventually present is four (radiale, ulnare, distal carpal 3 and pisiform) and four digits are also formed, although the most postaxial of these is represented by only a relatively small metacarpal which soon fuses with the large adjacent element. It is clear that one of the full set of five digits is missing both in adult and embryo, but the question of which digit — number 1 or number 5 — has not been satisfactorily resolved (Hinchliffe 1977). Palaeontologists, impressed by the similarity of coelurosaurian dinosaur and *Archaeopteryx* forelimb skeletons (see Chapter 2), take the view that number 5 is missing, but embryologists, by contrast, have tended to regard number 1 as missing (Summerbell and Tickle 1977; Montagna 1945), and this convention will be followed here.

There is even more confusion as to the number of carpal precartilaginous con-densations present in birds which has been variously claimed as 13, 11, 9, 7 (Parker 1888), 6 and 4 (review: Hinchliffe 1977). The accepted and most usually quoted view is that of Montagna, who suggested that 13 precartilaginous blastemata (Fig. 3.8) became simplified by fusion of some elements and loss of others to form four cartilaginous elements. This work was performed on haema-toxylin- and eosin-stained wax sections, which give rather poor resolution of condensations, and fail to distinguish clearly between those which are to become cartilage and those which are to become tendon or muscle.

Hinchliffe (1977) has recently re-analysed the precartilaginous carpal pattern in the chick using the rather more precise method of labelling those blastemata which will ultimately become cartilage with radioactive sulphate. The sulphate is

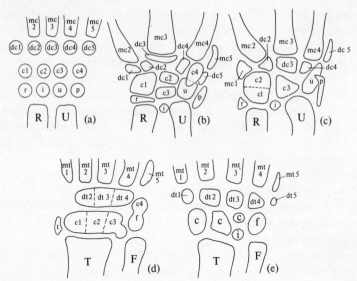

FIG. 3.8. Previous interpretations of prechondrogenic avian fore- (a–c) and hind-limb (d–e) pattern. (a) Montagna's schematic representation (1945) of the 13 embryo carpals arranged into a proximal row of four elements, a central row of four, and a distal row of five. (b) Montagna's diagrammatic representation (1945) of the 6-day embryonic carpals. (c) Holmgren's interpretation (1955) of the pre-chondrogenic elements of the wrist. (d) Holmgren's interpretation (1955) of the tarsus. (e) Lutz's interpretation (1942) of the tarsus in *Anser*. c = central carpals or tarsals 1–4, dc = distal carpals (1–5), dt = distal tarsals (1–5), F = fibula, f = fibulare, i = intermedium, mc = metacarpals (1–5), mt = metatarsals (1–5), p = pisiform, R = radius, r = radiale, T = tibia, t = tibiale, U = ulna, u = ulnare.

incorporated into chondroitin sulphate, which is initially widely synthesized in the developing limb bud (Searls 1965; Medoff 1967), but later sharply localized in precartilaginous condensations (Figs 3.9 and 3.10; Plate 9): this localization occurs just before mesodermal condensation can be detected histologically by the presence of cell packing. Hinchliffe found that the four cartilaginous con-densations were represented by four precartilaginous elements. The extra elements seen by Montagna are thus considered to be partly artifactual, due to the poor resolution of the technique, and may also include condensations repre-senting muscle and tendon.

The interpretation of the chick leg condensations follows similar lines. As in the case of the chick carpus, earlier workers claimed that the number of tarsal condensations was greater than the number of cartilaginous elements. Holmgren (1933, 1955) and Lutz (1942) identified ten carpal condensations (Fig. 3.8), and, since the number of cartilage elements is indisputably three (tibiale, fibulare and a single, distal tarsal), they explained the transition by a process of simplification, involving fusion. But if the more specific method of sulphate labelling of the condensations is followed (Hinchliffe 1977), it is clear that there

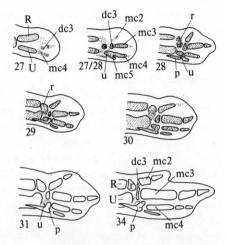

FIG. 3.9. The development of the pattern of precartilaginous condensations and cartilaginous elements in the chick forelimb. The pattern was established by autoradiographic mapping of $^{35}SO_4^{2-}$ uptake into chondroitin sulphate. (After Hinchliffe 1977, abbreviations as in Fig. 3.8.)

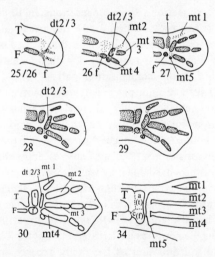

FIG. 3.10. The development of the pattern of precartilaginous condensations and cartilaginous elements in the chick hindlimb. The pattern was established by autoradiographic mapping of $^{35}SO_4^{2-}$ uptake into chondroitin sulphate. a = astragalus, c = calcaneum, other abbreviations as in Fig. 3.8. (After Hinchliffe 1977).

are only three, each representing a future cartilage element. There is no evidence for loss or fusion of condensations.

In contrast to the wing bud, there are five digits in the chick leg bud, but the fifth metatarsal is only present as a small round condensation whose growth is inhibited. This fifth metatarsal eventually fuses with the adjacent fourth meta-tarsal: there are no corresponding fifth digit phalanges.

The limb skeleton condensation and chondrification pattern (particularly at the carpus or tarsus level) have been investigated in a great variety of tetrapod species in the past. As was explained earlier (Chapter 2), one aim was to obtain information about the homology of the limb in relation to problems of phylogeny (review: Čihak 1972). Holmgren's wide-ranging survey (1933, 1955) represents the most useful compilation. In his view, the urodele limb is sufficiently different in its pattern of skeletal differentiation to warrant separation of urodeles from a second tetrapod group containing anurans and the amniotes. All limbs of members of the second group are considered to pass through an archetypal stage when the condensation pattern of carpus and tarsus is essentially similar, and corresponds with the pattern of the adult carpus and tarsus of the ancestral amphibians. In the case of the carpus, there is claimed to be a proximal row of three elements (radiale, ulnare and intermedium), a central row of four centralia, and then a row of five distal carpals, each with a corresponding meta-carpal (Fig. 3.8). Limb development then becomes specialized in different species by fusion and differential growth.

This conclusion must now be viewed with considerable scepticism. In con-ventionally stained wax sections, the condensations are ill-defined. Moreover, as has been explained (Chapter 2, section 2.10), the investigators were influenced by the prevailing doctrine of recapitulation, and expected to find that limb bud stages of tetrapods would be structurally identical, whatever the adult limb specializations, and that the condensation pattern would always reflect the primitive amphibian skeletal limb pattern. It now seems far more likely that − if chick limb development is typical − there is no carpus or tarsus 'archetype' pattern of condensations for all amniotes, but that this region has been repeatedly remodelled at the condensation stage during the adaptive radiation of the pentadactyl limb. Investigation of limbs of species other than the chick by the more specific methods now available may well show that the pattern and number of condensations is much closer to that of the adult skeletal pattern than has been realized previously. Once formed, the condensations acquire an individuality which is expressed in differential growth rates, perhaps involving competition between neighbouring elements, as is discussed in Chapter 7.

Later growth and individuation of the digits depend upon active processes taking place at the distal tip of each metacarpal or metatarsal blastema and upon changes occurring in interdigital areas. Digital mesoderm is gradually laid down at the distal end of the blastemata, and the adjacent AER is still a distinctive structure, though flatter than at earlier stages, whilst interdigital AER and meso-derm stop growing and ultimately degenerate. Digital length and phalangeal number seem to be controlled by the length of time that the AER of the particular digit remains active; once the ridge flattens, the number of phalangeal elements becomes fixed and the area of distal undifferentiated mesenchyme disappears. The possibility that cell death may play an important role in controlling the overall skeletal condensation pattern (discussed in section 3.9) through limiting the quantity of distal mesenchyme available should also be noted.

3.3. The development of joints

Chondrogenic condensations usually appear as continuous entities, not as anlagen of individual bones; it is, therefore, clear that joints must develop as specializations of a mesodermal condensation. The joint regions do not form cartilage as does the rest of the condensation, but persist as the 'interzonal' mesoderm. The fate of this tissue depends upon the type of joint to be formed. In non-movable synarthroses, such as the joints between the bones of the pelvis, the mesoderm becomes a unifying layer of connective tissue, or even cartilage or bone. Diarthrodial movable joints, which are in the great majority in the limbs, are characterized by a prominent joint cavity and a peripheral fibrous capsule.

The joint cavity is formed by a coalescence of peripheral clefts, which appear in the interzonal mesenchyme. The actual mechanism of cavitation has caused some controversy: according to one idea, cell death removes at least some of the intervening tissue. Dead cells have been observed during cavitation in the 6- to 8-day-old chick embryo (Mitrovic 1971, 1972, 1977), as has an acid phosphatase reaction (Milaire 1967a) of the mesenchyme (indicative of autolytic changes). Macrophages have also been seen at sites of cavitation in the digital rays of mouse embryos.

The articular faces on the ends of the bone retain their mesodermal covering for a period, although it is lost in the mature joint. The remaining peripheral interzonal mesenchyme forms the sleeve-like joint capsule, which is continuous with the outer layer of the bone blastema. Cells of the inner layers of the interzonal mesenchyme surrounding the joint cavity differentiate into the synovial membrane, which ultimately produces lubricative synovial fluid and is reflected onto the lateral faces of the bones, but does not cover their articular surfaces.

3.4. Development of bone

In some vertebrates the cartilaginous elements which develop from blastemata are retained as the main structural units. In the majority, however, they are replaced by bone. Most bones in the vertebrate limb form on a cartilaginous model, but certain parts of the girdles (e.g. part of the mammalian clavicle) and many bones of the dome of the skull betray their dermal origin (see Chapter 1), and form in dense connective tissue.

In dermal ossification a group of mesenchymal cells takes on the properties of osteoblasts (bone-forming cells) and lays down thin, irregular membranes or plates of dense fibrous, interstitial material, mainly collagen, upon which bone salts are deposited. These plates gradually expand at their margins and become thickened by the addition of further layers of bone on their inner and outer surfaces. In endochondral ossification, a cartilaginous model is replaced by bone. The cartilage cells towards the centre of a long bone cartilage model become hypertrophied. They swell and become arranged in columns; the matrix between the cells becomes calcified, and the cells die. Simultaneously, the perichondral cells at the hypertrophic cartilage surface become transformed into osteoblasts and begin to secrete the characteristic intercellular bone matrix. Thus, the central part of the cartilage element becomes surrounded by a bony collar. It has been suggested that the hypertrophic cartilage induces osteoblasts in the perichondrium (Fell 1956; Lacroix 1961; Hinchliffe and Ede 1968). This view is supported by evidence from mutants, and by experiments by Lacroix (1961) who found that cartilage blocks isolated from fracture callus and implanted in various sites elicited ossification from host connective tissue cells. *Creeper* (Landauer 1933) and *talpid* (Hinchliffe and Ede 1968) mutants of the fowl both show an association of retardation in cartilage hypertrophy with failure of periosteal ossification; membrane bones, by contrast, form normally. In both mutants the skeletal abnormalities have been attributed to the inability of the abnormal cartilage to induce osteogenic cells in the perichondrium.

But bone is not formed only by perichondral ossification. In addition the hypertrophic cartilage is replaced by bone. The honeycomb of calcified matrix which remains after the death of the hypertrophic chondroblasts is invaded by blood vessels from the surface, and osteoblasts, which enter with the blood vessels, begin to lay down bone. Ossification proceeds from the centre towards the ends of the bone. The process is extended in time because the cartilaginous model is still growing even as it is replaced: indeed, the ossification may never catch up, and the ends of the bone remain cartilaginous.

The process as described would lead to the eventual formation of a solid bony rod, with a central constriction like an hourglass. To rectify this anomaly, we find that further ossification takes place on the surface of the cartilage forming concentric layers of perichondral bone. Later still, bone may be modified into a hard mass of compact bone (which often forms an outer sheath), spongy (cancellous) bone, or layered lamellar bone. Bones are also continually reworked both during their development and adult life by osteoclasts, multinucleate cells which resorb bone and allow further growth (Fig. 3.11). This process involves great local specificity at present difficult to explain satisfactorily, but through which the shape of the adult bone emerges as a consequence of controlled processes of bone resorption in some parts and deposition in others (Bateman 1954). Characteristic of resorbing bone is the presence of Haversian systems consisting of small Haversian canals containing blood vessels surrounded by concentric bony layers. The formation of Haversian systems is preceded by resorption of a given area of bone: the large tubular spaces so formed are filled by concentric layers of bone deposited upon their walls. Enlow and Brown (1958) have argued that Haversian systems may be primary rather than secondary in some cases. Haversian systems are by no means universal, and their presence is often allied to calcium mobilization. An alternative view is that resorption of the compact

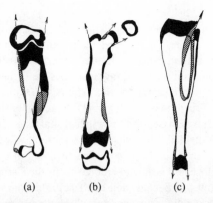

(a)   (b)   (c)

FIG. 3.11. Bone resorption is an extremely important part of bone growth. In these views of the mouse humerus (a), femur (b), and tibiofibula (c) bone which is added by accretion during growth is black, bone which is resorbed during the growth process is stippled. (After Bateman 1954.)

outer layer of bone necessary for growth may be accompanied by resorption of all bone exposed to ample vascular supply including that surrounding primary vascular channels within the bone. Lamellar deposition of new bone would then occur both on the periosteal border and around the recently eroded channels forming Haversian systems.

Many centres of ossification, for instance those in midshaft of long bones, are present in embryonic life, but others do not appear until much later. Many bones, such as those of the carpus and tarsus, ossify from a single centre but others have a primary centre allied to a number of secondary ones which may not start to ossify until late in life. A typical long bone, such as a tibia, will by the time of birth consist of an ossified shaft or diaphysis with cartilaginous ends or epiphyses within which secondary centres of ossification will later develop. As the latter enlarge, they come to occupy the whole of the end of the bone, except for a peripheral layer of articular cartilage and a disc of cartilage (the epiphyseal plate) which persists between diaphysis and epiphysis. Because of growth at the epiphyseal plate, the bone is capable of continued enlargement for a further period of time. When full stature has been reached, the growth mechanism is abolished by the ossification of the epiphyseal plate.

Although one secondary centre of ossification at each end of a bone is a common occurrence, many bones have more: for instance, the head of the human humerus ossifies from three secondary centres, which soon coalesce. In general, epiphyses occur in areas subject to pressure or pull by muscles or tendons (pressure and tension epiphyses respectively), or in places where they are thought to represent originally separate bones which have fused during the course of evolution (atavistic epiphyses).

3.4.1. *Epiphyses and evolution*

The pattern of primary and secondary centres of ossification described above is representative of mammals, but it must be remembered that bone growth in many vertebrates is accomplished without secondary ossification centres. In bony fishes, cartilaginous models of bony elements are formed and ossified from a central point perhaps equivalent to the mammalian primary centre of ossification. The ends of fish bones are capped by an extensive conical zone of cartilage, which extends well beyond the ossified shaft.

Tetrapods may be divided into two groups according to whether the epiphysis remains cartilaginous or secondary centres of ossification are present. Those in the first group comprise all fossil land animals from the Carboniferous to at least the Triassic (we know this because tell-tale fractured bones are sometimes preserved), chelonians, crocodilians, urodele amphibians, and most birds.

In fish, the cartilaginous growth plate for the shaft is flat (Fig. 3.12) and is found at the junction of the bony shaft and cartilaginous epiphyses: articular cartilage is found peripherally. This is evidently not a good weight-bearing arrangement, for in primitive reptiles and many amphibians the cartilaginous end of the bone has been reduced to a narrow cap below the articular surface, while the growth plate has become a cone, which bulges out beyond the shaft. The cells of this growth cone are arranged in clumps or columns orientated roughly perpendicular to the articular surface and contribute on the inner concave side to the shaft, on the outer convex side to the articular surface. When these cartilaginous columns are replaced, the columns of bone which are formed are also radially arranged. This is obviously a stronger structure with less undifferentiated cartilage; the radial arrangement of bone trabeculae is clearly dependent upon the reshaping of the growth plate.

The transition from fish type to cone type epiphysis can be seen during the development of the chelonian, and less clearly in the developing crocodile (Haines 1937). In a newly hatched turtle, the ends of the bone are capped by a zone of undifferentiated cartilage above a flat growth plate, the whole structure being reminiscent of that seen in fish, except that growth plate and cartilage cap are united by a zone of hypertrophied cartilage which anchors the epiphysis firmly to the shaft of the bone. This is later resorbed by means of a series of accessory marrow cavities which arise at sites of penetration of small blood vessels from the exterior. In the cavities so formed, secondary bone is deposited. The growth zone becomes conical by the addition of new cells on the outer surface and an increased resorption of cells from the inner one.

A similar type of structure is found in birds. Here, however, the hypertrophied cartilage uniting cap and shaft is resorbed via a ring of marrow processes, which arise within the periphery of the bone, rather than by secondary invasion from outside.

The radial arrangement of trabeculae is quite good mechanically; at any rate, it is better than the type found in fishes. It has one drawback, that the orientation of the trabeculae depends on the shape of the articular surface. The system

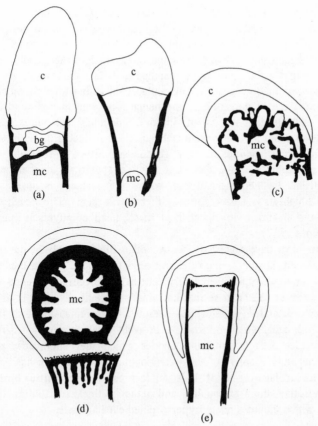

FIG. 3.12. The evolution of the epiphysis. In the fish (a), the end of the bone is capped by a cone of undifferentiated cartilage (c) and bone is added over a flat disc-shaped region (bg). A similar situation is found in the newborn chelonian (b), but in the part-grown chelonian (c), the amount of undifferentiated cartilage is much reduced and the region of bone growth is conical. In the mammal (d), a secondary centre of ossification with its own marrow cavity (mc) has been formed, and the growth of the articular surface and elongation of shaft are performed by different regions. (e) shows a specialization, the 'match-stick' epiphysis of the frog. (After Haines 1937.)

works well when the articulation is on the end of a bone, but less well when it is not, as, for example, in the head of the human femur where the articular surface is carried on a neck at an angle to the shaft. The answer to this problem seems to be a reversion to the situation seen in fishes, where separate areas of cartilage contribute to the articular surface and to the growth of the shaft. But we have already pointed out the lack of strength in the fish system: this is overcome by interposing another piece of bone, arising from the secondary centre, between the two growth regions.

This solution seems to have occurred independently at least five times in tetrapods: in amphibians, *Sphenodon,* lizards, birds, and mammals. In lizards and mammals, the system of remodelling cartilage has been further refined. The cells of the growth zone have become arranged in orderly columns, presumably by some mechanism which regulates the orientation of the spindle at mitosis. A regular, straight column of hypertrophied cells is then invaded by a narrow, straight process of bone matrix. This replaces the rather tortuous canals of other forms, which are of wider bore, and hence form weaker bone and often leave nests of cartilage cells unossified. In some mammals, the whole system is re-modelled yet again and new bone trabeculae are formed entirely independently of the original cartilaginous structure (Enlow and Brown 1958).

In the amphibians, we can find a wide spectrum of skeletal structure ranging from the neotenous types, where the cartilage is never secondarily eroded, to highly specialized forms, either with a large marrow cavity extending all along the shaft or a very specialized 'match head' epiphyses as found in many frogs (Haines 1937).

Modern birds have secondary centres of ossification only at the head of the tibiotarsus. But, in some types of chondrodystrophic mutants in the chick where growth is retarded, typical secondary centres may occur at the ends of other leg bones (Landauer 1927). It seems that birds may well have lost their secondary centres of ossification, possibly as a result of the replacement of the marrow cavity by air sacs, which occurs late in avian fetal development. These often extend further than the marrow cavities which they supercede, and project beyond the bony diaphysis; it is possible that this extension has appropriated the growth cartilage region of the secondary ossification centre. Birds have also failed to refine their trabeculae, and retain a thick scaffolding of calcified cartilage, which includes many hypertrophied cartilage cells.

3.4.2. *Bone growth*

Where secondary centres of ossification are present, they can be seen to be grow-ing faster than the cartilage in which they are embedded. The epiphyseal region, originally wholly cartilaginous, therefore becomes gradually converted to bone. Variation in the rate of this process occurs according to species, age, and sex. The rate also varies from bone to bone; were this not so, secondary centres of ossification would appear in strict decreasing order of size during development, which they do not.

One end of a bone often grows faster than the other: although a bone with two secondary centres of ossification initially grows at the same rate at each end, one often becomes dominant in early postnatal life. This was known to Hales (1727), and Bérard (1835) coined the jingle:

Au coude je m'appuis,
De genou je m'en fuis.

which, in its more familar English form:

To the elbow I grow
From the knee I flee.

has helped many generations of medical students to remember which are the 'growing ends' of the limb bones. In fact, the jingle refers to the path taken by the foramen of the nutrient artery: a full discussion of the relationship between this and bone growth is given by Brookes (1971).

'Growing ends' is, of course, a misnomer, as both ends of a long bone grow, albeit at different rates. What establishes the dominant end which is sometimes proximal, sometimes distal, is not understood. Growth cartilages also grow at different relative and absolute rates at different times.

Differences in relative growth account for the change in the angle between the shaft and neck of the human femur which occurs with age, and for the fact that growth cartilages often assume the shape of a concavoconvex disc, so that the epiphysis comes to resemble a shallow cup placed on the end of the shaft. The reciprocal shaping of the two bony surfaces on either side of this thin cartilaginous disc is often absolute, so that small ridges or irregularities of one surface are mirrored as convacities in the other. This reciprocity of fit clearly gives the growing bone resistance to shear forces, sufficient to survive the adolescent football or hockey game unscathed.

Differences in the absolute rates of bone growth occur with age: bone growth is rapid in human infancy, then decreases only to speed up again around puberty as the 'growth spurt'. This control seems to be largely hormonal (Williams and Hughes 1977): there seem to be no prenatal hormonal growth effects in mammals, but after birth bone responds to the pituitary growth hormone (GH), which acts on the epiphyseal growth plates; in hypophysectomized mice (which produce little or no growth hormone) growth plates become thinner, a situation remedied by supplying growth hormone. The effect is not a direct one, but is mediated by a second substance, somatomedin, which acts upon the cartilage cells. The situation is far from simple; thyroxine also stimulates limb growth, and the adolescent growth spurt is associated with the production of increasing amounts of sex hormones.

At the end of the period of growth, epiphysis and diaphysis fuse. The actively growing end of the main shaft of the bone seems to outgrow the cartilage, so that the growth plate is eroded by bone, mainly from the diaphyseal side (Haines 1975). The exact mechanism of fusion varies according to unknown factors, and several types of union have been described. The first stage appears to be the formation of plates of bone on either face of the growth cartilage. These were first seen as dense lines in early radiographs, and histological investigation showed them to consist partly of lamellar bone and partly of mineralized cartilage derived from the growth plate. Early union of these bony plates was seen to occur centrally in the small bones, which were chosen for sectioning in laboratory studies (presumably for convenience) and which included metacarpals, metatarsals, and phalanges. However, the early view that central union was the norm in mammals seems to have been based on this erroneous use of small bones, and peripheral union is now thought to be more usual (Haines, Mohuiddin, Okpa, and Viega-Pires 1967).

Since invasion of the growth plate by bone is preceded by mineralization, the first union between epiphysis and diaphysis is presumably by metaplasic bone without marrow cannaliculi: this stage must be rather brief, however, as it has not been demonstrated in man, although it has been described in some lizards (Haines 1941, 1969).

Peripheral invasion of the growth plate is of two types. Dawson (1925) found that the union of the radial head in man was characterized by the following stages: first, the formation of bony plates; secondly, the destruction of the intervening cartilage by a single peripheral perforation, which spreads inwards to remove the margins of the growth plate; thirdly, the retention of the cartilage columns of the plate until just before destruction; fourthly, the clean removal of the plate and its bony sheets, leaving no scar. Lassila (1928) found that, in the upper end of the femur of the dog, the following series of events could be seen: first, the formation of a strong basal bony plate on the epiphyseal surface of the growth plate, but absence or poor development on the diaphyseal side; secondly, thinning of the plate by sprouts from the diaphyseal marrow, disrupting cartilage columns; thirdly, multiple perforations scattered over a wide area; fourthly, long persistence of a bony scar.

The two types of union are inconsistent in distribution in different mammalian species: in the dog and man, metatarsals unite the Dawsonian way, but in the calf follow Lassila. In man and the rat, the main epiphysis at the distal end of the humerus unites according to Dawson, but in the dog according to Lassila. It has been suggested that the type of union described by Dawson is primitive in mammals, and that Lassila's modification is an improvement found in larger and later uniting epiphyses.

3.5. Blood supply

The earliest blood supply to the limb reflects its derivation from several segments. Blood vessels are first seen in mammalian embryos in the chorionic region, a fact probably correlated with the lack of yolk in mammals, and hence the need to extract oxygen and nutrients from the maternal circulation and to distribute them to all parts of the embryo. These first vessels are in the form of capillary beds which predate the formation of definite arterial and venous networks. The arteries and veins arise by enlargement and differentiation of selected parts of the network, depending upon both genetic factors and hydrodynamics; what determines exactly which channels are retained, which become arteries, and which veins, is poorly understood.

By the beginning of somite formation, paired axial primordia of the dorsal aortae and the corresponding umbilical and vitelline veins can be seen (Fig. 3.13(a)). The developing limb bud is fed by a capillary network, which is linked

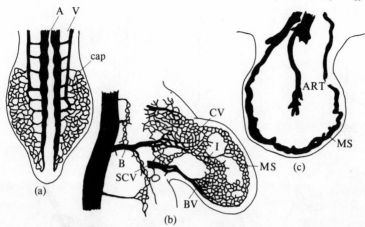

FIG. 3.13. (a) Posterior limb bud of 60-hour chick embryo showing developing blood vessels. The axial primordia of dorsal aortae (A) can be seen as can the vitelline veins (V). The mesenchyme of the limb bud is crossed by a network of capillaries (cap). (b) A slightly later stage (12-mm pig embryo). The capillary plexus is localizing in a number of areas and becoming much sparser elsewhere. Areas corresponding to the brachial artery (B), interosseous artery (I), and cephalic, basilic, and subclavian veins (CV, BV, SCV) can be recognized. (c) In the 12.5-day mouse embryo the blood system is clearly divided into a central artery (ART) and a marginal venous sinus (MS).

to the paired axial vessels by a series of intersegmental arteries and veins (Caplan and Koutroupas 1973). One of these pairs of vessels eventually comes to dominate the others, and reorganization of the capillary plexus forms the main vascular system of the limb (Fig. 3.13(b) and (c)). The definitive pattern of blood vessels is arrived at after an often complex process of annexation and replacement.

In the mammalian forelimb (Fig. 3.14), the main axial artery is the subclavian/axillary, which communicates via brachial and interosseous arteries with the plexus of the hand. The names of the various levels of this system have little significance at this stage; what we actually see is a single vessel running to the plexus, portions of which carry different names according to what they are to become in the adult. The median artery, which arises as a branch of the main stem, takes over the supply to the hand plexus, only to be usurped in turn by the developing ulnar and radial arteries.

A similar situation is seen in the lower limb (Fig. 3.15), except that the usurping vessel is not a branch of the original supply (the sciatic artery) but the adjacent segmental artery, the external iliac.

Turning now to the development of the venous pattern, the primitive capillary plexus of the developing limb bud gives rise to the important marginal or border sinus (Fig. 3.13(c)), which runs in the mesoderm beneath the apical ectodermal ridge and drains blood supplied by the developing axial vessels. The

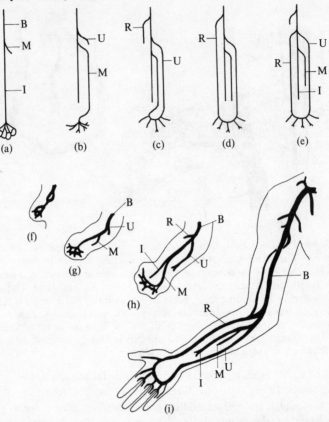

FIG. 3.14. (a)–(e) Diagrammatic representation of various stages of the development of the arterial blood supply of the human upper limb. For fuller explanation, see text. (f)–(i) Semi-diagrammatic views of the same stages of development. B = brachial artery, I = interosseous, M = median, R = radial, U = ulnar.

radial or craniad portion of this vessel tends to atrophy, but the ulnar portion is retained to form parts of the definitive subclavian, axillary and basilic veins. The marginal sinus drains originally into the posterior cardinal vein, but, as the heart moves forwards, transfers to the precardinal (jugular) vein. The veins of the radial side of the limb are secondary developments rather than relics of the marginal vein.

3.6. Lymphatics

The lymphatic circulation develops quite separately from the blood circulation system, and acquires its interconnections secondarily. Lymphatics originate as discrete spaces in the mesenchyme, which acquire an endothelial lining. Progressive fusion of these clefts forms channels which grow and branch to extend the system still further.

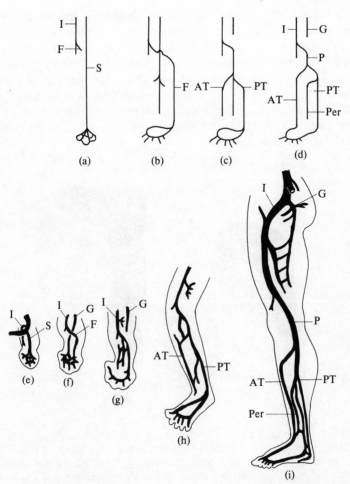

FIG. 3.15. Stages in the development of the arterial blood supply of the human lower limb (cf. Fig. 3.14). AT = anterior tibial artery, F = femoral, G = gluteal, I = iliac, S = sciatic, P = popliteal, Per = peroneal, PT = posterior tibial.

The earliest system of lymphatics is found distributed along the venous trunks of the primitive venous axis. The lymphatics of the forelimb are developed from paired jugular sacs, which arise lateral to the internal jugular vein, and those of the hindlimb from the posterior sacs, which arise in relation to the sciatic veins.

3.7. Development of muscles and tendons

Muscles and tendons, like skeletal elements, are derived from blastemata. We probably know less of the pattern of muscle development than of skeletal elements because of the sheer numbers of developing muscles involved, and because suitable skeletal preparations are easier to make; the chick wing contains about 50 distinct muscles and 30 tendons. However, despite its complexity, the process has been studied in detail in lizards (Romer 1944), newts (Romer 1942), turtles (Walker 1947), the opossum (Cheng 1955), and the chick (Romer 1927; Sullivan 1962; Wortham 1948). All these studies are in agreement that limb musculature is derived from dorsal and ventral premuscular masses. According to Romer's 'two mass' theory (1922), these masses correspond to the two muscle masses still to be seen in fish fins.

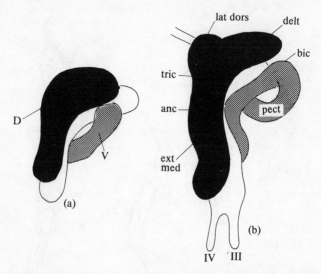

FIG. 3.16. Development of the muscle masses of the chick limb. (a) Hind-limb at 6 days, lateral view (after Romer 1927). (b) Right wing, stage 29 (after Sullivan 1962), lateral view. D = dorsal muscle mass, V = ventral muscle mass, anc = anconeus, bic = biceps, delt = deltoid, ext.med. = extensor medius, lat.dors. = latissimus dorsi, pect. = pectoralis group, tric = triceps, III and IV = third and fourth digital axes.

Although there are minor differences — hardly surprising considering the variation in musculature even within the same class (George and Berger 1966) — the general pattern of muscular development is remarkably similar wherever it has been studied. Premuscle blastemata develop into muscles by an orderly sequence of changes. Proximal muscles differentiate rather ahead of distal ones (Wortham 1948), more or less contemporaneously with the blastemata of the cartilaginous skeleton. Thus, at stage 27 in the chick (Shellswell and Wolpert 1977), when radius and ulna can be identified in sections as whorls of cells, the corresponding future muscular region is a dense condensation of cells with long cell contacts and reduced intercellular spaces. According to some authors, dorsal muscle masses differentiate ahead of ventral ones (Wortham 1948), although the reverse situation has also been described (Shellswell and Wolpert 1977). Dorsal and ventral muscle masses have been reported in the 6-day chick embryo (Romer 1927), or more precisely at stage 29 (Sullivan 1962) (Fig. 3.16). Thereafter, an orderly scheme of subdivision leads to the formation of definitive musculature. Sullivan's (1962) scheme in the proximal chick wing, Romer's (1927) for the chick thigh, and that of Wortham (1948) for the ventral part of the chick wing show obvious similarities. Actomyosin, the contractile protein of muscle, has been shown to be present by immunofluorescent technique at stage 28 in the chick (Thorogood 1973), though Medoff and Zwilling (1972) claim to have found it in the stage-23 limb bud, before muscle differentiates histologically.

Although the orderly pattern of division of flexor and extensor muscle masses is well-established, the factors controlling the division process are less well understood. Carey (1921), working on the developing hindlimb of the pig, suggested that muscle masses split in such a way that cells on the lines 'of optimum tension' for muscle differentiation (presumably those cells on the line of action of the forming muscle) continued to develop while the rest regressed. The splitting, in other words, was occasioned by tension produced in the muscle by elongation of the skeletal blastemata, and Carey noted that the splitting started opposite a joint (for example, the quadriceps extensor started to split opposite the hip joint), presumably because of the mechanical forces exerted in this region by the growing ends of the long bones. Shellswell and Wolpert (1977) report a different situation. They saw splitting of the muscle mass occurring first at mid-radial shaft level (stage 28). At this stage both dorsal and ventral muscle masses are contractile and can be activated by nervous stimulation. When the muscular splitting is completed (after about 24 hours) the intermediate region between muscle masses contains a few myoblasts, identified by the presence of contractile fibres, and cells with extensive cytoplasmic processes destined to form the connective tissue sheaths, endo-, peri- and epi-mysium.

The initial splitting of muscle masses was still found to occur even if the developing limb was amputated at the level of the wrist. This strongly suggests that early muscle development is autonomous and does not depend upon the tension generated by muscle attachments. These experiments do not rule out the possibility that later muscular development relies upon the presence of tendons of attachment, or upon tension generated within the muscle itself. Haines (1932) argues that such a mechanism must occur, at any rate in later stages of muscular development, in order to ensure correspondence between bone and muscle which is found even in the presence of congenital abnormalities.

Tendons also develop from muscle blastemata (Bardeen 1907; Butcher 1929, 1933; Leovy 1913) alongside 'their' muscles, being better differentiated proximally than distally. There is some experimental evidence (Shellswell and Wolpert 1977) to suggest that tendons also enjoy autonomy: distal tips from stage-24 chick wing buds grafted to chick flank produce well-formed hands; in these hands the tendon of flexor digitorum profundis is well developed and in its normal position, although no muscle is present. The position with regard to other, smaller tendons is less clear.

Mismatching of tendons (Shellswell and Wolpert 1977) by inverting a limb bud tip and transferring it from right to left showed that flexor muscles will unite happily with extensor tendons and vice versa. The attachments formed were between tendons 'in the same position both anteroposteriorly and with respect to distance from the ectoderm' which sounds like a simple coupling of cut surfaces with their nearest neighbours.

Minor differences are found between flexor and extensor tendons in the digits. The former are circular in cross-section and tend to appear earlier in development than the extensors, which are flatter in cross-section. There is no clear consensus about the origin of collagen fibres in this location, which have been described variously as originating in the intercellular space, within the cells themselves or at the cell membrane (Chaplin and Greenlee 1975). Vascular buds within the developing tendon can be seen by electron microscopy, at first too small in diameter to admit a blood corpuscle, then rather larger. There seems to be a specific difference in vascularity of tendons, as the tendon of the 13-day-old chick is said to be well-vascularized, whilst no blood vessels are seen in the new-born, nor indeed in the 30-day-old rat. The diameter of collagen fibrils is said to be 40 nm at birth in the rat, increasing to 80–160 nm at 30 days. In chick, the fibril diameter is variable at all stages of development.

3.8. Innervation

In our consideration of the developing fins of fishes, we saw that there is usually a direct relationship between a particular spinal nerve and the muscle it innervates, so much so that in axial fins an almost linear relationship is preserved. We noted that this arrangement became a little blurred in paired fins, and mentioned that it is preserved only in essence in the tetrapod limb. However, at some point in evolution, a major split seems to have developed between the urodele amphibians and all other tetrapods. Whereas in any non-urodele tetrapod the stimulation or cutting of a single nerve root produces contraction in or degeneration of the nerve supply to a single muscle, a similar experiment in a urodele produces a diffuse reponse. This is only one of a large number of differences which single out the urodeles as rather special vertebrates (Straus 1946).

Leaving aside the urodeles as a special case, most work on nerve development has been done on the anuran tadpole (because of its size and ease of access), on mammals, and on birds. The developmental pattern in these groups has many similarities, but is less well-described in higher tetrapods than one would like.

Within the spinal cord of the anuran tadpole are virtually two nervous systems, developing side by side. The first of these, concerned with axial locomotion, develops early; the other, concerned with the movement of the limbs, becomes fully functional at about the time of metamorphosis. Three phases of nervous development can be distinguished in the growing limb, a pre-motile period, a period of rapid development of limb movements, and finally a period of increasing organization and coordination.

The anatomical pattern of nerve supply is established early (stage 52 in *Xenopus*). In general, the nerves develop at the same time as the structures they supply. For example, the nerves supplying the digits of the frog, *Eleutherodactylus,* are visible before the digital mesenchymal condensations can be distinguished (Hughes 1965).

The limb is first penetrated by nerve fibres when it is still a hemispherical bud. The first fibres are naked; later Schwann cells migrate along them.

The question of what determines the paths followed by fibres as they grow into the limb is a fascinating, but vexed, one. It is an established feature of normal adult anatomy that the neurones which innervate a particular muscle are consistently located at a particular position in the spinal cord. This is manifested in the separate spinal roots through which fibres pass. The paths followed by fibres through the brachial or lumbar plexuses in the adult organism appear highly complex, but it is nonetheless possible that the initial neuromuscular connections are first established on the basis of propinquity. Given that these connections are formed very early during the outgrowth of nerve fibres and at a time when the structure of the limb bud is simple, fibres may do no more than innervate the first muscle rudiments they come to. Adult anatomy may be the result of pulling out of the nerve fibres by later elongation of the limb together with secondary compression of nerves into discrete trunks which later come to follow separate and indirect routes, the whole process being due to the later growth of intervening tissues of the limb (Horder 1978). Evidence in favour of such an interpretation comes from studies in which a limb bud is caused to become innervated by foreign sets of nerve fibres (Straznicky 1963, Fig. 3.17). A near-normal

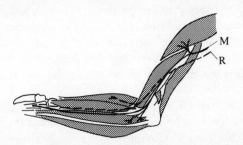

FIG. 3.17. Straznicky (1963) was able to remove the brachial level of the neural tube and replace it by other levels of the tube. If the lumbosacral section was grafted in place of the brachial level, the hatching chick had well-developed musculature with a normal pattern of innervation (M = median, R = radial nerves).

pattern of nerve trunks is formed. This cannot be due to any selective affinity between the fibres and the paths taken because none of the fibres are invading appropriate paths, but could be explained if fibres are constrained by the particular channels open to them between the intrinsic tissues of the limb. However, it must be stressed that claims have frequently been made during the long history of studies of this subject that fibres can be selectively guided to their appropriate targets. The reader is referred to the following reviews for further information: Horder (1978), Jacobson (1978), and Mendell and Hollyday (1976).

It is possible to present an invading axon with an abnormal environment. In the chick, for instance, modified limb buds can be manufactured with relative ease by operative surgery. Stirling and Summerbell (1977) operated on a series of chick limb buds, either truncating them or removing a whole segment or more and replacing the severed tip. They found that truncation of the developing limb also truncated its nerve supply: if the autopod was missing, then the nerve supply to the autopod was also missing. If a more proximal segment was deleted, then its nerve supply was also deleted. The migrating nerves can 'overleap' a gap in the developing limb, and innervate more distal parts normally. But this evidence does not clearly favour either of the rival theories of random innervation or selective affinity.

3.8.1. *Development of movement in anurans*

The first movements of developing limbs occur in conjunction with the presence of the first myofibrils in muscle cells. These movements are seen at first in *Eleutherodactylus* only during movements of the trunk, as uncoordinated wiping and clapping of the feet. A little later, two classes of movement can be distinguished, a reflex withdrawal after touch stimulation, soon followed by an extension or kick (often on the opposite side to that stimulated) and an unco-ordinated spontaneous movement produced without stimulation. During the course of a few days, the former develops into powerful symmetrical thrusts of the hindlimbs which, once they can be sustained over a period of time, become swimming movements. The spontaneous activity tends to develop into walking, with simultaneous movements occurring in diagonally opposed limbs. Such movements are fragmented at first: the developing frog may freeze in mid-stride and complete the movement (perhaps in several stages) after an interval of seconds or even minutes.

A similar state of affairs is seen in the toad, *Xenopus*. Random limb trembling is followed after a few days by a single bilateral flexure at the hip, with a passive recovery, the so-called 'flare' movement. This is never seen during swimming, but only at the end of a period of activity: it cannot be elicited by touch. The duration of swimming between each flare becomes shorter, until a mere change of posture is sufficient stimulus: at this stage, flaring can also be produced by a light touch on the tail or leg. Flare is superseded by alternate stepping move-ments of up to four consecutive cycles. Leg swimming first assists the axial locomotion of the tail (stage 60), then supersedes it (stage 63) as tail movement ceases.

In both *Eleutherodactylus* and *Xenopus,* the period of development of activity is short in relation to the time required to reach maturity (36 hours out of 14 days in the former, 15 out of 58 days in the latter). Both show limb flexion followed by extension being performed with increasing felicity.

3.8.2. *The central nervous connection – the ventral horn*

The correspondence between these two species is not confined to behaviour, but is mirrored in the developing spinal cord where motor neurons which innervate the limb musculature are developing in the ventral horns. In the Anura, the ventral horn is discrete, segmental and made up of relatively few cells – few enough to count. Inspection of serially sectioned material shows that, during the period of development, the number of cells in each ventral horn decreases (from 5000–6000 initially, to 1200 60 days later in *Xenopus*), but that the surviving cells increase in size (Prestige 1967). Non-surviving cells are seen as pycnotic regions within the developing horn. The extent of this degeneration can be shown experimentally in chick to depend on the degree of peripheral loading (simply, how much there is to innervate) (Fig. 3.18). The rate of cell death in the normal limb is highest during the period when movement is being developed (stages 54–59 in *Xenopus*).

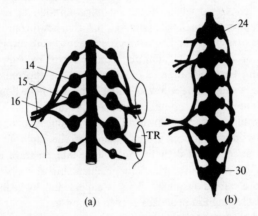

(a) (b)

FIG. 3.18. Increase and decrease in peripheral load affects the size of spinal nerve ganglia. In (a) an extra transplanted right wing (TR) has been added to a chick embryo; note the increase in size of ganglia 14–16 on the right side. In (b) the right leg was removed surgically at 2.5 days: the drawing represents the result at 6 days. Note the decrease in size of ganglia 24–30 on the right side of the body. (After Hamburger and Levi-Montalcini 1949.)

The two processes, increase in cell size and decrease in cell number, are separable experimentally. If larvae are starved of thyroxine, cell loss continues and differentiation ceases. By using this technique, it is possible to see that the growing horn increases in size by recruitment of cells at its posterior end. Observations on the amount of maternal melanin (a black pigment present in the egg and shared out amongst daughter cells at each division) in ventral horn cells also shows that the anterior part of the horn is ahead of the posterior part in development, and contributes neurons earlier to the developing limb. This craniocaudal gradient of development in the ventral horn matches the proximo-distal development of the limb bud, so that anterior segments tend to supply proximal structures.

The degree of differentiation of ventral horn cells is measured by their response to the amputation of the limb which they supply. In phase I, amputation halts the recruitment of further cells from the mantle layer of the cord; in phase II, cell death is rapid after amputation; but in phase III, there is more delay in reaction. The fate of a group of cells or a region of the horn after amputation can thus be used to asses its maturity. Phase II seems to be a short, critical stage, soon terminated by differentiation to stage III or by death; cells innervating more proximal parts of the limb and anterior in the horn pass through this stage earlier than those more posterior cells innervating distal areas.

3.8.3. *Functional innervation in Amphibia*

Functional contacts between nerve and muscle are presumably made only by those neurons which survive phase II of differentiation and go on to maturity. The functional contacts, which occur in a proximodistal sequence, can be recognized in sections specifically stained for the neurotransmitter-degrading enzyme cholinesterase in nerve fibres which come into contact with muscle cells.

At the time of its first contractions, a muscle will be supplied by a nerve bundle containing tens or hundreds of neurons, all of approximately the same diameter. Within a short time a few of these fibres will have doubled in size and further increases in neuron diameter occur up to maturity.

Electrical stimulation of the developing limb produces a concordant picture. At an early stage this produces either flexion of the hip followed by passive extension or an uncoordinated twitching: a little later, a stage is reached where the stimulation of an anterior ganglion produces hip flexion whilst posterior ganglia produce a varied response. This is superseded by a final stage where stimulation of each ganglion produces a fixed response.

The intermediate uncoordinated stage seems to indicate that, at some points during development, more responses to a given stimulus are possible than in the adult. This in turn presupposes a selective loss of connections within the CNS which is in fact seen histologically; a peak nerve size in terms of fibre number is reached in late embryology and is followed by a further phase of degeneration of neurons. This seems to be due to the removal of elements not necessary to the final plan of the fully developed nervous system.

Further information on nerve ontogeny can be obtained by establishing at what point antagonistic pairs of muscles (those with opposite effects) are first innervated separately. This can be determined by the administration of strychnine, which abolishes the normal inhibitory reflexes which prevent antagonistic muscles contracting together. The paralysing effect of the drug should thus become more and more marked as further reflex arcs develop. In *Xenopus* the flare movement is unaffected by strychnine, presumably because it has a passive rather than an active recovery, but stepping becomes increasingly strychnine-sensitive with time. Not surprisingly, the drug has no effect at stages where the embryo can flex but not extend its limbs at will, but response develops immediately active extension becomes possible. This suggests that the reflex arcs develop at the same time as functional innervation of muscle.

3.8.4. *Functional innervation in higher tetrapods and mammals*

In higher vertebrates, the situation is complicated by the fact that the ventral horn develops as a continuous tract of cells, which later becomes subdivided to supply each limb. Later still, the limb region of the horn splits into a series of columns thought to innervate muscles of similar function.

In the rabbit, Romanes (1941) described the development of the brachial horn supplying the forelimb; the process of splitting of the horn into columns occurs at the same time as the invasion of the limb bud by the first axons. No functional nerve:muscle connections can be seen at this stage. Subdivision of the horn continues, a new division being established as each successive proximodistal segment of the limb is innervated.

In the mammal, developing musculature can be stimulated electrically well before spontaneous movements occur. In the rat, response to electrical stimulation can be elicited at 15.3 days, whilst reflex responses to stretch are not seen for another 24 hours. The sequence of developing spontaneous muscle movements given by East (1931) shows abduction and adduction (movement away from and towards the side respectively) of the limb at 16 days with flexion and extension of the foot three days later. A similar sequence has been described in the rabbit (Pankratz 1939) and in the sheep (Barcroft and Baron 1939). In all cases, proximal muscles develop function before distal ones.

Degeneration of neurons in the ventrolateral motor horn is also seen in mammals. Harris (1965) described a wave of cell death in the mouse reaching a peak on day 14 (two days after the first appearance of columns) and which moved in a craniocaudal direction. This degeneration was complete before the onset of limb mobility. Whether or not there exists a final period of selection as seen in Amphibia is not known, but Gamble (1966) has described degenerating axons in the ulnar nerve of healthy 3-to-5-month-old human fetuses.

3.9. Limb shaping and cell death

We have seen the mode of development of the skeleton, muscular, vascular and nervous systems in the developing limb. But one of the major properties of the developing limb bud, the way in which it changes in shape during development, has not been considered. Besides the more obvious differential growth, there is another process of almost equal importance – differential cell death (Zwilling 1964a). This process seems to be significant only in amniotes, as one of the characteristic areas of cell death, the interdigital zone, which helps to delineate the amniote digit, is absent in amphibians (Cameron and Fallon 1977b).

The zones of mesenchymal cell death have been mapped out by vital staining of the embryo using Neutral Red or Nile Blue sulphate which is selectively concentrated by the macrophages which are engaged in mopping up the dead and moribund cells. These zones have been most widely studied in birds, where they are particularly prominent. In the early chick limb bud, there are initially three areas, the anterior and posterior necrotic zones (ANZ, PNZ) and the opaque patch. The ANZ and PNZ are situated at either end of the AER and the opaque patch within the central limb mesenchyme.

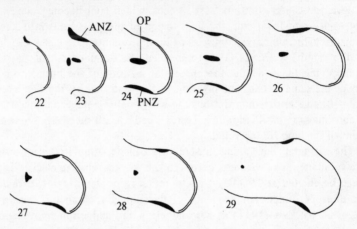

FIG. 3.19. Areas of mesenchymal cell death in the development of the chick wing bud (Hamburger–Hamilton staging). Note anterior and posterior necrotic zones (ANZ and PNZ) and opaque patch (OP). (After Saunders, Gasseling, and Saunders 1962; Hinchliffe 1974.)

In the chick wing bud, which is usually described (Saunders, Gasseling and Saunders 1962; Hinchliffe 1974*b*), the ANZ appears as two successive waves of cell death, a proximal one at stage 23 and a distal one at stages 25–26 (Fig. 3.19). The PNZ appears later, reaching a peak at stage 24, and then disappearing for some time. In later stages (27–31), ANZ and PNZ are still present distally, at either end of the AER. In the chick leg bud, there is a very prominent ANZ at stages 23 and 24.

In other avian species, the pattern of cell death in ANZ and PNZ differs from that in the chick, and the amount of cell death is somewhat reduced. In the duck wing bud, there is a prominent ANZ from stages 23–29, and in the leg bud from stage 25–28. In the herring gull wing bud, there is an ANZ from stages 23–31, but little cell death in the hindlimb until stage 26 (Hinchliffe 1980).

A comparative approach makes it possible to hazard a guess at the role of ANZ and PNZ. In the mouse and rat, Milaire (1971, 1977 *a, b*) has shown that, in both fore- and hind-limb, there are no areas corresponding to ANZ and PNZ, though there is a small necrotic area anteriorly, adjacent to the prospective first digit. Both mouse and rat have the full number of digits (five) typical of the pentadactyl limb. In birds, however, the digital number is reduced: there are essentially only three major wing and four leg digits. In birds, therefore, ANZ and PNZ may limit the quantity of distal mesenchyme available to digit formation and may thus control the pattern of skeletal development. There is, however, contrary evidence of Saunders (1966) that experimental suppression of the chick wing PNZ still results in the formation of a normal wing. The PNZ may, therefore, be dispensable in normal limb development. But the idea that skeletal pattern may be controlled by cell death in ANZ and PNZ is supported by other observations. According to Milaire, the necrotic area found anteriorly in rat and mouse is absent in the mole (*Talpa*) forelimb development (Milaire 1977*b*). This absence is correlated with the formation of the additional falciform digit of the mole (Fig. 2.20). By contrast in rats and mice the first digit is short. In various other mutants also, increases or decreases in areas of cell death are correlated with increases or descreases in digital number (Hinchliffe 1974, Fig. 4.30). Thus, in the *talpid* mutant, ANZ and PNZ are lacking and the resulting polydactylous limbs have up to 8 digits (Hinchliffe and Ede 1967; Cairns 1977), while the increased size of the ANZ in the wingless wing bud appears responsible for the *wingless* phenotype ranging from preaxial digital deficiencies to total winglessness (Hinchliffe and Ede 1973).

Another area of cell death is the 'opaque patch', so-called by its discoverers because it is opaque to transmitted light (Fell and Canti 1935). This has been found in fore- and hind-limb buds in a number of avian species, including the chick. It appears at the distal end of the proximal skeletal blastema – the humerus in the wing bud – and it has been suggested as a factor associated with the initial separation of radius and ulna (Dawd and Hinchliffe 1971). The opaque patch is at its largest at the time when radial and ulnar blastemata first appear. We know that the initiation of chondrogenesis requires cell adhesion, and one property of dead cells is that this adhesion is reduced and the cells round up. Thus, if there is a process of condensation along the central axis of the limb bud, and cell death intervenes distally, the axial blastema will become bifurcated and Y-shaped, as is the initial blastema of the limb long bones.

Later, at 8 days in the chick, further zones of cell death are formed (Fig. 3.20) in the developing footplate in the mesenchymal areas which separate the chondrifying digits (Saunders and Fallon 1967). Interdigital necrosis follows a precise developmental programme, different areas appearing at specific times. Thus, between chick toes 2 and 3, necrosis begins proximally between the digits, then an area appears distally under the AER, and finally the two areas coalesce (Pautou 1975). Such interdigital necrotic zones (INZ) have been found in all amniotes which have been investigated (Menkes *et al.* 1965), or at least those which have non-webbed digits. INZs have been found in human (Kelley 1970), mouse and rat (Ballard and Holt 1968) embryos, in avian species, and in reptiles (the lizard, *Calotes* (Goel and Mathur 1977), and the turtle (Fallon and Cameron 1977)). The morphogenetic role of the INZ in amniotes, as originally suggested by Saunders (Saunders and Fallon 1967), is unequivocally that of separating and shaping the digits. Confirmation of this is obtained from a number of sources, from mutants, from teratology and from web-footed birds, which provide a natural experiment in this context. In a number of mutants, for example the *talpid* fowl mutant (Hinchliffe and Thorogood 1974) and the poly-syndactylous mutant of the mouse (Johnson 1969), interdigital cell death is completely or relatively suppressed, with the consequence that the mutant limbs show soft tissue syndactyly: their digits are joined by webs of mesenchymal tissue. Teratological studies show that Janus Green, injected into the amniotic sac, has the effect of inhibiting interdigital cell death, once again resulting in soft tissue syndactyly (Saunders and Fallon 1967; Menkes and Deleanu 1964; Pautou 1976; Kieny, Pautou, and Sengel 1976). In web-footed birds, such as the duck and herring gull, considerable interdigital cell death is still present, but it is on a less substantial scale and its duration is shorter than in the chick (Hinchliffe 1980; Pautou 1974). This relative inhibition of INZ accounts for the survival of the webs of tissue linking the digits, and the fact that the INZs are not completely inhibited presumably accounts for the thinning of the interdigital webs. In both web-footed species, cell death is as intensive as in the chick between digits 1 and 2 where there is no web. After cell death in the interdigital tissue has ceased, it continues along anterior and posterior margins of the digits, further shaping them by removal of undifferentiated mesenchyme.

In the wing, the INZs have received less attention. Here cell death intervenes between digits 2 and 3, presumably separating them in a way similar to that of the feet INZ. Cell death between digits 3 and 4 follows a different pattern (Fig. 3.20). Here cell death begins proximally and spreads distally, but then the INZ thus formed and the PNZ posterior to digit 4 spread out and overlap, thus destroying undifferentiated mesenchyme distal to the last-formed phalangeal element of digit 4 (Hinchliffe, unpublished observation). As the specialized wing continues to develop, digit 3 differentiates further phalangeal elements, while digit 4, which was initially much the same size as digit 3, becomes relatively much smaller and does not add further phalangeal elements. Once again, our observations support the idea that cell death, by limiting the quantity of mesenchyme available for skeleton formation, is in effect a controlling factor governing the differentiation of skeletal pattern.

To developmental biologists familiar with the idea of differentiation involving constructive processes of growth and gene specification of characteristic, tissue-specific proteins, the concept of cell death is paradoxical. How do cells prepare their own death, or, as it were, suicide? Histological, histochemical, and ultra-structural studies on necrotic areas of chick limb buds (Dawd and Hinchliffe 1971) and on rat INZ (Ballard and Holt 1968) give at least a partial answer (Plates 10 and 11). Not all mesenchymal cells die simultaneously; scattered cells undergo a deterioration involving both chromatin condensation within the nucleus and cytoplasmic vacuolation. Viable neighbouring mesenchyme cells then take up, or phagocytose, the dead cells, this process apparently inciting the viable cell to further phagocytic activity, since it takes up more dead cells, eventually becoming a fully-fledged macrophage (Kieny and Sengel 1974). Such macrophages may contain some 12–20 dead cells within vacuoles where they undergo lysosomal digestion. These vacuoles are described as heterophagic (their

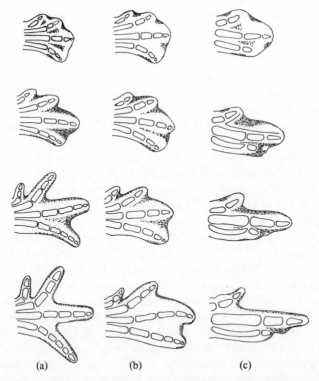

(a)   (b)   (c)

FIG. 3.20. Interdigital cell death in development of (a) chick leg, 7.5, 8.25, 9.25, and 10 days (partly from Pautou 1974 ,)(b) duck leg, 8.5, 9.5, 10.5, and 11.5 days (partly from Pautou 1974), (c) chick wing, 7.25, 7.75, 8, and 8.75 days (original, Hinchliffe). Note the shaping by interdigital cell death of the digital contours of the chick foot, the relative inhibition of interdigital cell death during webbed-foot development, and the intervention of cell death to limit the growth of digit 4 in the wing.

contents are from outside the cell), and contain lysosomal enzymes such as acid phosphatase, β-glucuronidase, and non-specific esterase, all of which are acid hydrolases engaged in the digestion of different cellular constituents. In many instances of morphogenetic cell death outside the limb, it appears that deteriorating cells synthesize additional lysosomal enzymes via an active Golgi body, and these are initially localized in autophagic vacuoles into which cytoplasmic organelles are sequestrated (Lockshin and Beaulaton 1974). Later, the lysosomal enzymes 'leak' out of the vacuoles into the adjacent cytoplasm which thus deteriorates, the cell at this stage fragmenting, a process described as 'apoptosis' by Kerr, Wyllie, and Currie (1972). A recent reinvestigation (Hurle and Hinchliffe 1978) of the chick wing bud PNZ has shown lysosomal involvement at an early stage of deterioration together with all the features just described, at least so far as acid phosphatase is concerned. Stereoscans and transmission electron micrographs suggest that mesenchymal cell fragmentation may well be an active process, rather than simply a consequence of confluence of cytoplasmic vacuoles.

3.10. Development of limblessness

Scattered observations have been made on the development of limblessness in the cetaceans while there has been more thorough investigation of the development of various limbless reptiles. In cetaceans, hindlimb buds appear and reach a stage where the digital plate is formed, but the limb buds regress before the formation of cartilaginous skeletal elements. This has been observed in porpoises and the humpback whale (Andrews 1921). The causes of initiation of the regression of the limb buds (e.g. AER regression) are not known. It is interesting that hindlimb buds reach a more advanced stage in the Odontocetes than in the Mysticeti, since rather more of the pelvic limb persists in the internal vestiges of the former.

Much more is known of the development of reptile limblessness, owing to the studies of Raynaud and his co-workers. The reptiles studied can be divided conveniently into three groups: lizards (e.g. *Lacerta viridis*), which form a normal limb bud which develops into a pentadactyl limb, legless lizards (e.g. the slow-worm, *Anguis fragilis*), which forms fore- and hind-limb buds which then regress, and the snakes (e.g. *Python reticulatus*), in which there is no forelimb bud but sometimes a small hindlimb bud which ceases to grow after the small femur (and, in *Python*, a fused tibia–fibula) has been formed (see Fig. 2.1).

The regression of the slow-worm forelimb bud has received particular attention. The first detectable deficiency is in the number of somites: while lizards with normal legs generally have eight somites contributing cells to the somatopleure (somite numbers 6–13 in *Lacerta viridis*) during limb bud initiation, the slow-worm has only four (Raynaud and Vasse 1972; Raynaud 1969). Even so, this reduced cellular contribution is in some way defective, since the cells from the distal part of the somite processes undergo degeneration (Raynaud, Adrian, and Kouprach 1973; Raynaud and Adrian 1975). Raynaud (1977) has found experimentally that, in *Lacerta viridis,* the somitic contribution exercises a stimulatory effect on the proliferation of the somatopleure cells since removal of somites 6–9 results in the absence of the thickening of the somatopleure and thus absence of the limb rudiment at that somite level. The initial cause of regression in the slow-worm is thus attributed by Raynaud to somitic deficiency.

In spite of this deficiency in the slow-worm, a small limb bud capped by an ectodermal ridge forms and, for a brief period, grows normally. The ridge soon begins to degenerate, but for three further days the mesoderm continues to proliferate, and the bud to grow. Then growth ceases; there is reduced protein and RNA synthesis in the mesoderm where cell death begins in the more proximal parts and then spreads distally (Raynaud and Vasse 1972). Thus the limb bud disappears. Raynaud (1976) considers that there is deficiency in the mesodermal factor maintaining the ridge (see Chapter 4.6), which therefore regresses, failing to stimulate continued outgrowth of the mesoderm.

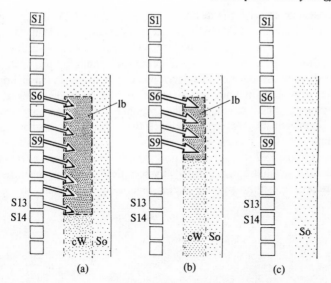

FIG. 3.21. Schematic representation of the relations between somites (S) and somatopleure (So) at the level of the forelimb bud (lb) in three types of reptiles. (a) Lizard with normal legs. Eight somitic processes (S6–13) contribute to the limb bud mesoderm. (b) Slow-worm (*Anguis fragilis*). Four somitic processes (S6–9) contribute to the reduced limb bud. (c) True snakes (e.g. *Python*). There are no somitic processes, no somatopleural thickening, and no forelimb bud. cW = crest of Wolff, lb = mesodermal thickening of the limb bud. Somitic processes are shown by arrows. (After Raynaud 1972.)

A similar picture emerges in other legless lizards. Three species of *Scelotes* show the same pattern of reduced somite number, a deficiency or degeneration of the somitic contribution, a poorly developed ectodermal ridge which soon degenerates and mesodermal regression. Raynaud (1977) draws a parallel with the development of wingless chick mutants (Zwilling 1974) in which the limb mesoderm fails to maintain the ectodermal ridge which flattens, thus failing to stimulate the outgrowth of underlying wing mesoderm (see Chapter 4.5). On the other hand, the mesodermal cell death in these lizards seems to be a secondary event, and is not due to extension of existing areas of normal cell death, as found in the sex-linked *wingless* mutant of the fowl (section 3.9) (Hinchliffe 1976).

In the true snakes, no attempt is made to form a forelimb bud: even the somites at the presumed forelimb level fail to produce processes. But in the hind-limb bud of *Python,* a snake with rudimentary pelvic appendages (cf. Fig. 2.19c and d), there are indications of somitic contributions to the early stages of a hindlimb bud. Within the mesoderm, a small femur and fused tibia-fibula form, but no elements more distal. As in the slow-worm, the ectodermal ridge soon degenerates and further growth ceases (Raynaud 1972*b*, 1974, 1976). Even those chondrogenic elements which have been formed grow very little, and this failure is associated with the death of a considerable proportion of cells in the pelvic girdle and in the femur (Renous, Raynaud, Gasc, and Pieau 1976).

Many aspects of this process of limb reduction remain puzzling. Why, for example, should cetaceans form a well-developed hindlimb bud, while snakes do not, though both are on the same developmental pathway towards limblessness? Does the reduction in somitic processes at the limb level make available mesenchyme for the increased somitic number which invariably accompanies reptilian limblessness? We cannot answer these questions: perhaps we should concentrate on the general conclusion we can draw. In apodous reptiles, Raynaud (1972*b*, 1977) emphasizes that the deficiency always affects the initial developmental mechanism, i.e. firstly by somitic deficiency, secondly by ecto-dermal ridge regression, and he argues that these deficiencies are genetically controlled.

4 Experimental embryology

4.1. Introduction

Turning from description to experiment, we find that progress in analysing limb development has depended largely on advances in techniques. The pioneers of experimental limb embryology relied heavily on amphibian material since the developing embryos can readily be cultured outside their vitelline membrane and very little specialized culture equipment is needed. Grafting is relatively easy since the embryo's wounds heal quickly. One drawback is that amphibian embryos tend to regenerate missing parts: a piece of tissue removed for experimental reasons may regrow before data on the effects of its absence can be collected.

Harrison (1921) established an experimental approach to limb development with a series of classical grafting experiments using urodele larvae. The chick limb is less accessible because of the presence of the extra-embryonic membranes, and in later stages it is prone to bleed heavily after operation. However, Murray (1926) made successful grafts of early chick limb buds and found that he could demonstrate relatively full differentiation of the skeleton. Murray grafted limb buds to the richly vascularized chorio-allantois (the embryonic 'lung') of a host embryo. The grafts in turn became vascularized and could be cultured for about 10 days. Hamburger (1938) pioneered the still widely used technique of intra-coelomic and flank grafting in chick embryos. Limb buds were implanted by inserting the base into a slit made in the host embryo's flank at 3 days of development, or into the coelom itself. The limb bud had to be inserted through chorion and amnion, but these were able to heal.

Fell (1929) initiated an organ culture approach (still in use in modified form) which allowed limb components (such as early chondrogenic elements) to be grown *in vitro* on a clot of embryo extract and blood plasma. However, the present intensive work on chick limb development undoubtedly derives from Saunders's discovery (1948) that the importance of the apical ectodermal ridge could be demonstrated by removing it surgically. A major step forward was Zwilling's (1955) discovery that trypsin or versene could be used to separate the two principal chick limb bud components, ectoderm and mesoderm. Zwilling and Saunders were then able to analyse the phenomenon of mesodermal/ectodermal interaction by combining tissues of different ages, origin, genetic potential, or even species. In this way, chimeric limb buds could be flank grafted to other embryos to reveal their developmental potential. (By this time flank grafting had replaced the less reliable chorio-allantoic graft.) Grafting, and the recombination of various limb components, is still a popular experimental approach, although requiring manual dexterity of a high order, since the host embryo must be operated on within the egg. Techniques of whole chick embryo culture *in vitro*, such as those of New (1966) and Spratt (New 1966), unfortunately do not permit limb development to proceed very far.

The precision of grafting techniques in chick is greatly increased by labelling either host or graft, either by autoradiography or more recently using the natural marker provided by the distinctive quail nucleolus (le Douarin 1971). Quail and chick are sufficiently similar to allow the growth of chick/quail combination limbs, and this technique has been much used recently in French laboratories.

A novel approach pioneered in particular by Ede (1971, 1976) has been to study events in early chondrogenesis by disaggregating mesenchyme cells and analysing their reaggregation in culture in the belief that such a system provides a model of the aggregation of mesenchymal cells seen during the formation of prechondrogenic condensations. Another recent approach is biochemical analysis (Goetinck and Pennypacker 1977) of developing limb cartilage constituents in normal, mutant or teratogen deformed embryos.

Organ culture of the whole limb bud still yields disappointing results, since the growth and development of limb buds without a blood supply is severely limited. Though considerable chondrogenic differentiation can take place (e.g. in mouse limb buds: Lessmöllmann, Neubert, and Merker 1975), normal bone will not form. For this reason, and because of the problems of operating on living mammalian embryos, even *in vitro*, mammalian limb development has been little analysed. However, Gulamhusein and Beck (1978) have recently obtained promising results from ferret limbs. Some insight is also possible through analysis of the 'natural experiments' provided by mutations, particularly in the mouse (Grüneberg 1963). Analysis of amniote limb development is thus mainly dependent on the experimental analysis of chick limb buds.

4.2. The limb field and the development of the limb axes

A developing limb has a definite orientation. It has a proximal and a distal pole, an anterior and posterior side, and a dorsal and ventral surface. What process of development determines the establishment of these axes, and when does it occur? Is the mesoderm or the ectoderm primarily responsible? These questions were asked by Harrison (1921) and his colleagues (reviewed by Huxley and de Beer 1934), who were able to establish a number of important principles about urodele limb development by carefully controlled experiments in which the location of the prospective limb bud area was changed relative to the host axes (Fig. 4.1). In this way it can be seen whether the polarity of the limb is already determined in the grafted prospective limb bud, or whether it can be influenced by the host axes.

Detwiler (1933) found that the area capable of limb formation was determined early in development (at the middle gastrula stage, long before limb buds can be recognized), and that this limb bud field was considerably larger than the area which usually forms limbs. Within the limb field there was no regional specificity:

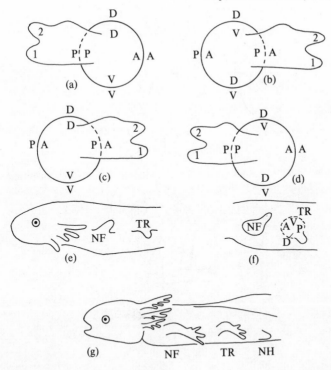

FIG. 4.1. Establishment of polarity in Axolotl limbs. The axes of both host and limb disc are represented by the abbreviations: A = anterior, P = posterior, D = dorsal, V = ventral. The circles represent the grafted limb discs, transferred immediately after neurulation, and the orientation of the resulting limb is shown at the 2 digit stage. In (a) the limb disc has been replaced in its original orientation. In (b)–(d) the A–P axis of the graft is determined by that of the disc, but the D–V axis is controlled by the host. The D–V axis does stabilize with the tail bud stage. In the representative experiment (e)–(g), a right forelimb bud has been transplanted to the left side: it differentiates according to its own antero-posterior axis, but according to its host's dorso-ventral axis ((e) host embryo after graft, (f) axes of graft, (g) resulting graft development). NF = normal forelimb, TR = transplant, NH = normal hind. (After Harrison 1921; Swett 1927.)

half a limb field, either transplanted or left *in situ*, regulates to form a whole limb. The specific properties of the limb field become stabilized gradually; first the limb type, then the antero-posterior axis, and lastly, the dorso-ventral axis. These specific properties reside in the mesoderm rather than the ectoderm.

Hamburger (1938) showed that in the chick, limb fields also had the property of self-differentiation well before the limb bud is recognizable. As early as stage 12 a prospective wing bud transplanted to the flank region differentiates into a limb whose dorso-ventral and antero-posterior axes correspond to those of the graft rather than those of the host (Fig. 4.2). The determination of the axes in the chick limb bud is also in general a mesodermal responsibility. If prospective

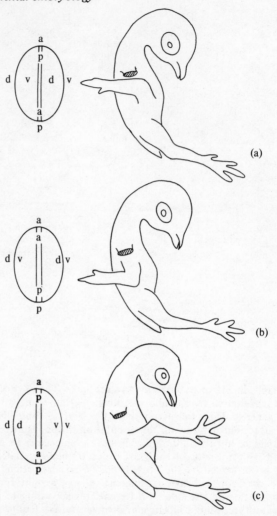

FIG. 4.2. Hamburger (1938) showed that stages 15–18 chick limb buds transplanted into the flanks of hosts of the same age had their antero-posterior and
dorso-ventral axes already determined at the time of transplantation. In the
experiments illustrated the orientation of the graft in relation to the host is
shown diagrammatically on the left, and the resulting development of the grafted
limb on the right. The grafted limbs develop in accordance with their own axes,
and their development is not influenced by the host axes. In (a) a transplanted
wing bud has both antero-posterior and dorso-ventral axes in opposition to those
of the host (apdv), in (b) the orientation of the wingbud is aadv, and in (c) the
orientation of the leg bud is apdd. For clarity the host wing is not drawn. a =
anterior, p = posterior, d = dorsal, v = ventral.

wing bud mesoderm (stage 12–17) is transplanted to the flank so that flank ectoderm heals over it, a wing develops whose axes are again determined by the

orientation of the mesodermal graft rather than by the host (Saunders and Reuss 1974).

In its turn, the self-differentiating ability of wing bud mesoderm depends upon earlier influences from the adjacent somitic mesoderm (Pinot 1970; Kieny 1969, 1971). Kieny showed that prospective wing bud mesoderm inserted into a slit made in the flank of a host embryo will form a wing when the graft is transferred at the 11-somite stage along with its adjacent somitic mesoderm. If the prospective limb bud is grafted without its somitic mesoderm, it forms a wing only after the 13-somite stage. The differentiation of the mouse limb bud is similarly enhanced by the presence of the associated somites (Agnish and Kochhar 1977).

Mesodermal responsibility for the wing axes is also shown by experiments of Zwilling (1956a), in which ectodermal caps of stage 19 limb buds were separated from their mesodermal cores using trypsin, and replaced either in their original orientation or upside-down and back-to-front. The mesoderm determined all axes of the resulting limbs. It has been pointed out recently (MacCabe, Errick, and Saunders 1974) that Zwilling examined these limbs at too early a stage to analyse responsibility for the dorso-ventral axis of the most distal limb parts. In fact, as a result of more recent investigations (MacCabe *et al.* 1974; Pautou and Kieny 1973; Pautou 1977), his conclusions must be modified since the ectoderm has been shown to be polarized dorso-ventrally and to exert a controlling influence on the development of the dorso-ventral axis of the distal limb parts. The dorsal and ventral aspects of the chick foot differ externally in the curvature of the claws, and the size and pattern of scales. Internally, mesodermal derivatives such as the musculature and skeleton are also affected. If the ectodermal cap of a 3.5-day limb bud is inverted with reference to its mesodermal core, then the dorso-ventral axis of the distal limb parts is reversed (Fig. 4.3). By 5.5 days the mesoderm has lost its capacity to respond to ectodermal control, since recombination of 5.5-day mesoderm with 3.5- or 5.5-day ectoderm results in a limb orientated entirely by the mesoderm.

Searls (1976) and Stark and Searls (1976) also found that pieces of limb ectoderm when reorientated could affect adjacent developing mesodermal structures. They grafted pieces of stage 22–23 limb ectoderm (together with the underlying mesoderm necessary for technical reasons) into the dorsal surface of a stage 22–24 wing bud, in either reversed or normal orientation. The host humerus developed abnormally in all cases except those in which graft and host ectoderm matched exactly. An abnormal humerus might frequently be short, or might develop ectopic cartilages. Thus the limb ectoderm can also affect proximal limb mesoderm; but this effect is seen only when discontinuities are created within the ectodermal cap by changing the position of pieces of ectoderm. Changing the relative position of the ectodermal cap as a whole does not affect proximal mesodermal differentiation (Zwilling 1956a).

These findings that some aspects of mesodermal differentiation are controlled by the ectoderm (Gumpel-Pinot 1973) are somewhat surprising. In general in

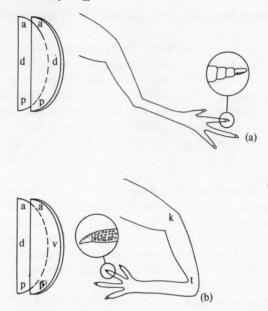

FIG. 4.3. Reversal of the dorso-ventral axis of the ectoderm with respect to that of mesoderm results in this axis of the distal parts of the developing limb being governed by ectoderm (MacCabe *et al.* 1974; Pautou and Kieny 1973; Pautou 1977). In the control, in which ectoderm and mesoderm dorso-ventral axes are unchanged relative to one another, a foot develops with one side showing only dorsal features (such as the large dorsal scales of tarsometatarsus) and the other only ventral features (such as the small tubercular scales and phalangeal pads). In (b) the dorso-ventral axes of ectoderm and mesoderm are changed relative to one another. Here, the resulting limb has its two surfaces changing their character from dorsal to ventral and from ventral to dorsal along the proximo-distal axis. Thus, the thigh feathers and knee-joint flexion (= k) follow the pattern of right asymmetry of the mesoderm, but the flexion of the tibiotarsal (= t) joint is of left asymmetry. The differentiation of the distal ectoderm of the surface illustrated is typically ventral, composed of small tubercular scales, and has followed the ectodermal, and not the mesodermal, axis. (Based on MacCabe *et al.* 1974.)

development, ectodermal differentiation is under mesodermal control, and it is rare for ectoderm to control mesodermal differentiation in a specific way (Sengel 1971).

4.3. The Saunders–Zwilling hypothesis of ectodermal–mesodermal interaction

Following the technical advances made by Saunders and Zwilling which enabled them to isolate the various factors operating in early chick development, a hypothesis of vertebrate limb morphogenesis was put forward. This hypothesis, which has been widely accepted as a theoretical basis for some twenty years, was set out in detail by Zwilling (1961) in a classic paper which is still the most widely quoted account (see also Saunders 1969). In recent years there has been a major modification of the hypothesis by the addition of a further element, the zone of polarizing activity (ZPA) and its control (in grafts) of antero-posterior differentiation.

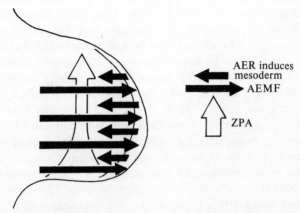

FIG. 4.4. The Saunders–Zwilling hypothesis. AER, apical ectodermal ridge, which induces outgrowth in the underlying mesoderm. AEMF, apical ectodermal maintenance factor, a mesodermal factor necessary for AER survival and concentrated postaxially. ZPA, zone of polarizing activity, responsible when grafted preaxially, for the antero-posterior axis of limb development. (Its role in normal development is controversial, see text.)

In its latest form the main features of the Saunders–Zwilling hypothesis are (Fig. 4.4):

1. Initially the AER is induced in the ectoderm by the underlying prospective limb mesoderm.

2. The AER induces the outgrowth of the underlying mesoderm, which forms progressively more distal structures.

3. The AER is not autonomous, but is itself maintained by a mesodermal factor, the apical ectodermal maintenance factor (AEMF). The AEMF is transmitted in a proximo-distal direction and is thought to be more concentrated in the postaxial mesoderm than preaxially. Anomalous limb formations, such as an increase or decrease in the number of digits, are due to a change in the amount or distribution of AEMF.

4. The limb type is controlled by the mesoderm.

5. The posterior margin of the limb (or ZPA) when transplanted to the preaxial margin acts as the source of a morphogenetic gradient imposing a secondary antero-posterior axis of differentiation. Control of the normal antero-posterior axis by the ZPA *in situ* has not been unequivocally demonstrated.

In subsequent sections we shall discuss some of the evidence upon which this hypothesis is based.

4.4. Induction of the AER by the mesoderm

Kieny (1960, 1968) found that, when early limb bud mesoderm (stages 17 and 19) or prospective mesoderm (stages 15–16) stripped of ectoderm was implanted under flank mesoderm, an AER was induced, and a limb developed. Normally, the flank ectoderm does not develop a ridge. Later Dhouailly and Kieny (1972) refined the technique, rolling up the prospective limb bud mesoderm 'in carpet fashion' and wedging it into a slit in the flank somatopleure so that one end projected into the coelom. In these experiments, the grafted prospective limb mesoderm was labelled, either by autoradiography or with the quail nucleolar marker. While many graft cells died, others survived and migrated, taking a few flank cells with them, towards the flank ectoderm where they induced an AER. Thus, under these conditions, some flank cells were persuaded to take part in limb development. Prospective chick wing mesoderm from stage 11 embryos and leg mesoderm from stage 13 have acquired the capacity to induce ridge formation. Younger mesoderm required associated somitic tissue to produce a ridge, and older material loses its inductive capacity at stage 17 (wing), or 18 (leg) (Dhouailly and Kieny 1972; Kieny 1971). The competence of the flank ectoderm to respond is lost after stage 19. Ability to induce a ridge is thus lost by mesodermal cells at about the same time that they acquire the ability to maintain an existing ridge. Induction and maintenance of the ridge by the mesoderm would, therefore, seem to be two distinct properties.

In Saunders's laboratory (Reuss and Saunders 1965) a different analytical technique has been adopted, which yields essentially similar results. In these chick embryo experiments, the flank ectoderm was removed and a slit made in the mesoderm along the antero-posterior axis. Prospective wing mesoderm, stripped of its ectodermal coat, was placed in the slit with its external surface facing outwards and the ends of the graft wedged into the slit. Regenerating flank ectoderm soon heals over the graft. In a high proportion of cases a ridge is induced over the graft, which then develops into a supernumerary wing. Wing mesoderm induces a ridge in flank ectoderm if both are from stages 12–17, but the inductive property is lost after stage 17.

For a brief period after its formation the ridge can be regenerated. If the AER is extirpated at stage 17 or 18 in wing buds, or stage 17 in leg buds, it is replaced and a normal limb is formed. Later excision results in non-regeneration of the ridge and consequent failure to form distal limb parts (Saunders and Reuss 1974).

The experimental evidence from both French and American laboratories indicates clearly that prospective wing mesoderm initially induces the AER but loses this property at stage 17, soon after the first appearance of the AER. At the same time it acquires the property of ridge maintenance. Shortly after the loss of inductive capacity by the mesoderm, both flank and limb ectoderm also lose their ability to respond to the mesodermal message.

4.5. The inductive influence of the AER

Saunders (1948) investigated the effect of the AER on the development of the limb by removing it surgically. He found that in the absence of the AER distal limb components were not formed (Fig. 4.5). If the AER was removed at an

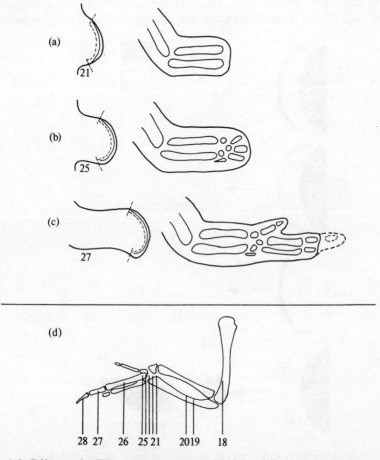

FIG. 4.5. Effects of AER excision at stages 21, 25, and 27 in preventing formation of distal wing skeletal elements (Saunders 1948; Summerbell 1974*b*). Note the quantitative relationship: the earlier the AER excision, the greater the distal deficiency. In (c) the dotted line indicates the normal limb outline and the missing phalageal element. The summary diagram (d) shows the level of truncation corresponding to AER excision at each stage between 18 and 28. (After Summerbell and Lewis 1975.)

early stage both distal parts were affected. Later Summerbell (1974, 1977*b*) made a quantitative analysis of the effect of AER excision (see Fig. 4.5), and found that removal at stage 20 prevented the formation of skeletal structures distal to the wrist, at stage 21–24 truncated the limb at the wrist, and at stage 27 only prevented the formation of a single phalangeal element.

Saunders' experimental findings in the chick were confirmed by Zwilling's discovery (1949) of the *wingless* (*wg*) chick mutation, in which, although wing buds initially form, the AER regresses on the third day, and the limb buds fail to make any further growth. Zwilling (1956*c*) separated 3-day-old mutant ecto-derm and mesoderm chemically, and recombined them with normal components (Fig. 4.6). When a normal ectodermal cap was combined with *wingless* mesoderm

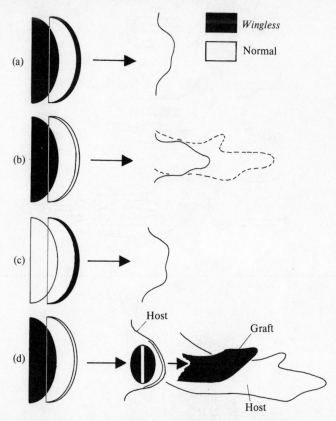

FIG. 4.6. Reciprocal interchanges of wingless (*wg*) and normal wing bud com-ponents show that *wingless* mesoderm lacks AEMF and provide evidence for both the role of AER and AEMF in normal development (Zwilling 1949, 1956*c*, 1974). Mutant mesoderm and a normal AER (which survives for 2–3 days) give more outgrowth (b) than controls. Normal mesoderm and *wg* ectoderm give no more outgrowth (c) than when both components are *wg* (a). Mutant mesoderm plus normal AER placed in a distal position on a normal wing bud form a defective wing including recognizable metacarpals and phalanges.

the AER survived for 2–3 days, then regressed, and distal outgrowth ceased (although formation of proximal skeletal parts was greater than in undisturbed *wingless* wing buds), but when *wingless* ectoderm was combined with normal

mesoderm no AER and no further limb development was seen. Zwilling interpretated these experiments in terms of a postive contribution by the AER
towards limb outgrowth.

Convincing further evidence of this contribution (Zwilling 1956*d*) came from
later experiments in which a single mesodermal core has a ridge grafted on each
lateral face (Fig. 4.7(a)). Outgrowth of the original distal mesoderm ceases:
instead there is now mesodermal outgrowth under each grafted AER. Similarly,
if the AER is rotated through 90° (Fig. 4.7(b)), the axis of mesodermal outgrowth changes so as to conform to the AER.

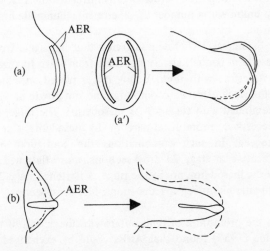

FIG. 4.7. Experiments of Zwilling (1956*a*) showing the effect of the AER in
controlling mesodermal outgrowth. In (a) two AERs have been placed on the
lateral sides of the mesodermal core ((a′) shows the combination viewed distally).
The resulting limb develops two sets of distal structures. In (b) the original AER
has been rotated 90°. Limb outgrowth takes place at right angles to the original
axis, and conforms to the new position of the AER. The dotted line indicates
the normal limb outline for this stage.

Confirmation of the results obtained by creating two parallel AERs comes
from studies on a chick mutant, *eudiplopodia* (Goetinck 1964). In this mutant,
a second AER develops on the dorsal aspect of the leg bud, parallel with the
first (Plate 12). Under the influence of this second AER, the underlying mesoderm grows out, and a supernumerary limb tip develops. When mutant ectoderm
is combined with normal mesoderm, two ridges and subsequently two parallel
wing tips are again formed. Normal ectoderm grown over *eudiplopodia* mesoderm produces only one ridge and a normal limb. *Eudiplopodia* adds further
support to the idea that the AER induces outgrowth of distal mesoderm.

Apical ectodermal ridges appear to have a specific affinity for limb
mesenchyme. Zwilling (1968) found that, when he dissociated labelled mesoderm from the limb bud and unlabelled mesoderm from elsewhere and placed

a pellet of randomly mixed cells under an ectodermal jacket complete with ridge, the limb mesoderm cells aggregated beneath the ridge. The AER also seems to exert a specific attraction on limb mesoderm cells cultured as a monolayer (Globus and Vethamany-Globus 1976). Such an attraction may be responsible for the limb outgrowth.

Supported by experimental evidence of this nature, Zwilling's theory that the AER has an inductive influence became widely accepted. He was careful to point out that the term induction, far from implying that a known mechanism is involved, 'merely indicates that a ridge is active in promoting limb outgrowth' (Zwilling 1961). Although the nature of this influence of AER on mesoderm is still essentially unknown, a number of experiments illuminate important aspects of the mechanism.

Rubin and Saunders (1972) demonstrated that the signal from AER to the underlying mesoderm is qualitatively constant from stage to stage since there is no change in its effect with time. Young ridges placed on a mesodermal core had precisely the same effect in promoting limb outgrowth as older ones (stage 23–28 AER combined with stage 18–23 mesoderm). The ridge, therefore, does not specify successively more distal parts in the mesoderm as development and elongation proceed. In such combinations the configuration of the ridge (markedly projecting in stage 23 cross-sections, more flattened at stage 28) is determined by the mesoderm, not by the ridge. A flattened stage 28 AER grafted on to stage 23 mesoderm regains the nipple-like cross-section, appropriate to that stage.

Apart from the promotion of limb outgrowth, the action of the ridge is permissive. Zwilling (1953) found that AERs could be exchanged between wing and leg bud without affecting the wing or leg pattern of the developing mesoderm. If the antero-posterior axis of the AER is reversed with reference to the mesoderm, the pattern of mesoderm differentiation is again unchanged (Zwilling 1956a).

Further evidence of the permissive and non-instructive nature of the ridge signal is obtained from experiments in which limb ectoderm from different species of birds, or even from mammals, is placed over chick mesoderm. Such combinations (when flank grafted) produce well-developed limbs. For example, Zwilling (1956b) found that, when duck leg bud mesoderm was covered with chick ectoderm, a typical duck leg resulted. When the ectoderm was from 13-day-old rat embryos and the mesoderm from 3-day-old chicks, a well-formed limb develops in a small number of cases with a characteristic chick wing skeleton covered by rat-like skin (Jorquera and Pugin 1971).

Recent evidence from Saunders' laboratory suggests strongly that mesodermal outgrowth is controlled specifically by the AER rather than adjacent distal ectoderm. Errick (1977) removed the AER from an ectodermal cap in such a way that the edges of the wound adhered, forming a 'pressure suture'. When a mesodermal core was provided, an AER was reconstituted and a complete limb developed. But, if the AER was removed along with rather more of the adjacent ectoderm, no new AER was constituted, and no limb develops. This suggests that AER outgrowth-inducing ability is found only in the AER itself, and is not shared by the surrounding distal ectoderm. Secondly, Errick and Saunders (1976) placed a strip of dissociated AER cells apically on a chick mesodermal core and covered the combination with chick back ectoderm. After grafting to a host embryo, an AER was reconstituted and limb outgrowth took place. A distal vascular sinus was formed, and later toes and claws (Fig. 4.8). Use of quail

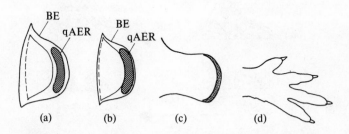

FIG. 4.8. (a) Dissociated AER cells of quail (q AER) are sandwiched between chick stage-22 non-limb back ectoderm (BE) and chick stage-22 leg bud meso-derm. (b) The ectoderm shrinks tightly to the limb mesoderm, binding the AER cells to its apex. (c) Following grafting, a well-vascularized leg bud-like out-growth is formed which later develops into a typical foot (d). (After Errick and Saunders 1976.)

AER cells showed that the reconstituted ridge was mainly of quail origin. In controls, reaggregated non-ridge ectoderm replaced AER cells, and outgrowth was feeble and lacked a vascular sinus. Once again the property of outgrowth induction is restricted to the ridge, and is not found in non-limb ectoderm.

An isolated quail AER grafted to the dorsal surface of a chick wing bud can be persuaded to induce a secondary mesodermal outgrowth, which continues to be capped by quail AER (Saunders, Gasseling, and Errick 1976). These experi-ments emphasize cell continuity within the AER over a period of time, and contradict the view that the AER is simply a transitory structure composed of distally sliding ectoderm cells.

One of the least equivocal experiments indicating a definite effect of AER on distal mesoderm was performed by Cairns (1975). Small pieces of distal limb mesoderm were dissected from early limb buds and cultured in isolation. After ten hours of culture, the explants were seen to be dying (Fig. 4.9). If placed in contact with pieces of AER, they were, in most cases, still alive after 24 hours. Non-ridge distal ectoderm does not have the same effect of inhibiting cell death. The phenomenon seems to be due to a secretion produced by the AER: the influence persists even if the tissues are separated physically. Isolated ridges suspended in a small basket in culture medium over the mesenchyme fragments caused them to remain healthy for a longer period than controls.

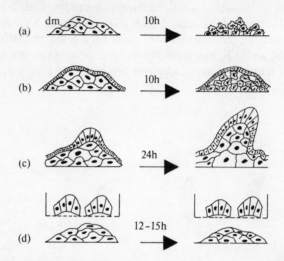

FIG. 4.9. Isolated distal limb mesoderm fragments (= dm) survive in culture for only a brief period (a), even if associated with distal ectoderm (b). If it is associated with AER, either in contact (c) or physically separated (d), the mesoderm survives longer. (After Cairns 1975.)

In summary, it is the AER rather than adjacent distal ectoderm which appears to control mesodermal outgrowth. The ridge, which shows cell continuity throughout its existence, acts in a non-specific way, and does not control the pattern of mesoderm differentiation.

4.5.1. *Inductive influence of the AER and apical ectoderm in the amphibian limb bud*

By contrast with the extensive studies on chick limb development just reported, experimental analysis of amphibian limb development has produced meagre results. There are two main difficulties. It has not yet proved possible to devise a chemical procedure for separating cleanly the two limb bud components. Secondly, while the significance of the chick AER can be determined by extirpation since it does not usually regenerate, in amphibians the limb bud epidermis regenerates readily, and special measures are necessary to separate limb mesenchyme and ectoderm.

Tschumi (1957) analysed the tissue interactions in *Xenopus* limb development in which there is a distinct epidermal ridge, though less marked than the chick AER. First it was necessary to map the prospective areas of the *Xenopus* hind limb bud, by insertion into the mesenchyme of carbon particles. As in the chick, development of the skeletal parts follows a proximo-distal sequence, with a rapidly growing distal tip in which areas prospective for the distal elements can be found only at later stages of limb bud morphogenesis (Fig. 4.10). Tschumi used forceps to strip off the ectodermal covering of the limb buds whose mesodermal core he subsequently inserted into sites away from the host epithelium within

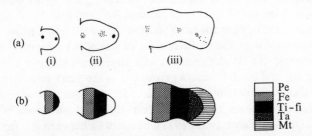

FIG. 4.10. Analysis of prospective areas of hindlimb bud of *Xenopus,* redrawn from Tschumi (1957). In (a) three mesenchymal areas have been marked with carbon particles, which are recognizable in subsequent stages (i) 0.35 mm bud, (ii) 0.8 mm bud, (iii) 1.4 mm bud. In (b) the prospective areas are shown, as deduced from the marking experiment, in the same limb bud stages as (a). Pe = pelvis, Fe = femur, Ti-fi = tibia, fibula, T = tarsus, Mt = metatarsals.

the abdominal areas of the host tadpole. Control limb buds with intact epithelium developed a normal hind limb skeleton at whatever size they were grafted. However, the experimental limb buds failed to develop more distal structures, and the degree of deficiency was greater the earlier the limb bud which was used (Fig. 4.11). The skeletal parts which formed were those which had already been

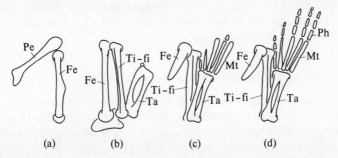

FIG. 4.11. The skeletons which developed from isolated mesenchyme of *Xenopus* limb buds of different stages, (a) 0.54 mm, (b) 1.0 mm, (c) 1.55 mm limb bud. (d) 0.42 mm control limb bud with intact epidermis. For abbreviations, see Fig. 4.10. (After Tschumi 1957.)

laid down as prospective areas. Tschumi emphasized the distinction between 'apical growth' and 'growth of material already laid down' since these can be dissociated experimentally. The proximal prospective areas continue their growth but apical proliferation is suppressed in the experiment. When control limb buds, similarly stripped of epidermis, were implanted in either abdominal wall or head, with the distal tip exposed, the graft rapidly became covered by host epithelium and underwent normal development. Tschumi always found there was a close relationship between the presence of the ectodermal ridge and the marginal vein: those grafts lacking epidermis which later developed distal deficiencies always lacked a marginal vein. In an experiment paralleling that of Zwilling (1956a), Tschumi rotated the ectodermal ridge through 90°, and found that the developing digital plate developed in the same plane as the re-orientated ridge.

Tissue interactions in the urodeles seem to follow the pattern of the anura. In experiments on the Axolotl, early paddle stages were stripped of their overlying epidermis, and inserted into a groove cut in the flank musculature of the tadpole, so that they developed out of contact with the host epidermis. The proximal skeletal elements differentiated, but the distal parts such as the digits were absent (review: Faber 1965, 1971). Similarities between the properties of Axolotl limb buds and regeneration blastemas are emphasized in experiments of Stocum and Dearlove (1972). In this case, limb regeneration blastemas were deprived of their epidermis, and inserted into tunnels bored into the dorsal fin connective tissue so that they developed out of contact with host epidermis. The later the stage of development of the limb bud regeneration blastema, the more complete in its distal development was the graft skeleton. Once again, if the grafted mesenchyme made contact with host epidermis, which then regenerated an epidermal coating for the limb bud, a fuller distal skeleton developed.

These experiments demonstrate clearly that the distal epidermis and, more specifically, the epidermal ridge controls the proliferation of the distal mesenchyme and also its polarity. The ridge is thus indispensible for the distal growth of the amphibian limb bud and it plays a morphogenetic role similar to that of the chick AER. Because of the technical difficulties, it is not possible to say yet whether the role is permissive (as in the chick) or instructive in determining mesodermal skeletal differentiation.

4.6. The apical ectodermal maintenance factor (AEMF)

The AER is not autonomous: its persistence depends on the presence of a mesodermal factor, the apical ectodermal maintenance factor (AEMF). If limb mesoderm is removed from a limb bud, replaced by non-limb mesoderm (such as flank lateral plate or posterior somites) and the combination suitably grafted, then the AER degenerates within two days of the operation (Zwilling 1961, 1972). But if in this experiment a small piece of limb mesoderm is added beneath a part of the AER, then that part of the ridge survives.

The controlling influence of the mesoderm on the AER was demonstrated by Zwilling (1956d). The AER is thickest along its central portion, and is lower at each end. Zwilling placed two or three thick central AER sections in tandem along an early limb mesoderm core, creating an AER which was abnormally thick at each end. In due course, the AER assumed the normal configuration, with the thicker regions at each end flattening out, and a normal limb resulted. In other words, the normal configuration of the AER is imposed by the underlying mesoderm.

Other experiments have been interpreted as suggesting that the AEMF is not distributed evenly throughout the mesoderm, but is more concentrated post-axially. The postaxial half of the limb develops a longer AER and undergoes more mesodermal growth then the preaxial half, where some regression of the ridge takes place. If a sheet of mica is inserted transversely at an early stage in the distal apex of the limb (Fig. 4.12), it is found to migrate preaxially as development proceeds, due to greater growth on the postaxial side (Zwilling and Hansborough 1956).

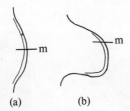

(a)   (b)

FIG. 4.12. A mica plate (= m) inserted in the mid-distal postion of an early chick limb bud (a) later becomes located preaxially (b).

Experiments by both Saunders (Saunders, Gasseling, and Gfeller, 1958) and Amprino and Camosso (1959), leading to duplication of distal limb parts, are interpreted as demonstrating the asymmetrical AEMF distribution. If a distal limb tip is grafted to a new limb site so that graft/host axial relationships are un-changed, normal skeletal parts develop. If the distal tip is rotated through 180° and replaced on the stump, duplication of the limb takes place (Fig. 4.13). The preaxial AER becomes longer, and outgrowth of mesoderm is stimulated pre- and post-axially. The eventual result is a mirror image hand with a digital sequence of 43234. The suggested redistribution of AEMF is shown in Fig. 4.13(d).

Various mutations, in which the number of digits is greater (Goetinck 1966) or less than normal, have provided further evidence for the AEMF theory. In the *duplicate* (Po^d) mutant of the fowl (Landauer 1956*b*), the fourth-day AER is abnormally extended preaxially with accompanying excess preaxial mesenchyme. In more extreme cases, this leads to the duplication of the wing, with mirror imaging (Fig. 4.14). The genetically produced anomaly thus resembles closely the experimental duplication illustrated in Fig. 4.13.

Responsibility for the genetical *duplicate* condition has been shown (Zwilling and Hansborough 1956) to lie in the mesoderm. Early in development, while the *duplicate* limb buds still showed a normal outline, mesoderm and ectoderm were separated and combined with tissues from normal chicks. The resulting chimeric limb buds were flank grafted. The results (Table 4.1) showed clearly that a factor in the *duplicate* mesoderm produces a more extensive AER which in turn leads to excessive preaxial outgrowth of the limb. Zwilling interpretated

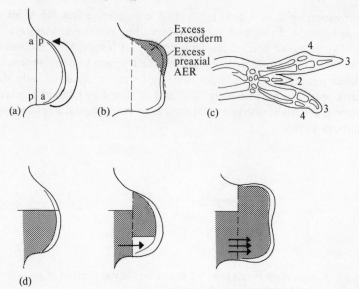

FIG. 4.13. Turning the distal tip of the chick wing bud through 180° (a) results in greater than normal preaxial extension of the AER and an excess of preaxial mesenchyme (b). Eventually there is duplication of the wing tip, with the supernumerary preaxial tip mirror imaging the normal tip (c). (a,p = antero-posterior axis, the digits are numbered). The interpretation of the experiment is given in (d). A preaxial concentration of AEMF (hatched) is created leading to preaxial AER extension, while the formerly preaxial mesenchyme (initially devoid of AEMF) is infiltrated by AEMF from the postaxial stump. (After Saunders, Gasseling, and Gfeller 1958; Saunders and Gasseling 1968.)

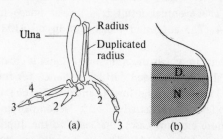

FIG. 4.14. The *duplicate* mutant: (a) right forearm with complete duplication of the radius (after Landauer 1956*b*). (b) Interpretation of development of duplicate. Shaded area represents area of mesenchyme producing or distributing AEMF. N = normal area, D = additional preaxial area in duplicate.

these results as showing that there was a genetic modification of the normal pattern of AEMF distribution and that the AEMF was present in preaxial regions of the limb mesenchyme from which it was normally absent.

A rather similar case is provided by the *talpid* (*ta*) mutants (Goetinck and

Table 4.1.

| Mutant | Composition of composite limb bud | | Character of resulting limb |
	Ectoderm	Mesoderm	
Duplicate	Duplicate	Normal	Normal
	Normal	Duplicate	Duplicate
	Duplicate	Duplicate	Duplicate
talpid^2	talpid^2	Normal	Normal
	Normal	talpid^2	talpid^2

Polydactyly in the two mutants Duplicate (Zwilling and Hansborough 1956) and talpid^2 (Goetinck and Abbot 1964) is due to the mesoderm, probably through alteration in AEMF distribution. The table shows the type of limb development resulting from chimeric limb buds.

Abbott 1964; Hinchliffe and Ede 1967), where there is pronounced polydactyly of both wing and leg: of the 8–10 digits in the footplate, none is identifiable as a specific finger or toe. As in *duplicate*, there is an excessively long AER and a distal excess of mesenchyme. Here again, reciprocal recombination of normal and *talpid*^{2} limb components by Goetinck and Abbott (1964) showed that the mesoderm is responsible (Table 4.1) and AEMF may again be redistributed. It should be noted that Goetinck's interpretation could be modified by subsequent findings on *talpid* mesenchyme behaviour which are discussed elsewhere (see Chapter 6.4). In the polydactylous *diplopodia* mutation also, the extended AER is due to mesodermal influence (MacCabe, MacCabe, Abbott, and McCarry 1975).

Zwilling (1956a) interpreted his original experiments on the *wingless* mutant (Fig. 4.6) as supporting the concept of an AEMF. The failure of a normal AER to survive over *wingless* mesoderm suggests this is failing to supply AEMF and that the AER is not autonomous. In a further experiment he found that *wingless* mesoderm combined with normal ectoderm grew much better if transplanted to a dorsal location on a normal wing bud than elsewhere (Zwilling 1974). He suggested that, in this location, host limb AEMF was transmitted through the mutant mesoderm to the normal ectodermal ridge which thus promoted limb outgrowth.

Experiments by Saunders and Gasseling (1963) with millipore filters are consistent with the idea that AEMF is transmitted through the mesoderm in a proximo-distal direction. If the tip of a wing bud is turned through 180°, insertion of a filter between stump and tip (Fig. 4.15) does not prevent the thickening of the repositioned preaxial AER. Thickening and subsequent duplication occurred in 75 per cent of experiments using a 25-μm thick filter of pore size 0.8μm. A pore size of 0.45μm lowered the frequency of duplication, and one of 0.05μm suppressed it almost completely. An impermeable film allows no duplication.

Saunders and Gasseling (1963) concluded that the activity of the maintenance factor could not be explained in terms of free diffusion of small molecules, since

Fig. 4.15. Insertion of a Millipore filter (f) (Saunders and Gasseling 1963) between the postaxial part (p) of the wing bud stump and the reorientated formerly preaxial distal part (a).

its transmission was affected by filters, whose porosity should not affect diffusion. Cell-to-cell contact is also unlikely to be involved, since the cell processes do not appear to penetrate far into filter pores. Instead, the authors suggest that what passes (or fails to pass) through the filter is structured material, 'a part of the continuum which is the embryonic ground substance, produced by the cells, dependent on their properties and reflecting their specificities'. But the material nature of the maintenance factor remains to be defined.

4.7. The AER induction hypothesis challenged: Amprino's theory of a bio-mechanical role for the ectoderm

Amprino, who in private conversation charmingly describes himself as 'the bad boy of limb morphogenesis', has strongly challenged the view that the AER has an inductive role in limb outgrowth (Amprino 1965, 1974, 1977). In his view, the AER consists of ectodermal cells (some of which are dying) which have 'piled up' distally during growth in which the distal movement of the ectoderm is greater than that of the mesoderm. This ectodermal sliding provides a distal space which is constantly filled by mesoderm. Limb outgrowth is thus controlled, not by the AER, but by the topography of the whole ectodermal cap which shapes the enclosed mesoderm. The outgrowth and differentiation of the mesoderm are an expression of the intrinsic properties of this tissue within which morphogenetic control is exerted by the more proximal regions on the more distal, and does not depend on the inductive influence of the ridge.

To a certain extent the difference between the theories is one of semantics. Amprino objects particularly to Saunders and Zwilling's use of the term induction to describe the action of the ridge. These authors are careful to state that 'induction' is not used in the classic sense (meaning that the AER causes a switch from undifferentiated to a differentiated cell type) but to suggest merely that the ridge is active in promoting limb outgrowth. Since both early and late ridges have the same effect on mesodermal outgrowth, and since the source of ridge may be wing or leg, or even from a different species, without influencing limb type, Zwilling's hypothesis makes it clear that the ridge is *not* specifying successively more distal parts in the limb mesoderm as outgrowth proceeds.

Amprino supports his theory both with a critique of the existing experimental evidence for the hypothesis of induction by the AER and by setting out experimental evidence which cannot, in his view, be reconciled with the induction theory. As Amprino suggests, the results of many of Saunders and Zwilling's early experiments do not distinguish between a theory of ridge induction and one of ectodermal moulding of mesodermal growth. For example, a fragment of prospective thigh mesoderm placed under the AER in the wing apex forms toes (Saunders, Gasseling, and Cairns 1959). This 'distalization' may be due to the influence of the ridge, as Saunders claims, but may equally be due to the influence of the surrounding distal mesoderm as Amprino (1965) suggests. The changed axis of the mesodermal outgrowth following a 90° rotation of the ectodermal cap (Fig. 4.9) could be due to the new axis of the AER or to mesodermal reshaping caused by the rotated ectodermal cap. Much of the experimental evidence is equally equivocal.

As experimental evidence Amprino (1965) quotes an investigation of limb mirror imaging produced by rotation of the limb apex. Camosso and Roncalli (1968) found that after 15 hours the mesoderm repositioned preaxially had increased its proliferation *before* there was any increase in the thickness of the overlying AER (Fig. 4.16). He argues that, if the induction theory is correct, thickening of the ridge should precede the stimulation of outgrowth of the underlying mesoderm.

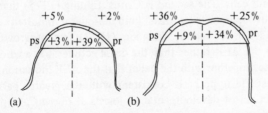

FIG. 4.16. Experimental duplication of the chick wing obtained in Amprino's laboratory (Amprino 1965; Camosso and Roncalli 1968). The diagrams show changes in thickness of the ectodermal ridge and in the rate of proliferation of the apical mesoderm (a) 13–18 h and (b) 34–8 h after reorientation of the wing bud apex. The anterior part of stump lies to the left. The thickness of the preaxial (pr) and of the postaxial (ps) part of the reorientated ridge is expressed as per cent increase over the thickness of corresponding sectors of the ridge in control wing buds fixed at the time of the operation. The values for proliferation of the mesoderm in the reorientated apex are expressed as per cent increase of the mitotic rate over that of corresponding regions of the apex of the normally growing contralateral wing bud.

The quantitative relationship between the stage at which the AER is excised and the resulting degree of distal skeletal deficiency has always been considered strong support for the AER induction hypothesis. Amprino claims (1965) that ridge excision damages the distal mesoderm leading to vascular deficiency, lowered mitotic rate, and cell death: he attributes the resulting skeletal deficiencies to this mesodermal damage. Saunders (1977) has countered this criticism, quoting the work of Cairns (1975) which shows that the wave of cell death (which is certainly present in exposed mesoderm) does not affect the distal tip, but is some distance below the surface. Cell death is not affecting the distal mesoderm which would normally form terminal limb parts.

Amprino further contends that the ridge merely represents a migrant population of ectodermal cells in the process of being sloughed off. It is certainly true that during the period of supposed inductive activity there is considerable cell death along the distal margin of the AER of the chick (Jurand 1965; Hinchliffe and Ede 1967) and of other amniotes (Milaire 1967, 1970; Kelley and Fallon 1976), but there is also cell division (Kelley and Fallon 1976), and evidence of cell continuity in the AER throughout its life (Errick and Saunders 1976: see section 4.5).

Recently, Amprino (1977) has been able to show that, if ectodermal 'pouches' are created in the limb bud, limb mesenchyme cells will migrate to fill them, even though there is no inductive ridge present.

Amprino's critique has been invaluable in leading to more precise formulation of the AER induction hypothesis. By no means all of his objections have been answered: there are, however, a handful of crucial experiments which suggest that the distal ectoderm does more than mechanically shape the distal mesoderm. One is Zwilling's experiment (1968) suggesting that the ridge has a specific affinity for limb cells. The second is Cairns' finding (1975) that AER cultured adjacent to, but separate from, distal limb mesoderm inhibited cell death. There is also the evidence set out by Saunders (1977) that outgrowth is controlled specifically by the AER rather than the distal ectoderm as a whole. On the basis of this evidence, together with the belief that the AER induction theory offers a precise and testable hypothesis consistent with the greater part of the experimental evidence, most developmental biologists at present accept the Saunders/Zwilling hypothesis.

4.8. Mesodermal control of limb type

We have already seen that the action of the AER is permissive, and that the axes of the developing limb are determined largely by the mesoderm. It therefore comes as no surprise to learn that the specific character of a limb, whether it is a wing or a leg, webbed or with free digits, is also determined by the mesoderm. Chemical separation of chick mesoderm and ectoderm allows combinations of wing and leg tissue to be flank grafted. Zwilling (1955) showed that wing ectoderm combined with leg mesoderm develops into a leg, whilst leg ectoderm combined with wing mesoderm develops a wing. Pautou (1968) analysed the development of chick/duck composite limb buds (Fig. 4.17), and found that development was typical of the species contributing the mesoderm. Thus, the reduction in cell death in the duck foot which leads to the survival of the inter-

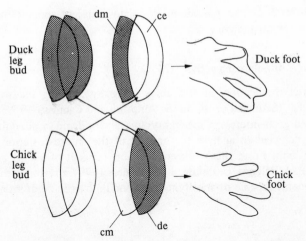

FIG. 4.17. The limb type is controlled by the mesoderm. Chimeric duck/chick hindlimb buds develop according to the species which contributes the mesoderm. c = chick, d = duck, e = ectoderm, m = mesoderm. The duck foot is webbed, but not that of the chick. (After Pautou 1968.)

digital webbing is determined by the mesoderm. (It should be noted that this contradicts the earlier conclusions of Zwilling (1959) who found some residual webbing in limbs made up of chick mesoderm and duck ectoderm. Pautou suggests that this was due to partial syndactyly of the digits resulting from abnormal experimental conditions: but we have already seen the effect of the ectoderm on the determination of distal parts of the limb axis: perhaps its involvement in distal webbing should not be disregarded too lightly.)

Species specific control by the mesoderm extends even to the type of feathers produced, even though the feathers are almost entirely formed from ectoderm. When duck ectoderm develops over chick mesoderm the feathers produced are recognizable chick feathers (Dhouailly 1967; Sengel 1971).

There is some discussion as to whether limb quality (i.e. leg or wing) is imposed on the somatic mesoderm by the adjacent somitic mesoderm, as Dhouailly and Kieny (1972) have suggested. The *material* contribution of somites to the limb bud (and specifically to the musculature) is now clearly established (see Chapter 3). Is this contribution related to the morphogenetic control of limb quality? It is agreed that, before a certain stage, limb prospective somatic mesoderm can only form a limb if associated with somitic mesoderm from the same level (see section 4.2). Prospective leg somatic mesoderm associated with somitic mesoderm of the same stage, but from the neck region, cannot form a leg (Kieny 1971). But neither can it form either leg or wing if associated with somites from the wing area. But Pinot (1969, 1970*a*, *b*), using a different technique, found that heterotopic combinations of somatic and somitic mesoderm from wing and leg levels did form limbs, and that limb type was always determined by the source of the somatic mesoderm. She concludes that, while limb level somitic mesoderm stimulates adjacent somatic mesoderm, it does so in a non-qualitative way.

4.9. The zone of polarizing activity (ZPA)

Experimental duplication of the chick wing by rotating the wing bud tip through 180° (Saunders *et al.* 1958; Amprino and Camosso 1959: see section 4.6) aroused great interest in the embryological world and inspired much experimentation designed to analyse the control of the antero-posterior axis of the developing limb. From this work emerged the concept of a zone of polarizing activity (ZPA) (Balcuns, Gasseling, and Saunders 1970), a region within the postaxial mesoderm capable of specifying a second limb axis and of interacting with the AER.

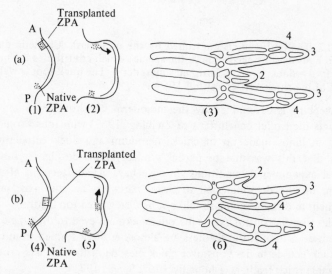

FIG. 4.18. Wing duplication resulting from transplantation of ZPA from donor wing bud to the preaxial (a) or distal central (b) position in the wing bud apex. The adjacent preaxial AER thickens and stimulates the outgrowth of the adjacent mesoderm (2) and (5). The antero-posterior axis of the duplicated limb tip is determined by the position of the grafted ZPA: digit 4 is always adjacent to the graft. These results have been obtained in the laboratories of both Saunders (1–6) and Wolpert (1–3).

Saunders and Gasseling (1968) found that transplantation of the mesoderm from the posterior margin of the wing bud into a preaxial site mimicked rotation of the whole tip, and produced the same preaxial AER thickening and mirror imaging (Fig. 4.18(a)). Initially, only the mesoderm was transplanted; later experiments used mesoderm and overlying ectoderm (for technical reasons) with the same result. If the graft is made to the distal tip of the wing bud instead of to the preaxial margin (Fig. 4.18(b)), the preaxial AER anterior to the graft thickens and a supernumerary wing tip is again induced: in this case, the digits are not mirror imaged but in series with those of the host wing.

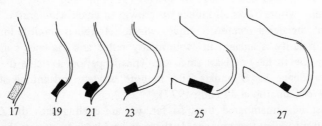

FIG. 4.19. Distribution of ZPA in chick wing buds from stage 17 to 27. The area shaded at stage 17 has less polarizing activity than that of the later stages, grafts of which cause more than 50 per cent of duplications. (After MacCabe, Gasseling, and Saunders 1973.)

ZPA activity is shown strongly by the posterior wing bud border between stages 19 and 28 (Fig. 4.19). At least 50 per cent of host wing buds responded to apical or preaxial ZPA grafts with duplications. Weak activity can be detected as early as stage 15 (MacCabe, Gasseling, and Saunders 1973). The specific properties of the ZPA are not shared in this experiment by other areas of wing mesoderm, as control grafts of other limb mesoderm preaxially or apically fail to produce duplication (Fallon and Crosby 1975*b*). However, Saunders (1977) has shown recently that ZPA properties are also possessed by a large area of 4-day chick flank and ventral mesoderm.

The polarizing effect of the ZPA is shown very dramatically by its effect on dissociated wing mesoderm (MacCabe, Saunders, and Pickett 1973). If dissociated mesoderm cells are packed in an ectodermal jacket and flank grafted, digits are formed, but these cannot be identified as specific wing digits, each of which has a characteristic morphology. If a ZPA is added, a much more normal skeleton results, with recognizable digits, the most posterior of which (number 4) is closest to the ZPA graft.

In the leg bud there is a similar polarizing zone which again causes duplication of the limb when transplanted to a preaxial position (Saunders and Gasseling 1968; Summerbell and Tickle 1977). As with AERs we can, therefore, interchange ZPAs between wing and leg, and with rather similar results. Yet again, the response of the limb to the signal (whatever that may be) generated by the ZPA depends upon the origin of the mesoderm receiving the signal. The ZPA from the chick leg bud transplanted to the chick wing bud stimulates the growth of supernumerary wing digits (Balcuns *et al.* 1970). Thus, wing and leg ZPAs may emit the same signal, the specificity residing in the response of the mesoderm.

The ZPA appears to be a general feature of the posterior border of amniote limb buds. Two rodents, hamster and mouse (MacCabe and Parker 1976*a*; Tickle, Shellswell, Crawley, and Wolpert 1976) have ZPAs which cause wing-like duplications when grafted into the chick wing bud. Mouse ZPA will also induce wing duplications when grafted into pheasant and guinea-fowl wing buds. Fallon and Crosby (1977) list a range of species (snapping and painted turtles, pig, ferret, man), whose ZPAs all induce outgrowth in chick wing grafts. They conclude that the signal–receptor complex which determines amniote limb antero-posterior polarity is ancient in evolutionary terms and has been conserved (as shown by the turtles) at least since the Triassic period. Outside the amniotes there is evidence for a similar ZPA in both urodele and anuran amphibians (Slack 1976; Cameron and Fallon 1977).

It must be remembered that, so far, we are dealing with the ZPA transplanted to a foreign environment. Is there any evidence to suggest that the ZPA is active *in situ*? The obvious experiment is to remove the ZPA and to follow the development of the ZPA-less wing or leg. We would expect reduced digit development, or, at best, the production of unspecialized digits. Disturbingly, excision of the ZPA at a stage when it is active as a graft has little effect on the development of the wing. In one series of experiments (Fallon and Crosby, 1975a; MacCabe, Gasseling, and Saunders 1973), the ZPA was removed from stage 17–24 forelimbs, resulting in 50 per cent normal wings and 50 per cent normal wings with postaxial defects. The possibility of ZPA regeneration can be ruled out: ZPA removed at stage 21 is not regenerated later. Thus, it appears that the ZPA has no direct role in normal development between stages 17 and 24. It was suggested that the ZPA normally exerted its effect only during the early stages of limb bud differentiation (i.e. during determination by the somites as claimed by Kieny (1971)). In transplantation experiments, properties of the ZPA which are latent at this stage in normal development are being utilized, perhaps reawakened by the trauma of transplantation. But it is still difficult to explain why the activity of the transplanted ZPA should be weak at a time when it is considered to influence normal development, and strong when it has ceased to do so. Fallon and Crosby's (1975a) experiments, together with the finding of ZPA activity in non-limb mesenchyme, have led Saunders (1977) to doubt that the ZPA plays an antero-posterior polarizing role in *normal* development.

The nature of ZPA action still remains to be determined, although some work by MacCabe and Parker (1976b) and Calandra and MacCabe (1978) suggests that it involves chemical diffusion. MacCabe has developed an *in vitro* assay for ZPA activity involving culture of the test material in contact with stage 21–22 preaxial wing bud tissue. In a successful test, the preaxial AER remains thick instead of flattening, and there is little cell death in the underlying mesoderm. MacCabe has demonstrated a gradient of activity in the 4-day chick wing bud, ranging from marked activity near the posterior border (the ZPA), through an intermediate central level, to no detectable activity near the anterior margin. Insertion of an impermeable barrier of Mylar film (Fig. 4.20) blocks the spread of ZPA activity anteriorly, but a 0.45-μm millipore filter does not. Thus, the activity of the central block depends on where the impermeable barrier is

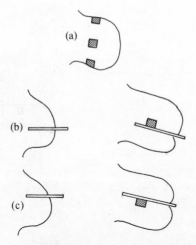

FIG. 4.20. MacCabe and Parker's (1976*b*) experiment demonstrating a morphogenetic gradient in polarizing activity along the limb bud antero-posterior axis. (a) shows the sites assayed for activity. In (b) a barrier is placed just posterior to the centre, and in (c) just anterior to the centre. In both cases the position of the central area is shown in relation to the barrier after 24 hours, when the central area is assayed.

inserted in relation to the ZPA. MacCabe suggested that the gradient of activity is established by the movement, perhaps the diffusion, of a factor originating from the ZPA. Preliminary attempts to identify this factor produced apparently equivocal results (MacCabe, Calandra, and Parker 1977). It appears as a low molecular weight, soluble component in culture medium conditioned by exposure to posterior wing bud tissue, but as a large molecular weight fraction from homogenisates of the tissue itself. Perhaps the active component is bound to a carrier molecule when present within the ZPA and free when it migrates.

The barrier insertion technique has also been used by Summerbell (1979) to support his view that the ZPA organizes the antero-posterior axis in normal development. He regards the postaxial deficiencies frequently obtained by Fallon and Crosby (1975*a*) following ZPA removal as indicating a polarizing role for the ZPA in normal limb development. Fallon and Crosby on the other hand consider that the ZPA overlaps the prospective posterior digit tissue, which may thus be removed in the operation. Summerbell's view is that the digits are specified by particular levels of a hypothetical morphogen diffusing from a ZPA high point to a low point anteriorly. Thus, the digit IV is specified by a high morphogen level, digit II by a low level. Insertion of an impermeable barrier causes the morphogen to build up postaxially and decline preaxially. The resulting changes in digital pattern (e.g. the failure to form digits anterior to a centrally inserted barrier, Fig. 4.21(b)) are interpreted in terms of changes produced by the barrier in the normal gradient of the morphogen.

Ingenious though Summerbell's gradient model is, it by no means solves the

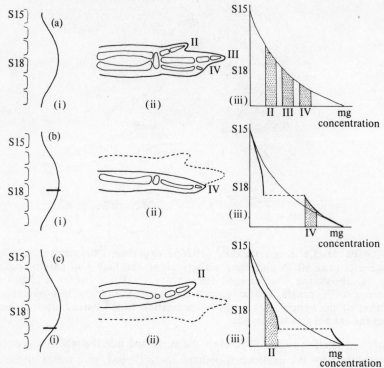

FIG. 4.21. Experiments by Summerbell (1979) support the theory that the antero-posterior axis is controlled by a diffusible morphogen from the ZPA in normal development. (a) In controls a cut in a stage-17 limb bud heals and the skeleton (ii) develops normally. The digits are regarded as specified by different levels of a diffusible morphogen (mg) continually produced by the ZPA and declining anteriorly where it is gradually removed (iii). (b) A centrally placed impermeable barrier at stage 17 results in elimination of more anterior skeletal structures (ii). Summerbell interprets this result (iii) as showing that anterior to the barrier the level of morphogen drops below the level necessary to specify anterior skeletal elements, while posterior to the barrier, the morphogen accumulates. (c) A more posteriorly placed barrier allows only digit II (and radius) to develop anteriorly (ii), while posteriorly the morphogen level is regarded as too high for specification of digit IV (iii). In (iii) of (b) and (c), the heavy line indicates the interpretation of the changed level of morphogen.

problems presented to it by Fallon and Crosby's experimental results. Even if digit IV is missing following ZPA removal, digits II and III are always present, whereas with the Summerbell model, they too would surely be lost.

One rather curious feature of the ZPA is that, although the posterior margin of the limb bud has polarizing properties over a long period (stages 15–28), the active area moves in a proximo-distal direction (Saunders 1972; MacCabe, Gasseling and Saunders 1973) (Fig. 4.19). Since limb development proceeds by the division of distal cells which lay down first proximal, then progressively more distal structures, the cells of the later ZPA seem unlikely to be the descendents of the earlier ZPA. The new ZPA seems to arise through the influence of the existing one, since a preaxially grafted ZPA initiates polarizing activity in host mesoderm distal to the graft.

The relationship of ZPA and AEMF is unclear. Since the original duplication experiments were explained in terms of redistribution of AEMF, and the same results are obtained by ZPA transplantation, it has been argued that the ZPA is the source of AEMF (Wolpert 1976). But evidence that grafting ZPA beneath AER leads to regression of the latter (Gasseling and Saunders 1964) suggests that this is not the case. An alternative view is that ZPA induces AEMF in surrounding mesenchyme. We have seen that limbs produced by packing disaggregated mesoderm into ectodermal jackets lack an antero-posterior axis (MacCabe, Saunders, and Pickett 1973; Pautou 1973; Zwilling 1964). These limbs must be considered to have AEMF without ZPA activity. It seems best, at present, to regard maintenance activity and polarizing activity as two distinct entities, with the ZPA perhaps being able to modify the distribution of AEMF.

4.10. Determination and regulation in the limb

Developing embryos or organ systems are frequently classified as *mosaic* (isolated parts from the same structures as *in ovo*) or *regulatory* (removal of material from, or addition of material to, the system fails to alter its ability to form a normal organ or organism). Organ rudiments of vertebrates frequently pass through a labile stage in which the parts are not determined, and the rudiments regulate for lost or added material: later the parts become determined and regulatory ability is lost.

We have already seen how Harrison (1921) demonstrated the regulatory nature of the early amphibian limb field (section 4.2). As a result of the first experiments on the early chick limb bud, this was considered initially to be a mosaic system (review, Huxley and de Beer 1934). Murray (1926) and Murray and Huxley (1925) grew both whole and part limb buds on chorio-allantoic membrane and obtained relatively normal whole or partial skeletal development.

Later work, which was directed at altering the positions or proportions of the proximal or central mesoderm whilst leaving the AER and distal mesoderm intact, has emphasized the regulatory nature of the wing bud, particularly up to stage 24 or 25. Limb material can be taken away from or added to the central section and the limb is able to regulate and develop relatively normally (Wolff and Kahn 1947). If 20–30 per cent of the central section of the leg bud (corresponding to the knee–ankle) is removed at stage 19–20, a normal limb develops, apart from frequent absence of the fibula. If the excised slice is grown on chorio-allantois, it develops distal femur and proximal ends of tibia and fibula (Fig. 4.22) (Hampé 1959). Extra material may be added to a limb bud by grafting a stage 18 leg bud (which includes all prospective skeletal elements) on to a stage 21–22 leg bud whose distal tip (prospective tarso-metatarsal material) has been removed (Fig. 4.23). This excessively large leg bud, incorporating two

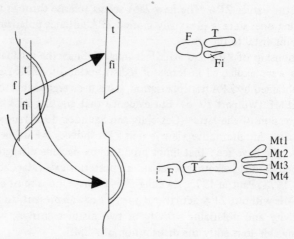

FIG. 4.22. Regulation in the early leg bud is demonstrated by removal of a central segment, including prospective tibia/fibula, which, cultured in isolation, develops according to its normal fate. The depleted leg bud regulates, forming a normal limb (apart from the absence of fibula), including tibia and all distal elements (Hampé 1959, p. 429). f, t, fi = prospective femur, tibia, fibula. F = femur, T = tibia, Fi = fibula, Mt = metatarsals.

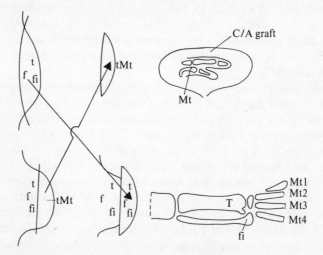

FIG. 4.23. Regulation in the early leg bud is demonstrated by addition of a stage 18 leg bud to a stage 21–22 leg bud, thus forming an excessively large leg bud containing two sets of prospective tissue for femur, tibia, and fibula. The leg bud regulates forming a normal limb (apart from the increased fibula size) (Hampé 1959, p. 454). f, t, fi = prospective femur, tibia, fibula. Fi = fibula, Mt = metatarsals, T = tibia.

doses of prospective femur, tibia and fibula, is able to regulate sufficiently to produce a normal leg, albeit with an enlarged fibula (Hampé 1959).

Analysis of regulation was carried further by Kieny (1964*b*) who combined stage 18–22 wing and leg bud parts in such a way that presumptive stylopods and zeugopods were duplicated (Fig. 4.24). Regulation was more perfect for

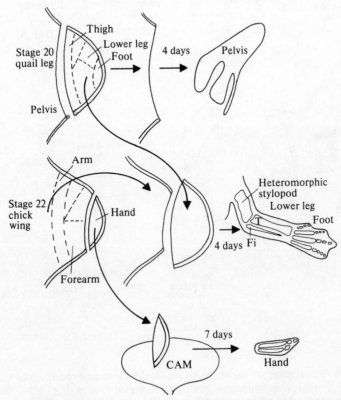

FIG. 4.24. Regulation of excess mesenchyme in an experimental limb bud in which both prospective stylopod and zeugopod are duplicated. Use of quail graft cells with their nucleolar marker enables the contribution of host and donor tissue to be analysed. Prospective chick zeugopod, now placed proximal to prospective quail zeugopod material, has its prospective fate shifted to the formation of more proximal stylopod structures. CAM = chorio-allantoic membrane, Fi = fibula, T = tibia. (After Sengel 1975.)

external limb form than in the skeleton, and more feeble in wing than in leg bud. Recently these results have been confirmed using quail/chick combinations which allow the precise contribution of each tissue to be assessed (Kieny and Pautou 1976). Where presumptive stylopods and zeugopods are duplicated, it is clear that tissue blocks placed in the base have their fate shifted to produce structures more proximal than normal. In recombinations lacking prospective zeugopod, prospective distal material is persuaded to form both intercalated proximal structures as well as normal distal parts (Fig. 4.25) (Kieny and Pautou 1976; Sengel 1975).

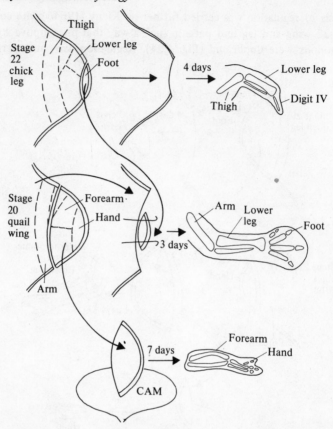

FIG. 4.25. Regulation of depletion of mesenchyme in an experimental limb bud in which prospective zeugopod has been removed. As in Fig. 4.24, 'labelled' quail cells are used in a heterospecific graft. Prospective chick autopod (normally forming foot paddle elements only) regulates and, in addition to foot paddle, forms also the intercalated zeugopod elements: thus, the prospective fate of some of these cells is shifted to development of more proximal structures. (After Sengel 1975.)

Wolpert and his co-workers have made similar composite limb buds using wing material, but their results (Summerbell, Lewis, and Wolpert 1973; Wolpert, Lewis, and Summerbell 1975; Summerbell and Lewis 1975; Summerbell 1977*a*) are in striking contrast to those of Kieny. They placed stage-19/20 wing buds (which contain prospective skeletal tissue of limb elements distal to the humerus) on wing buds of various ages (stages 22-26) from which only the distal part had been removed. The composite limb bud contained two sets of zeugopod, and the limb which developed (Fig. 4.26(a)) had two sets of radius and ulna. In other experiments a mesodermal deficiency was created. A young wing bud (stage 19/20) had its tip replaced by the tip of an older wing bud (stage 22-26). In this way, the prospective parts of stylopod and zeugopod were removed. The limb

which developed (Fig. 4.26(b)) lacked the skeletal material corresponding to
the excised tissue. Wolpert interprets these results as supporting his hypothesis
that, once mesenchyme leaves the area under the AER, its fate has become
determined (Chapter 6).

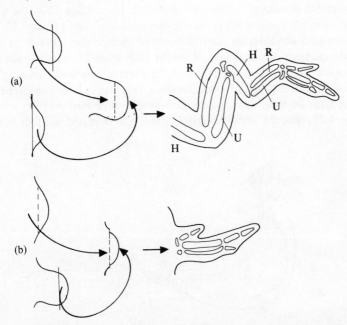

FIG. 4.26. Composite wing buds made by Wolpert and his colleagues (Wolpert *et al.* 1975; Summerbell *et al.* 1973) fail to show regulation. In (a) the tip of a stage 19 wing bud has been pinned on to a stage 24 wing bud base, thus forming a composite wing bud with two prospective stylopods and zeugopods. The resulting limb has two sets of stylopods and zeugopods. In (b) the tip of a stage 24 wing bud has been added to a stage 19 base, thus forming a composite wing bud lacking prospective stylopod and zeugopod. Only wing digits are formed. H = humerus, R = radius, U = ulna.

The different results obtained by the two groups of workers may be partly
explained by differences in grafting procedures (maximal graft-stump contact
is necessary for regulation according to Kieny) or by the fact that wing buds (as
used by Wolpert) were found by Kieny (1964*b*) to give a lower frequency of
regulation than leg buds. Nevertheless, it is still difficult to explain why similar
experiments have given such contradictory results supporting two mutually
exclusive hypotheses.

4.11. The determination of cell type

An alternative approach to this problem is to look at the specialization of
mesenchyme cells. Apparently homogeneous mesoderm gradually becomes

specialized in the developing limb until distinctive cell types can be recognized, either histologically or biochemically. When and how does determination take place?

Small blocks of mesenchyme may be transplanted to new sites in the limb bud, or grown in culture (review, Searls 1973). Up to stage 22 in the wing bud the mesenchyme appears histologically homogeneous, but by stage 23 there is both increased condensation and synthesis of chondroitin sulphate by the pre-cartilaginous areas of the zeugopod, whilst from stage 25 chondrogenic cells are recognizable due to the appearance of the metachromatically staining matrix. Labelled prospective chondrogenic regions transplanted to non-chondrogenic areas of stage 24 wing bud regulate according to their new position up to stage 24 (Fig. 4.27). But this tissue from later stages is determined and fails to regulate

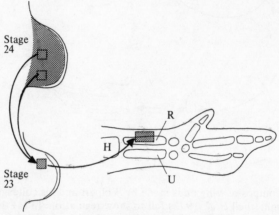

FIG. 4.27. The limb bud is able to regulate for tissue type up to stage 24 (see Searls and Janners 1969). In the experiment shown, a labelled block of stage 24 potentially chondrogenic tissue or potentially soft tissue transplanted to a different position in stage 23 limb bud develops harmoniously in relation to host tissue. Part of the graft forms chondrogenic tissue, part non-chondrogenic tissue. There is no evidence for cell movement from or to the implanted tissue block. The experiment also shows that cell migration (e.g. involving segregation from a mixed population of pre-cartilage and non-cartilage cells) is not involved in cartilage differentiation in the limb (Searls 1967). H = humerus, R = radius, U = ulna.

in its new position where it forms ectopic cartilage (Searls 1967). Searls also concluded that skeletal differentiation does not take place by the segregation together of pre-cartilage cells from an initially randomly mixed population of pre-cartilage, pre-fibroblasts and pre-myoblasts. The blocks of tissue maintained their integrity, with no migration from host to graft or vice versa. Zwilling (1966) considered that differentiation of chondrogenic and myogenic regions was not determined in stage 22–24 limb buds. He divided mainly the proximal parts of limb buds into small, central, prospectively chondrogenic fragments and outer fragments, which he regarded as myogenic (but which were probably prospective soft tissue). Fragments from both sources were grown either in tissue culture or as grafts. Tissue samples, from whatever source, developed cartilaginous centres in 67 per cent of cases (Fig. 4.28). Zwilling's conclusion

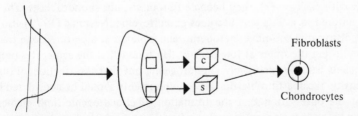

Fibroblasts

Chondrocytes

FIG. 4.28. Tissue properties stabilize late in the limb bud. Proximal fragments isolated from various regions (c = chondrogenic, s = soft tissue) from stage 22–24 limb buds grown in tissue culture all tend to develop chondrogenic centres (Zwilling 1966).

that prospective myogenic cells can form cartilage is unsound (because the tissue used was probably not pre-myogenic), but the experiments emphasize that large areas of the limb bud can form cartilage if isolated *in vitro,* and that stabilization of limb tissue types is a relatively late event, the limb bud being able to regulate at zeugopod level until stage 25.

While these results of Searls and Zwilling show clearly that prospective fibro-blasts and chondroblasts can change their developmental pathway according to their position in the limb, there is no unequivocal evidence that cells prospective for these tissues can form myoblasts, or vice versa. Newman (1977) has tried to establish the source of the precursor cells of each of the three main limb meso-dermal phenotypes. He points out that the distribution of muscle in the limb varies according to position: the largest muscle masses are associated with the humerus, while the digits have little muscle associated with them. The important question is whether or not the muscle differentiates *in situ* from the same pool of cells as those giving rise to cartilage and fibroblasts.

Newman investigated the differentiation of blocks of sub-ridge mesoderm removed at different stages and grown in culture under conditions suitable for both chondroblast and myoblast differentiation. When the mesoderm was taken from stage 17-18 wing buds, both tissue types appeared in the explants. Ex-plants from stage 21–22 always produced cartilage, but gave muscle in only 50 per cent of cases. At stage 25, when the mesoderm is prospective only for the hand, myoblasts were never formed. He concludes from this evidence that pre-chondroblasts are not also pre-myoblasts. One possible model is that the muscle primordia increasingly fail to populate the sub-ridge mesoderm of later stages.

The conclusion that chondrocytes and fibroblasts on one hand and myoblasts on the other are derived from two separate cell lines is supported by the experi-mental work of Christ *et al.* (1977; see Chapter 3), which shows that chondrocytes and fibroblasts are derived from somatopleural and myoblasts from somitic mesenchyme respectively. (See Dienstman, Biehl, Holtzer, and Holtzer 1974.)

The choice between chondroblast and fibroblast seems to be determined by cell density, at least in culture. If stage 25 apical mesoderm is dissociated and the cells grown at less than confluent densities (i.e. so that the cells do not make contact with each other), they become fibroblasts, not chondroblasts. The same tissue cultured as a fragment becomes chondrogenic. Newman (1977) also completely dissociated sub-ridge mesoderm, and pelleted and cultured one fraction, while culturing the other at low density. He found that the aggregates prepared from pellets became exclusively chondrogenic, but that the fraction cultured at low density became fibroblastic. These experiments should be considered in the light of the observation that the formation of chondrogenic limb elements is heralded by a phase of mesodermal condensation, in which there is extensive and intimate cell contact (Thorogood and Hinchliffe 1975; Ede and Flint 1972). Studies, such as those of Ede (Ede, Flint, Wilby, and Colquhoun 1977; Ede and Flint, 1972), who has analysed in culture the initial close association of pre-chondrogenic cells, and Holtfreter (1968), who emphasizes that aggregation of pre-chondroblasts is necessary for amphibian cartilage differentiation, support Newman's hypothesis (Fig. 4.29) that differentiation is, in this case at any rate, modulated by the presence or absence of cell interaction.

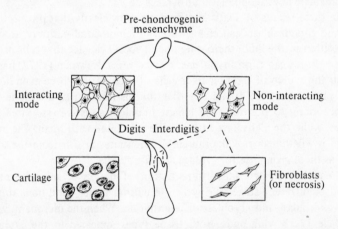

FIG. 4.29. Diagram illustrating Newman's hypothesis (1977) that the interacting mode of the distal limb mesenchyme determines differentiation, whether *in vivo* or *in vitro*.

To sum up, it appears that myoblasts are derived from one cell line, constituted by primordia of somitic origin invading the limb bud from its base, while chondrocytes and fibroblasts are a second line derived from sub-apical mesoderm which is somatopleural in origin. The skeletal pattern is determined by the choice (which remains open proximally until stage 25) between differentiation as chondrocytes or fibroblasts made by this second line of cells and governed by position within the limb and at the local level by the type of cell association.

4.12. The programming of cell death

We described in Chapter 3 (section 3.9) how cell death helps to shape the developing limb, particularly in the interdigital regions. We must now ask ourselves how these areas of cell death are determined, and whether death of a cell can be legitimately regarded as the goal of a pathway of differentiation.

Saunders *et al.* (1962), in a classical study, analysed the process of determination of cell death in the posterior necrotic zone of the chick wing bud. The PNZ co-exists in time and space with the ZPA (section 4.9), but its morphogenetic activity is thought to be independent of the cell death process (Saunders and Gasseling 1968). It first appears amongst healthy mesenchyme as a scattering of dead cells and macrophages at stage 24. The death of the cells within the PNZ has been shown to be controlled by the local cellular environment. If the healthy prospective PNZ cells are excised at stage 17 and flank grafted, the cells die on schedule after the appropriate interval. But if the prospective PNZ is removed between stages 17–22 and grafted to the dorsal surface of a host wing in contact with central limb bud mesoderm, the 'death clock' is stopped and cells survive. After stage 22 their fate is sealed, and they die even if grafted as described.

The inhibition of cell death by central limb mesenchyme was further analysed by Saunders and Fallon (1967) using organ culture. Prospective PNZ isolated in organ culture dies *in vitro* at the same time as does the control PNZ on the unoperated side of the host. But, as in the grafting experiment, prospective PNZ grown with central limb mesoderm (but not with somitic mesoderm) survives. An interposed millipore filter of pore size $0.45\mu m$ permits central mesodermal inhibition of PNZ cell death, but, if the pore size is reduced to $0.05\mu m$, death supervenes. It appears that a diffusible factor is involved in the control process, and that, once again, position in the limb controls differentiation.

Although cell death is irreversibly programmed by stage 22, the autophagic and autolytic activity (Hurle and Hinchliffe 1978) resulting in cell fragmentation and ingestion by macrophages (see section 3.9) does not take place until stage 24. In this gap between determination and expression, DNA and RNA synthesis in the PNZ decreases by stage 22 (Pollack and Fallon 1974) and protein synthesis by stage 23 (Pollack and Fallon 1976). The PNZ cells appear to be shutting down their genome before cytological changes are detectable.

Saunders (1966) has tried to determine whether the PNZ is specifically involved in limb shaping. If the prospective PNZ is excised before cell death takes place, a normal wing is formed. If the PNZ cells are prevented from dying by the insertion of a small piece of central mesoderm, a normal wing is again formed. He concluded that the PNZ was dispensible as far as limb shaping was concerned.

The PNZ makes only a fleeting appearance compared with the anterior necrotic zone (ANZ), and Saunders' experiments do not rule out the possibility that the ANZ is involved in wing shaping (see section 3.9). Unfortunately, corresponding experiments using the ANZ have not been performed.

There is ample evidence from chick embryos carrying mutant genes that the areas of cell death in the limb are under direct or indirect genetic control (Fig. 4.30), and that changes in their extent produce changes in limb shape (Ede, 1968; Hinchliffe 1974). In the *talpid*[2] and *talpid*[3] mutants, ANZ and PNZ are eliminated, there is excessive elongation of the AER, and the resulting limbs are polydactylous (Hinchliffe and Ede 1967; Cairns 1977). Survival of the ANZ and PNZ cells is clearly related to the distal excess of mesenchyme at 5–6 days which allows supernumerary digits to be formed at 8–9 days. The inhibition of cell death in *talpid*[3] extends even to interdigital zones, and produces soft tissue syndactyly (Hinchliffe and Thorogood 1974). Talpid mesoderm cells have been shown to be more resistant than normal to various treatments, such as removal of the AER or dissociation (Cairns 1977; Ede and Flint 1972), both procedures which will kill a proportion of normal mesodermal cells.

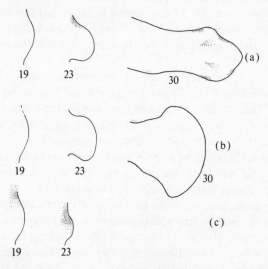

FIG. 4.30. Areas of cell death are under genetic control, and changes in the pattern of cell death are associated with changes in limb shape (Hinchliffe 1974*b*). (a) normal wing bud, (b) *talpid*[3] wing bud (note the excess of distal mesenchyme associated with inhibition of cell death: Hinchliffe and Ede 1967, Hinchliffe and Thorogood 1975). (c) *wingless* wing bud (note the precocious and enlarged ANZ: Hinchliffe and Ede 1973). By stage 30 there is no wing. Areas of cell death are stippled (Hamburger–Hamilton stages).

In other mutants, areas of cell death are enlarged. In the sex-linked *wingless* mutant (*ws*) the ANZ makes a precocious appearance and is larger than normal (Hinchliffe and Ede 1973). The legs are also frequently affected, and it is clear that the size of the leg bud ANZ is correlated with the reduction of the leg bud and with later deletions of distal skeletal elements. In *ametapodia* (Ede 1976*a*) the ANZ is suppressed, but the PNZ is enlarged during stages 23-25, and later there is massive cell death in more distal limb parts.

Even though the precise morphogenetic role of several of these areas remains obscure, there is now sufficient evidence to consider cell death in the limb in terms of classical developmental biology. Cell death may be regarded as the prospective fate of a group of competent cells progressively determined by a hierarchy of genetic, spatial, and temporal factors. (Reviewed Menkes, Sandor, and Ilies 1970; Saunders 1966.)

5 Limb regeneration

5.1. Introduction

In previous chapters we have discussed the events which occur during the development of vertebrate limbs. For many vertebrates this is a once-and-for-all process, but in other species a limb which has been accidentally lost or experimentally removed can regrow (for a recent review see Grant 1978). Limb regeneration occurs most readily in urodele amphibians. It is also found in the larvae of anurans, but not usually in adults (excepting certain primarily aquatic forms such as *Xenopus* and *Hymenochirus*, where an amputated limb regenerates only partially). Reptiles have very limited powers of limb regeneration, and birds and mammals do not usually regenerate lost limb parts, although there is at least one report (Mizell 1968) of experimental limb regeneration in the pouch young of the opossum, and two of partial regeneration in laboratory rodents. In the opossum, the forelimbs are developed precociously so that the young can climb into the mammary pouch. The relatively undeveloped hindlimbs can be made to regenerate at this stage by the addition of neural tissue.

Clearly mammalian limb regeneration is a subject of great practical importance, since man is intensely interested in the possibility of restoring his own lost limbs and digits. Apart from the work on the opossum, the best results achieved so far consist only of the regeneration of parts of individual bones. Becker and Spadaro (1972) noted that bone is laid down along the lines of greatest mechanical compression, and found that these compressions are transduced to electrical currents. Implantation of electrodes into the stump of rat limbs amputated two-thirds of the way down the humerus led to regeneration of the distal end of the bone if a suitable current was passed through the stump. Deuchar (1976) has made a preliminary investigation of the ability of 11.5-day rat limb buds to regenerate following amputation. She claimed to have obtained limb bud regeneration following whole embryo culture for 2 days. This interpretation must be treated with caution since only in 25 per cent of experiments is AER regenerated, and since the developmental potentiality of the regenerated limb bud is not revealed over this short period of culture.

The phylogenetic limitation of regeneration to the lower tetrapods has aroused interest since Morgan (1906) stated the problem. As we shall see (section 5.2.8), nerves are important for regeneration, and Singer (1973) suggests the following hypothesis: volume for volume, the limb of a newt is much more richly innervated than that of a mammal, whilst its CNS is less elaborate. The mammal has achieved better and more useful control of its limb by developing the CNS without a concomitant increase in peripheral nerve supply. The bulkier mammalian limb may be sub-threshold for the regeneratory effect of the nerves, but swifter running, reflex activity, and interpretation of sensory information is apparently of greater survival value in protecting the limb from amputation by predators than is the ability to regrow it after the event.

Growth of the limb the second time around has obvious similarities to and obvious differences from the initial process of limb formation. Regeneration of the limb of a salamander proceeds from a population of mesenchyme cells forming a bud (the blastema) on the amputated stump. This has a similar appearance to a limb bud and differentiates in a similar way. The limb bud, however, is not exposed, as the blastema is, the the constant presence of fully differentiated stump tissue. There is evidence of continuous interaction between stump and blastema during differentiation. The cells of the blastema are derived from differentiated cells; although the possibility that there is a contribution from embryonic stem cells has not been rigorously excluded, there is no good evidence to support this view. Can the differentiated cells undergo a metaplastic reorganization, involving a change of tissue type? And finally, there is strong evidence that the regenerating limb (but not the developing limb) relies on the presence of both nerves and hormones for its successful development.

5.2. Phases of limb regeneration

Although this is not the place for an extensive discussion of the phenomenon of regeneration for its own sake, we must, if we are to compare and contrast regeneration and primary development, be acquainted with the basic course of events in a regenerating limb. These have been divided into various phases (Thornton 1968) (Figs 5.1 and 5.2) with the proviso that the scheme outlined represents a statistical average rather than a precise staging without overlaps.

5.2.1. *Trauma*

Limbs do not regenerate spontaneously. The process of regeneration is initiated by trauma. Usually in nature or in the laboratory the trauma takes the form of amputation, but ligature, irradiation, the presence of foreign tissue or of a cut nerve will all act as triggers. Needham (1941) proposed that the trauma released a 'wound factor' as a result of tissue injury, but the nature of this substance (if it indeed exists) is unknown. Extensive traumatization can induce regeneration at sites where simple amputation would not suffice. Polezajew (1936) found that extensive pricking of the wound stump of tadpoles in metamorphic climax would initiate regeneration, and Rose (1944) found that irritation of the amputation stumps of adult frogs with sodium chloride solution had a similar effect.

Implantations of foreign tissue will often promote the formation of supernumerary limbs. Ruben (1960) suggested that the foreign tissue activated the host's tissue rejection system, again causing massive trauma to the implant, and secondarily to the host tissue surrounding it. In fact, supernumerary limbs are most often formed as a response to genetically 'foreign' tissue which might be expected to produce massive rejection by the host. Boiling the tissue (kidney is

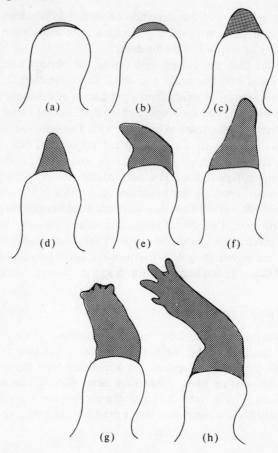

FIG. 5.1. Regeneration of the forelimb of the newt. (a) early bud stage – about 10 days after amputation, with swollen end to stump. (b) 12 days after amputation – early regenerate bud. (c) 14 days medium bud, (d) late bud, about 18 days. (e) and (f) Palette stage 3–5 weeks. (f) Lateral view showing flattening of the presumptive hand region. (g) early finger stage (6 weeks), (h) advanced functional regenerate (8 weeks).

often used) before implantation destroys its ability to induce extra limbs, but freeze-drying does not, suggesting that a protein fraction may be involved (Carlson and Morgan 1967; Stevens, Ruben, Lockwood, and Rose 1965).

5.2.2. Wound healing

This phase is characterized by closure of the wound surface by the migration of epidermis from adjacent regions to cover the injured area. Within 12 hours the whole surface is covered by one or two layers of cells. This is achieved without extra cell division, but once the wound has been closed, mitoses become common and the thickness of the epithelium increases beyond the three or four

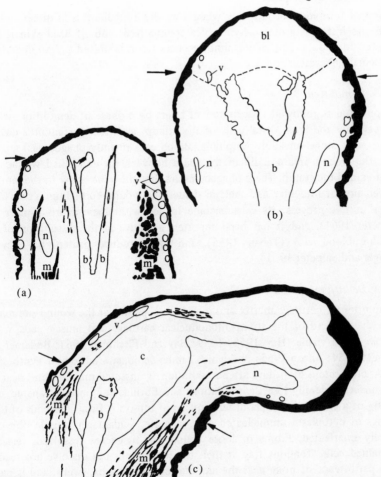

FIG. 5.2. (a) Longitudinal section through a regenerating stump 7 days after amputation. Arrows indicate original level of amputation. (b) After 14 days, at the early bud stage of regeneration, note the presence of a blastema (bl), the absence of muscle in the stump and the pitted, eroded bone end (b). The ectoderm is thickened over the amputation site. (c) A longitudinal section through palette stage regenerate. Note extensive cartilage (c) found at the end of existing bone, and the newly formed muscle (m). n = nerve, v = vessels.

layers of the normal adult epithelium, and it may become 12–16 cells thick. This thickened wound epidermis has been called the apical ectodermal cap and may be analogous to the apical ectodermal ridge of the developing limb. It should be remembered that the basal membrane and fibrous dermis present beneath normal epidermis are initially absent from wound epithelium and that cells subjacent to this epidermis may be influenced by it. All the traumatic procedures described in section 5.2.1 lead to the formation of a wound epithelium, and blastemal formation occurs only when a wound epithelium is in direct contact with the histolysing mesenchyme of a traumatized limb. If head skin is substituted for wound epithelium, limb regeneration is inhibited and no underlying blastemal aggregate is formed.

5.2.3. Demolition

Amputation is followed in a matter of hours by a phase of demolition, which affects only the most distal cells of the stump, and lasts for about 2 days in larvae, but longer in adult Amphibia. Blood cells (mainly phagocytes) migrate into the wound area and fill in the space between the thickened wound epithelium and the stump. These phagocytes are thought to be active in the removal of remains of muscular and skeletal tissue. The wound epithelium also participates in this process: its cells become loaded with tissue debris (Singer and Salpeter 1961), and it has been reported as active in the dissolution of the ensuing blood clot (Taban 1955), and may produce proteolytic enzymes (Singer and Salpeter 1961).

5.2.4. De-differentiation

Dissolution of cartilage matrix and muscle sarcoplasma at the wound site release into the cut end of the stump mononuclear cartilage and muscle cells, which appear to be viable (Hay 1958, 1959; Hay and Fischman 1961; Bodemer and Everett 1959; Anton 1965), and which can be demonstrated to have synthesized DNA and protein by 4 days after amputation. Transected muscle fibres near the cut surface generally lose their striations and fibrillae and become tapered, consisting of a string of cytoplasm with nuclei at intervals. From the ends of these strings of cytoplasm uninucleated cells separate. Undamaged muscle fibres are usually unaffected. Fibres of loose connective tissue are dissolved, releasing contained cells. Tendons fray at their transected ends but dissolve less readily. The periosteum of bone near the amputation site loosens, swells, and is partly broken down, releasing some cells. The bone itself becomes pitted and eroded by the action of nests of osteoclasts.

Histolysis spreads proximally into the stump for only a few millimetres. The release of high molecular weight cellular debris into the wound area leads to fluid retention and infiltration, and swelling follows, fluid sometimes collecting as a large blister.

In the salamander the released cells develop a discontinuous and vesicular endoplasmic reticulum and become indistinguishable on morphological grounds, whether they originated in muscle, cartilage, bone or tendon. In fact, they come to resemble closely the mesenchyme of the developing limb. Since they arise from de-differentiated adult cells and their developmental potential is not well understood, they are best referred to as mesenchymatous cells, or cells of regeneration. But as they are indistinguishable from each other, an intriguing point arises: is there metaplasia (change of cell type), or will cells derived from cartilage ultimately produce cartilage, and cells derived from muscle ultimately produce muscle? It should be remembered that we have come across the important concept of independent cell lines for muscle and cartilage before (see section 4.11).

The earliest attempts at an answer to this question are based on the experiments of Butler (1935) who established that blastemal cells are of local origin by transplanting limbs from a normal to an irradiated host. Irradiated hosts were incapable of regeneration, but the grafted limb, if re-amputated, regenerated; its blastema must have formed from local healthy tissue (Fig. 5.3). Similar

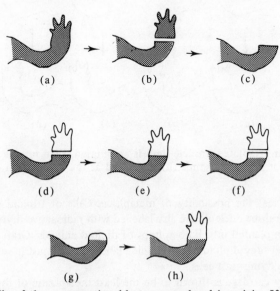

FIG. 5.3. Cells of the regeneration blastema are local in origin. If a limb which has been X-irradiated (shading (a)) is amputated (b), no regeneration of the stump occurs (c). If an unirradiated hand is grafted to an irradiated stump (d), allowed to heal (e), then amputated at a slightly more distal level (f), the unirradiated cells remaining on the end of the stump (g) will form a complete regenerate (h).

experiments identified the area of origin of the blastemal cells as the cut surface of the amputation stump, but said nothing as to cell type. Irradiation could be used to this end, however, if tissue masses of a single cell type were grafted onto the amputation stump of a suitably irradiated host (Fig. 5.4). In these experiments (Umanski 1937; Thornton 1942), muscle, bone, cartilage, or skin (dermis + epidermis) often produced regenerates, arguing for metaplasia. This evidence is suggestive but not conclusive. The host animals had been locally irradiated (i.e. irradiation had been confined to the limb to be amputated), and there is evidence that locally irradiated areas can regain regenerative ability through contact with normal tissues or after traumatization (see Thornton 1968 for a full discussion of this point).

In more recent work, double labelling of the implanted tissue has been

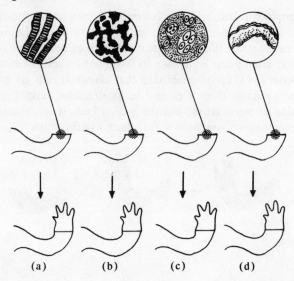

FIG. 5.4. If an irradiated urodele limb is amputated, then muscle (a), bone (b), cartilage (c), or skin and dermis (d) implanted at the amputation site will form a blastema.

employed to test the possibility of metaplasia. Cells of triploid origin, whose nuclei contain three nucleoli, are also labelled with radioactive thymidine. Tissue can then be implanted into limb stumps of diploid animals. Graft cells must be double-labelled: any diploid but thymidine-labelled cells must have incorporated the label from dying graft cells.

In this way cartilage is shown to be the least metaplastic of the three tissue types. If double-labelled cartilage cells are implanted in place of the humerus in a limb stump, then in the regenerating limb most of the graft cells give rise to cartilage (Steen 1968). A few labelled perichondrial cells and fibroblasts indicate a small degree of metaplasia may occur. But most de-differentiated cartilage cells become cartilage again.

Perhaps in that experiment de-differentiated chondroblasts do not have their metaplastic potential tested fully, since other host cells are available, which can differentiate non-cartilage cell types. Wallace, Maden, and Wallace (1974) and Maden and Wallace (1975) tested the metaplastic potential of cartilage with a more rigorous challenge. They isolated blocks of pure cartilage from the Axolotl humerus and implanted these into an irradiated limb stump. Previous experiments enabled them to discount any host contribution to re-generation. Thus, if there is to be regeneration at all, it must come from the cartilage graft. Regeneration was very variable, but, in some experiments, small but recognizable hands were obtained. The authors claim that the grafted cartilage provides all the mesodermal tissues of the regnerates: cartilage, muscle, and connective tissue. Perhaps cartilage is only metaplastic when the alternative is no regeneration at all.

Muscle appears to be more labile. When labelled muscle tissue is implanted, the resulting blastema is composed mainly of labelled cells which then differentiate into all cell types, including cartilage. But it is not certain that myoblasts after de-differentiation can form cartilage. Muscle contains connective tissue, which is highly metaplastic, and the non-muscle tissue in the regenerate may originate from this.

If labelled connective tissue from the tail fin of a salamander is grafted into an irradiated and amputated limb, then most tissue types in the regenerate are labelled. Connective tissue cells can thus differentiate as muscle, cartilage, peri-chondrium, or connective tissue. Metaplasia has been most clearly established for connective tissue, since it is difficult in many of the experiments on cartilage and muscle to eliminate entirely the possibility of connective tissue contamination.

Consistent with the importance of connective tissue in regeneration are the results obtained by Chalkley (in Thornton 1959), who estimated the contribution of different cell types to the regenerate by counting mitoses in each. The most mitosis was seen in connective tissue (85 per cent) with muscle (<8 per cent), periosteum (<8 per cent), and nerve sheath (<4 per cent) also contributing. It is a matter of speculation, however, if this is a valid method of assessing contribution to the blastema.

We do know that, of all the tissues making up the limb stump, only the skeleton may be removed without affecting regeneration (Goss 1961). Removal of the humerus from a stump does not prevent the regeneration of a new humerus, nor the presence of more distal bones in the regenerate. Weiss (1925) made a slit through the skin and muscle of the arm of a newt and removed the humerus (Fig. 5.5). The wound healed, then the limb was amputated through the upper arm. A regeneration bud re-formed all the tissues of the limb distal to the amputation level, including the distal part of the humerus. In another experiment, Weiss (1927), removed a circumferential strip of skin from the arm of a newt and replaced it by trachea turned inside out, so that the tracheal epithelium replaced the skin. Amputation through this 'collar' again produced a complete regenerate. Not all elements of the limb pattern have to be present in the stump for successful regeneration.

A comparable experiment with muscle is less easy to do. Liosner and Woronzowa (1936) removed arm muscles as completely as possible from an amputation stump and packed the space with tail muscle. This produced abnormal regeneration and a structure resembling a tail.

There are, of course, other alternatives, given that regenerate cells originate locally. One is the presence of stem cells (Table 5.1), another that they may be derived from the epidermis.

The presence of undifferentiated stem cells amongst the tissues of the body has been demonstrated in *Hydra* and in other invertebrates, and was used as a basis for one theory of the origin of malignant tumours. According to this theory, amongst the cells of the normal limb are scattered undifferentiated

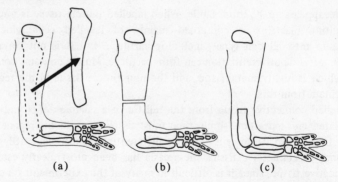

FIG. 5.5. If the humerus is removed from a newt's limb (a) and the limb is subsequently amputated (b), the regenerate will contain a humerus distal, but not proximal, to the level of amputation, and a complete set of distal skeletal elements.

TABLE 5.1. The possible origins of regenerate cells

1. Muscle cell $\longrightarrow$	Blastemal cell $\longrightarrow$	Muscle
Cartilage cell $\longrightarrow$	Blastemal cell $\longrightarrow$	Cartilage
Connective tissue cell $\longrightarrow$	Blastemal cell $\longrightarrow$	Connective tissue
2. Muscle cell		Muscle
Cartilage cell $\Rightarrow$	Blastemal cell $\rightleftarrows$	Cartilage
Connective tissue cell		Connective tissue
3. Undifferentiated reserve cell $\longrightarrow$	Blastemal cell $\rightleftarrows$	Muscle
		Cartilage
		Connective tissue

embryonic cells, possibly multipotential, waiting for the signal inducing them to differentiate. The experiments of Goss (1961) mentioned above have been used to support this theory; the fact that absence of skeletal tissue does not affect the formation of a perfect regenerate suggests that 'reserve' cells capable of forming skeletal tissue must have been present. This argument, of course, fails to distinguish between derivation from reserve cells and the possibility of metaplastic de-differentiation. The reserve cells might, of course, be fibroblasts.

Another possible, though rather unlikely, source of blastemal cells is the wound ectoderm. Rose (1971) showed that, at the time when the blastema was forming, the increase in mesenchymatous cells corresponded numerically to a decrease in ectodermal cells, and postulated that ectodermal cells descended into the underlying tissue, becoming transformed *en route* into mesenchymatous cells, which then differentiate into the usual tissue types. Labelling of epidermal cells with ^{3}H-thymidine (Rose and Rose 1965) produced labelled muscle and cartilage nuclei after three to five cell generations. Such a transformation of an epidermal tissue into cells which are, in the normal limb, clearly mesodermal in origin would surprise most embryologists and, in fact, other evidence fails to support this idea. Steen (1970) implanted cells labelled both with ^{3}H-thymidine and an extra set of chromosomes (triploid) into regenerating blastemata and subsequently recovered diploid cells with thymidine label. The label must have migrated from cell to cell. Other ^{3}H-thymidine labelling studies of epidermis (Hay and Fischman 1961) have failed to locate labelled blastema cells. Perhaps the neatest experiments were those of Riddiford (1960). She infused tritiated thymidine directly into the regenerating limb of *Triturus*, thus labelling both ectoderm and mesenchyme. A similar regenerate on the other side of the animal remained unlabelled. Surgical removal and exchange of epidermis side for side gave a labelled ectoderm on an unlabelled mesenchyme and vice versa. If Rose was right, then labelled cells should percolate from the labelled ectoderm to the unlabelled mesenchyme after a suitable period of time. This did not occur, but the reverse movement, from mesenchyme to epidermis already mentioned, was clearly demonstrated. Dead mesenchyme cells were seen to ascend into the ectoderm, where they were phagocytosed.

The idea that cells circulating in the blood stream contribute to the blastema has been periodically fashionable since the beginning of the century, perhaps its latest champions being Becker and Murray (1970). The Schwann cells forming nerve sheaths have also been seen to round up after amputation and follow their regenerating axons in to the blastema; their fate there is a matter for speculation.

The origin of the cells of the blastema thus seems fairly clear. There is evidence that the differentiated cells of the stump de-differentiate, and there is also evidence suggesting that the epidermis does not contribute cells to the blastema. As to which cell becomes what within the regenerating limb, the evidence is equivocal. We know that skeletal tissue may be replaced, but we do not know from what. We know that labelled cartilage cells in the stump prefer to produce mainly cartilage in the regenerate, but, that when they are the only source of cells for regeneration, they can be metaplastic. Connective tissue on the other hand appears to be readily metaplastic, but there is no good evidence as to whether muscle produces only muscle, or whether it can also be the source of the cells which replace the missing cartilage.

5.2.5. *Blastemal cells and the ectoderm*

The mononuclear mesenchymatous cells, whose origin was discussed above, accumulate at the stump tip to form the blastema, which rapidly increases in size due to the high rate of mesenchymatous cell division. This phase marks the end of degenerative change in the limb regenerate and signals the onset of the beginnings of reconstruction.

The role of the ectoderm overlying the blastema in its further development has attracted much attention because of the known role of the apical ectodermal ridge in amniote limb development. Is the thickened apical cap analogous to the apical ectodermal ridge?

The idea of analogy between the thickened ectoderm of the regenerate and the AER was tested by removal of the apical cap of regenerating limbs of *Ambystoma maculatum* larvae (Thornton 1957) (a process which had to be repeated daily as the cap promptly regenerated!). Daily removal slowed regeneration and blastema formation, but did not entirely obliterate it. But the time taken for the cap to regenerate in this species is only 12 hours, and daily removal allowed the cap to do whatever it does do for 12 out of 24 hours. In *Ambystoma tigrinum* larvae, the cap takes 24 hours to regenerate, and here daily removal abolished both cap and blastema formation. Careful ultraviolet irradiation (so as not to damage the underlying mesoderm) also abolished both cap and blastema formation (Thornton 1958). The obvious objection to these experiments is that tissue-damaging doses of ultraviolet light are not a normal part of the environment, and may damage the limb in unknown ways. A better experiment would be to move the cap and to see if it induced a blastema at its new site. This is possible in amphibians because of the way in which wound healing takes place; an epidermal wound is covered by migration of the adjacent epidermis. By making a wound adjacent to a newly amputated limb, it was possible to make the thicker wound epidermis migrate to an abnormal position where blastemal cells accumulated beneath it. This seemingly conclusive experiment is also open to objection; nerve fibres play an important part in regeneration (see section 5.2.8) and many sensory nerve fibres enter the wound epidermis. These might have migrated along with the epidermis to its new position, and acted as 'highways' along which blastemal cells could migrate. The objection is overcome by using as experimental material limbs that initially developed without a nerve supply (Yntema 1959), but which regenerate normally. If the experiment is repeated with limbs which have never been innervated, an asymmetrical blastema is still formed (Thornton and Steen 1962).

The importance of the epidermis in regeneration has also been stressed by other workers. Skowron and Walknowska (1963) noted that a transplanted blastema and ectoderm produced regenerates only if mesoderm and ectoderm did not become separated, and Jordan (1965), who transplanted blastemata to *Xenopus* brain, noted that they formed only cartilaginous nodules in the absence of epithelium. Frog kidney (Ruben and Frothingham 1958) will induce supernumerary limb formation only if the wound through which it is implanted subsequently develops a thickened wound epithelium. The close parallel between regeneration and embryonic blastemas in their dependence upon intact epithelium for growth has already been noted (Chapter 4.5.1).

5.2.6. *Blastemal proliferation*

Once degeneration of the amputation stump is halted, the blastema proliferates by mitosis. Increased mitotic rates have been observed as soon as 4 days after amputation (Chalkley 1959) in the newt. Hearson (1966) calculated the mitotic index for four zones of tissue at important stages of regeneration: early bud (10 days), mound (13 days), cone (16 days), and paddle (19 days) (Fig. 5.6). By the nineteenth day after amputation, mitosis is at a peak in the distal half of the regenerate, suggesting the presence of an 'apical growth cone' similar to that seen in the regenerating tail (Holtzer, Holtzer, and Avery 1955).

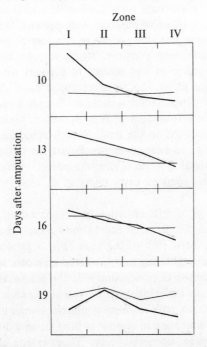

FIG. 5.6. Graphic representation of mitotic index (thick line) and cell density (thin line) of the four longitudinal zones (I apical zone to IV proximal) of the Axolotl blastema at four stages of regeneration (after Hearson 1966).

5.2.7. *Morphogenesis of the blastema*

In all important respects the morphogenesis of the regenerating limb blastema resembles that of the developing limb, but it must be stressed again that re-generation takes place in conjunction with an adult limb stump. In the absence of a stump, blastemata can be induced to grow as grafts, but they then show distalization, i.e. develop more distal structures than they would have done *in situ* (Mettetal 1939; Faber 1960; Pietsch 1961). Thus, early bud stage blastemata develop only one or two digits with phalanges and metacarpals, mound stages develop 1–4 digits, cone stage digits, carpals and one or two forearm elements, and paddle blastemata normal limbs minus the humerus. If paddle stage blastemata are divided into proximal and distal halves and grown as grafts, then both halves regenerate distal elements with equal frequency (Pietsch 1937). Faber (1965) postulated the presence, and interaction, of a 'distal field' centred on the blastema and a 'proximal field' centred on the stump to account for these findings. However, more recent work has shown that the distalization is more apparent than real, and due to the initial regression of the transplant. Stocum (1968) has found that, under suitable conditions, blastemata can produce all structures distal to the amputation surface (see Chapter 6), and de Both (1970) made up for any loss of mesoderm by implanting a compound bud made up of mesoderm from several blastemata topped off with wound ectoderm. Again, all structures distal to the level of amputation were present. Stocum thought that any apparent distalization was due simply to the loss of proximal mesoderm destined to differentiate into proximal structures; de Both that a simple deficiency of mesodermal mass was enough to account for the phenomenon. Although interpretations differ, the facts are concordant: distalization can be eliminated by suitable experimental technique. Stocum's technique to reduce tissue regression was to introduce a graft composed of mesoderm and its own ectoderm into a flank wound in the host. Wound epidermis was thus formed at the junction of graft and host epidermis. Whilst the transplanted mesoderm always produced proximal structures, the mesoderm immediately below this wound epidermis often produced extra digits at an angle to the original limb axis.

The first physical sign of differentiation in a regenerating limb is the formation of cartilage around the cut bone end to form a cap. The cap extends so as to replace the missing distal ends of the bone (Fig. 5.2): with further growth, cartilaginous centres corresponding to more distal elements appear. Much later, this cartilage is transformed to bone. Alongside the regenerating cartilages new muscle fibres are seen to differentiate from regenerate cells. These increase in number and size so as to replace missing muscle elements. In addition, the muscle fibres of the stump start to regrow at their tapered distal ends, formerly a source of mononuclear regenerate cells. They extend across the line of amputation into the regenerate, recruiting mesenchymal cells as they grow.

Tendons, epidermal glands, and dermis all appear, and the regenerate is invaded by a network of small blood vessels, later coalescing to reproduce the original vascular pattern. Nerves also return as outgrowths of the many axons transected at amputation. Each of these grows into the regenerate and, as with blood vessels, the original pattern of innervation is restored. In fact, nerve regeneration has been noted as early as 2 days after amputation, when sensory axons invade the epidermal cap in profusion, rendering the regenerate sensitive to mechanical stimulation and thus protecting it from injury. Nerves are particularly plentiful in the ventral and posterior quadrants of the regenerate, and it is in these areas that maximum growth and cell division are found. One is tempted to ask if nerves play any special part in regeneration.

5.2.8. *The influence of nerves*

In a classic series of experiments, Singer (see Thornton (1968) for bibliography) demonstrated that regenerative ability in the limb of the newt was a function of the quantity of nerve fibres present at the wound surface of the stump. The neuronal influence is a local one (Kamrin and Singer 1959) and does not depend on the presence of the CNS, although CNS fibres can supply the neural stimulation if implanted together with a blastema (Thornton 1956). The quantitative level necessary to induce regeneration seems to be higher in larval newts than in adults (Karczmar 1946). In *Notophthalmus*, which is unusual in going through two metamorphoses, Peadon and Singer (1965) found thresholds of 75.5 fibres per $100\mu m^2$ amputation surface in first larvae, 47.6 in small land phase, and 27.7 in adult newts respectively. This is contrary to the expected result that the threshold should rise with increasing maturity: the apparent contradition stems from the fact that larvae are better innervated than adult forms. Van Stone (1964) found that the loss of regenerative capacity in developing *Rana* tadpoles was not accompanied by a drop in innervation level per unit area. Singer (1954) found that lost regenerative capacity could be re-invoked in young adult frogs by increasing the total number of fibres present in the forelimb stump by diverting the sciatic nerve (Fig. 5.7). But, on the other hand, the forelimb of

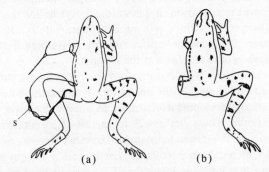

(a)   (b)

FIG. 5.7. When the forelimb of an adult frog is amputated (a) and the sciatic nerve (= s) dissected free from the hindlimb and brought up under the skin to the forelimb stump (b), then imperfect regeneration of the forelimb will occur (after Singer 1973).

Xenopus (which normally regenerates imperfectly to form a spike) reacts badly to superinnervation, and regenerates less well than normally (Konieczna-Marczynska and Skowron-Cendrzak 1958).

The presence of 'nerve factor' is most critical in the early stages of regeneration, when its absence leads to extensive tissue necrosis and regression of the stump, especially in larvae; adult stumps seem less affected. Thus, the presence of nerves may limit the process of de-differentiation. Innervation is not required for the initial process of wound healing and demolition. But the blastemal stage is affected. In denervated limbs few blastemal cells accumulate, and, as shown by their DNA synthesis, they do not continue dividing. If a normal blastema is formed and the limbs then denervated, continued division of the blastemal cells (which would otherwise decrease their DNA synthesis) may be obtained by an infusion of brain extract (Jabaily and Singer 1977). However, once a blastema is well-established, it becomes independent of nerve supply. Schotté and Butler (1944) found that de-innervation inhibited larval regeneration if performed on days 1-7 after amputation, but not if delayed until day 9. Singer and Craven

(1948) found that in the adult newt denervation inhibited regeneration on day 13 but not on day 17.

The way in which nerves exert their influence on regenerates has been subject to much speculation and experimentation. Impulse transmission may be ruled out, since, if the ventral nerve roots are cut, isolating the limb neurones from the central motor connections but retaining sensory connections, limbs will still regenerate. Sensory neurones are as effective as motor neurones in regeneration. Singer and his school (Singer 1960) suggested that the active factor was a neurotransmitter, but were unable to demonstrate (Taban 1955) that acetylcholine and other neurotransmitters supported regeneration. Blockers of acetylcholine metabolism inhibited regeneration, but only in such large doses as to kill tissues within the stump. Furthermore, acetylcholine is present in greater amounts in motor than in sensory nerve fibres, yet a quantity of motor nerve fibres insufficient to support regeneration supplies more acetylcholine than an equivalent quantity of sensory fibres which *will* support regeneration. Other neurotransmitters could be implicated since various molecules have been shown to be transported down nerve axons for release at the synapse.

As already mentioned, regeneration can occur in certain conditions without the benefit of a nerve supply. If the neural tube is surgically removed from early *Ambyostoma* larvae, development continues in some individuals, which develop non-innervated limbs. These limbs will regenerate if amputated. Limb tissues must acquire neurotrophic dependence in development. Because of this behaviour of aneural limbs, it has been postulated that trauma is the governing factor in regeneration, and that limbs with sub-threshold quantities of nerve fibres might be induced to regenerate by increased traumatization, and indeed this has been demonstrated several times (Bodemer 1960; Singer and Mutterperl 1963; Singer 1965). Singer (1965) has postulated that whatever is produced by nerve cells is also produced, albeit in lesser quantities, by other cells. Normally the supply from nervous tissue inhibits production by other tissues. Aneuronal limbs would, therefore, require the same level of stimulation as other limbs to support regeneration, and this would have to be supplied by other cells conditioned to overproduce. In the case of sub-threshold innervation, one can see that excess trauma might lead to injury to a large number of cells and release of stimulant to the tissue fluids.

5.2.9. *The influence of hormones*

By contrast to limb development in the embryo, where hormones have no known role, limb regeneration is dependent upon the integrity of the hypophysis and, in some cases, the thyroid gland. The exact stages at which these glands act have been the subject of extensive experimentation. In *Notophthalmus* (Richardson 1945), regeneration fails when hypophysectomy is performed at the same time as, or before, amputation. If delayed to 3 days or more after amputation, it has no effect, or at least imperfect regeneration takes place. The proportion of positive regenerations increases with the time between amputation and hypophysectomy, suggesting perhaps that hypophysectomy is concerned with the wound healing and de-differentiation stages of regeneration rather than the phases involving growth. ACTH, growth hormone, NIH, and possibly prolactin (Berman, Bern, Nicoll, and Strohman 1964) may all be involved. Schotté (1961) suggested that the stress of amputation might trigger ACTH release, which in turn stimulates cortisone production. The role of cortisone in limb regeneration is, however, equivocal (Thornton 1968).

In anuran tadpoles, thyroxine given before amputation inhibits regeneration, but promotes it if given to blastemal stages. In urodeles, the situation is quite different, thyroxine having no effect pre-amputation, but being inhibitory post-amputation. However, thyroidectomy 10–30 days prior to amputation considerably stimulates regeneration (Schmidt 1958a, b), to such an extent that blastemal cells aggregate precociously.

It is difficult, at present, to integrate the results showing hormonal control of regeneration into a coherent story. One problem is that some of the hormones are probably acting via the extracellular matrix, whose state is known to affect cell activity in morphogenesis. Another problem is that the pituitary role is difficult to analyse because of secondary feedback interactions with other dependent endocrine glands.

5.3. Limb regeneration versus primogenesis

Before we look at the similarities and differences between regeneration and primary growth, it might be as well to summarize our current views on limb regeneration. It seems clear that the cells of the blastema are derived from the limb stump, and that these 'de-differentiated' cells often retain tissue specificity (especially cartilage), although morphological identity is lost. But even cartilage can be metaplastic, and connective tissue usually is. The metaplasia which does occcur (e.g. connective tissue giving rise to cartilage) is not limited to regenerating tissue, but is a fairly common pathological change. Connective tissue is notoriously plastic: in a fractured bone, connective tissue forms callus, etc. The main question which arises is how does a conglomeration of mixed cell types reorganize itself to reform a limb? This, of course, is the same question that we must ask ourselves with reference to the developing limb, where we know there are also at least three tissue types (ectoderm, somitic mesoderm, and lateral plate mesoderm). The major difference between limb bud and regenerate is the presence of the stump. The stump initially supplies blastemal cells and later governs how much limb is regenerated, but a regenerating blastema transferred to a foreign site still produces limb elements; once programmed by the stump, it becomes self-differentiating.

Perhaps the influence of stump upon graft is best seen as a back-up system, ensuring harmonious regeneration, by allowing the correlation of pre-existing and newly formed elements into a working limb. Limbs amputated at different levels develop different structures; an amputation in mid-humerus causes regeneration of distal tissues only, as does an amputation in mid-radius/ulna. Faber (1971) suggested that blastemata which grew on distal amputation stumps were smaller than those growing on proximal ones; this led to the idea that the amount of tissue regenerated depended upon the amount of blastemal mesenchyme present, and lent support to the experiments of de Both (1970), who combined blastemal mesenchymes into a 'super' blastema which was able to produce structures proximal to the original line of amputation. Faber's statement was challenged by other workers (Iten and Bryant 1973; Lewis, Smith, Crawley, and Wolpert 1974), who considered that blastemata were the same size regardless of the level of amputation. Maden (1976) set out to resolve this controversy and found that in *Ambystoma* mid-arm and mid-forearm amputations gave rise to blastemata with identical growth characteristics. No significant differences were found in cell volume, cell number or cell cycle. The only significant difference was in the appearance of cartilage a day earlier in proximal than in distal blastemata.

Clearly the blastemata of proximal and distal amputations are initially identical. Clearly the stump, or an interaction between stump and blastema, is able to specify in some way the level at which regeneration should commence, because stump and regenerate are always a perfect fit. Clearly the blastema is organized in some way so as to produce the right number of the right structure, just as the limb bud is organized to do exactly the same thing. There are considerable similarities here with the interpretation of chick limb bud regulation by the French school (see Chapter 4), whose experiments show that regulation of excesses or deficiencies in limb buds involves exchange of information between stump and grafted bud. Stocum (1975) argues that developmental mechanisms are conserved in urodele ontogeny, and that the same mechanisms may be acting in both developing limb bud and regenerating blastema. If this is so, then the regenerating limb forms a valuable tool for the developmental biologists and, more important, solving the problems of limb regeneration also solves the problem of limb development.

In the next chapter we shall discuss the concept of pattern in the limb, both developing and regenerating, and look at the models that have been proposed to account for limb development.

6   Pattern in the limb

6.1. Introduction

The elements which go to make up the vertebrate fin or the tetrapod limb are not arranged randomly. Each bears a special relationship to the other. In terms of the elements of which it is constituted, the human arm is very like the human leg, with x per cent skeletal material, y per cent muscle, z per cent connective tissue, etc., but each is immediately recognizable as arm or leg. The chick wing and leg are also similarly constituted, but strikingly different, both from each other and from their human counterparts. In the chick with man comparison, of course, the genetic make-up of the cells within the limbs is very different; but the cells composing the wing and leg of a particular individual hen, or those composing the arm or leg of a particular man, are identical in genotype and have been exposed to very similar conditions during development.

Yet they differ. In this chapter we shall try to see how and why cells, initially histologically indistinguishable, come to differ. The difference we see between arm and leg is one of form, or of pattern. It will, therefore, be necessary for us to try to define what we mean by these terms. Once defined, we must try to find how the expression of this pattern is governed, and whether the pattern is inherent within these cells or imposed upon them from without.

All this is within an invidual. We must also consider the range of variation in the pattern between individuals, i.e. the gene pool of a species. It is upon this variation that evolution works in the present and has worked in the past. The differences between the final shape of a chick wing and a human arm must depend upon variations in the mechanism controlling the pattern, for it is this which is inherited, not the final shape. And, if we understand a little of the ways in which living species differ from each other by studying their embryology, perhaps we can hazard a few informed guesses about the past, about the evolutionary history of the developing limb. This has left few traces in the final product, the adult limb, or in the meagre fossil record, and no direct evidence at all of the developing pattern or its control mechanisms at the crucial stages of limb evolution.

6.2. Form and pattern

What is pattern and what is form? Waddington (1962) suggested that form implies cell movement and changes in shape. Pattern, which focuses attention on spatial relationships of the parts of the developing form, concerns differences which do not involve cell movement. In practice, of course, any embryological situation will involve at least some cell movement, so the distinction cannot be an absolute one. In general terms the problem is this: how can an ensemble of more or less identical cells be organized so that they differentiate to form a well-defined spatial pattern? Why, in any species, is a particular three-dimensional arrangement of bones, muscles, nerves, and vessels preferred to all other possible arrangements, and how is it reproduced generation after generation? We must also ask about differentiation. Why did these particular cells become muscle instead of connective tissue or cartilage?

The methods of forming biological and non-biological patterns that we see about us may be classified in many different ways. One possible classification (Waddington 1962) sub-divides patterns into these categories:

1. *Unit generated forms.* The type of the unit generated form is the inorganic crystal, whose units (ions and atoms) are held together by valency forces. The unit could be as large as a living cell; but the forces available for holding such an array together depend upon very accurate spacing, falling off with the square (or with even higher powers) of the distance apart. A system made up of particles in this way can be of any shape. Globular protein molecules with two asymmetrical patches of stickiness, for example, would assemble themselves into a helix. If the units are cylinders, like the insulin molecule (Fig. 6.1(a)), then the shape generated might be a four-lobed fibre. Fibres may be monotypic (that is, made up of one sort of unit) like collagen, or polytypic, like a muscle fibre. It is easy to see that a suitable unit might also be built up into a two-dimensional sheet or membrane.

2. *Instruction generated forms.* It is also possible to make a structure from a series of units plus a set of instructions on how to assemble them. Think of a bricklayer using a plan and a pile of bricks to make a house. The way in which the bricks are assembled is not a function of the shape of the bricks (as it would be in a unit generated form) but of the plan. Bricks are assembled one by one, diachronically (that is, spaced out in time) to form the finished structure. But the process could also be synchronic (assembled in very little time); a sergeant-major shouting 'Fall in' (instructions) can generate a line of soldiers (pattern) in very little time. Waddington (1962), from whom the above illustration is taken, argues that in biological systems this method is most likely to consist of a set of instructions in the form of a material structure in whose immediate vicinity the new structure will be formed. An analogy would be an architect, pegging out his plan directly on the ground instead of providing the builder with the usual scale plan. Such a system forms a special category of instructive systems which we can define as 'template systems'. These are important in biological systems, and worthy of separate consideration.

3. *Template generated forms.* We may define this as the assembly of a number of units in the vicinity of a pre-existing structure whose pattern determines their orderly arrangement. The assembly of a hen's egg (Fig. 6.1(b)) is a diachronic example, depending on the proximity of the forming egg to an ordered series of regions of the oviduct where the various layers of albumin, membranes, and shell are serially added. Such an assembly line is rare in animals, however, and in most

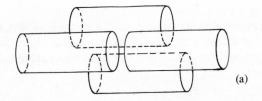

(a)

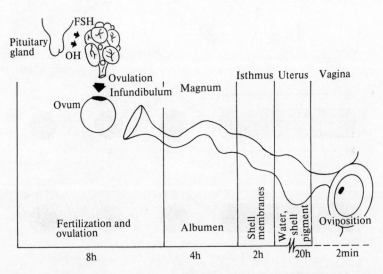

FIG. 6.1. (a) The insulin molecule is made up of four sub-units which determine its shape. (b) A hen's egg achieves its final form by controlling passage down the female reproductive tract, where successive layers of material are slowly added.

biological templates the various elements act synchronically. Perhaps a more important distinction is that between structures produced which are exact copies (or simply coded replicas) and structures ('non-copies') which are quite different from the template and related to it only by a complex coding relation. An example of such a non-copy is seen in experimental analysis of primary embryonic induction in amphibians: a transplanted blastopore dorsal lip (the template) implanted in presumptive epidermis induces from it a secondary neural tube (the non-copy). Examples of generation of copies are seen in the replication or transcription of DNA or the translation of mRNA. The copy may be identical to the master as in replication (DNA copying DNA) or non-identical as in transcription and translation (RNA copying DNA, mRNA assembling protein) through suitable coding.

4. *Condition generated forms.* These are not related to the structure of the units from which they are made, nor formed from a set of instructions, but arise from the interactions of a number of spatially distributed conditions. As an illustration imagine a cylindrical mass of tissue, upon which we impose the following

conditions (Fig. 6.2):
   (i) precartilage cells congregate along the axis (Fig. 6.2(b), stippled);
   (ii) when the density of these cells reaches a certain level they die;
   (iii) the threshold for death decreases as we move along the axis (Fig. 6.2(c), shaded black).

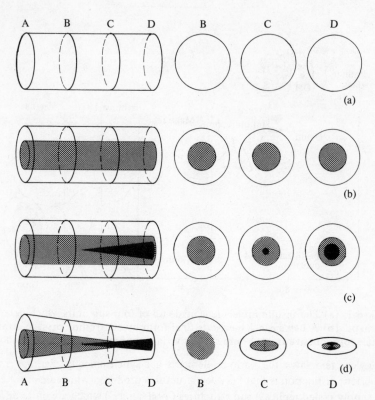

FIG. 6.2. A condition generated pattern. For explanation, see text.

What happens if these conditions are met? First, precartilage cells will accumulate into a central rod. At the end with the lowest threshold for death, cells will begin to die. If we further stipulate that at this end the cylinder is flattened a little (Fig. 6.2(d)), the cartilaginous rod will split in two, with a region of cell death between the two cartilaginous areas. We have generated a diachronic pattern not incorporated into any of the conditions imposed, and which also serves as a formal model of early limb chondrogenesis (Dawd and Hinchliffe 1972).

Different aspects of the genesis of limb pattern may be assigned to one of these major divisions. Collagen fibres in the extracellular matrix of cartilage assemble because of the molecular properties of tropocollagen: they are unit generated. Within limb cells, as within all living cells, template replication of

DNA and RNA is occurring. The induction interaction of mesoderm and ecto-derm may be regarded as involving template generation of non-copies. However, when we look at skeletogenesis, the experimental analysis of its control and theoretical explanations, it becomes clear that the model with greatest potential is the diachronic condition generated pattern.

6.3. Where is the pattern?

It may well be that the pattern which we are looking for is not common to all elements of the limb, but is confined to a small number, or even just one cell type. We can, for instance, rule out the circulatory system (Searls 1968) as it differentiates rather late from an apparently unpatterned capillary net, and the final, rather undisciplined arrangement of arteries and veins is clearly subsidiary to other structures (though Caplan and Koutroupas (1974) give a contrary view). The nerves can also be ruled out, because aneurogenic limbs can be produced which, although non-functional, are perfectly shaped. We think that the ecto-derm can also be ruled out; the AER has, of course, special outgrowth-inducing properties, and the non-AER ectoderm seems to be concerned with establishing the dorso-ventral axis of the limb (Pautou, 1977), but the main ectodermal effect is non-specific: leg ectoderm will induce the outgrowth of wing meso-derm; chick mesoderm can even be induced by rat AER. This influence is clearly concerned with growth rather than pattern.

If we look at the patterned limb bud just prior to ossification, the types of mesoderm present are muscle, cartilage, and fibroblasts from soft connective tissue. Having excluded everything else, our pattern should lie in one or other of these cell types. We have already described Newman's work (1977), which suggests that, distally in the limb bud, the mesenchyme has only chondrogenic potential (see section 4.11). Pre-chondroblasts, he argues, are not pre-myoblasts. It is likely, therefore, that the skeletal patterning which takes place distally is produced by the non-myogenic pre-cartilage. Because of the absence of pre-myoblasts in the digital region, patterning must be confined to the pre-chondro-blasts. And if this is true in one area of the limb, it is likely to be so elsewhere. More proximally, the pre-chondroblasts and pre-myoblasts are in close spatial proximity but, although morphologically indistinguishable, have different destinies, forming distinct muscular and chondrogenic patterns. One important question is the relationship between the two patterns: does the formation of the chondrogenic pattern 'cause' the associated muscle pattern in the adjacent mesenchyme? As we have seen, the chondrogenic pattern can be duplicated experimentally (section 4.9), and when this happens the myogenic pattern is also duplicated (Shellswell and Wolpert 1977). Is this because both prospective chondrogenic and myogenic cells can form their appropriate pattern indepen-dently? Or does the forming pre-chondrogenic pattern impose the related myogenic pattern on the pre-myogenic cells? We can pose the question but we cannot, from the evidence presently available, answer it.

The cells which form the pattern must also be suitably distributed in space, and sufficient in number to produce a limb. We are looking for a system of patterning which (a) allows the correct number of the correct type of cell to be present at the right time, and (b) causes the elements of the pattern to arise at pre-determined points in the limb bud. (a) and (b) may be two parts of the same process, or they may be entirely separate phenomena.

6.4. Growth and shaping of the limb bud

It is quite easy to suggest the parameters of cell behaviour which may govern the shaping of the limb bud: mitosis and cell migration spring immediately to mind. The mitotic index is an obvious variable to look at in a growing system (Mohammed 1978). Mitotic index is fairly easy to measure, but progress in this field was hampered by the physical difficulty of dealing with the huge cell numbers involved. The limb bud may, for instance, contain at a conservative estimate somewhere in excess of a million cells. The recent introduction of digital computers has made it possible to perform manipulations involving very large numbers in a reasonably short time. It is now quite possible to simulate developmental events by modelling a group of cells with a computer, and to build in to the program factors allowing the rate of mitosis, the migration of cells, and other factors to be varied either together or independently. One such simulation was performed by Ede and Law (1969). They set out to model limb shapes. In such a model the area (the studies are far more easily performed in two dimensions than in three) which the 'cells' could occupy was limited by the capacity of their computer to an array of 80 X 80 spaces (equivalent to 100 chess boards). The resolution of this model is such that one computer 'cell' was equivalent to about 100 actual cells.

Ede and Law started out with a line of 40 cells placed in the centre of one edge of the array, representing the flank mesoderm. The computer was instructed to scan the array repeatedly counting cells, and to cause each rth cell to divide. The two products of cell division were placed one in the original space occupied by the dividing cell, and the other in the nearest available empty space. Mitotic rate could be changed by altering the value of r. In practice (Fig. 6.3), the model produced a simple beehive-shaped mass which corresponds quite well with the chick limb bud up to stage 22, where the mitotic index is uniform throughout (Fig. 6.6; Janners and Searls 1970; Hornbruch and Wolpert 1970). To obtain a simulation of further development another factor had to be added. The mitotic rate was changed, not uniformly by varying r, but by making r have different values in different parts of the array; that is, by introducing a gradient of mitotic index. When this was done, and a small amount of distal migration built in to the model (by making the second division product of a cell move one or two rows distally before looking for a space) further limb-like shapes were produced (Fig. 6.4).

Later modelling of the shape of the limb became more sophisticated. Wilby

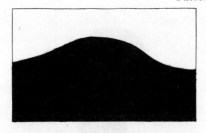

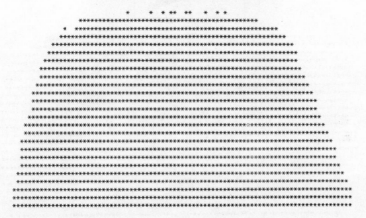

FIG. 6.3. Ede and Law's computer simulation of chick limb development (*below*) was able to produce a beehive-shaped mass similar to the 3-day chick limb bud (*above*).

and Ede (1975) compared outlines of growing chick limb buds by superimposing tracings of them so as to maximize the concentricity of the distal tips and the alignment of growth axes, and to minimize the overlap between outlines (Fig. 6.5). Doing this enabled the growth of the limb bud to be seen as (a) an initial polarized distal expansion phase (stages 18-24), (b) a proximal elongation phase (stages 24-30), (c) a more uniform distal expansion phase (stages 26-30). Distinct gradients in mitotic rate are found in practice (Fig. 6.6) in both subapical and differentiating regions. The fact that removal of the AER halts distal expansion but does not interfere with proximal elongation (Saunders 1948; Summerbell 1974*b*) suggests that the two phases of growth might be differently controlled, the AER exerting an effect on distal expansion while the proximal tissue develops autonomously.

Wilby and Ede used a two-dimensional model, and simulated control of cell division by an all-or-none method, i.e. certain cells were 'allowed' to divide by the computer, others not. An array of 60 × 60 'cells' was used, starting from a central row of 10 on the left-hand edge, a scale of approximately 1 : 100. An added sophistication is that, where Ede and Law's earlier model found the nearest free space after division and placed a daughter cell in it, the later model

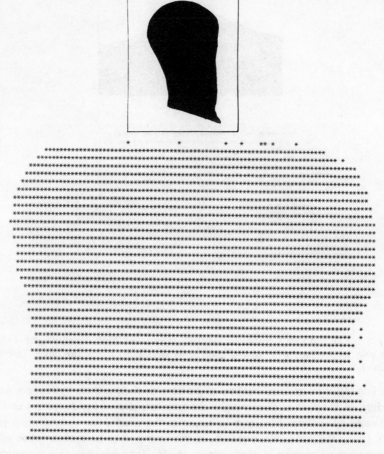

FIG. 6.4. A rather more sophisticated program (which included factors for distal migration and for regional variation in rates of cell division) allowed the production of an elongated stem region capped by a digital plate (*below*) similar to the 5-day chick limb bud (*above*). (After Ede and Law 1969.)

finds the nearest free space, then juggles the cells already present, by the shortest possible route, so that daughter cells stay adjacent to each other. The type of simulation produced is seen in Fig. 6.7.

We have seen that, using mitotic index alone, successful simulation of limb development does not proceed very far, but that when distal migration has been built into the system, a later stage limb bud is simulated. Ede and Law (1969) also tried the effect of changing the rate of distal migration in their computer model. If it was reduced, the limb bud became broader and shorter, of a type resembling that of the *talpid* mutant which develops extreme polydactyly from its initially broad limb buds (Fig. 6.8). *In vitro* investigation of the behaviour of

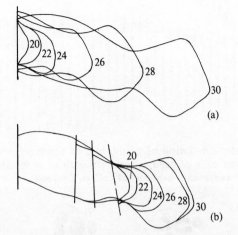

(a)

(b)

FIG. 6.5. Growth patterns of the chick limb. Tracings of the outlines of stages 20–30 chick hindlimbs may be superimposed in various ways. In (a) the super-imposition is such that all limbs are assigned a common baseline. In (b) the limb buds are aligned more realistically to give maximum correspondence of major axis and maximum overlap. This demonstrates the relative lack of change in the footplate at later stages and the great elongation of the proximal region. (After Ede 1976*b*.)

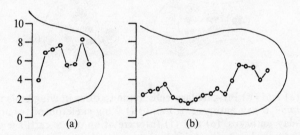

(a)   (b)

FIG. 6.6. Mitotic index (scale is in dividing cells per hundred) at different levels of stage 23 (a) and stage 29 (b) chick wing buds. Note the association in (b) of low mitotic index with chondrogenesis proximally. (After Wilby and Ede 1976.)

talpid limb mesenchyme cells showed that they were more adhesive and less motile than normal cells (Fig. 6.9) (Ede and Agerbak 1968; Ede and Flint 1975*a, b*). It is thus possible to show that, in this mutant, a defect in cell behaviour, presumably affecting the cell surface and inhibiting outward migration of limb mesenchyme, is related to the emerging limb shape. Computer simulation studies thus support this interpretation by providing a model which confirms that small changes in outward cell migration will produce consequent changes in limb bud outline.

It should be borne in mind that not only cell division, motility, and adhesiveness play a governing role in shaping the limb bud. Cell death is another cellular activity by which the limb bud is shaped (Chapter 3.9). Indeed, the broad limb

FIG. 6.7. Computer simulation of a limb bud of the type produced by Ede and Law when daughter cells of each mitosis are allowed to remain adjacent to each other (see text). * represents a quiescent cell; o, a mitosis.

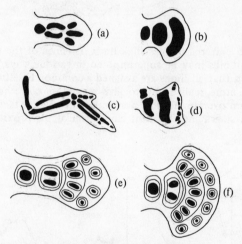

FIG. 6.8. (a) and (b) Pre-cartilage cell condensations in wing buds of (a) normal and (b) *talpid³* 6-day embryos. (c) and (d) Wing skeleton of (c) normal and (c) *talpid³* 11-day embryos. (e) and (f) Interpretation of pre-cartilage condensation fields in (e) normal and (f) *talpid³* limb buds. Cells migrate from the outer circle to the inner black region in normal, but in *talpid³* cells, movement is inhibited and they do not reach the inner region. (After Ede and Kelly 1964; Ede 1971.)

buds of the *talpid* mutant may result partly from inhibited outward migration, partly from the survival of pre- and post-axial mesenchyme normally dying.

This sort of computer model, programmed to take into account rates of cell division and migration, produces an adequate facsimile of limb bud shape. We can also see how varying these factors alters limb bud shape and thus mimics mutant development, suggesting these rates are under strict genetic control. The next step in patterning involves changes of cell type within the mesoderm.

6.5. What governs condensation?

We can rephrase this question in more general terms and ask 'What sorts of

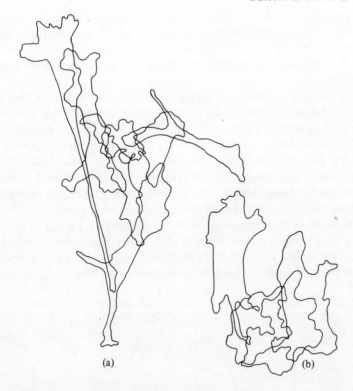

(a)   (b)

FIG. 6.9. Tracings from time-lapse cine film superimposed to show movement of (a) normal and (b) *talpid³* mutant limb bud mesenchyme cells in culture over the same time period. (After Ede 1974.)

properties do cells have that can affect their behaviour towards other cells?' Let us look at a series of simple experiments. A number of cells (in relative terms, say 1 million) of differing types can be mixed together in the laboratory and encouraged to survive by supplying a suitable environment. The cells aggregate together, at first in twos and threes, and then in larger numbers. Eventually, they segregate into regions containing only one cell type (Moscona 1960), or of different cell types arranged in a particular way; if placed within ectoderm jackets even further differentiation occurs if these aggregates are grown in suitable places (such as the chorio-allantois of the chick) and very complete organs may be formed (Zwilling 1964*b*; Pautou 1973). What the cells recognize as 'like' for sorting purposes seems to vary. In a mixture of kidney and chondrogenic tissue from both mouse and chick, aggregates were made up of kidney cells (from both animals) or chondrogenic cells. In other experiments using cells from various newts, aggregation was according to species. How the cells 'recognize' each other remains an open question, but we do know that the recognition can vary with time. Curtis (1961) found that *Xenopus* embryonic cells disaggregated in mid-blastula stage normally reaggregate with ectoderm outside, endoderm inside and mesoderm between the two. If the ectoderm is allowed to reaggregate alone for 4 hours before the other tissues are added, the resultant mass has a mesodermal core with a mixed ectodermal and endodermal coating, and after 6 hours the endoderm is outside, mesoderm inside, and ectoderm forms the middle layer.

Cell adhesiveness seems to be highly specific, but do 'like' cells have regions which fit exactly in some way on to other cells of the same kind, as in lock and key or antigen and antibody, or is the property just unspecific stickiness? Whatever the mechanism, a mass of cells with differing adhesive properties would eventually sort themselves out into cell types. Embryonic cells which stay together over a long period tend to reinforce this adhesiveness by developing more elaborate fixing devices, complicated interdigitations of membrane or connecting bars resembling the desmosomes seen in adult tissues.

An increase in adhesiveness amongst the members of a group of cells would lead to progressively greater areas of their membranes coming into contact and the cells would be drawn closer together. This in fact is a formal description of the process of condensation seen in precartilaginous (Fig. 6.10, Plates 6–8) or

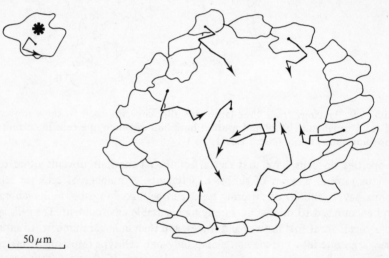

50 μm

FIG. 6.10. Outlines of cells drawn from the projection of films of the development of a condensation in a culture of normal limb mesenchyme cells. The outlines are taken from a frame at the beginning of each film. Outlined cells are at the periphery of the condensation. The path which each cell (marked at the beginning of the path with a dot) followed during approximately 30 hours of culture is indicated by a series of lines. Three groups of cells were followed: those at the perimeter of the condensation, those at its centre, and those away from it (starred). Note the inward migration of the peripheral cells. (From Ede *et al.* 1977.)

premuscular blastemata. Could localized changes in adhesion produce blastemata? Anikin (1929) described the appearance of the condensations forming the digits within the limb bud of the newt. Each of the five digital condensations is small at first, starting with a single row of cells. When other cells joined the condensation, Anikin noted that their nuclei showed a variety of deformations from the kidney shape seen in the original row of cells (Fig. 6.11) which he was able to

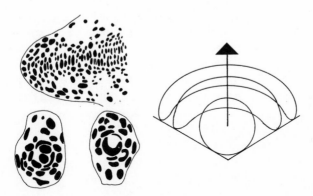

FIG. 6.11. Shapes of nuclei in the pre-cartilage cells of a longitudinal section (*left, above*) and two transverse sections (*left, below*) of a toe of a developing newt. *Right,* Anikin (1929) supposed that these compressed nuclear shapes were generated by movement of nuclei away from a central axis, and represented his ideas graphically.

describe geometrically, and that the cells formed the swirling pattern later described in other blastemata (Ede 1976*b*). Surely the explanation of this is simple. The original line of cells had sub-spherical nuclei; peripheral cells are simply flattened so as to present as great an area of cell contact as possible. The cells are concavo-convex in cross-section, and their nuclei are deformed accordingly, simply reflecting the cell configuration.

Searls (1972, 1973) has examined the hypothesis that the condensing cells might show specifically different adhesive properties from the undifferentiated mesenchyme of the limb bud. He tested the ability of single cell suspensions from various sources in the chick limb to segregate according to origin. Not surprisingly, late stages of differentiation were able to segregate. Thus, 7-day limb cartilage cells segregated from 12-day muscle cells, and both these cell types segregated from undifferentiated mesenchyme. But chondrogenic cells from stages 24 and 25, and even as late as 26 when matrix is present, were unable to segregate from stage 20–22 limb bud mesenchyme. The ability of chondrogenic cells to segregate thus appears as a late feature of differentiation, after cytodifferentiation has begun. It may be that the adhesive changes in the condensing cells are too subtle to be identified in this experimental test of segregation capacities.

At this point it is worth digressing to consider a process analogous to condensation in a different but well-studied organism. *Dictyostelium discoideum* is a slime mould. Part of the life history of this organism is spent as a collection of free-living amoeboid cells, part as a slug or grex. The similarity with the limb bud lies in the aggregation of the amoebae which occurs when food reserves are depleted. During this aggregation *in vitro* on plates of nutrient agar, the cells form circular or spiral patterns resembling those seen in a cartilaginous condensation. In *Dictyostelium* the mechanism is known. Certain cells (and it is not known what makes these cells special) are believed to produce cyclic pulses of AMP. Cells within a certain threshold of this initiating cell respond by relaying the signal; they produce a pulse of AMP too, and move towards the signal. Cells further from the signal origin do not relay it, but simply move towards the source (Durston 1973). If the source is a point source (i.e. one cell) signalling at regular intervals, it will produce a circular wave (Fig. 6.12) of a fixed wavelength.

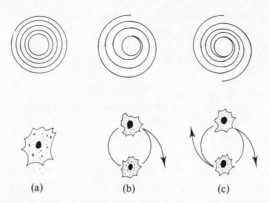

(a)   (b)   (c)

FIG. 6.12. Aggregation in slime moulds, a process perhaps analogous to condensation, is governed by signals sent out by certain cells. A single signalling cell (a) may produce a series of circular wavefronts like ripples in a pond. Two or more signalling cells can generate a single spiral wavefront (b) or a nest of interlocking spirals (c).

Adjacent cells all signalling, however, would tend to form a closed loop. If one signal is relayed around and around, a single spiral wavefront will radiate from the loop. If more than one, then multiple 'nested' spirals will form. Also pairs of opposed spirals could be generated from pairs of opposed signalling loops. All these classes have been observed in *Dictyostelium*.

By analogy it has been suggested that the three-dimensional aggregation of cells around a condensation centre in a hand or a foot is generated in the same way, simply because the pattern generated is similar. There is no evidence to suggest that blastemal core cells secrete cyclic AMP, but it does look as if they secrete something — a product which changes the behaviour and properties of adjacent cells. Ede *et al.* (1977) showed that re-aggregating chick cells grown in culture formed chondrogenic foci, and that surrounding cells moved towards these growing foci in a rather zig-zag pattern (Fig. 6.10). Cells near the centre of a condensation travelled at the same speed but followed a circular path. This is comparable with the behaviour of *Dictyostelium* amoebae. Toole

(1972) considers the condensation involves cell immobilization following removal by hyaluronidase of hyaluronate whose presence is associated with cell mobility (reviewed, Hall 1978).

Once again, the *talpid³* mutant provides an interesting 'control' to compare with normal condensation. Abnormal cell behaviour can be seen to result in aberrant condensation. The *talpid* mutant has not merely a very broad limb bud, but in addition the pattern of both the pre-cartilage condensations and chondrogenic elements is affected. Both of these are poorly defined, and elements along the same antero-posterior axis are fused (e.g. radius-ulna, carpals, and metacarpals form three broad bands — see Fig. 6.8), while distally there are ill-defined polydactylous digits. As we know, *talpid* mesenchyme cells are more adhesive and less motile than normal. Ede (1971) argues that this probably accounts for the failure to form well-defined condensations, in that the aggregation movements may be insufficient to establish a clear separation between neighbouring rudiments. Rather similar evidence comes from studies on the mouse by Elmer (1976) on the *brachypod* mutation and by Flint (1977) on the *amputated* mutant. In the *brachypod* mutant, the limbs (especially the hind) are micromelic, the distal skeletal elements being particularly affected, and the blastemal condensations abnormally small (see Chapter 7). *In vitro* studies showed that *brachypod* limb bud mesenchyme failed to aggregate normally, forming only irregular clusters rather than typical cartilage nodules. Elmer concludes that the *brachypod* cell surface has been altered so that cell adhesion is disturbed, thus causing anomalous development. Deviation from normal cell surface properties which appear to be genetically controlled thus has dramatic effects on the emerging chondrogenic pattern.

In normal condensations, this change in adhesiveness, or more accurately in cell-to-cell contact, has been reported in detail in pre-chondrogenic cells (Thorogood and Hinchliffe (1975), though see Searls *et al.* (1972) for a contrary view). In areas of prospective cartilage the cells undergo a substantial change in their contacts with each other. During the stages when these cells (which may become either chondroblasts or fibroblasts) are capable of becoming cartilage if left *in situ* or of becoming fibroblasts if moved to a prospective soft tissue area (Searls 1967), contacts between cells are mediated through long, thin filopodia and there is extensive intercellular space. In later stages the cells have large areas of close surface contact and become closely packed (Plates 7 and 8). This change may be interpreted as a consequence of differentiation of pre-cartilage cells, or as an obligatory step in the process. If it is obligatory, then we have an answer to the problem of why pre-chondroblasts cultured at low density will not form cartilage (Newman 1977).

Subsequently, of course, the phenotypes of cartilage cells and fibroblasts diverge even more. We may follow this step by looking at the way in which the collagen produced varies. Both condroblasts and fibroblasts produce collagen, but the type of collagen differs. Fibroblasts produce collagen described as $[\alpha 1(1)_2 \alpha 2]$, that is with two different protein chains, presumably produced by two different genes. Cartilage produces $[\alpha1(11)]_3$ collagen, containing only the $\alpha1(11)$ sub-chain. If cells are grown in culture, the $\alpha1:\alpha2$ chain ratio can be obtained, and used as an indicator of cell type. Mesoderm of an appropriate stage cultured intact shows a rise in this ratio from the 2:1 characteristic of fibroblasts to 10:1 or higher (Newman 1977), indicating that most of the collagen being synthesized is of the cartilage type. Cultured at low density, cells from a piece of mesoderm retain a fibroblastic 2:1 ratio. This is only one of a number of changes seen in the cells at a biochemical level.

Notwithstanding these indications of biochemical divergence, the aspect of the phenotype or pre-chondrogenic cells which interests us at present is a physical one, or more accurately a biochemical one resulting in a simple change in cellular behaviour since what causes cells to aggregate is a change in their surface properties. Pattern, in this instance, seems to be expressing itself as a change in the adhesiveness of certain cells (Anikin's original line of pre-blastemal cells) which seem to involve other cells around themselves at second hand.

Once again we have had to introduce an element of non-uniformity. In the production of mesodermal condensations we have specified that some cells were stickier than others, just as in Ede and Law's model we had to specify that some cells divided more often than others. These seem to be two of the conditions which govern the formation of our condition generated pattern. This non-uniformity could arise in two different ways. Whatever 'tells' the cells to divide more often, or to become sticky, could reside within the cells, or be imposed from outside them. The cells which form the heart of a mesodermal condensation could be older or younger than their fellows (in terms of cell divisions) or they could have originated from a slightly different place in the embryo. They could form a clone, a group of descendents from one original cell which was quite literally switched on to become cartilage. The alternative view is that cells which find themselves in a particular location, which is destined to become cartilage, differentiate as cartilage cells. Similarly, mitotic rate, which remains higher in later sub-ridge mesoderm than elsewhere (Ede 1971), could be elevated either by a morphogen, a product of the AER which affects sub-adjacent mesoderm cells, or could be higher in this area because the cells ancestral to those which form the sub-ridge mesoderm had been programmed to divide a little more frequently than their fellows.

6.5.1. *The overall pattern of condensation*

While the cell behaviour which leads to the formation of individual condensations is by now reasonably well-understood, what determines the overall pattern of condensations within the limb remains essentially unknown. One feature which stands out is that the number of condensations formed in the pentadactyl limb is related to the width of the limb bud, or at least to the ratio of antero-posterior (AP) axis to dorso-ventral (DV). When the limb bud is essentially circular in cross-section, as it is proximally in the stylopod, one element (femur or humerus) is formed. Where the AP axis is perhaps twice the DV, two elements are formed, as in the zeugopodium, while where the AP axis is much greater than the DV, as in the autopod, four or five elements are formed.

Mutants also support the idea that the number of chondrogenic elements is related to limb bud width. In extreme forms of winglessness in the chick, where the leg bud is reduced in width due to increased ANZ area, the leg may have only 2 or 3 digits instead of the normal 4 (Hinchliffe and Ede 1973). On the other hand, if the distal part of the limb bud is broader than normal, then polydactyly results. This is shown clearly by the *talpid* mutant in the chick and also by polydactylous mutants of the mouse such as *extra-toes* (Johnson 1967).

Regular spacing of condensations is a property even of isolated limb mesenchyme which no longer has any points of reference within the limb. Thus Ede (1971) found that dissociated limb mesenchyme cells following re-aggregation formed spaced chondrogenic centres whose number was related to the width of the aggregate. The same rule is followed whether the cells are within or outside the limb.

Impressive evidence of a spacing mechanism is provided by experiments of Pautou (1973) in which limb mesenchyme cells from two avian species were disaggregated, mixed, and rejacketed in an ectodermal cap. Limbs developed which lacked specifically identifiable digits, perhaps because such points of reference as the ZPA has been lost. But the cartilage clearance preparations showed clearly that, as these limbs broadened out from the base, so the number of digital rays increased (Fig. 6.13). Ability to form spaced condensations thus appears to be a fundamental property of limb mesenchyme, expressed in a number of abnormal situations.

FIG. 6.13. Experimental limb skeletons obtained by Pautou (1973) from mixed chick/duck leg bud mesenchyme cells.

6.6. Intrinsic patterns and development

The suggestion that the fate of a particular group of cells depends on their cell lineage follows from a large body of work which suggests that, in development, nuclear activity and, more specifically, gene-directed synthesis of macromolecules, is controlled by factors in the cytoplasm. Gurdon's (1974) elegant nuclear transplantation experiments show that at least some differentiated cell nuclei, such as those from tadpole gut epithelial cells, are totipotent, i.e. they have the capacity to support the whole range of cellular differentiation when placed in the cytoplasm of the unfertilized *Xenopus* egg. In other experiments, nuclei from cells which normally synthesize RNA had this activity repressed when transplanted to egg cytoplasm. Early *Xenopus* eggs do not synthesize RNA. Since many aspects of development are controlled by similar interactions *within* the cell, Bonner (1952) has argued in the following way: first, that differentiation consists of an ordered sequence of repression and de-repression of genes. If changed circumstances are imposed upon a differentiated region, a different pathway may be selected, and different genes repressed and de-repressed. Secondly, that the normal result of the sequential switching of these genes is a flower or a foot. Thirdly, that the formation of a flower or a foot is one of a series of sub-routines constituting the life-cycle of an organism. For a plant, he suggested the sub-routines of Table 6.1 were necessary.

TABLE 6.1. Sub-routines required for the execution of the plant life cycle (after Bonner 1952)

Sub-routine		
	1	Cell life
	2	Embryonic development
	3	How to be a seed
	4	Bud development
	5	Leaf development
	6	Stem development
	7	Root development
	8	Reproduction development

If we accept all, or even some, of Bonner's views on the nature of pattern formation, with their implicit assumption that the pattern is specified from within the cell, then we must also accept the proposition that clonal development is important in embryology. The progeny of a single cell forms a clone. During a period of development, when cell proliferation predominates over cell movement, most of a clone will stay together. If two adjacent clones had differing instructions, say to become chondrocytes or to become fibrocytes, then the spatial distribution of the clones would be conditional for the formation of a pattern. If we accept that clones can give rise to patterns, then cloning should be demonstrable in the developing embryo.

In recent years it has become possible to investigate the presence or absence of clones by manufacturing chimeric mice. A chimera, in this sense, is an embryo which is formed from cells derived from two zygotes, and which consequently has four parents (McLaren 1976). If we make such a mouse (say) by fusing early embryonic stages of two or four cells, then the chimeric mouse will differ in the genetic make-up of many of its differentiated parts. Because the fusion was made so early, clones derived from a single cell will resemble one or other of the original zygotes in genetical make-up, and the mouse will be 'patchy' for one or other parental genotype. It should, therefore, be possible to identify such clones, if they are provided with suitable genetic markers. This technique has been widely applied with success for such markers as coat colour and various enzyme phenotypes. Moore and Mintz (1972) extended this concept, and took as their marker the vertebral shape of two inbred strains of mice. When chimeras were made between these strains, it was possible to classify each half of each vertebra as belonging to one or other parental strain. Most vertebrae were symmetrical, and there were strong correlations between neighbouring vertebrae. Moore and Mintz were able to hypothesize that each vertebra was formed from a minimum of four clones of cells. As each vertebra is made up of one posterior half somite and one anterior half somite, this implies that somites may also be made up of a minimum of four clones: the important fact is they they are clonal. These observations on mammals are especially illuminating in the light of the influence which the somitic mesoderm has over limb development. We saw in Chapter 3 that the somite makes a contribution to the muscles of the limb, but there is also evidence that it may be important in pattern determination. Agnish and Kochhar (1977) grew mouse forelimb buds, both with and without adjacent somites. Limb differentiation was much better if the somites were left attached to the limb buds, when girdle elements, humerus, radius, ulna and a condensation representing digits were formed. Without somites only a cartilage mass formed, or, at best, a small scapula and thin humerus.

This evidence does not stand alone. Pinot (1970) found that in the chick the stimulatory action of somites was restricted to those adjacent to the limbs, and Raynaud (1977) was able to show that the excision of somites adjacent to the presumptive limb region of the lizard, *Lacerta viridis,* inhibited the usual thickening of the somatopleure and formation of the apical ectodermal ridge. Interestingly, this thickening and the AER formation did take place in the region of somites left intact immediately behind the operation site. Other workers have also suggested somitic influence on the limb bud (Kieny 1971; Raynaud and Adrian 1975) and we have already discussed the chick/quail transplants of Christ *et al.* (1977) (described in Chapter 4) which show that the limb musculature (though not the tendons) is of somitic origin. Chevallier (1977), using similar techniques, demonstrated that, in addition, somites contribute to the scapula, while clavicle, coracoid, sternum, and pelvic girdle all take origin from lateral plate mesoderm. In fact, the contributions to the scapula from the somites could be recognized at 2 days of incubation, i.e. before somitic segmentation occurs, and ahead of muscular determination. There is thus considerable evidence that the somites make a clonal contribution to limb development, supporting Newman's (1977) view that there are two main cell lines: one somatopleural chondrogenic and fibroblastic, and the other somitic and myogenic.

6.7. Signals and signalling

The second of our alternatives, that instructions are impressed upon the cells from without rather than from within, is currently the subject of intense discussion and has given rise to a number of models of limb development.

6.7.1. *The existence of pre-patterns*

The more conventional explanations of the genesis of pattern (Turing 1952; Stern 1968; Maynard Smith 1960; Gmitro and Scriven 1966; Waddington 1962) involve postulating the distribution throughout a field of one or more chemical messages or morphogens. The features represented within the pattern depend upon features present in the prepattern. Thus, a digit which is to appear in the pattern must be represented by a local increase, or perhaps decrease, in morphogen. Turing (1952) showed how two morphogens initially evenly distributed in a given field would eventually come to equilibrium. A sudden increase in the concentration of either morphogen would create a disturbance which led, in some cases and in some places, to a long-lasting increase or decrease in morphogen concentration. The re-arranged distribution of morphogens was usually in the form of random spots (Fig. 6.14), but in some cases periodic patterns

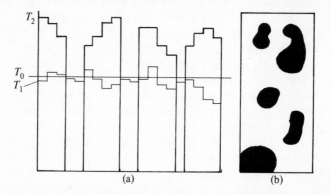

(a)   (b)

FIG. 6.14. Turing (1952) was able to show (a) that a morphogen initially distributed between a row of cells (concentration 1.0 units at time T_0) need not remain homogeneous but could, over a period of time (T_1, T_2), develop discontinuities. In a two-dimensional field (b) two morphogens could become distributed in such a way as to form a spotted pattern.

were formed. Bard and Lauder (1974) have pointed out, however, that Turing's model is complex and suggested that it has insufficient precision to generate a series of digits. To give greater precision Goodwin and Cohen (1969) suggested a 'thunder and lightning' model based on the generation of two waves of different velocities from a boundary perimeter cell. One wave (the faster, equivalent to the light of a lightning flash) would reach a given point ahead of a second, slower wave (the sound of the thunder). A cell could then receive information by sensing the lag between the arrival of the two waves, just as starting to count when we see a lightning flash and stopping when we hear thunder tells us how far off the lightning is. This model would, of course, operate in a two-dimensional field (Wolpert 1971).

Wilby and Ede (1975) suggest a Turing-style method of generating a periodic pattern based on standing waves (Fig. 6.15). This pattern is generated by the following set of rules:

(1) cells are sensitive to their internal concentration of freely diffusible morphogen M;

(2) at concentrations of M below a lower threshold T_1 cells are inactive;

(3) at concentrations of M between T_1 and T_2 cells make M;

(4) at concentrations of M above T_2 cells destroy M;

(5) transformation in inactive to active and active to destructive are irreversible.

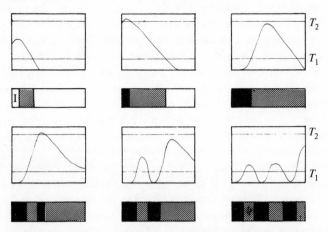

FIG. 6.15. The development of Wilby and Ede's periodic gradient. I = initator, black = destruction, stippled = synthesis. For further explanation, see text.

Computer simulation techniques have enabled investigation of the results of applying these rules to a one-dimensional array, and by implication to the developing limb (Ede 1976*b*). An initiator region proves to be essential, since without it random initiation produces the same periodicity but with variable positioning of the peaks. The initiator region propagates a constant velocity wave of M. The first gradient peak grows behind the wave front and then splits in two as the upper threshold is attained and destruction triggered. As determined by the rules, interactions of destruction, synthesis, and diffusion cause the 'trailing' peak to move backwards and downwards until it stabilizes, while the 'leading peak' moves forwards and upwards until it sets in train the same cycle of destruction behind the wave front. The end result is a periodic gradient initiating a periodic pattern. Thus, given an initiator region (the ZPA?), and applying the rules just described, we have a model which could control programmes of growth and differentiation needed to produce, say, the spaced chondrogenic elements of the digits.

6.7.2. *Positional information*

As long ago as 1900, Driesch formulated the view that development was a function of position, based on his experimental studies on regulation of isolated blastomeres of sea-urchin embryos. Recently, embryologists attempting to explain pattern, perhaps disappointed by the insights provided by molecular biology into this field, have returned to this view, that 'developing cells know their position' (Wolpert).

Wolpert (1969, 1971) argues that the existence of a pre-pattern is not necessary to govern the formation of a pattern. He states the problem of pattern in one dimension as follows: given a line of cells, intercommunication between them, and that each has the capability of differentiating into one of three states, described for purposes of discussion as blue, white or red, how do we ensure that a tricolour is always formed no matter how many cells are in the line (Fig. 6.16(a))? The solution is positional information; each cell is assigned, by appropriate signals, a position with respect to the two ends of the line. The cells interpret this signal by turning on appropriate genes and becoming red, white or blue. Wolpert takes a universalist view, that all positional fields are the same in essence, differing only in size and boundary conditions. What varies is the response of the cells. Neural tissue transplanted to a foreign site might thus differentiate as forebrain if placed in a proximal position, and hindbrain if placed distally. Wolpert (1971) estimated that the size of the field might be of the order of 50 cells, or 1 mm^2, and gives examples of many fields of this order of magnitude. Crick (1971) has argued that, for fields of this size, a very simple signal, governed by diffusion, would suffice. On this hypothesis, the signal substance would diffuse from its source at one end of the gradient to a sink at the other end which mops up or inactivates the signal. In such conditions a gradient of signal molecule will be set up which will soon stabilize. Munrow and Crick (1971) investigated the physics of this model and found that for a signal of molecular weight of about 500 a gradient would stabilize over a field of 1 mm in a few hours.

It has been pointed out (Wilby and Ede 1975) that a single linear gradient, although simple in theory and therefore good as a model, does involve practical difficulties. If we think of the long axis of the limb as a series of cartilages with non-cartilaginous regions between (Fig. 6.16(b), then to produce three bands of cartilage six thresholds must be recognized by the cells of the mesoderm — T1– T2, T3–T4, T5–T6 specifying cartilage and T2–T3 and T4–T5 non-cartilage. If the six cartilaginous regions of the chick are to be specified, a very stable and rather complex system is needed.

Positional information in the chick limb. The concept of positional information was applied to the chick limb by Summerbell, Lewis, and Wolpert (1973). They proposed the idea of a two stage process, specification of position followed by appropriate differentiation by the cells concerned. The initial positional information model had to be modified because of an important property of limb buds: they grow. It was suggested that the key to positional specification was an area of mesoderm, the 'progress zone' lying beneath the apical ectodermal ridge. The AER is thought of simply as a means of preserving the progress zone rather than

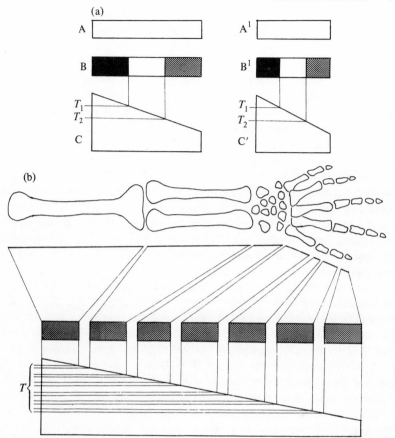

FIG. 6.16(a). The French flag problem. A line of cells (A) or a rather shorter line (A^1) differentiates so that one third of each is blue (left), white (centre) or red (right) respectively. This may be achieved if the cells interpret their position on a simple gradient (C, C^1) with fixed boundaries, the ultimate 'colour' of the cell being determined by the thresholds T_1, T_2 for the blue-white, white-red transformations. (After Wolpert.)

FIG. 6.16(b). The concept of positional information as applied to the generalized tetrapod limb. If each segment of the limb is represented by a 'colour' of the French flag, then one obvious problem is the large number of thresholds (T) involved.

determining mesenchyme differentiation patterns. As the limb grows, positional values are assigned by the progress zone to cells leaving it, and these values become progressively more distal with the passage of time. At the same time, the progress zone serves as a source of new cells. Cell division could (and does) also occur outside the progress zone.

In this model the positional value of any cell depends on how long it has spent within the progress zone. If the rate of change of the signal is linked in some way to cell division, then growth and pattern would be interlocked, and pattern would always be appropriate to the size of the system. Changes in external temperature, for instance, would not affect the pattern of a developing anuran limb.

In fact, this model fits the longitudinal outgrowth of the chick wing quite well. The primordia of proximal elements are laid down before those of distal ones, and the proximal end of each primordium before its distal end. Below the AER is a zone of mesoderm which seems to remain undifferentiated until around stage 28 and proliferates fairly rapidly; this is interpreted by Summerbell *et al.* as the progress zone. Rubin and Saunders (1972) showed by transplantation that variation in the age of the AER alone did not change the fate of the sub-ridge mesoderm. But what happens if the ridge and progress zone are transplanted together? According to the model, grafting on a late host limb bud stump to produce limb buds with additional prospective areas should result in limbs with skeletal duplications. Experimental limb buds lacking prospective areas should lack the corresponding skeletal parts (see Chapter 4.10). In the hands of Wolpert's school, in fact, these predictions are realized, but experiments carried out in France (Hampé 1959; Kieny 1964*a, b*; Kieny and Pautou 1976) have not confirmed their findings. Kieny found that chick limb bud regulated well for defects or for serially repeated excess material. According to Summerbell *et al.*, the defect regulation was due to the fact that the width of the grafting pieces used by French investigators was less than the depth (claimed to be 0.3 mm) to which the influence of the AER penetrates the mesoderm. Thus, they argue that the AER could have reacted with the host stump, rendering positional information values in it labile. But this explanation is not altogether convincing. First, many of Kieny's experiments (Kieny and Pautou 1976) involve grafting of whole early limb buds, whose proximo-distal axis is considerably greater than 0.3 mm. Regulation in these experiments is clearly taking place in regions beyond the reach of the progress zone. Moreover, when Kieny grafted a prospective autopod to stylopod, so that prospective zeugopod was absent, the intercalated zeugopod which appeared was made up of both stump and graft cells. According to the progress zone theory, stump cells already specified as stylopod by a number of divisions in the progress zone would not be expected to form more proximal zeugopodal material. Equally, graft cells (prospective for distal differentiation) adjacent to the stump are capable of being reprogrammed to form structures more proximal then their normal fate. This result cannot be explained satisfactorily by the 'progress zone' theory.

The concept of distal addition of new territory to the limb has also been challenged. It has been established by means of carbon particles inserted into the mesenchyme of developing limbs (Saunders 1948) that proximal territories were represented in limb buds but not distal ones, as carbon particles could subsequently not be found in the most distal areas. A more direct study by Stark and Searls (1973) using ^{3}H-thymidine as a label, showed that prospective hand cells could be located as a narrow (3-5 cells wide) strip of apical mesoderm.

Each region localized in their fate map grows, but the more distal the region the longer it continues to grow.

Faber (1971) has recently proposed a modification of Wolpert's ideas on positional information, which has itself been further modified by Stocum (1975). Faber takes as a starting point Wolpert's original model, with the boundaries of the limb field formed by the AER and the cells of the flank, with the former as a source and the latter as sink. Wolpert's gradient was uniform throughout; Faber's has a definite peak during growth which is induced by the AER in the mesoderm beneath it (Fig. 6.17). At early stages of development the gradient would be very

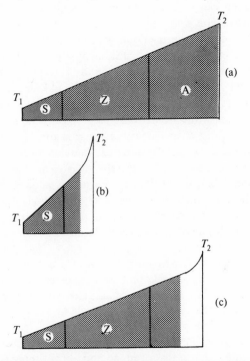

FIG. 6.17. Positional information in the limb according to Faber (1971). In the adult limb (a) the positional gradient rises uniformly from T_1 at the base to T_2 at the tip of the digits. S = stylopod, Z = zeugopod, A = autopod. At two intermediate stages of development (b, c), the values of T_1, T_2 are unaltered but the longitudinal axis is compressed and the gradient rises steeply just below the AER. Shading indicates differentiated tissue.

compressed but all levels would be represented. This is consistent with the ability of transplanted limb discs to self-develop (Harrison 1918; Hamburger 1938; Murray 1926) and with Stark and Searls' labelling experiments (1973). Although a full range of positional information can be read by the cells already present, the values cannot be expressed until growth supplies enough cells to stabilize the pattern. The AER is not assigned any responsibility to maintain an active sub-ridge zone of mesoderm: the mechanism of outgrowth is not specified. Growth is seen by Faber as of two types: the first to establish the pattern, and the second to increase the pattern to its full adult size. The latter is seen as a late-occurring phenomenon, possibly dependent upon systematic factors such as hormones (Williams and Hughes 1977). The steeply rising gradient beneath the AER in this model helps to explain the out-of-phase developments of stylopod and zeugopod. The autopod begins its expansion later than the more proximal areas because its prospective cells are contained in the compressed steepest region of the gradient which itself would not expand until later in development.

Defect regulation can be explained on this model (Fig. 6.19). A distal part brought into contact with a proximal part would steepen the gradient, and result in cells on both sides of the operation site having their positional values re-specified. Intercalation of an additional segment would cause prospective zeugo-pod stump cells to be re-specified as stylopod. This is in accordance with the result of the mixed regenerates of Kieny (1964*a*) and Kieny and Pautou (1976). It should be emphasized that incorporation of defect regulation into the model represents a major departure from Wolpert's progress zone model, according to which programming is irreversible once the 'progress zone' is left.

Because distal parts of undifferentiated limb buds can differentiate when amputated and transferred to a foreign site, it is clear that any non-limb will serve as a proximal boundary or sink; the positional value at that boundary will always be a little lower than that of the base of the bud. Also the part of the gradient remaining after surgical removal of the AER is stable, as the limb elements which do differentiate after such treatment are of normal shape and size.

Positional information and regeneration. If we take the wider view that the initial development of the urodele limb and its power of regeneration are the two sides of the same coin, then a hypothesis like positional information which sets out to explain the genesis of the limb should also be capable of explaining regeneration (Faber 1971).

What actually happens in regenerating urodele limbs has been confused in the past by the regression due to loss of blood and nerve supply (see Chapter 5). It is now clear that regression can be avoided by suitable technical manipulations, and is not part of the regenerative process proper. It need not, therefore, be built into any model of regeneration, although Faber's model, in fact, allows it to be taken into account. During normal limb regeneration (Fig. 6.18) the wound epithelium assumes the distal boundary value, and a new and steeper gradient is established along the limb axis. This will contain only those positional values lost by amputation, and will re-specify the pattern for the missing parts which will regrow exactly in the same way as in the developing limb. Regression can be accounted for like this; if little or no regression occurs, the regenerating blastema would contain all positional values necessary to make a perfect limb. If there was extensive degeneration of the blastema, then the gradient would be disorganized. On reorganization the remaining mesoderm would occupy the

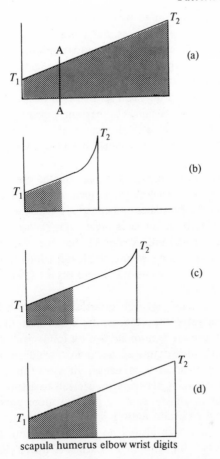

FIG. 6.18. Amputation of the limb according to Faber (1971) at a level AA (a) causes a rapid rise in positional value to T_2 in the blastema (b). This value is retained in the sub-ridge mesoderm during regeneration (b)–(d).

upper part of the gradient and form digits.

The only difference between regenerate and developing limb bud on this hypothesis is that the proximal boundary is constant in the latter but varies in the former according to the level of amputation. Because the regenerate normally contains those structures distal to the level of amputation (Rose 1974), we can suggest that the level of the proximal boundary is governed by a property of the stump cells, and that the stump may signal to the blastema. This idea is reinforced by experiments (de Both 1970; Carlson 1974) suggesting that on occasion blastema cells can form structures *proximal* to their level of origin; the mass of the regenerate may be a factor here (de Both 1970). Some experiments of Stocum (1975a, b) throw some light on this apparent violation of the law of distal transformation (Rose 1962). He found that if undifferentiated wrist blastemata of *Ambystoma maculatum* were grafted on to upper limb stumps (and upper limb blastema on to wrist stumps), more or less perfect regulation occurred in a large number of cases, but there was no violation of the rule of distal transformation. Regeneration differed according to whether the blastema was relocated at a level proximal or distal to its original site. Upper arm blastemata, capable of forming upper arm, arm, and hand were only slightly delayed after grafting on to a wrist stump and formed only hands. There was no evidence of destruction of tissue destined to become upper arm, necrosis or graft resorption. The prospective fate of these grafts had shifted distally due to interaction with the wrist stump, and cells destined to become upper arm in fact became hand.

In the reciprocal experiment, wrist blastematas grafted on to upper arm stumps, regeneration was delayed by a week or more. During this period the upper arm stump de-differentiates and contributes cells to the regenerate. Again, there is little necrosis, the stump cells augmenting rather than replacing the graft cells. Marking with ^{3}H-thymidine showed that the graft cells formed exactly what they would have formed *in situ*, the hand, whilst the stump cells formed the upper arm. Dinsmore (1974) and Iten and Bryant (1973) present very similar sets of experimental data.

Stocum draws a parallel between urodele regeneration and chick regulation experiments. He suggests that the results show that the ultimate proximal boundary of the regenerate is normally set by level specific cell properties, and that interaction with the stump can occur in 'forbidden' situations where the rule of distal transformation is in danger of violation, i.e. where there is a hiccough in the gradient. A blastema transferred to a stump of more proximal positional level cannot regulate so as to produce more proximal structures, but the stump can and does produce distal structures, through intercalary regeneration. When a blastema is transplanted to a more distal stump, it can regulate for excess within itself, deleting unwanted proximal elements (Fig. 6.19).

Maden (1976) suggests a slightly different concept of limb regeneration derived partly from insect regeneration studies (section 6.10). He suggests that the components of adult limb have a positional value which is impressed upon them during development. He gives this information a numerical value with the ectoderm represented by 0 and the limb base by 10. The normal situation is thus:

Ectoderm 0 1 2 3 4 5 6 7 8 9 10

On amputation the ectoderm re-grows over the stump and the situation is then (say)

0 4 5 6 7 8 9 10 or 0 8 9 10

Because there are large steps in this series, Maden suggests that, at cell division in the regeneration blastema, cells whose neighbours on either side differ in positional value by more than 1 follow an 'averaging law' and assume an intermediate value thus:

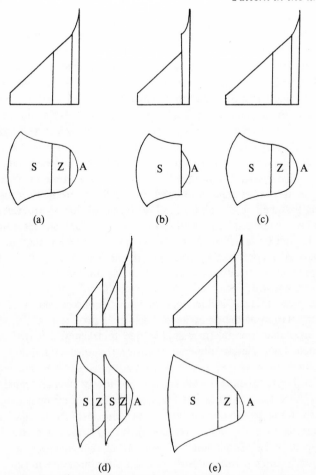

FIG. 6.19. Regulation in the embryonic chick limb bud after grafting, using Faber's modified positional gradient. A normal stage 22 limb bud (a) has a partially extended positional gradient. If the prospective zeugopod is removed (b), the limb regulates (c). If the distal region of one stage 20 limb bud is capped with the whole of another (d, e), then the excess is regulated for by producing a larger than normal stylopod. (After Stocum 1975.)

		0 4	5 6 7 8 9 10								0	8 9 10		
		0 2 4	5 6 7 8 9 10							0 4	8 9 10		
	0 1 2 3 4	5 6 7 8 9 10							0 2 4 6	8 9 10		
(blastema)		(stump)					0 1 2 3 4 5 6 7	8 9 10		
								(blastema)		(stump)	

until the gradient is restored. This implies local negotiation at the cellular level after amputation, and perhaps more fundamentally suggests that the means of creating the gradient during development is not necessarily the same as that used to recreate it during regeneration. This is at odds with a fundamental tenet of those interested in limb development and regeneration: that the two processes are essentially similar.

The joint regions. It is clear that the dorsoventral axis of a developing limb consists of a series of cartilaginous elements and a series of joint regions. We know (or strongly suspect) that the elements are specified by some form of pattern-generating mechanism, but what of the joints? Does a joint merely form in the space between two specified elements or is it itself specified as part of the pattern? At stage 36 in the chick, the elbow region consists of the cartilages of humerus, radius, and ulna separated by a region of flattened, darkly staining cells which will ultimately surround the synovial space. Are these cells flattened by growth of the surrounding primordia, or are they flattened because they are specified as flattened cells? Holder (1977a) reasoned that if structures distal to the elbow joint were surgically removed at an early stage (in fact, stage 24) and the humerus and its joint cap developed normally, then opposed growth could be excluded as a contributing factor in its development. Also, if the elbow region were to be surgically removed at stage 24, and fusion of humerus, radius, and ulna subsequently occurred, the joint could only be formed from joint-determined cells. In fact, Holder was able to demonstrate both of these conditions. Amputation at the elbow level at stage 25 produced subsequent humeri a little shorter than normal (presumably due to trauma) but with lateral and medial epicondyles clearly present. Removing a slice containing the elbow region at stage 24 produced fusion of humerus, radius and ulna as predicted. Wolff (1958) and Hampé (1959) have previously demonstrated that the prospective knee joint in chick has the capacity for self-differentiation at stage 20 (by explanting slices of limb bud to the chorio-allantoic membrane), and Holder suggests that the elbow is determined by stage 24 at the latest, and possibly by stage 19 (Summerbell 1974b). It should, however, be noted that for the French workers the capacity for self-differentiation in limb bud slices does not exclude the capacity for regulation in composite limb buds formed from stage 20–22 material (Kieny 1964a, b). Exclusion of opposed growth as a factor in joint formation is not the same as support for the theory that the joint region is specified at the time it leaves the 'progress zone'.

One surprising feature about the elbow joint is that, although it occupies only a small volume of the adult limb, the prospective elbow forms a substantial fraction of the mesenchymal volume of the early limb bud. Lewis (1977) has shown, using tritiated thymidine labelling, that the forearm region grows between stages 27 and 29 considerably more than the elbow region: at the earlier stage the elbow region is one-third of the volume of the forearm region, but later amounts to only 7 per cent of forearm volume. This phenomenon of differential growth is discussed later in Chapter 7.6.

6.8. The antero-posterior axis

So far we have considered only the proximo-distal axis of the limb, the difference between humerus and finger. But we must also note that there are differences in a second axis at right angles to the first, specifying digit I as opposed to digit V. Once we have a mechanism capable of generating element–space–element–space along the long axis of the limb, we must superimpose a second gradient specifying the number of elements at each level (Fig. 6.20). But an alternative, simpler view is possible. Could not one gradient produce both axes of the pattern?

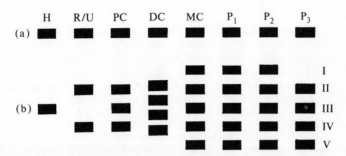

FIG. 6.20. A proximo-distal gradient (a) will specify the different limb segments (H = humerus, R/U = radius/ulna, PC = proximal carpals, DC = distal carpals, MC = metacarpals, P_1–P_3 = phalanges), but a second gradient at right angles to the first is necessary to specify the two-dimensional limb pattern (b).

Wilby and Ede (1975) applied their standing wave pattern (as discussed above) to a two-dimensional limb field, neglecting the dorso-ventral axis (Fig. 6.21). If they placed their source of signal (*M*) along the posterior boundary of the

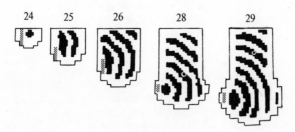

FIG. 6.21. Wilby and Ede's (1976) first attempt to simulate the cartilaginous pattern of the limb produced pattern similar to this (see text). Stippled area = initiator area (equivalent to ZPA).

field (corresponding with the ZPA position), then they produced a series of ever-widening 'ripples of destruction' of *M*. If the axis of orientation is changed, so that the source of *M* is the whole posterior edge of the limb and arrays of cells resembling actual limb shapes are placed within the field, early simulations are encouraging. Outlines of stage 24 or 25 limb buds treated in this way produced parallel proximo-distal 'long bone' elements (Fig. 6.22), but distally there was

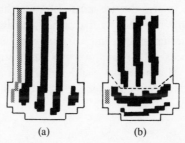

(a)   (b)

FIG. 6.22. Further modifications to simulate more realistic pattern included (a) the extension of the initiator zone to include the whole of the posterior limb edge — this produced a series of proximo-distal 'long bones' but a poor representation of distal areas and (b) the combination of a patterned proximal region (above dotted line) with an unpatterned distal region containing an initiator, and resulting in a series of transverse distal bands. This is due to initiation of the distal pattern by the proximal pattern, which is much more efficient in simulating patterns than the initiator region. (After Ede 1976*b*.)

little resemblance to the real thing. This was unsurprising since time had not been built into the model: the aim was to produce a whole limb pattern in one step, a situation not very close to that found in nature where the pattern gradually arises a little at a time. A modification of the model (Fig. 6.23) consists

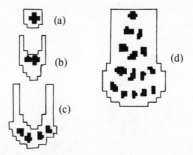

(a)

(b)

(c)

(d)

FIG. 6.23. By far the most realistic patterns were obtained by removing the already differentiated pattern from the field at each stage, i.e. by removing an area corresponding to the previous extent of the limb bud. Thus (a) represents a stage 24 limb bud, (b) a stage 25 minus stage 24, and so on, The final pattern is shown in (d). (After Ede 1976*b*.)

of excising those parts where pattern formation has already occurred from the model. In effect, these are said to be no longer responsive to the ZPA, which is supposed active only on those parts of the limb which are growing. These excised zones can then be re-united to give a representation of the final pattern. In this model, a series of elements is formed resembling quite closely the initial pattern of cartilage condensations. Growth can be added on to the simulation to give even more resemblance to the final limb pattern, but this is not generated by the model.

The effect of changing the limb shape, but keeping the other constants unchanged, has also been tested. In a broadened limb bud a polydactylous pattern is simulated which resembles that found in *talpid*[3] limb development.

This model shows similarities to the proximal/distal positional information one discussed above, but with the gradient along a different axis. It should be noted that *one* gradient will generate a passable two-dimensional representation of the cartilage pattern of the limb. The model predicts that the cartilage pattern is dependent upon limb shape, the position of the initiator region (ZPA) and the rate of synthesis of M. It demands that proximal parts of the pattern are not interfered with by developing distal areas and that M diffuses more readily in an antero-posterior axis than in a proximal distal one.

An alternative model put forward by Tickle, Summerbell, and Wolpert (1975) and Summerbell (1974*a*) is that there are two gradients, the proximo-distal one of Summerbell *et al.* (1973) with a superimposed postero-anterior gradient centred on the ZPA. (Saunders' (1977) reservations about a ZPA role in normal development should be recalled, however.) Tickle noted the findings of Saunders and Gasseling (see Chapter 4) on the grafting of an additional ZPA in to a developing limb bud. When this was added to the pre-axial limb bud border, extra digits were induced; those between the two ZPAs were in mirror-image symmetry (Plate 13). Tickle suggested that the ZPA was a boundary or reference region for the A–P axis of positional information, perhaps a source of diffusible signal substance as suggested by Summerbell's barrier experiments (1979) (see section 4.9). A second ZPA (Fig. 6.24) would induce other digits according to

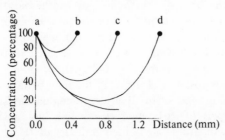

FIG. 6.24. Concentration of a morphogen along the antero-posterior axis. The source (a) at the ZPA is fixed at 100, and other conditions chosen so that 1 mm away the concentration of morphogen is 10. If a second source is incorporated (b, c, d) at various distances from the first, the diffusion gradient is modified.

its distance from the existing field. If 4 is the top value of the gradient, the effect of a second ZPA grafted anteriorly would be seen as initiating in nearby mesoderm a new digit 4. As the two zones moved nearer, between the zones sequences such as Z432234Z, Z4334Z, Z4Z would occur. Tickle was able to graft an additional ZPA at various sites along the pre-axial limb bud apex (using somites as a marker) and obtained most of the predicted results.

Such discrepancies as there were between prediction and experimental result can be explained if the actual shape of the limb bud is considered. First, the AER is not symmetrical (it is larger posteriorly, perhaps because of the presence of the ZPA) and secondly, the presence of a second ZPA interferes with normal growth. Tickle explains that the introduction of a second ZPA anteriorly would, in fact, raise the level of signal midway between the two zones to above digit 2 level, thus preventing formation of anterior digits along the central limb axis and interfering with the experimental testing of the hypothesis. In fact, the extra growth induced by the second ZPA moves the original and transplanted zones further apart and restores an intermediate low level of signal.

Slack (1977*a*, *b*) has re-investigated the antero-posterior polarity of the Axolotl forelimb and pattern formation within the limb, obtaining results which support those of Tickle *et al.* (1975). Slack took as his starting point the classic experiments of Harrison (1918) (see Chapter 4), who looked at the establishment of the three limb axes in the Axolotl. In contrast to Harrison, Slack was able to demonstrate that the limb disc was not equipotential, but consisted of two distinct parts, prospective limb and prospective flank (an area defined by Slack in this context as lying between fore- and hind-limb buds). He postulates that the anterio-posterior axis is established (1) by the splitting of the primordia into 'limb' tissue and 'flank' and (2) by the latter signalling to the former. Normally, 'flank' lies posterior to 'limb': re-duplications can occur if 'limb' tissue has 'flank' tissue on either side. This condition is fulfilled in urodeles (as in chick ZPA transplantation) by the grafting of a strip of flank tissue to the anterior edge of a limb disc (Fig. 6.31). Small changes in the positioning of this extra flank tissue can lead to quite large changes in the nature of the re-duplicated limb. Slack assumes that two thesholds govern the position of a skeletal element (Fig. 6.25(a)). The grafting of an extra piece of flank anteriorly can (1) set up a gradient in which the element is not represented (Fig. 6.25(b)), (2) set up a gradient where it is broader than normal (Fig. 6.25(c)), and (3) set up a gradient where it is present twice (Fig. 6.25(d)). Grafts of this nature should always have the more posterior elements in the limb pattern represented twice, the configuration of the rest of the limb depending on the 'sag' of the gradient and the distance apart of its boundaries. Typical duplicated limbs in Slack's experiments were reduplicated along their entire length (Plate 13), the humerus, for instance, consisting of two posterior halves. It was noticed, however, that in a given limb the configuration of the proposed gradient was not constant; a limb with a double posterior humerus might well have 8 digits, suggesting that the 'sag' of the gradient changed along the proximo-distal axis, perhaps due to the widening of the proliferating zone in more distal areas.

The evidence for the gradient which these experiments on the Axolotl and those of Tickle *et al.* (1975) on chick suggest to be present is not restricted to these two species. ZPA activity has also been found in *Xenopus* limbs (Cameron and Fallon 1977*a*), and in all the three major amniote groups (Fallon and Crosby

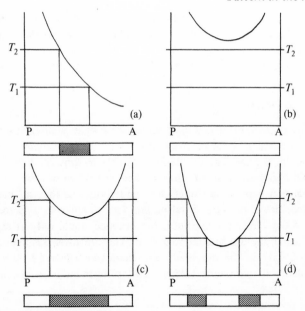

FIG. 6.25. If we specify two thresholds (T_1, T_2) between which a cartilaginous element is specified by a single ZPA (a), then grafting in a second ZPA anteriorly gives the following possibilities: the gradient may not fall below T_2 (b), the gradient may fall to a minimum level between T_1 and T_2 (c), and the gradient may fall to a level below T_1 (d). In (b) no cartilaginous element is specified, in (c) a broad one, and in (d) two of almost normal size. (After Slack 1977*a*).

1977). The gradient can be interpreted in a number of ways. The active zone within the flank of urodeles could be the precursor of the amniote ZPA. Or the flank could induce a ZPA from limb mesoderm. Or the ZPA could be a position in space, rather than a specific set of cells: differences in environment between flank and limb bud could result in the highest concentration of a morphogenetically active substance always being found posteriorly. At present, there is no strong evidence as to which of these alternatives (if any) may prove to be correct. Although attractive, this hypothesis deals only with the anterior limb. Clearly in the posterior limb active flank tissue would be anterior not posterior, and it is presumably necessary to add a sub-hypothesis, either that the situation is reversed in the hindlimb (unlikely, because we know that amniote hindlimbs have ZPAs) or that a second posterior inducer exists caudal to the hindlimb (perhaps another dose of the same inducer), the two limbs being separated by a sufficient distance to preclude interference.

We have seen how mirror imaging may be produced by ZPA or flank grafts, but in amniotes there is also a small group of mutants which show very similar effects. Is it possible that this condition is due to a duplication of the ZPA?

Amongst this group is Strong's *luxoid* (Forsthoefel 1963*b*) which in homozygous mice causes preaxial polydactyly and duplication of radius or tibia (Fig.

7.4(h), (i)). In the chicken, mirror-image limbs are also produced by the *duplicate* allele (*Po^d*) (Fig. 4.24). One possibility is that, in these mutants, the properties of the ZPA are also present in the preaxial mesenchyme, but unfortunately this hypothesis has yet to be tested experimentally.

6.9. The dorso-ventral axis

Although the dorso-ventral axis is usually ignored by modellers of limb development, it should really be taken into consideration in any scheme purporting to explain how limbs grow. Pautou (1977) was able to show that the ectoderm of the limb bud is polarized dorso-ventrally, and able to control the formation of a dorso-ventral axis, providing that the underlying mesoderm had not yet differentiated into a proximo-distal pattern (see Chapter 4.2). Ectoderm taken from 3.5–5.5-day-old chick leg buds, for instance, could only affect the distal portion of a 3.5-day-old mesodermal core. The dorso-ventral determination is stable by 5.5 days in the mesoderm and cannot be affected by the ectoderm. The influence of the ectoderm tended to be stronger and longer-lasting in dorsal than in ventral areas.

6.10. The polar co-ordinate model

Yet another model based on positional information in development involves ignoring the three conventional axes and looking at the regenerating system end on (Bryant, Bryant, and French 1977). If we do this, and assume for the sake of simplicity that the limb bud is a cone (Fig. 6.26), then any point on the surface of the cone can be specified by two coordinates, say A–D, along the major axis of the cone and 1–12 around its circumference. To fit experimentally determined facts the intervals are unequal. We may further simplify the model if we look at a section through the cone at a given level, in which case we see a disc (whose size depends on the level of amputation) upon which the numbers 1–12 can be arranged rather like a clock-face for reference. This model is once again two-dimensional as it does not distinguish between the locations A, B, and C (Fig. 6.26). This is equivalent to saying that pattern is determined by the outside boundary layer. In the limb this would be the epidermis, or at any rate the sub-epidermal mesoderm: not too drastic an assumption when we remember the superficial location of the AER and ZPA.

Two rules are needed to specify the behaviour of cells in this field. The first is this: if cells with non-adjacent positional values come to lie side-by-side, the incongruity induces growth at the junction which continues until cells with the appropriate positional values have been intercalated. The shortest set of possible numbers is intercalated. For example, if a cell of positional value 3 finds itself next to a cell of positional value 6, then cells carrying values of 4 and 5 are produced in preference to 6 7 8 9 10 11 12 1 2 3. The second rule states that cells at any proximo-distal level can give rise to new cells with a more distal positional

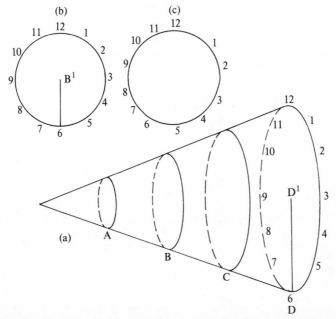

FIG. 6.26. In the model of Bryant, Bryant, and French (1977), the limb is seen (a) as a cone with a base (proximal) and an apex (distal), the position of a point is specified by its level (A–D), and its position on the clock face at that level. For instance, the point D has a level value D and a clock-face value of 6. All the information is assumed to lie on the surface. All points along the lines D D^1 and B B^1 (b) have the same positional value. In practice, the spacing of the numbers on the clock-face has to be modified somewhat (c).

value, but this can only occur when a complete series of positional values has been exposed, as in amputation.

This model has essentially emerged from studies on insect limb regeneration where it predicts accurately the outcome of an exhaustive series of elegant experiments on larval cockroaches. If a longitudinal strip of integument is removed from the circumference of the larval femur, the cut edges heal bringing together cells which are normally separated. There is localized growth, and the deleted structures are regenerated: a simple demonstration of the shortest inter-calation rule (Fig. 6.27). This rule is also demonstrated if pieces of integument are transplanted to an abnormal position bringing together cells not normally neighbours at the edges of the graft. Once again, there is growth, and structures which would normally lie along the shortest of the two possible routes between host and graft circumferential positions are intercalated (Fig. 6.28).

Intercalation also occurs proximo-distally. If non-adjacent levels within a leg segment are placed together, there is localized growth and intercalary regenera-tion of the deleted structure (Fig. 6.29(a), (b)). The regenerated section has been shown by using colour marked cuticle to be derived from both graft and host tissue. Further experiments demonstrate that the system of polar co-ordinates

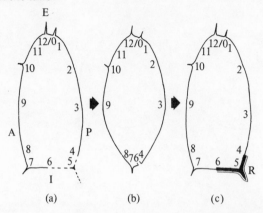

FIG. 6.27. Intercalary regeneration is demonstrated in deletions from larval cockroach legs. (a) represents a schematic section through the femur in which A,P represent anterior and posterior surfaces, and E,I external and internal surfaces. Numbers 0–12 have been allocated arbitrarily around the circumference. In (a) epidermis between 4 and 6 has been removed; in (b) the cut surfaces have healed; in (c) intercalary regeneration (= R) of the missing structures, visible after moulting, has taken place. (After Grant 1978.)

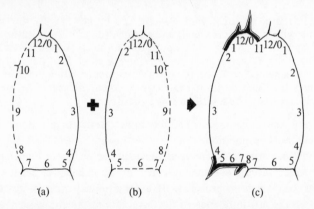

FIG. 6.28. A posterior surface of a femur from one side (a) has been grafted into the anterior face of a femur of the other side (b). (Discarded parts are dotted, and the heavy line represents the graft.) The result after two moults (c) shows that intercalary regeneration has taken place, following the shortest route rule.

appears to be repeated in each limb segment. Thus, if host femur is cut in mid-segment and combined with donor tibia also cut in mid-segment, there is no intercalary regeneration (Fig. 6.29(c), (d)).

This model predicts quite well the events which follow disturbance of the antero-posterior axis in newts. For example, if a left leg is transplanted to a right leg stump, a conflict of polarity occurs at the amputation site (Fig. 6.30). This results in the growth of two supernumerary limbs, both right ones, at the points of maximum incongruity. Amputation of a limb, followed by rotation through

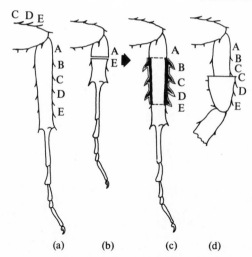

FIG. 6.29. Intercalary regeneration also takes place along the proximo-distal gradient of the larval cockroach leg. (a) The letters A–E represent arbitrary values along the tibial sequence (see Fig. 6.26). Both diagrams show graft combinations and the result after two moults. In (b) a mid-section of the tibia has been removed, and intercalary regeneration of the missing section takes place between the normally non-adjacent positional values of the cut surfaces (c). Both graft and host tissue contribute. In (d) a mid-line cut is made in the tibia, to which is grafted a femur, also cut in the mid-line. Since the positional values are the same at both surfaces, there is no regeneration. (After Grant 1978.)

180° and regrafting back to its own stump, can also give rise to supernumerary limbs, this time a right and a left, according to position. Such limbs were noted in the early transplantation work of Harrison (1918). He attributed the supernumeraries to the trauma of the operation. Bryant *et al.* (1977) point out that if anterior and posterior values (3 and 9) are established first, followed by 6 and 12, then the rule of intercalation will ensure the formation of two new complete 1–12 arrays at the base of the limb. Bryant's model also correctly predicts the position of supernumeraries if the graft is orientated at angles other than 180° to the host stump. It must be pointed out, however, that Harrison's findings also fit very well with Tickle's hypothesis that an antero-posterior axis is established first, followed by a dorso-ventral one.

Bryant (1976) and Slack and Savage (1978) have obtained differing results from two rather similar experimental tests of the clock-face model. Bryant, by means of surgery, made urodele limbs composed of two posterior halves which, according to the model, should possess two sets of positional values from 6–12 (Figs 6.26 and 6.31) healed in mirror symmetry. As no complete set of numbers would be exposed if such a limb were to be amputated, Bryant predicted that no regeneration should occur. This was tested experimentally and found to be correct, regeneration either failing to occur or producing only small cartilaginous nodules.

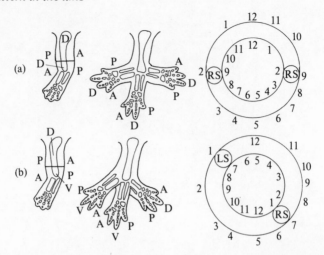

FIG. 6.30. According to the model of Bryant, Bryant, and French (1977), and Bryant and Iten (1976), supernumerary limbs will occur where intercalation of missing parts has no shortest route, i.e. a 6 and 12 brought into apposition will intercalate 7–11 and 1–5 to produce a complete 1–12 sequence equivalent to a limb base: a supernumerary limb will form on this site. According to the model, the two amputations and graftings performed above (a) transplantation of a left limb to a right stump, D–V axis maintained, and (b) transplantation of a right limb to a right stump with 180° rotation so as to interfere with the D–V axis will produce regenerates of a different handedness or different locations.

Slack and Savage (1978) made superficially similar limbs in a rather different way by grafting pieces of flank tissue to the anterior edge of the limb rudiment (Fig. 6.31), or by grafting the central part of the limb rudiment to the flank of tail-bud stage Axolotl larvae. At this stage, no limbs have appeared. The limbs which subsequently developed had a digital formula of 4 3 2 3 4. If these limbs are amputated, more than 67 per cent regenerate limbs with the same digital sequence, whilst the remainder regenerate normal limbs. Slack and Savage point out that (a) if the clock-face model applies to both development and regeneration, then duplicate posterior limbs should not have developed in the first place and (b) the absence of anterior elements implies a gap in the clock-face which should not have allowed regeneration on Bryant's model.

Maden and Turner (1978) have also presented evidence that the Bryant, Bryant, and French model is not applicable to the Axolotl. They rotated the blastema after amputation of the axolotl forelimb. According to the Bryant clock-face hypothesis, supernumeraries should occur only in certain well-defined positions, when the difference between stump and graft values is maximal. Supernumeraries should also occur in pairs. Maden and Turner found that, if blastemata were rotated through 180° there was no preferred position for the regenerate, and that 46 per cent of experimented animals produced only

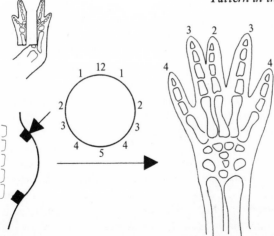

FIG. 6.31. Double posterior limbs (*right*) in urodeles may be made either by grafting (*above, left*) or by adding a second polarizing zone (arrow) anteriorly in the developing limb bud. According to Bryant, Bryant, and French (1977), these should not regenerate after amputation. If made by grafting, this appears to be true. But limbs produced by the grafting of a second polarizing zone (which should not differentiate at all in this hypothesis) once amputated, regenerate to give another double posterior limb (Slack and Savage 1978).

one supernumerary limb. Rotations of 20, 45, 75, 90, 105, 120, 135, and 150° gave 1–3 supernumerary limbs which again should not occur on Bryant's model.

In the light of these apparent contradictions (Cooke 1978), the clock-face model cannot be accepted uncritically. At present, much experimentation inspired by the model is in progress, and only time will resolve these discrepancies.

6.11. The choice of model

It seems that none of the models described above fits all the available facts on limb genesis and regeneration. The existence of a pre-pattern has been criticized because of the complexity necessarily involved in its generation and maintenance. Wilby and Ede's model based on short-term interactions between cells where differentiation is governed by reference to the cell's immediate neighbours and to its internal state seems to be workable, but appears complex and simulates only some features of the developing chondrogenic pattern. The concept of positional information which appears simpler has also had its critics. Here, the claim is that the signal is simple if not universal in developing systems. But limbs individually and collectively are complex. Thus, the price paid for a simple signal system is that the whole responsibility for generating complex patterns is loaded on to the mechanism of interpretation. And we have even less inkling of how this mechanism works than of the signalling mechanism. Moreover, the contradictory results obtained by Wolpert and his colleagues and the French school need further elucidation.

Brenner (1975) likens the positional information concept to a system which first produces a series of empty boxes which are arranged in three-dimensional space: after a computation involving the relationship of these boxes to each other and to objects outside the system, properties are written on the boxes, the allocation of which depends on their position. The non-positional information concept would be of a similar pile of boxes, but, in this case, the properties written on each box depend, not on its position, but upon its history and origin. In the first case, the external signal develops the system from a series of identical units, in the second, a series of apparently identical units start to show that they do in fact differ from each other. Positional information models of limb development such as Wolpert's also demand the interaction of two gradients along the major axes (at least: the dorso-ventral axis has been omitted from the model and may well demand a third gradient). Ede (1978) contrasts his model with positional information models: he emphasizes that it involves only short-range interactions between cells. On the other hand, both models use the ZPA as a reference point. Ede is attempting to define the conditions necessary to generate limb-like patterns, and this assumes the limb fits best the category described by Waddington as condition-generated pattern. Clonal explanations of limb development are used to explain the origin of the musculature and perhaps also of the ZPA, fitting Brenner's non-positional concept.

The clock-face model of the Bryants is interesting in that it unites developmental concepts in insects and vertebrates, and thus reinforces Wolpert's idea that the signal system is very old and universal in application. But this model fails to fit all the experimental evidence, and therefore cannot be adopted uncritically.

7 Limb development, mutants, and the process of evolution

7.1. An overall view

It should be clear from the discussion of limb models listed above that none of them accurately describes all aspects of limb development. This is hardly surprising. The modeller starts with a simple, elegant concept and, by reasoning and experiment, tries to see how good is the fit between the concept and the hard facts provided by the developing limb bud of chick or mouse, or the regenerating limb of the Axolotl. The rationale of these models and experiments is that there is a single mechanism for specifying pattern in these species which has persisted more or less intact throughout tetrapod evolution, throughout many millions of years, at least from the point where the ancestors of laboratory species diverged from a common stock (see Maderson 1975).

If we consider that evolution, although directed by selection, and therefore sometimes appearing as a goal-directed process, is dependent upon variation, and that variation itself depends upon mutation, which is random, it is hardly surprising that a precise mathematical model is a poor fit to a process which must have been modified extempore upon many occasions in the past. A study of the nature of biological phenomena leads us to an understanding that they are not always organized in the simplest and most economic way: there are often duplications, modifications, and complications which seem to have arisen by this opportunist process of evolution seizing upon the available material and using the variation in it made available by mutation.

As the neat mathematical model seems to fail us, an inevitable consequence of biological complexity and variety, it is necessary to widen our net a little and to admit information from sources other than experimental embryology. Obviously, we must consider the whole vertebrate kingdom: all living species and all the fossils of which we have records are potential raw material in our search for the pattern. But we must remember that each living species and each fossil represents a successful, highly evolved, and highly modified animal: we shall not find our archetypal ancestral limb attached to a living vertebrate or embedded in a rock. All we can do is to build it ourselves on the bassis of probability.

Besides the extinct and extant hordes of vertebrates, there is one other source of information available to us: this resides in the gene pool of the living vertebrates. In fact, we have comprehensive information about the variability contained here in only a few species; a handful of rodents, the chick (Hutt 1949), a few amphibians, and patchy knowledge from a few domestic mammals and pets. Taken all together, this information is quite enought to enable us to make a few suggestions about the developmental mechanisms involved in limb evolution. But first, how can it help us?

Consider a Miocene landscape where a herd of three-toed *Merychippus* are besporting. If we could sample the limbs of these beasts, a biologist would surely predict that the size of the lateral toes would exhibit variation. Standing in the very privileged position of having both fore- and hind-sight relative to the time we have chosen, we can classify those with the shorter and narrower lateral toes as being more like the modern horse descendants of *Merychippus,* and those with longer wider toes as more like his ancestors.

The same reasoning could be applied to the modern horse. We have no fore-sight as to the direction of horse evolution over the next million years or so, but we do have the hindsight to identify the occasional atavistic three-toed foal which is born (Ewart 1894*b*). And the same reasoning can be applied to laboratory rodents and chicks: the variation in the present day genome will contain rough sketches (to be modified by selection and genetic background) of possible future mice, as well as of possible ancestral mice. There will, of course, be other mutations, grossly deformed, very inviable. We shall have to use our discretion as to which forms we select. Once we accept that mutations do not necessarily lead to the formation of new patterns, but can sometimes recreate, roughly, an ancestral state (the extra toes of an atavistic horse are not *new* toes − they represent perhaps the repeal of a gene suppressing toes), a pattern that may have been present in an ancestral form, we may go fossil-hunting in the genetic literature. Moreover, the ways in which genes modify limb development in these mutants will give us insight into the developmental mechanisms which are the basis of the adaptive radiation of the pentadactyl limb.

7.2. The size and extent of the limb bud

While form and pattern are clearly interrelated, we will follow the useful distinction between size and form of the limb, and pattern of mesodermal condensations. Let us first examine some variations in limb bud size seen both in normal and mutant vertebrates.

Even before the formation of the AER during the thickening of the somato-pleure mesoderm, genetically controlled factors are known to be involved. Somites contribute cells to the early limb bud and the quantity of this contribution is important, as shown by the studies of Raynaud (1972*b*) on lizard limbs. Once formed, the limb bud comes under the influence of the AER which it induces from the ectoderm. According to the Saunders/Zwilling hypothesis (section 4.3) the AER induces limb outgrowth through its action on the meso-derm, perhaps by maintaining in it a high mitotic rate and directing outward migration. Such outgrowth induction by the AER is a most important factor in determining limb form. The antero-posterior orientation of the ridge deter-mines the fact that the limb bud is wider along its A–P than D–V axis. The length of the ridge is important in determining the width of the limb bud, and the duration of its period of activity is important in determining the length of the proximo-distal axis.

The length of the ridge, according to Zwilling, is related to the supply of maintenance factor (AEMF) from the mesoderm. Greater concentration of the factor postaxially in the normal chick limb bud leads to AER regression pre-axially. Zwilling interprets various chick mutants as varying the distribution of the maintenance factor (see section 4.6). Thus, the polydactylous mutant (Po^d) involves extension of the ridge which induces an excess of distal preaxial mesenchyme. This excess is then available for formation of additional preaxial digits (Fig. 7.1). The *wingless* (*wg*) mutant involves variation in the other

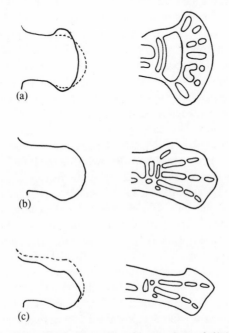

(a)

(b)

(c)

FIG. 7.1. Mutants of the fowl show that the number of digits is related to the quantity of distal mesenchyme available. (a) *Talpid*[3] mutant hindlimb at 5 and 7 days; (b) normal hindlimb at 5 and 7 days; (c) *wingless* mutant hindlimb (severe effect) at 5 and 7 days. (Dotted outline indicates normal limb shape.)

direction: inhibition of AEMF supply leads to AER collapse, failure of mesenchymal outgrowth and regression of the limb bud. In other mutants, not subjected to analysis by experimental recombination, there is the familiar pattern of elongated AER, limb bud enlargement and ensuing polydactyly (see section 7.4.1).

Ridge length in avian limb buds is also related to the presence of the anterior and posterior necrotic zones (section 3.9). The causal relationship is still unclear, but this mesenchymal cell death may well block AEMF and lead to regression of adjacent AER. In the normal chick limb bud, ANZ and PNZ may thus control AER length and hence the length of the AP axis. It is certainly true that AER length in the narrow limb buds of the chick is much less than that in the wider limb buds of rat and mouse where ANZ and PNZ are lacking (Milaire 1977*b*). The chick forelimb develops only three main digits, while rats and mice have five. Moreover, in a number of mutants, these zones are affected (section 4.11). In *talpid* chick embryos, ANZ and PNZ are absent, and the AER and the distal part of the limb bud are elongated along the AP axis. *Wingless* (*ws*) chicks have a precocious and enlarged ANZ, and the anterior part of the limb bud is suppressed. Whether acting directly or via the AER, the ANZ and PNZ seem to act as end stops limiting the A–P dimension of avian limb buds.

The period during which the AER is active is also significant in determining the limb bud form along its proximo-distal axis. In the chick, the AER is active over a long period, from 2.5 to 7 days, during which five proximo-distal rows of skeletal elements (stylopod, zeugopod, and the three parts of the autopod) form in the mesenchyme. Disappearance of the ridge is always associated with completion of the definitive number of phalanges in the digit and disappearance of the distal undifferentiated mesenchyme. Thus in the 7.5-day leg, a ridge is still visible over the more posterior digits which are still adding phalanges distally, when the more anterior elements, whose smaller phalangeal number has been completed, have lost their AER (JRH, personal observation). At the other end of the scale, in the legless slow worm (in which a small limb bud is formed, but regresses) the first sign of this regression is the degeneration and death of the AER (Raynaud and Vasse 1972). In the anlage of teleost fish fins, the apical crest of the trout makes only a brief appearance (Geraudie and François 1973), sufficient to generate enough mesenchyme to form the single row of radials.

Whatever the precise mechanism for controlling the period of activity of the AER and its length, it is clear that its length in particular varies, in different mutants and in different species, and that this variation is related to the size and form of the limb bud. In this context we should emphasize the evidence from fish fins where there is great variation in form associated with simple skeletal patterns. As we saw in section 3.1, the axis of fin development is determined by a primitive ectodermal ridge, the Wolffian ridge, which often initially runs the whole length of the body and becomes invaded by mesenchyme. The outgrowing buds of the paired fins, capped by an AER-like ridge (described in the trout by Bouvet (1968)) become restricted to certain regions of the initial primitive ridge. In many fish (e.g. *Scyllium*, Figs 3.1–3.3), they occupy initially an area larger than one they will occupy finally since shortening of the base occurs through the formation of the posterior notch. The ridge is very variable in extent, and very long along the AP axis in some fishes, even reaching (e.g. in *Torpedo*, Goodrich 1930) the point at which the anterior and posterior fin buds almost unite. If we count only digits in tetrapods, then for both these and fish we can make the same generalization, that along the AP axis the number of skeletal elements forming within each bud is correlated with its AP dimension. Further, in fish and reptiles, at least, the number of somitic contributions made to each bud is also proportional to bud size. Quantitative changes in limb size can clearly become qualitative skeletal changes if pattern generation then takes place in the way suggested by Ede's standing wave model (section 6.7.1).

7.3. Somite number and digit number

Is it possible to explain the formation of the spaced chondrogenic elements within the developing limb or fin bud by reference to the metameric segmentation of the somites which are making a material contribution? One possibility is a direct relationship between the number of digits and the number of contributing somites. According to this theory the 'striped' somitic mesoderm patterns the somatic mesoderm. Since the somitic 'stripes' soon lose their integrity such patterning by the somites of the somatic material must be indirect.

The first question to settle is: how many somites are involved in limb formation? This can be done in two ways. First, we can actually observe the contributions of somites in reptiles, because of the distinctive morphology of the somite process. If we do this, we find the number of somites sending contributions is rather constant (Table 7.1). These will not, of course, be the same somites in

TABLE 7.1. Somite numbers contributing to reptile limbs.

Species	Forelimb	Hindlimb
Lacerta viridis	8	
L. agilis	8	
L. muralis	8	
L. sicula	8	
Testudo graeca	8	
Emys orbicularis	8	
Scelotes gronovii	7–8	
Scelotes brevipes‡	5	
Ophisaurus apodus‡	4–5	3†
Anguis fragilis‡	4–5	3†
Trophidonotus tessalata‡	0	
Vipera aspis‡	0	
Calotes versicolor	5†	5†

Data from Raynaud (1977), or (†) from Goel and Mathur 1977.
‡Limbless or reduced limbs

every case (see Chapter 2). The number of somites contributing material in species with a full allocation of digits seems to be eight for the reptilian forelimb. In the chick embryo, the processes are less distinct, but it is estimated (Chevallier, Kieny, Mauger, and Sengel 1977) that six somites contribute to the forelimb, and seven to the hindlimb. This number is in excess of the digital number, but we should remember that cell death reduces the width of the chick limb bud. Five somites contribute to the mouse forelimb bud (Milaire 1976).

We can also get a slightly different estimate if we consider the number of nerves contributing to the limb plexus (Table 7.2). If we do this, we see that in a wide variety of species the number of nerves involved in limb plexuses is five or less.

TABLE 7.2. The numbers of spinal nerves contributing to the limb.

Species or class	Forelimb	Hindlimb
Anura		
Rana sp.	3	3
Reptilia		
Pseudopus	3	–
Trionyx	3	
Phrynosoma	4	6
Crocodilus	5	5
Chamaeleo	5	
Aves		
Columba	6	
Anser	5	
Cygnus atratus	5	
Mammalia		
Homo	5	5

(Data from Goodrich 1930.)

Thus, the AER in tetrapods tends to overlie and influence the lateral plate mesoderm adjacent to a fixed small number of somites. It seems an obvious next stop to suggest that the five rays of the primitive tetrapod limb are related in some way to the five somites closest to the AER.

In the fish fin bud, at least in elasmobranchs, the metameric segmentation, or one-to-one relation between somites and the radials of the fin skeleton is clear. The classic studies of Balfour and Goodrich on elasmobranchs emphasize that development is segmental (see Chapter 3.1), with precartilaginous radial condensations developing between dorsal and ventral segmental muscle buds which emerge from the somites, while even the apparently non-segmental basal elements show initial faint indications of segmentation. The segmental patterning is only clearly shown initially in the musculature, since the segmental cartilaginous radials appear within a single plate of condensed mesenchyme. In some adult fish (e.g. many elasmobranchs such as *Cladoselache*, Fig. 1.10), the direct relation between metameric segmentation and the number of the radials (which are parallel and unfused) is clear.

Unfortunately, when the evolution of fin and limb is considered, this clear relationship becomes obscured. First there is the evolution of a posterior notch and fusion of basal skeletal elements, followed by the appearance in some forms of the postaxial radials (see section 1.8, Fig. 1.12). In crossopterygian fish, the identification of the radials is uncertain and, in one species, *Eusthenopteron*, the supposed radials have double elements distally (Fig. 1.13). In their descendents, the tetrapods, the problems of identifying segmental elements in the limb skeleton multiply. In the hypothetical transition from lungfish to primitive amphibian, only the stylopod, zeugopod, and proximal carpal (tarsal) elements of the amphibian limb are thought to have been represented in the crossopterygian fin paddle (Holmgren 1933; Gregory and Raven 1941). The distal parts, including metacarpals (or tarsals) and phalanges are supposed 'neomorphs', so that tetrapod digits cannot be considered homologous with fish fin radials. There is also the problem of not knowing if an adult skeletal structure was formed from a single corresponding mesenchymal condensation or through fusion.

Evolution, in its exploration of the potentialities of simpler patterns has taken the tetrapod limb patterns far away from their origin in the simpler fish fin skeleton. There is now no longer a direct one-to-one relationship between the limb somites and the digits. But the simpler, metamerically segmented basis to elasmobranch fin development should be borne in mind when we try to explain the spaced digital condensations of the tetrapod limb. The mechanism which spaces out the somite-related fish radials may survive in tetrapods where, with different constraints, it spaces out the condensations of the digital rays.

7.4. Genetic effects on the patterning of the limb skeleton

Now let us consider the evidence as to the way genes affect the pattern of the limb skeleton by altering its development, bearing in mind that we are looking for mechanisms which will explain some of the evolutionary changes undergone by the limb. Our genetic effects can be divided into three major groups: (i) effects on the size of the limb bud (which may be decreased or increased) which only secondarily involve the pattern of mesenchymal condensations, (ii) effects on pattern through changes in the allocation of mesenchyme to the initial condensation, and (iii) systemic effects on cartilage affecting the overall growth of the limb.

7.4.1. *Mutants changing the skeletal pattern through effects on limb bud size*

A large group of mutants involves changes in limb bud size. The distal foot plate is particularly vulnerable to size changes: an excess or deficiency in mesenchyme appears to affect distal rather than the first-formed proximal regions. Such alterations are usually preaxial.

Decreased limb bud size. The consequences of decreased footplate size may be either a squashing together of blastemal condensations forming too close to each other, or, where the condensations try to maintain their normal spacing, loss or reduction of digits, usually pre-axially. The first group are syndactylous, the second oligodactylous.

As examples of syndactylism, we can consider a group of mutants studied by Grüneberg (1963). Shaker with syndactylism (*sy*) is recessive, and affects particularly the hindlimb in which digits 2 and 3, or 3 and 4 (or all three) are fused at the phalangeal (but not metatarsal) level. In development, the footplate of the mutant is narrow distally and the periphery is reduced: within the reduced mesenchymal area the condensations of the affected phalanges have no separate existence, being fused from their initial appearance (Fig. 7.2(c)). The recessive *syndactylism* (*sm*) mutant is very similar in its effect: within the reduced distal mesenchyme of the limb bud, the blastemata of the middle

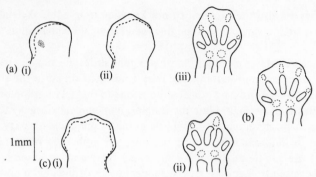

FIG. 7.2. Genetic effects reducing limb bud size. (a) *Oligosyndactylism*: the forelimb bud (dotted line) is already reduced preaxially compared with the normal (solid line) at 11 days (i) and 12 days (ii). In (i) the increased area of pre-axial mesenchyme cell death is shown (dots). In the narrowed footplate at 13 days digit 2 is either absent or unusually close to digit 3 (iii). (b) Normal 13-day forelimb. (c) Shaker with syndactylism (*sy*): the hindlimb footplate (i) dotted line) is smaller than normal (solid line) at 12.5 days, and at 13 days (ii) a single phalangeal element represents those of digits 3 and 4. (After Grüneberg 1956, 1960, 1962; Milaire 1967*a*.)

digits are pushed together so that phalanges are fused (Fig. 7.4(c) Grüneberg 1956, 1960). *Oligosyndactylism* (*Os*) is a semidominant mutant in which there is both loss and fusion of digits (Figs 7.2(iii) and 7.4(e)). The hind foot ab-normality is more pronounced, and there is a range of expression from fusion of the basal phalanges of digits 2 and 3 to an extreme form where digit 2 including its metatarsal is lost completely. In development, mutant limb buds have a preaxial mesenchymal deficiency recognizable as early as 11 days (Fig. 7.2(i)). Later an anomalous pattern of chondrogenic blastemata appears in this reduced distal mesenchyme. The blastemata of digits 2 and 3 are close together (Fig. 7.2(iii)) or, in more extreme forms, the digit 2 blastema is reduced or missing. The preaxial mesenchymal deficiency is considered by Milaire (1967*a*) to be due to an extension in the area of normal cell death in the mesenchyme underlying the preaxial AER (Milaire 1963, 1970, 1976*b*).

Both *oligosyndactylism* (Freye 1954) and post-axial *hemimelia* (Searle 1963) also have a reduced footplate but here the mesenchymal deficiency and the missing digits are post-axial.

Increased limb bud size: polydactyly and luxations. Increase in limb bud size seems invariably to result in polydactyly, which may be postaxial, or, more commonly, preaxial (review, Hinchliffe and Ede 1967). One type of preaxial polydactyly is particularly striking: these are the '*luxate*' or '*luxoid*' mutations in which polydactyly is associated with a preaxial reduction in more proximal limb parts such as radius or tibia (Fig. 7.3).

Let us consider Carter's *luxate* (1954) as an example since it has been so fully described. The gene is semidominant, affects +/*lx* mice moderately and *lx*/*lx*

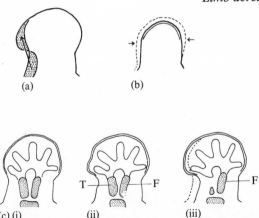

FIG. 7.3. Development of the luxate mutants in the mouse. (a) Interpretation of luxate hindlimb development. Mesenchyme is shifted from making tibia to making preaxial digits. (b) At 11 days the initial limb bud (solid outline) is narrower and has a shorter AER than normal (dotted outline: arrows indicate AER length). This example is *dominant hemimelia*, redrawn from Rooze (1977). Later, the mutant limb buds are frequently able to overcompensate, producing a preaxially elongated AER accompanied by preaxial mesenchymal excess. This is illustrated by the *luxate* mutant (Carter 1954) in (c) at 12.5 days: (i) normal, (ii) *luxate* heterozygote with preaxial growth of mesenchyme and AER, and (iii) *luxate* homozygote in which the tibia is almost completely absent, but there is also preaxial growth of both mesenchyme and AER (dotted line: normal limb outline). F = fibula, T = tibia.

rather more severely. The manifestation of the gene is also very sensitive to genetic background. The $+/lx$ mouse may have completely normal feet, or the hallux (the effects are confined to the hind feet) may have three phalanges instead of the normal two, or be divided into a hallux and pre-hallux. In the homozygotes, the effects are more marked, with up to seven toes. More severely affected individuals have a reduced number of toes, down to four or three. In the proximal limb skeleton $+/lx$ is always normal, but lx/lx shows a progressive reduction of the tibia while the calibre of the fibula increases. Sometimes the femur and even the os pubis may be reduced. These changes in the leg skeleton are found both in animals having polydactyly and those with preaxial reduction of digits. In homozygous embryos, limb buds are narrower than normal at the base at 11 days, before blastemata can be identified. Carter claims that, in homozygotes at 10.5 and 11.5 days, the AER is reduced preaxially, but later his drawings suggest that, by 12.5 days, the AER is extended preaxially (Fig. 7.3(c)). Certainly the AER-covered circumference is longer and preaxial extension at this stage is typical of the other luxate mutations (e.g. *lst,lu*, Forsthoefel 1963*b*, 1959; *Dh*, Rooze 1977). In older embryos, the tibial blastema is seen to be reduced or absent (Fig. 7.3(c)). If it is merely reduced, excess preaxial digital condensations appear; if it is vitually absent, then no extra condensations are seen.

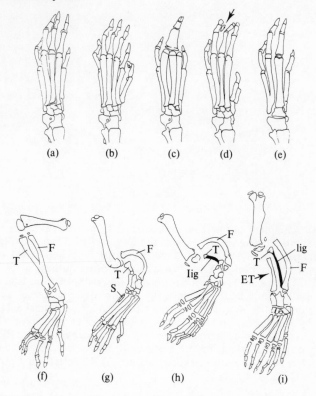

FIG. 7.4. Mouse mutants show us that the limb skeletal pattern can be altered: (a) normal left hindfoot, (b) *extra-toes* (*Xt*/+) with preaxial polydactyly, (c) syndactylism (*sm/sm*) with fusions between digits and in tarsus, (d) *poly-syndactyly* (*Ps*/+) with an extra element (arrowed) inserted between digits 3 and 4, (e) *oligosyndactylism* (*Os*/+) with fusions of metatarsals and tarsals. *Luxate* mutants are represented by (f) and (g), which are Green's *luxoid* (*lu*/+ and *lu/lu* respectively) and by (h) and (i), which are Strong's *luxoid* (*lst/lst*). In mild expression of the luxate phenotype, there is preaxial polydactyly, but in severe forms, this is achieved at the expense of the tibia. ET = extra tibia, F = fibula, T = tibia, lig = ligament, s = splint. (Redrawn from Grüneberg 1963; Johnson 1967, 1969; Strong 1961.)

A whole group of essentially similar mutants has the same features (Grüneberg 1963). In Green's *luxoid*, the effects on the hindlimb are very similar to those just described for *luxate* (Fig. 7.4(f), (g)). Forsthoefel (1959) found here that there is sometimes preaxial mesenchymal excess and AER extension, sometimes preaxial mesenchymal and AER deficiency. In *dominant hemimelia* (*Dh*), the hindlimb effects are similar to *luxate,* but more severe (Searle 1963). In develop-ment, the limb buds are initially smaller than normal, due to preaxial deficiency, and the AER is short (Fig. 7.3(b)). Later, as in Carter's *luxate,* some mutant limb buds appear able to overcompensate by forming a preaxial excess of mesenchyme accompanied by an elongated AER attributed by Rooze (1977) to absence of the normal process of AER preaxial regression described by Milaire (1967*b*, 1970, 1977*a*). Milaire (1970) considered that the preaxial *Dh*/+ mesenchymal excess was due to absence of the normal preaxial area of mesenchymal necrosis which in his view was suppressed by the AER hyper-activity preaxially.

Essentially, then, this phenotype consists of tibia reduction, sometimes com-pensated by polydactyly. Its development can be explained as follows: the initial limb bud is small, perhaps through delay or absence of preaxial AER initiation. The tibia blastema suffers from an inadequate supply of proximal preaxial meso-derm. If the AER does not recover from this delay then preaxial digits are also lost, giving the most severe expression of the mutant phenotype. Frequently, however, the preaxial AER does not regress in the normal way and through this late preaxial extension it is able to make good the initial deficiency in total mesenchyme. But this new mesenchyme is wrongly positioned, and is then used to form the excess preaxial digits. Effectively, mesenchyme has been shifted from making the tibia to making preaxial digits (Fig. 7.3(a)). We may regard these mutants as involving shifts in the boundaries of the prospective areas (pre-axial digits gaining at the tibia's expense). Such shifts have followed from out-of-sequence development of mesoderm associated with first shortened and later lengthened AER.

This explanation is not a complete one. It does not explain, for example, why some individual mutant embryos make good their initial mesenchymal deficiency while others with the same gene fail. Moreoever, in the absence of experimental evidence, it fails to specify precise mechanisms. Is the initial deficiency due to limitation in AEMF, or reduced somite contribution? Is the primary defect in the mesoderm, with AER reflecting mesodermal misdirection? Other explana-tions have been put forward. Carter (1954), noting the slight cranial shift of the hindlimb, has proposed that the 'hindlimb inductor' is shifted anteriorly in relation to the limited extent of competent mesoderm. Rooze (1977) explains *dominant hemimelia* by a rather similar scheme in which relative positions of prospective limb somites and somatopleure are altered. However, the cranial shift theory explains the hemimelia, but not the polydactyly, and in addition the various hemimelias move the limb cranial, or caudal, or not at all (Grüneberg 1963). Zwilling and Ames (1958) point out the shift theory is not consistent with many experimental results from chick limb buds. They prefer to suggest a shift in AEMF is involved, as shown experimentally in the *duplicate* chick mutant, but in the absence of experimental evidence, this explanation remains purely formal for the mouse luxations.

Reviewing luxate mutations by no means exhausts the polydactylous mutants, but the remaining ones form a rather heterogeneous group. Chang (1939) studied a strain of preaxial polydactyly in the mouse preceded by preaxial mesenchymal and AER excess. In *polysyndactyly* of the mouse, Johnson

(1969) described the intercalation of an additional digit within the normal pattern of new-born mice (Fig. 7.4(d)). Such intercalation within the pattern is rare in comparison with the numerous cases of preaxial polydactyly. Mention should also be made of the 'polydactylous monster' gene in the guinea-pig which in the heterozygote restored the pentadactyl pattern of both fore- and hind-limb skeleton (Wright 1945; Scott 1937, 1938). The guinea-pig normally has four front digits (lacking number 5) and three hind digits (lacking numbers 1 and 5). Homozygotes were extreme monstrosities: each foot had about 10 toes. Poly-dactylous mutants of the fowl have already been discussed because some of them provide important experimental evidence in the analysis of normal development (section 4.6). Some have additional preaxial digits (*diplopodia*: Landauer 1956*a*), others attempt to duplicate the whole limb (see Fig. 4.14) (e.g. *duplicate*, Launder 1956*b*; Zwilling and Hansborough 1956) while yet others do not have identifiable normal digits (*talpid*). All have the familiar enlarged limb bud capped with elongated AER, and the experimental evidence implicates anomalies in AEMF distribution.

Amidst this welter of morphological anomaly and theoretical speculation, what conclusions can we draw concerning the genetic patterning of the skeleton when the limb bud size is altered? The mutants affect primarily limb bud size, especially distally. In reduced limb buds, digital condensations are squeezed together or missing completely. Limb buds are mainly enlarged distally and pre-axially which is where the supernumerary digits appear. Genes affecting the limb skeleton seem to act primarily in changing the shape and size of the early limb bud since these changes predate any change in skeletal blastema pattern. An initial quantitative change in distal mesenchyme thus becomes a qualitative skeletal anomaly. Genes do not seem commonly to act directly on parts of the skeletal pattern, e.g. by forming supernumerary blastemata within a normally shaped limb bud. There is frequently a simple relationship between digits and mesoderm in that the normal digits number themselves off from the postaxial margin (Forsthoefel 1963*a*), and any excess mesoderm produces additional anterior digits. This theory is consistent with the hypothesis that the post-axially located ZPA controls the anteroposterior axis of the limb. In the luxate group, the preaxial mesenchyme is often 'stolen' from more proximal levels, i.e. the prospective tibia. Various developmental mechanisms have been put forward to explain these anomalies, but all lack rigour to some extent. But the defects in our understanding of the mechanisms need not worry us unduly in relation to our purpose. These mutations make it clear that there is a pool of developmental variation where limb mesenchyme can be taken away here, and added there, perhaps by a process of competitive redistribution, in such a way that the limb skeleton is qualitatively changed with elements deleted, or added or changed in proportion. We can now consider a case where such a redistribution takes place within a normally shaped limb bud.

7.4.2. *Mutants changing the proportions of prospective skeleton areas*

Grüneberg and Lee's study (1973) of the *brachypod* mouse shows a normal axial skeleton associated with a markedly reduced limb skeleton. Different segments of the limbs are shortened by differing amounts, the ulna/tibia being mildly shortened, the humerus and the femur rather more, and the manus and pes more still. Obviously, a simple proximo-distal gradient is not at work here. Embryological studies showed that, by contrast with the group we have just discussed, the *brachypod* limb bud is the same size and form as the normal until the digital contours and their blastemal condensations emerge at 13.5 days. The authors suggest that what goes wrong (although complicated by later events) involves the misallocation of material between the various sections of the limb. The stylopod and metapod receive less than they should to the benefit of the zeugopod and the phalanges respectively. Thus, at the time of chondrification, the metacarpal is normally longer than the two phalanges, but in *brachypod* the reverse situation applies, with the phalanges represented by a single long pencil-thin element (Fig. 7.5). As early as 13 days, the digital condensations of *brachypod* limb buds are distinctly thinner than normal, while the metacarpal-phalangeal joint is shifted proximally. This misallocation of material is significant as it possibly represents a disruption in the usual pattern determining where joints are to occur in the limb. One interesting point about *brachypod* is that one of the primary lesions present in mutant animals is thought to be a change in cell adhesion (Elmer 1977; see section 6.5). Could it be that this property, already shown to be important in individual blastema formation, also governs the allocation process whereby the overall blastemal pattern is initiated?

The *brachypod* mutant gives us an important model suggesting that the process of allocation of limb bud mesenchyme to the various skeletal blastemata is under genetic control, and that the normal pattern can be varied. Maps of the prospective areas of the chick limb bud have been constructed (Saunders 1948; Stark and Searls 1973) and we may speculate that a similar map produced for *brachypod* (were that possible) would show some rearrangement of the areas, perhaps through changing the position of the joints. We have here a developmental mechanism whereby changes in proportion of adult limb bones may be achieved.

7.4.3. *Systemic effects on cartilage growth*

In a large number of mutants there is a systemic upset in the growth potential of the cartilaginous skeleton. The effects of this growth restriction are most marked in the limb skeleton. These mutants also affect the proportions of the limbs. Earlier studies on chondrodystrophy showed histological abnormalities: recent analysis is at the molecular or ultrastructural level. Abnormalities in the histogenesis of cartilage, in matrix production, in hypertrophy, or in forming the chondrocyte rows of the epiphyseal plates will all clearly result in defects of the adult limb bones (Warkany 1971).

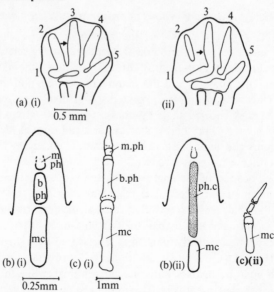

FIG. 7.5. The development of the *brachypod* mutant, which involves misallocation of mesenchyme between limb blastemata. (a) (i) normal and (ii) *brachypod*
forelimb buds in 13-day embryos. Note the slimness of the brachypod digital
condensations, and the relatively proximal positioning (arrow) of the metacarpal-
phalangeal future joint. (b) (i) normal and (ii) *brachypod* third digital rays from
the forelimb bud of 14-day embryos. Note in *brachypod* the small chondrogenic
metacarpal and the single mesenchymal blastema representing a phalanx (equivalent to the basal and middle phalanges of the normal digit). (c) (i) normal and
(ii) brachypod third digit after birth. In *brachypod* there is a normally sized
distal phalanx, but there is only one very small other phalangeal element
between this and the reduced metacarpal. b.ph. = basal phalanx, mc = metacarpal, m.ph. = middle phalanx, ph.c. = phalangeal condensation. (Redrawn from
Grüneberg and Lee 1973.)

Cartilage appears particularly vulnerable to defects in its metabolism. Thus, in
short-legged *nanomelic* chicks (Landauer 1965), ultrastructural studies show an
abnormality of the matrix in that proteoglycan granules are absent. Although
the mutant chondroblasts had the capacity for both collagen and chondroitin
sulphate synthesis, they synthesized only small amounts of proteoglycan, in
which the chondroitin sulphate chains are linked to a protein backbone (Goetinck
and Pennypacker 1977).

By contrast, in *chondrodysplasia*, a chondrodystrophic mutant of the mouse,
the collagen component of cartilage is affected with the fibrils showing ultrastructural abnormalities (Seegmiller, Fraser, and Sheldon 1971). In *cartilage
anomaly* in the mouse, the cartilage matrix is sparse while in the epiphyseal
plate the cartilage columns are poorly aligned (Johnson and Wise 1971), and at
17 days of development, protein synthesis (and in particular collagen synthesis)
is depressed (Johnson and Hunt 1974). In another chondrodystrophic mouse,

stumpy, the cartilage has an increased mitotic rate, but the chondrocytes fail to move apart and ultrastructural study shows them to have interdigitating membranes (Johnson 1977). Thus, the chondrodystrophic phenotype can be produced by one of a number of quite different anomalies at the ultrastructural or biochemical level.

Interesting as are these ultrastructural and biochemical studies, from our point of view they reveal less than the extensive classical analysis by Landauer of the *creeper* chondrodystrophic mutant of the chick. Heterozygous creepers (*Cp*/+) are viable but have short legs and, to a lesser extent, wings (Landauer 1927). The distal bones are more reduced than proximal ones, but in addition to this, the longer a bone is normally, the greater its length reduction. *Creeper* heterozygote embryos can first be identified only on the seventh day of incubation at which time the relative shortening of the cartilage rudiments representing the leg long bones as compared with those of normal chicks is already established. Landauer (1934) studied the subsequent growth of the long bones up to 26 weeks and found that the growth of *creeper* bones did not fall further behind that of normal bones. In other words, the mutant long bones were, both initially and finally, 80 per cent of the length of normal long bones. Mutant cartilage becomes histologically abnormal, with a delay in central hypertrophy and late irregularities in the formation of the columns of flattened cartilage cells (Landauer 1931). Periosteal ossification takes place but shows some abnormalities, probably secondary to the cartilage anomaly. Homozygous creepers are even more severely affected, with greater reductions and fusions of the long bones, and cartilage which is extremely abnormal histologically (Landauer 1933).

As far as evolutionary potential goes, the various chondrodystrophies appear negative, apart perhaps from a regressive role. It should be remembered, however, that certain artificially selected changes in domestic animals probably involve selection of similar mutants. The short-legged Ancon sheep, preferred in the eighteenth century because it could not leap over fences, is alas extinct, but a similar recent mutation of sheep has shortened limbs with distal elements particularly reduced in a pattern similar to the *creeper* mutant. The relative shortening of the bones is present in the embryo and does not increase after birth (Grüneberg 1963). Dogs also have been selected for shortening of the legs, controlled in the dachshund and basset hound by a single gene. Since the axial skeleton is not affected, a systemic effect on cartilage growth can be ruled out. However, direct developmental proof of anomalies in cartilage growth in the limb is lacking (Grüneberg 1963).

Changes in proportion between corresponding bones in different species were one of the problems tackled by D'Arcy Thompson (1917) in his then revolutionary book, *On growth and form.* He saw that it was possible to apply Cartesian transformation (a system involving the superimposition of a regularly spaced grid on the outline of a bone, and the subsequent deformation of the grid in various ways — Fig 7.6) to, say, the cannon bone of a sheep, and produce a

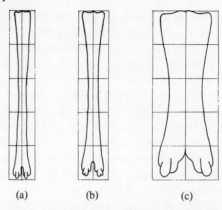

FIG. 7.6. Differences between species in the configuration of a single element are often a matter of simple proportions. D'Arcy Thompson (1917) was able to transform the cannon bones of a giraffe (a), sheep (b), and ox (c) by varying the ratio of length:breadth.

structure closely resembling the cannon bone of an ox, the latter being simply a transformed version of the former. He was also able to show that whole limbs could be treated similarly (Fig. 7.7) and, in this case, different parts of the limb has to be deformed by different amounts. It can thus be seen that alteration of the growth potential of different bones in the limb produces spectacular differences in the form of the limb finally produced.

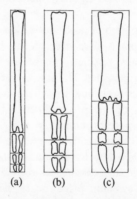

FIG. 7.7. Differences in configuration of a whole limb rather than a single bone cannot be expressed by a simple change of length:breadth ratio. In this case the limbs of a giraffe (a), sheep (b), and ox (c) can only be made equivalent by changing the length:breadth ratio of each segment independently.

It is clear that disproportionate growth has been at work in a positive way in various orders of the vertebrates. We noted in Chapter 2 the tendency to elongation of distal elements in animals adapted for speed; obvious elongations of parts of the pattern appear in flying forms, birds, bats, and pterosaurs. The deformations of growth of limb bones we have just analysed all result in defective use of the limb. But these chondrodystrophic mutants (e.g. *creeper*), the *luxate* group, and *brachypod,* which involve changes in proportions of the prospective skeletal areas, provide models of the genetically controlled developmental mechanisms for generating this disproportion.

7.5. Regression and fusion of skeletal elements

Less drastic than the large scale reorganization of pattern following from changes in limb bud size or mesenchymal allocation processes, are the changes involving loss of individual elements or their fusion with their neighbours. In fact, many evolutionary changes involve fusion and loss of the elements of the primitive pentadactyl limb.

Since bones during development go through a process first of mesenchymal condensation and then chondrification, an element to be suppressed or fused can be eliminated at one of a number of stages in skeletogenesis. Two examples from normal development will illustrate this point.

In many fossil reptiles (but not in modern ones) the proximal row of carpals was made up of three elements: the radiale, ulnare, and intermedium (see Chapter 1). In *Calotes,* which has no sign of an intermedium in the adult, a mesenchymatous condensation appears at stage 33 in the embryo (Goel and Mathur 1977) (Fig. 7.8). In the hind limb, the analogous centrale is also seen in mesoderm, but in neither case do the elements chondrify. In contrast in the chick wing (Hinchliffe 1977) the only mesenchymal blastemata present in the wrist are the four which chondrify; at a later stage the cartilaginous ulnare becomes pycnotic and disappears. Thus, in two examples we have seen three methods of suppression of an element:

(i) absence of mesodermal condensation;
(ii) mesodermal condensation present but regresses;
(iii) cartilaginous element regresses.

Presumably, absence of an element represents an elimination which is older phylogenetically than regression.

Grüneberg (1963) has pointed out that a reduction in the size of a blastema leads to certain consequences: delay in chondrification, delay in histogenesis of cartilage, and delay in ossification. Reduced blastemata give rise to cartilages of reduced size or (if below a critical size) fail to chondrify at all.

Studies of various mutants where syndactylism or fusion of bony elements occurs suggest that this condition may also be the product of interactions at different embryological stages. The syndactylism may be affecting only soft tissue (i.e. the bony elements of two digits may be united in a single ectodermal envelope) or involve the bones themselves. In the *syndactylism* mouse (Grüneberg 1956) the condition occurs in the forefeet as a soft tissue syndactylism and in the hindfeet as bony fusions (Fig. 7.4(c)). Osseous fusion involves the phalanges (but not the metacarpals or metatarsals) and the tarsals. Fusions between the

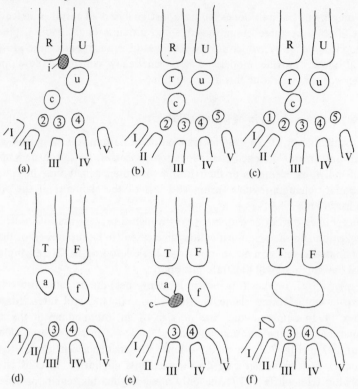

FIG. 7.8. Elements may be deleted from the limb pattern in various ways. In this diagram of the development of (a–c) fore- and (d–f) hind-limbs of *Calotes versicolor,* the intermedium (i) is seen as a pre-cartilaginous blastema which later disappears. In the hindlimb the centrale (c) appears as a pre-cartilaginous blastema which fuses with that for the astragalus (a). R = radius, U = ulna, T = tibia, F = fibula, f = fibulare, r = radiale, u = ulnare. (After Mathur and Goel 1976; Goel and Mathur 1977.)

phalanges are inevitably primary, that is a single centre of chondrification, derived from a single blastemata representing a fusion of the two elements from the start (Fig. 7.4c(ii)), but fusions between tarsals involve late union of two independent cartilaginous entities.

The implication is quite clear: syndactylism and the apparent reduction in digital number can be due to coalescence of mesodermal blastemata (due to reduction of the footplate — see section 7.4.1) or to secondary fusion of cartilaginous elements.

7.6. The individuality of the skeletal blastema

Skeletal blastemata are frequently indistinguishable from each other histologically at condensation and chondrogenic phases, yet one of their most striking features is their very different rates of growth. We have already seen that the wrist region as a whole grows much more slowly than, say, the zeugopod region (Summerbell 1976), but to illustrate the principle for the individual blastema we can consider a much older piece of work.

Ewart (1894*a, b*) was interested in the way in which specialization of the pentadactyl limb occurred, an issue which arises with particular acuteness in the development of the horse limb in which essentially a single digit survives in the adult. In the early horse embryos studied by Ewart, three metacarpal cartilages (2, 3, and 4) are present. All three are approximately the same length, but the third (which survives in the adult) has twice the diameter of the second and fourth. The longitudinal growth rate of the third is much the greater, however, since in the adult skeleton the second and fourth are represented by narrow splint bones, by now much shorter than the 'dominant' metacarpal. As in the chick, the metacarpal growth rate exceeds that of the carpal region; initially metacarpal 3 is twice the length of the carpal region, but in the adult it is five times its length. Ewart (1894*a*) also identified transient phalanges of the second and fourth digits. Initially there are three chondrogenic phalanges to the second digit, with rather poorly differentiated joints between, but these grow only very slowly and soon fuse to give a single cartilaginous element which later fuses with the distal end of the metacarpal. Thus, cartilages initially rather similar in size show very different growth rates, and the metacarpal and phalanges of digit 3 become dominant.

The development of the tibia and fibula in the chick embryo is another striking example of the individuality of skeletal blastema. Initially, at 5 days, the condensations of tibia and fibula are of similar length, though the tibia is always slightly larger in diameter. But the growth of the tibia is much faster (Table 7.3(B)) than the fibula which by 8 days has become a narrow splint of bone, half the length of the tibia. Fortunately, the culture of tibia and fibula *in vitro* is not difficult, and in this way, together with other experiments, it has been possible to attempt analysis of their differential growth. One idea that has been put forward by Wolff (1958) and his co-workers is that a competitive relation exists between the two rudiments.

Analysis of regulation in the limb (see section 4.10) by Wolff (1958) and Hampé (1959, 1960) demonstrated that in these experiments the fibula was relatively unstable compared with the tibia. In conditions of mesenchymal excess, the fibula was much larger than normal (Fig. 7.9), but where there was mesenchymal deficiency, a normal tibia formed while the fibula was often absent. According to the competition theory, the dominant tibia appropriates the necessary number of mesenchyme cells, while the 'weak' fibula is only formed if sufficient material remains. Insertion of a mica plate between the centres at stage 24 results in the fibula becoming much larger (Hampé 1960). Presumably, intermediate cells normally recruited by the dominant tibia can no longer by attracted away from near the fibula. Irradiation of the limb produces a result similar to mesenchymal deficiency. The fibula is more sensitive to radiation

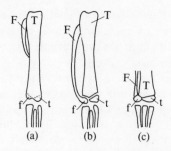

FIG. 7.9. The final morphology of a limb depends on the amount of mesoderm present in the limb bud. The normal chick leg (a) can be changed by the surgical addition of more mesoderm (b). According to the competition model of Hampé (1959), the 'strong' tibia recruits cells more successfully than the 'weak' fibula. Mesenchymal excess enables an enlarged fibula (= F) to form. These changes also reinstate a separate fibulare (= f) and tibiale (= t) which normally fuse with fibula and tibia (= T) respectively. The altered skeleton according to Hampé resembles that of the leg of the ancient bird–reptile, *Archaeopteryx* (c).

damage to the mesenchyme than is the tibia (Wolff and Kieny 1962).

Other work (reviewed by Hall 1971, 1975) has suggested that once a blastemal condensation is formed, its subsequent differentiation is determined. Such programming extends even to the details of secondary bone remodelling. A recent study by Holder and Wolpert (1978) showed that the different growth rates of chick wrist and radius were already determined at stage 27, as shown by isolation in organ culture.

Hicks, in unpublished work at Aberystwyth, found that, once tibia and fibula had formed, their respective high and low growth rates were also determined. Cartilage elements of tibia and fibula isolated with adjacent perichondrium at stage 28 (6 days) cultured *in vitro* grew respectively quickly and slowly (Table 7.3(C)). Estimates of the cartilage volume change during growth showed that the tibia was initially four times the volume of the fibula, but that after 6 days growth *in vitro* the tibia was twelve times the volume of the fibula.

There is evidence that the differential growth is genetically controlled. In the *diplopod* (dp^4) mutant of the fowl at 19–21 days, the tibia is shorter than a normal tibia by 35–45 per cent, but the mutant fibula is the same length as the mutant tibia. Thus, the mutant fibula must have a higher than normal growth rate relative to the tibia. This changed growth rate is determined by 7 days since at that stage isolated *diplopod* fibulae in organ culture became considerably larger than mutant tibiae (or normal fibulae) similarly cultured, and in some cases even form a distal epiphysis (Kieny and Abbott 1962).

By what cellular mechanism does the tibia in the normal embryo grow so much faster than the fibula? There are a number of possibilities:

(i) differential recruitment by the condensations and later chondrogenic blastemata from neighbouring mesenchyme (Wolff's competitive interaction theory);

TABLE 7.3. Analysis of differential growth of chick tibia and fibula.

(A)	Stage	Tibia:fibula ratio of $^{35}SO_4^{2-}$ incorporation (*in vivo*)
	5 days	3.3
	7 days	7.1

(B)	Stage	Tibia:fibula ratio of volume (*in vivo* growth)
	5 days	2.57
	7 days	7.03

(C)	Day of culture	Tibia:fibula ratio of volume (*in vitro* growth)
	0 days	4.0
	6 days	11.5

(A) Ratios of labelled $^{35}SO_4^{2-}$ extracted as chondroitin sulphate from tibia and fibula grown *in vivo* following pulse labelling. The increase in the rate of synthesis by the tibia is much greater than by the fibula. The increase approximately parallels the change in ratio of the volumes measured *in vivo* at the same two stages as shown in (B). (C) The growth rates of tibia and fibula blastemata are determined. At 6 days of development isolated chondrogenic blastemata with intact perichondrium are organ cultured by the grid method. The tibia grows at about 2.5 times the speed of the fibula. (All three tables from Hicks, unpublished.)

   (ii) different cell division rates within condensation and chondrogenic rudiment;

   (iii) different rates of synthesis of intercellular matrix;

   (iv) changes in the cell volume of the chondrocytes during hypertrophy.

Hicks has examined the possibilities of competitive interaction and differential matrix synthesis. Matrix synthesis was monitored by measuring the incorporation of ^{35}S-sulphate into chondroitin sulphate in the two elements at different stages *in vivo* following a labelled pulse of $^{35}SO_4^{2-}$. Measurements of the ratio of the radioactivity of chondroitin sulphate extracted from tibia compared with that from fibula at 5 and 7 days showed that the tibia increased its rate of synthesis of chondroitin sulphate much more than the fibula in this period (Table 7.3). However, the rate of synthesis of each element when considered on a per volume basis can be seen to be very similar in tibia and fibula.

   The competitive interaction model of Wolff was also investigated. Tibia and fibula cartilage elements (with intact perichondrium) were grown in closely associated pairs of like or unlike elements (Ti + Ti; Ti + Fi; Fi + Fi – Fig. 7.10). The growth rate of each element was unaffected by the associated element of the pair. Thus, a tibia continued to grow strongly, even in association with another tibia, while a fibula grew slowly even when associated with another 'weak' fibula. These results suggest that, if the competition model is correct, this must affect recruitment to the initial condensation only, since tibia and fibula cartilage rudiments, as soon as it is technically possible to isolate them, have a strictly determined growth rate.

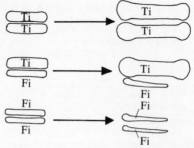

FIG. 7.10. Skeletal blastema of tibia or fibula isolated at 6 days and organ cultured in pairs for 6 days have a determined growth rate, irrespective of the other element of the pair. At this stage there is no evidence for competitive interaction of 'strong' tibia with 'weak' fibula. Fi = fibula, Ti = tibia. (Hicks, unpublished.)

Cell division rates and volume changes in tibia and fibula are currently being investigated. One feature which undoubtedly contributes to slow growth of the fibula is the absence of a distal epiphysis. Holder (1977*b*), in fact, considers this as fully as explaining the fibula growth relative to the tibia, but Hicks finds the slow growth rate is apparent in organ culture before the epiphyses are formed. Holder examined the cellular mechanisms in another region: the differential growth of the radius and the wrist cartilages of the chick wing between stages 28 and 37 (Summerbell 1976). The much greater growth of the radius was attributed to hypertrophy or enlargement of the cells in the mid zone, where the average cell volume relative to the small cells of the epiphysis is 27:1. Epiphyseal chondrocytes remained small and are separated from the growing mid-zone by flattened cells. In the slow-growing wrist cartilage, the radiale, there was no cell hypertrophy, and the cells remained small. The increase in cell number in the radius over this period was estimated to be only 1.3 fold. Holder thus attributes the faster growth of the radius to the enlargement of the mid zone cells, cell division and matrix secretion playing a lesser role.

The cellular mechanisms controlling blastemal individuality (or 'non equivalence', the term used by Lewis and Wolpert (1976)) remain, therefore, unclear. If competitive recruitment is important, it appears to affect only the initial condensation phase. The rate of hypertrophy is likely to be a crucial factor, while cell division and rates of matrix synthesis appear less important. Uncertainty as to cellular mechanisms should not obscure the central conclusion, that simple mesenchymal condensations behave as different entities through the acquisition of individual growth programmes, presumably genetically controlled. Here we have another important mechanism by which, starting from a simple pattern of chondrogenic elements perhaps common to large numbers of related tetrapods, the D'Arcy Thompson 'transformations' of skeletal elements can be achieved and important differences in the structure (and therefore in the function also) of the pentadactyl limb can arise.

The later process of replacement of hypertrophic cartilage by bone affords further opportunity for genetic modification of the shaping process. Growth is eventually restricted to the cartilaginous epiphyseal plates where differences in cell division rates and organization of the chondrocyte columns will be important in determining the final size and form of bones. The chondrodystrophic mutants, such as *creeper* in which there is a systemic defect of chondrogenesis, affect the histogenesis of the epiphyseal growth plates. Later, the bone remodelling process allows further functional adaptation of the element. This process too appears to be genetically controlled, as shown by the *grey lethal* mutant (Bateman 1954).

7.7. Some of the rules

From the study of mutants and from normal embryology, we can begin to put forward a set of rules for modification of limb pattern, which would produce some of the variations present in the vertebrates. As we have seen, many of the factors listed are under genetic control, thus providing the ontogenetic variation available for the evolutionary modification of the limb pattern by natural selection.

(i) The formation of a limb blastema (whose size is critically important) depends on the control of the quantity of mesoderm by such factors as somitic contribution, rate of cell division and cell death, and cell surface properties affecting mesenchyme motility and adhesiveness.

(ii) Further shaping of the initial limb bud is dependent on an AER of a specific length, controlling mesoderm division and migration rates through its inductive effect. An elongated AER leads to formation of excess distal mesoderm and to polydactyly. Localized reduction of the AER at either end leads to reduction in digital number, while AER abolition leads to abolition of the limb bud. The length of time during which the AER operates is also important in determining the number of elements laid down along the proximo-distal axis.

(iii) Rule (ii) implies that there is a regular spacing mechanism, 'placing' the condensations whose number is related to the width of available mesenchyme. In this way, by the interaction of conditions, a quantitative change (excess of distal mesenchyme) may be converted into a qualitative change (polydactyly).

(iv) There is a process of allocation of mesoderm to the blastema, whose size is an indication of the size of the later chondrogenic element. Thus, the tibia is always slightly larger than the fibula, even at the condensation stage, while the small wrist cartilages start as small condensations. It is this allocation process which we see upset in mutants such as *brachypod*, where more proximal blastema may 'steal' distal mesenchyme.

(v) Blastemata, once formed, acquire their own individuality which is expressed as a different growth rate as in the case of the fast-growing chick tibia and slow-growing fibula. Blastemata may also be able to compete with each other for mesoderm, the 'winner' taking mesoderm at the expense of the 'loser'.

(vi) A blastema which is smaller than its fellows may lag in later stages of development, and may regress completely. A certain critical size is necessary: in some mutants this is not achieved and the element disappears, another case of a quantitative difference becoming qualitative. A blastema may appear but not chondrify, or chondrify but then regress, while some (which might be expected on phylogenetic grounds) may simply not appear at all.

(vii) Blastemata may fuse either early or late (as cartilage or bony entities) to form a single bony unit.

(viii) Further genetically controlled processes of modelling the skeletal element take place during cartilage hypertrophy and its replacement by bone during histogenesis of the epiphyseal growth plates, and during the final secondary remodelling of the bone.

Thus stated, the process of limb development seems intolerably complex. Perhaps insight into it is provided by recent interpretation of insect development (Morata and Lawrence 1977; Kauffman, Shymko, and Trabert 1978). Essentially, this falls into two stages. The first is the process of compartmentalization, in which groups of cells are set aside as imaginal discs, which will later form adult structures. These cell groups are related by spatial proximity rather than by clonal ancestry. The compartments have boundary lines, corresponding to adult structures, which are not crossed by dividing cells in development. Compartment formation is thus a process in which homogeneous populations of cells are split into sub-populations, which have different developmental potential. The second phase is the development of the cell groups into one or other body part, a process which is gene-directed, as has been demonstrated by homoeotic genes. Homoeotic genes transform one body part into another, e.g. the mutant *bithorax* transforms the group of cells which would normally form the anterior part of the haltere into anterior wing. Traditionally, genes have been thought to control synthetic activities, but here we have genes which at our present stage of knowledge it is best to regard as pattern-controlling. Homoeotic mutants are described as single loci determing the developmental pathway taken by groups of cells.

We do not know at present whether compartments and homoeotic genes exist in vertebrates. But much of the evidence we have discussed suggests that limb development follows a similar two-stage process: an initial patterning of homogeneous cells into spaced condensations, perhaps related to the initial process of somite compartmentalization, followed by the acquisition of individuality by the condensations whose differentiation is now determined and whose subsequent developmental potentiality is very different, as in the case of tibia and fibula. This second process may be determined with reference to certain boundaries in the limb field, such as the ZPA, and, once individuality is achieved, each blastema follows its specific genetic programme.

References

ABBOTT, J. and HOLTZER, H. (1966). The loss of phenotypic traits by differentiated cells. III. The reversible behaviour of chondrocytes in primary cultures. *J. Cell Biol.* **28**, 473–8.

AGNISH, N. D. and KOCHHAR, D. M. (1977). The role of somites in the growth and early development of mouse limb buds. *Devl. Biol.* **56**, 174–83.

ALEXANDER, R. Mc. (1975). *The chordates.* Cambridge University Press.

AMPRINO, R. (1965). Aspects of limb morphogenesis in the chicken. In *Organogenesis* (eds. R. L. De Haan and H. Ursprung) pp. 255–81. Holt, Rinehart and Winston, New York.

—— (1974). Developmental ability of the apical mesoderm of the chick embryo limb bud in sectors deprived of the ectodermal ridge. *Nova Acta Leopoldina,* **217**, 235–70.

—— (1977). Morphogenetic interrelationships between ectoderm and mesoderm in chick embryo limb development. In *Vertebrate limb and somite morphogenesis* (eds. D. A. Ede, J. R. Hinchliffe and M. Balls), pp. 245–55. Cambridge University Press.

—— and CAMOSSO. M. (1959). Observations sur les duplications expérimentales de la partie distale de l'ébauche de l'aile chez l'embryon de poulet. *Archs. Anat. microsc. Morph. ex.* **48**, 261–305.

ANDREWS, R. C. (1921). A remarkable case of external hind limbs in a humpback whale. *Am. Mus. Novitates* **9**, 1–6.

ANDREWS, S. M. and WESTOLL, T. S. (1968). The post-cranial skeleton of *Eusthenopteron foordi* Whiteaves. *Trans. R. Soc. Edinb.* **68**, 207–329.

—— (1970). The post-cranial skeleton of rhipidistian fishes excluding *Eusthenopteron. Trans. R. Soc. Edinb.* **68**, 391–489.

ANIKIN, A. W. (1929). Das morphogene Feld der Knorpelbildung. *Arch. Entw.mech. Org.* **114**, 549–78.

ANTON, H. J. (1965). In *Regeneration in animals* (eds. V. Kiortsis and H. A. L. Trampusch). North Holland, Amsterdam.

ASHTON, E. H., FLINN, R. M., OXNARD, C. E., and SPENCE, T. F. (1976). The adaptive and classificatory significance of certain quantitative features of the forelimb in primates. *J. Zool. Lond.* **179**, 515–56.

BAKKER, R. T. (1971). Ecology of the brontosaur. *Nature, Lond.* **229**, 172–4.

—— and GALTON, P. M. (1974). Dinosaur monophyly and a new class of vertebrates. *Nature, Lond.* **248**, 168–72.

BALCUNS, A., GASSELING, M. T., and SAUNDERS, J. W. (1970). Spatiotemporal distribution of a zone that controls antero-posterior polarity in the limb bud of the chick and other bird embryos. *Am. Zool.* **10**, 323.

BALFOUR, F. M. (1881). On the development of the skeleton of the paired fins of elasmobranchs considered in relation to its bearings on the nature of the limbs of vertebrates. *Proc. Zool. Soc. Lond.* **3**, 656–71.

BALLARD, K. J. and HOLT, S. J. (1968). Cytological and cytochemical studies on cell death and digestion in fetal rat foot: the role of macrophages and hydrolytic enzymes. *J. Cell. Sci.* **3**, 245–62.

BARCROFT, J. and BARON, D. H. (1939). The development of behaviour in fetal sheep. *J. comp. Neurol.* **76**, 477–502.

BARD, J. and LAUDER, I. (1974). How well does Turing's theory of morphogenesis work? *J. theor. Biol.* **45**, 501–31.

BARDEEN, C. R. (1907). Development and variation of the nerves and the tendons musculature of the inferior extremity and of the neighbouring regions of the trunk in man. *Am.J. Anat.* **6**, 259–390.

BATEMAN, N. (1954). Bone growth: a study of the grey-lethal and microthalmic mutants in the mouse. *J. Anat.* **88**, 212–62.

BECKER, R. O. and MURRAY, D. G. (1970). The electrical control system regulating fracture healing in amphibians. *Clin. Orthop.* **73**, 169–98.

—— and SPADARO, J. A. (1972). Electrical stimulation of partial limb regeneration in mammals. *Bull. N.Y. Acad. Med.* **48**, 627–41.

BÉRARD, A. (1835). Mémoire sur le rapport qui existe entre la direction des conduits nourriciers des os longs et l'ordre suivant lequel les épiphyses see soudent au corps de l'os. *Archives générales de Médicine*, Series 2, **7**, 176–83.

BERMAN, R., BERN, H. A., NICOLL, C. S., and STROHMAN, R. C. (1964). Growth promoting effects of mammalian prolactin and growth hormone in tadpoles of *Rana catesbeiana. J. exp. Zool.* **156**, 353–60.

BODEMER, C. W. (1960). The importance of quantity of nerve fibres in development of nerve-induced supernumerary limbs in *Triturus* and enhancement of the nervous influence by tissue implants. *J. Morph.* **107**, 47–59.

—— and EVERETT, A. B. (1959). Localisation of newly synthesised proteins in regenerating newt limbs as determined by radiographic localisation of injected methionine-S^{35}. *Devl. Biol.* **7**, 327–42.

BONNER, J. J. (1952). *Morphogenesis, an essay on development.* Princeton University Press.

BOUVET, J. (1968). Histogenèse précoce et morphogenèse du squelette cartilagineux des ceintures primaires et des nageoires paires chez la truite (*Salmo trutta fario* L.). *Archs. Anat. microsc. Morphol. exp.* **57**, 35–52.

—— (1978). Cell proliferation and morphogenesis of the apical ectodermal ridge in the pectoral fin bud of the trout embryo (*Salmo trutta fario* L). *Wilhelm Roux Arch. EntwMech.Org.* **185**, 137–54.

BRENNER, S. (1975). Discussion to L. Wolpert, J. Lewis, and D. Summerbell. Morphogenesis of the Vertebrate limb. p. 124. CIBA Foundation Symposium 29, *Cell patterning.* Elsevier, Amsterdam.

BROOKES, M. (1971). *The blood supply of bone.* Butterworth, London.

BRYANT, P. J. BRYANT, S. V., and FRENCH, V. (1977). Biological regeneration and pattern formation. *Scient. Am.* **237**, 67–81.

BRYANT, S. V. (1976). Regenerative failure of double half limbs in *Notophthalmus viridiscens. Nature, Lond.* **263**, 676–9.

—— and ITEN, L. E. (1976). Supernumerary limbs in amphibians: experimental production in *Notophthalmus viridiscens* and a new interpretation of their formation. *Devl. Biol.* **50**, 212–34.

BUTCHER, E. O. (1929). The development of the somites of the white rat and the fate of the myotomes, neural tube and gut in the tail. *Am. J. Anat.* **44**, 381–439.

—— (1933). The development of striated muscle and tendon from the caudal myotomes in the albino rat, and the significance of myotomal cell arrangement. *Am.J. Anat.* **53**, 177–90.

BUTLER, E. G. (1935). Studies in limb regeneration in X-rayed *Ambystoma* larvae. *Anat. Rec.* **62**, 229–307.

CAIRNS, J. M. (1960). Depth of penetration of growth-stimulating factor from apical ectodermal ridge into the limb bud mesoderm of the chick. *Anat. Rec.* **138**, 339.

—— (1975). The function of the apical ectodermal ridge and distinctive characteristics of adjacent distal mesoderm in the avian wing bud. *J. Embryol. ex. Morph.* **34**, 155–69.

—— (1977). Growth of normal and *talpid*² chick wing buds: an experimental analysis. In *Vertebrate limb and somite morphogenesis* (eds. D. A. Ede, J. R. Hinchliffe, and M. Balls), pp. 123–37. Cambridge University Press.

CALANDRA, A. J. and MACCABE. J. A. (1978). The *in vitro* maintenance of the limb-bud apical ridge by cell free preparations. *Devl. Biol.* **62**, 258–69.

CAMERON, J. A. and FALLON, J. F. (1977a). Evidence for polarizing zone in the limb buds of *Xenopus laevis. Devl. Biol.* **55**, 320–30.

—— —— (1977b). The absence of cell death during development of free digits in amphibians. *Devl. Biol.* **55**, 331–8.

CAMOSSO, M. E. and RONCALLI, L. (1968). Time sequence of the processes of ectodermal ridge thickening and of mesodermal cell proliferation during apical outgrowth of the chick embryo wing bud. *Acta Embryologica et Morphologicae Experimentalis* **10**, 247–63.

CAPLAN, A. I., and KOUTROUPAS, S. (1973). The control of muscle and cartilage development in the chick limb: the role of differential vascularization. *J. Embryol. exp. Morph.* **29**, 571–83.

CAREY, E. G. (1921). Studies in the dynamics of histogenesis IV. Tension of differential growth as a stimulus to myogenesis in the limb. *Am. J. Anat.* **29**, 93–115.

CARLSON, B. M. (1974). Morphogenetic interactions between rotated skin cuffs and underlying stump tissues in regenerating Axolotl forelimbs. *Devl. Biol.* **39**, 263–85.

—— and MORGAN, C. J. (1967). Studies on the mechanism of induced supernumerary limb formation in urodeles. II. The effects of heat treatment, lyophilization, and homogenization on the inductive capacity of frog kidney. *J. exp. Zool.* **164**, 243–50.

CARTER, T. C. (1954). The genetics of luxate mice. IV. Embryology. *J. Genet.* **51**, 1–35.

CHALKLEY, D. J. (1959). The cellular basis of limb regeneration. In *Regeneration in vertebrates* (ed. C. S. Thornton), pp. 34–58. Chicago University Press.

CHANG, T. K. (1939). The development of polydactylism in a special strain of *Mus musculus. Peking nat. Hist. Bull.* **14**, 119–32.

CHAPLIN, D. M. and GREENLEE, T. K. (1975). The development of human digital tendons. *J. Anat.* **120**, 253–74.

CHENG, C. C. (1955). The development of the shoulder region of the opossum *Didelphys virginiata*, with special reference to the musculature. *J. Morph.* **97**, 415–71.

CHEVALLIER, A. (1977). Origine des ceintures scapulaires et pelviennes chez l'embryon d'oiseau. *J. Embryol. exp. Morph.* **42**, 275–92.

—— KIENY, M., and MAUGER, A. (1977). Limb–somite relationship: origin of the limb musculature. *J. Embryol. exp. Morph.* **41**, 245–58.

—— —— —— and SENGEL, P. (1977). Developmental fate of the somitic mesoderm in the chick embryo. In *Vertebrate limb and somite morphogenesis* (eds. D. A. Ede, J. R. Hinchliffe, and M. Balls), pp. 421–32. Cambridge University Press.

CHRIST, B., JACOB, H. J., and JACOB, M. (1977). Experimental analysis of the origin of the wing musculature in avian embryos. *Anat. Embryol.* **150**, 171–86.

ČIHAK, R. (1972). Ontogenesis of the skeleton and intrinsic muscles of the human hand and foot. *Advances in anatomy, embryology and cell biology* **46**, 1–194.

COOKE, J. (1978). Embryonic and regenerating patterns. *Nature, Lond.* **271**, 705–6.

CRICK, F. H. C. (1971). The scale of pattern formation. In *Control mechanisms of growth and differentiation. Society for Experimental Biology Symposium* 25, 429–38. Cambridge University Press.

CURTIS, A. S. G. (1961). Timing mechanisms in the specific adhesion of cells. *Exp. Cell Res.* (suppl.) 8, 107–22.

DALGLEISH, A. (1964). Development of the limbs of the mouse. Ph.D. thesis, Stanford University, USA.

DARWIN, C. (1872). *On the origin of species.* (6th edn). John Murray, London.

—— (1909). *The foundations of the origin of species.* Two essays written in 1842 and 1844. (ed. Francis Darwin). Cambridge University Press.

DAWD, D. S. and HINCHLIFFE, J. R. (1971). Cell death in the 'opaque patch' in the central mesenchyme of the developing chick limb: a cytological, cytochemical and electron microscope analysis. *J. Embryol. exp. Morph.* 26, 401–24.

DAWSON, A. B. (1925). The age order of epiphyseal union in the long bones of the albino rat. *Anat. Rec.* 31, 1–18.

DEAN, B. (1896). The fin fold theory origin of the paired limbs in the light of the Ptychopterygia of Palaeozoic sharks. *Anat. Anzerger.* 11, 673–9.

DE BEER, G. R. (1958). *Embryos and ancestors.* (3rd edn). Oxford University Press.

—— (1971). *Homology, an unsolved problem.* Oxford Biology Reader no. 11. Oxford University Press.

DE BOTH, N. J. (1970). The developmental potencies of the regeneration blastema of the Axolotl limb. *Wilhelm Roux Arch. EntwMech. Org.* 165, 242–76.

DESMOND, A. J. (1975). *The hot blooded dinosaurs.* Blond and Briggs, London.

DETWILER, S. R. (1933). On the time of determination of the anteroposterior axis of the forelimb in *Ambystoma. J. exp. Zool.* 64, 405–14.

DEUCHAR, E. M. (1976). Regeneration of amputated limb buds in early rat embryos. *J. Embryol. exp. Morph.* 35, 345–54.

DHOUAILLY, D. (1967). Analyse des facteurs de la différentiation spécifique de la plume néoptile chez le canard et le poulet. *J. Embryol. exp. Morph.* 18, 389–400.

—— and KIENY, M. (1972). The capacity of the flank somatic mesoderm of early bird embryos to participate in limb development. *Devl. Biol.* 28, 162–75.

DIENSTMAN, S. R., BIEHL, J., HOLTZER, S., and HOLTZER, H. (1974). Myogenic and chondrogenic lineages in developing limb buds grown *in vitro. Devl. Biol.* 39, 83–95.

DINSMORE, C. (1974). Morphogenetic interactions between minced limb muscle and transplanted blastemas in the Axolotl. *J. exp. Zool.* 187, 223–32.

DRIESCH, H. (1900). Die isolirten Blastomeren des Echinodenkeimes. *Arch. EntwMech. Org.* 10, 361.

DURSTON, A. J. (1973). *Dictyostelium discoideum* aggregation fields as excitable media. *J. theor. Biol.* 42, 483–504.

EAST, E. W. (1931). An anatomical study of the initiation of movement in rat embryos. *Anat. Rec.* 50, 201–19.

EDE, D. A. (1968). Abnormal development at the cellular level in *talpid* and other mutants. In *The fertility and hatchability of the hen's egg* (eds. T. C. Carter and B. M. Freeman), pp. 71–83. Oliver and Boyd, Edinburgh.

—— (1971). Control of form and pattern in the vertebrate limb. In *Control mechanisms of differentiation and growth.* Society for Experimental Biology Symposium **25** (eds. D. D. Davies and M. Balls), pp. 235-54. Cambridge University Press.

—— (1976*a*). Limb skeleton deficiences in some mutants of the chick embryo. In *Mécanismes de la rudimentation des organes chez les embryons de vertébrés*, pp. 187-91. Colloques internationaux du CNRS **266**, Paris.

—— (1976*b*). Cell interactions in vertebrate limb development. In *The Cell surface in animal embryogenesis and development* eds. G. Poste and G. L. Nicolson), pp. 495-543. Elsevier, Amsterdam.

—— (1978). *An introduction to developmental biology.* John Wiley and Sons, New York.

—— and AGERBAK, G. S. (1968). Cell adhesion and movement in relation to the developing limb pattern in normal and *talpid*[3] mutant chick embryos. *J. Embryol. exp. Morph.* **20**, 81-100.

—— and FLINT, O. P. (1972). Patterns of cell division, cell death, and chondrogenesis in cultured aggregates of normal and *talpid*[3] mutant chick limb mesenchyme cells. *J. Embryol. exp. Morph.* **27**, 245-60.

—— —— (1975*a*). Intercellular adhesion and formation of aggregates in normal and *talpid*[3] mutant chick limb mesenchyme. *J. Cell Sci.* **18**, 97-111.

—— —— (1975*b*). Cell movement and adhesion in the developing chick wing bud: studies on cultured mesenchyme cells from normal and *talpid*[3] mutant embryos. *J. Embryol. exp. Morph.* **18**, 301-13.

—— —— WILBY, O. K., and COLQUHOUN, P. (1977). The pattern of pre-cartilaginous condensations in limb bud mesenchyme *in vitro* and *in vivo*. In *Vertebrate limb and somite morphogenesis* (eds. D. A. Ede, J. R. Hinchliffe, and M. Balls), pp. 161-79. Cambridge University Press.

—— and KELLY, W. A. (1964). Developmental abnormalities in the trunk and limbs of the *talpid*[3] mutant of the fowl. *J. Embryol. exp. Morph.* **12**, 339-56.

—— and LAW, J. T. (1969). Computer simulation of vertebrate limb morphogenesis. *Nature, Lond.* **221**, 244-8.

—— and WILBY, O. K. (1976). Analysis of cellular activities in the developing limb bud system. In *Automata, languages, development* (eds. A. Lindenmayer and G. Rozenberg), pp. 15-24. North Holland, Amsterdam.

ELMER, W. A. (1976). Morphological and biochemical modifications of cartilage differentiation in the brachypod and other micromelic mouse embryos. In *Mécanismes de la rudimentation des organes chez les embryons de vertébrés* (ed. A. Raynaud), pp. 235-42. Colloques internationaux du CNRS **266**, Paris.

ENLOW, D. H. and BROWN, S. O. (1958). A comparative histological study of fossil and recent bone tissues. *Texas J. Sci.* **10**, 187-230.

ERRICK, J. (1977). Quoted in Saunders (1977).

—— and SAUNDERS, J. W. Jr. (1974). Effects of an 'inside-out' limb bud ectoderm on development of the avian limb. *Devl. Biol.* **41**, 338-51.

—— and SAUNDERS, J. W. Jr. (1976). Limb outgrowth in the chick embryo induced by dissociated and reaggregated cells of the apical ectodermal ridge. *Devl. Biol.* **50**, 26-34.

EWART, J. C. (1894*a*). The second and fourth digits in the horse: their development and subsequent degeneration. *Proc. R. Soc. Edinb.* 185-91.

—— (1894*b*). Development of the skeleton of the limbs of the horse, with observations on polydactyly. *J. Anat. Physiol.* **28**, 236-56.

EWER, R. F. (1965). The anatomy of the theocodont reptile, *Euparkeria capensis* Broom. *Phil. Trans. R. Soc. B* **248**, 379-435.

FABER, J. (1960). An experimental analysis of regional organization in the regenerating fore limb of the Axolotl (*Ambystoma mexicanum*). *Arch. Biol.* (*Liège*) **71**, 1–72.

—— (1965). Autonomous morphogenetic activities of the amphibian regeneration blastema. In *Regeneration in animals and related problems* (eds. V. Kiortsis and H. A. L. Trampusch), pp. 404–19. North Holland, Amsterdam.

—— (1971). Vertebrate limb ontogeny and limb regeneration: morphogenetic parallels. *Adv. Morphog.* **9**, 127–47.

—— (1976). Positional information in the amphibian limb. *Acta biotheor.* **25**, 44–64.

FALLON, J. F. and CAMERON, J. A. (1977). Interdigital cell death during limb development of the turtle and lizard with an interpretation of evolutionary significance. *J. Embryol. exp. Morph.* **40**, 285–9.

—— and CROSBY, G. M. (1975a). Normal development of the chick wing following removal of the polarizing zone. *J. exp. Zool.* **193**, 449–55.

—— and CROSBY G. M. (1975b). The relationship of the zone of polarizing activity to supernumerary limb formation (twinning) in the chick wing bud. *Devl. Biol.* **43**, 24–34.

—— and CROSBY, G. M. (1977). Polarizing zone activity in limb buds of amniotes. In *Vertebrate limb and somite morphogenesis* (eds. D. A. Ede, J. R. Hinchliffe, and M. Balls), pp. 55–69. Cambridge University Press.

FARQUHAR, M. G. and PALADE, G. E. (1963). Junctional complexes in various epithelia. *J. Cell. Biol.* **17**, 375–412.

FELL, H. B. (1929). Experiments on differentiation *in vitro* of cartilage and bone. *Arch. exp. Zellfor.* **7**, 390–412.

—— (1956). Skeletal development in tissue culture. In *The biochemistry and physiology of bone* (ed. G. H. Bourne), pp. 401–41. Academic Press, London.

—— and CANTI, R. G. (1935). Experiments on the development *in vitro* of the avian knee-joint. *Proc. R. Soc. Lond.* B **116**, 316–51.

FLICKINGER, R. A. (1974). Muscle and cartilage differentiation in small and large explants from the chick embryo limb bud. *Devl. Biol.* **41**, 202–8.

FLINT, O. P. (1977). Cell interactions in the developing axial skeleton in normal and mutant mouse embryos. In *Vertebrate limb and somite development* (eds. D. A. Ede, J. R. Hinchliffe, and M. Balls), pp. 465–84. Cambridge University Press.

—— (1980). Ontogeny and phylogeny of the limb. (In preparation.)

FORSTHOEFEL, P. F. (1959). The embryological development of the skeletal effects of the luxoid gene in the mouse, including its interactions with the luxate gene. *J. Morph.* **104**, 89–142.

—— (1963a). Observations on the sequence of blastemal condensations in the limbs of the mouse embryo. *Anat. Rec.* **147**, 129–37.

—— (1963b). The embryological development of the effects of Strong's luxoid gene in the mouse. *J. Morph.* **113**, 427–51.

FRENCH, V., BRYANT, P. J. and BRYANT, S. V. (1976). Pattern regulation in epimorphic fields. *Science, N.Y.* **193**, 969–81.

FREYE, H. (1954). Anatomische und entwicklungsgeschichtliche Untersuchungen am Skelett normaler und oligodactyler Mäuse. *Wiss. Z. Univ. Halle. Math-Nat.* **3**, 801–24.

GALTON, P. M. (1970). The posture of hadrosaurian dinosaurs. *J. Paleo.* **44**, 464–73.

GAMBLE, H. G. (1966). Further electron microscope studies of human foetal peripheral nerves. *J. Anat.* **100**, 487–502.

GANS, C. (1975). Tetrapod limblessness: evolution and functional corollaries. *Am. Zool.* **15**, 455–68.

GASSELING, M. T. and SAUNDERS, J. W. JR. (1964). Effect of the 'posterior necrotic zone' of the early chick wing bud on the pattern and symmetry of limb outgrowth. *Am. Zool.* **4**, 303–4.

GEORGE, J. C. and BERGER, A. J. (1966). *Avian myology.* Academic Press, New York.

GERAUDIE, J. and FRANÇOIS, Y. (1973). Les premiers stades de la formation de l'ébauche de nageoire pelvienne de Truite (*Salmo fairo* et *Salmo gairdneri*). *J. Embryol. exp. Morph.* **29**, 221–37.

GLOBUS, M. and VETHAMANY-GLOBUS, S. (1976). An in vitro analogue of early chick limb bud outgrowth. *Differentiation* **6**, 91–6.

GMITRO, J. I. and SCRIVEN, L. E. (1966). A physiochemical basis for pattern and rhythm. *Symp. Int. Soc. Cell Biol.* **5**, 221–55.

GODMAN, G. C. and PORTER, K. R. (1960). Chondrogenesis studied with the electron microscope. *J. biophys. biochem. Cytol.* **8**, 719–60.

GOEL, S. C. and MATHUR, J. K. (1977). Morphogenesis in reptilian limbs. In *Vertebrate limb and somite morphogenesis* (eds. D. A. Ede, J. R. Hinchliffe, and M. Balls), pp. 387–404. Cambridge University Press.

GOETINCK, P. F. (1964). Studies on limb morphogenesis, II. Experiments with the polydactylous mutant eudiplopodia. *Devl. Biol.* **10**, 71–91.

—— (1966). Genetic aspects of skin and limb development. *Current topics in developmental biology* **1**, 253–83.

—— and ABBOTT, U. K. (1964). Studies on limb morphogenesis, I. Experiments with the polydactylous mutant, *talpid²*. *J. exp. Zool.* **155**, 161–70.

—— and PENNYPACKER, J. P. (1977). Controls in the acquisition and maintenance of chondrogenic expression. in *Vertebrate limb and somite morphogenesis* (eds. D. A. Ede, J. R. Hinchliffe, and M. Balls), pp. 139–59. Cambridge University Press.

GOODRICH, E. S. (1906). Notes on the development, structure and origin of the median and paired fins of the fish. *Q. Jl. microsc. Sci.* **50**, 333–76.

—— (1914). Metameric segmentation and homology. *Q. Jl. microsc. Sci.* **59**, 227–48.

—— (1930). *Studies on the structure and development of vertebrates.* Macmillan, London.

GOODWIN, B. C. and COHEN, M. H. (1969). A phase-shift model for the spatial and temporal organisation of developing sytems. *J. Theor. Biol.* **25**, 49–107.

GOSS, R. J. (1961). Regeneration of vertebrate appendages. *Advanc. Morphogenesis* **7**, 103–52.

GOULD, R. P., DAY, A., and WOLPERT, L. (1972). Mesenchymal condensation and cell contact in early morphogenesis of the chick limb bud. *Expl. Cell. Res.* **72**, 325–36.

—— SELWOOD, L., DAY, A., and WOLPERT, L. (1974). The mechanism of cellular orientation during early cartilage formation in the chick limb and regenerating amphibian limb. *Expl. Cell. Res.* **83**, 287–96.

GRANT, P. (1978). *Biology of developing systems.* Holt, Rinehart, and Winston, New York.

GREGORY, W. K. (1912). Notes on the principles of quadrupedal locomotion and on the mechanism of the limbs in hoofed animals. *Annals N.Y. Acad. Sci.* **22**, 267–94.

—— MINER, R. W., and NOBLE, G. K. (1923). The carpus of *Eryops* and the structure of the primitive Chiropterygium. *Bull. Am. Mus. nat. Hist.* **48**, 279–88.

—— and RAVEN, H. C. (1941). Studies on the origin and early evolution of paired fins and limbs. *Ann. N.Y. Acad. Sci.* **42**, 273–60.

GRUNEBERG, H. (1956). Genetical studies on the skeleton of the mouse. XVIII. Three genes for syndactylism (with an appendix by D. S. Falconer). *J. Genet.* **54**, 113–45.

—— (1960). Genetical studies on the skeleton of the mouse. XXV. The development of syndactylism. *Genet. Res. Camb.* **1**, 196–213.

—— (1961). Genetical studies on the skeleton of the mouse. XXVII. The development of Oligosyndactylism. *Genet. Res. Camb.* **2**, 33–42.

—— (1962). Genetical studies on the skeleton of the mouse. XXXII. The development of shaker with syndactylism. *Genet. Res. Camb.* **3**, 157–66.

—— (1963). *The pathology of development.* Blackwell, Oxford.

—— and LEE, A. J. (1973). The anatomy and development of brachypodism in the mouse. *J. Embryol. exp. Morph.* **30**, 119–41.

GULAMHUSEIN, A. P. and BECK, F. (1979). Development of ferret limb buds in organ culture. *J. Anat.* **127**, 645.

GUMPEL-PINOT, M. (1973). Culture in vitro du bourgeon d'aile de l'embryon de poulet: differenciation du cartilage. *Annee Biol.* **12**, 417–29.

—— (1974). Contribution du mésoderme somitique a la genèse du membre chez l'embryon d'Oiseau. *C.r. hebd. Séanc. Acad. Sci. Paris D.* **279**, 1305–8.

GURDON, J. B. (1974). *The control of gene expression in animal development.* Oxford University Press.

HAINES, R. W. (1932). Laws of tendon and muscle growth. *J. Anat.* **66**, 578–85.

—— (1937). The primitive form of the epiphysis in the long bones of tetrapods. *J. Anat.* **72**, 323–43.

—— (1941). Epiphyseal structure in lizards and marsupials. *J. Anat.* **75**, 282–94.

—— (1969). Epiphyses and sesamoids. In *Biology of the reptilia* (eds. C. Gans, A. d'A. Bellairs, and T. S. Parsons). Academic Press, London.

—— (1975). The histology of epiphyseal union in mammals. *J. Anat.* **120**, 1–25.

—— MOHIUDDIN, A., OKPA, F. J., and VIEGA-PIRES, J. A. (1967). The sites of early epiphyseal union in the limb girdles and major long bones of man. *J. Anat.* **101**, 823–31.

HALE, L. J. (1956). Mitotic activity during early skeletal differention of the scleral bones in the chick. *Q. Jl. Microsc. Sci.* **97**, 333–53.

HALES, S. (1727). *Statical Essays,* Vol. 1. *Vegetable Staticks* W. Innys and Woodward, London.

HALL, B. K. (1971). Histogenesis and morphogenesis of bone. *Clinical Orthopaedics* **74**, 249–68.

—— (1975). Evolutionary consequences of skeletal differention. *Am. Zool.* **15**, 329–50.

—— (1978). *Developmental and cellular skeletal biology.* Academic Press, New York.

HAM, A. W. (1969). *Histology.* J. B. Lipincott, Philadelphia.

HAMBURGER, V. (1938). Morphogenic and axial self-differentiation of transplanted limb primordia of 2-day chick embryos. *J. exp. Zool.* **77**, 379–400.

—— and HAMILTON, H. L. (1951). A series of normal stages in development of the chick embryo. *J. Morph.* **88**, 49–92.

—— and LEVI-MONTALCINI, R. (1949). Proliferation, differentiation and degeneration in the spinal ganglia of the chick embryo under normal and experimental conditions. *J. exp. Zool.* **111**, 457–502.

HAMPÉ, A. (1956). Sur la régulation des pièces excédentaires dans le bourgeon de membre de l'embryon de poulet. *C.r. Séanc. Soc. Biol.* **150**, 1726-9.

—— (1959). Contribution a l'étude du dévelopment et de la régulation des deficiences et des excédents dans la patte de l'embryon de Poulet. *Arch. Anat. micr. Morph. exp.* **48**, 345-478.

—— (1960). Le compétition entre les elements osseux du zeugopode de Poulet. *J. Embryol. exp. Morph.* **8**, 241-5.

HARRIS, A. E. (1965). D. Phil. thesis. Cambridge University, England.

HARRISON, R. G. (1918). Experiments on the development of the forelimb of *Ambystoma*: a self differentiating equipotential system. *J. exp. Zool.* **25**, 413-61.

—— (1921). On relations of symmetry in transplanted limbs. *J. exp. Zool.* **32**, 1-136.

HAY, E. D. (1958). The fine structure of blastema cells and differentiating cartilage cells in regenerating limbs of *Amblystoma* larvae. *J. Biophys. Biochem. Cytol.* **4**, 583-91.

—— (1959). Electron microscope observations of muscle differentiation in regenerating *Amblystoma* limbs. *Devl. Biol.* **1**, 555-85.

—— and FISCHMAN, D. A. (1961). Origin of the blastema in regenerating limbs of the newt *Triturus viridescens*. *Devl. Biol.* **3**, 26-59.

HEARSON, L. (1966). An analysis of apical proliferation in the fore limb regeneration blastema of the Axolotl *Ambystoma mexicanum*. Ph.D. thesis, State University, East Lansing, Michigan.

HEILMANN, G. (1926). *The origin of birds*. Witherby, London.

HEPTONSTALL, W. B. (1970). Quantitative assessment of the flight of *Archaeopteryx*. *Nature, Lond.* **228**, 185-6.

HILFER, S. R., SEARLS, R. L., and FONTE, V. G. (1973). An ultrastructural study of early myogenesis in the chick wing bud. *Devl. Biol.* **30**, 374-91.

HINCHLIFFE, J. R. (1974). The patterns of cell death in chick limb morphogenesis. *Libyan Journal of Science* **4A**, 23-32.

—— (1976a). 'Rudimentation', reduction and specialisation in the development and evolution of the bird wing. In *Mécanismes de la rudimentation des organes chez les embryons de vertébrés*, pp. 411-14. Editions du CNRS 266, Paris.

—— (1976b). The development of winglessness (ws) in the chick. In *Mecanismes de la rudimentation des organes chez les embryons de vertébres*, pp. 173-85. Editions du CNRS **266**, Paris,

—— (1977). The chondrogenic pattern in chick limb morphogenesis: a problem of development *and* evolution. In *Vertebrate limb and somite morphogenesis* (eds. D. A. Ede, J. R. Hinchliffe, and M. Balls). Cambridge University Press.

—— (1980). Cell death and the development of limb form in the developing wing and webbed foot of the Herring Gull, *Larus argentatus*. *J. Embryol. exp. Morph.* (In press.)

—— and EDE, D. A. (1967). Limb development in the polydactylous *talpid*³ mutant of the fowl. *J. Embryol. exp. Morph.* **17**, 385-404.

—— —— (1968). Abnormalities in bone and cartilage development in the *talpid*³ mutant of the fowl. *J. Embryol. exp. Morph.* **19**, 327-39.

—— —— (1973). Cell death and the development of limb form and skeletal pattern in normal and *wingless* (ws) chick embryos. *J. Embryol. exp. Morph.* **30**, 753-72.

—— and THOROGOOD, P. V. (1974). Genetic inhibition of mesenchymal cell death and the development of form and skeletal pattern in the limbs of *talpid*^{3} mutant chick embryos. *J. Embryol. exp. Morph.* **31**, 747–60.

HOLDER, N. (1977*a*). An experimental investigation into the early development of the chick elbow joint. *J. Embryol. exp. Morph.* **39**, 115–27.

—— (1977*b*). The control of growth and cellular differentiation in the developing chick limb. Ph.D. thesis, University of London.

—— (1978). The onset of osteogenesis in the developing chick limb bud. *J. Embryol. exp. Morph.* **44**, 15–29.

HOLMGREN, N. (1933). On the origin of the tetrapod limb. *Acta. Zool. Stock.* **14**, 185–295.

—— (1955). Studies on the phylogeny of birds. *Acta. Zool. Stock.* **36**, 243–328.

HOLTFRETER, J. (1968). Mesenchyme and epithelia in inductive and morphogenetic processes. In *Epithelial mesenchymal interactions* (eds. P. Fleischmajer and R. E. Billingham). Williams and Wilkins, Baltimore.

HORNBRUCH, A. and WOLPERT, L. (1970). Cell division in the early growth and morphogenesis of the chick limb. *Nature, Lond.* **226**, 764–6.

HORDER, T. J. (1978). Functional adaptability and morphogenetic opportunism, the only rules for limb development. *Zoon.* **6**, 181–92.

HOLTZER, H., HOLTZER, S., and AVERY, G. (1955). Morphogenesis of tail vertebrae during regeneration. *J. Morph.* **96**, 145–71.

HUGHES, A. (1965). A quantitative study of the development of the nerves of the hind limb in *Eleutherodactylus martinicensis*. *J. Embryol. exp. Morph.* **13**, 9–34.

HURLE, J. and HINCHLIFFE, J. R. (1978). Cell death in the posterior necrotic zone (PNZ) of the chick wingbud: a stereoscan and ultrastructural survey of autolysis and cell fragmentation. *J. Embryol. exp. Morph.* **43**, 123–36.

HUTT, F. B. (1949). *Genetics of the fowl.* McGrawHill, New York, London.

HUXLEY, J. S. and DE BEER, G. R. (1934). *The elements of experimental embryology.* Cambridge University Press.

ITEN, L. E. and BRYANT, S. V. (1973). Forelimb regeneration from different levels of amputation in the newt *Notophthalmus viridescens*: length, rate and stages. *Wilhelm Roux Arch. EntwMech. Org.* **173**, 263–82.

—— —— (1975). The interaction between the blastemata and stump in the establishment of the anterior–posterior and proximal–distal organisation of the limb regenerate. *Devl. Biol.* **44**, 119–47.

JABAILY, J. A. and SINGER, M. (1977). Neurotrophic stimulation of DNA synthesis in the regenerating forelimb of the newt, *Triturus*. *J. exp. Zool* **199**, 251–5.

JACOBSON, M. (1978). *Developmental Neurobiology* (2nd edn). Plenum Press, New York.

JACOBSON, W. and FELL, H. B. (1941). The developmental mechanics and potencies of undifferentiated mesenchyme of the mandible. *Q. Jl. microsc. Sci.* **82**, 563–86.

JANNERS, M. Y. and SEARLS, R. L. (1970). Changes in the rate of cellular proliferation during the differentiation of cartilage and muscle in the mesenchyme of the embryonic chick wing. *Devl. Biol.* **23**, 136–65.

JARVIK, E. (1960). *Theories de l'evolution des vertébrés (reconsiderés à la lumière des recents decouvertes sur les vertébrés inferieurs) l'origine des nageoires paires*. Masson et Cie., Libraires de l'academie de Médicine, 129 Boulevard Saint-Germain, Paris VIe.

JOHNSON, D. R. (1967). Extratoes: a new mutant gene causing multiple abnormalities in the mouse. *J. Embryol. exp. Morph.* **17**, 543–81.

—— (1969). Polysyndactyly, a new mutant gene in the mouse. *J. Embryol. exp. Morph.* **21**, 285–94.

—— (1977). Ultrastructural observations on stumpy (stm), a new chondrodystrophic mutant in the mouse. *J. Embryol. exp. Morph.* **39**, 279–84.

—— (1978). The growth of femur and tibia in three genetically distinct chondrodystrophic mutants of the house mouse. *J. Anat.* **125**, 267–75.

—— and HUNT, D. M. (1974). Biochemical observations on the cartilage of achondroplastic (can) mice. *J. Embryol. exp. Morph.* **31**, 319–28.

—— and WISE, J. M. (1971). Cartilage anomaly (can); a new mutant gene in the mouse. *J. Embryol. exp. Morph.* **25**, 21–31.

JORDAN, M. (1965). Investigations on the differentiation of blastemas implanted into the brain of amphibia. *Folia Biol (Warsaw)* **13**, 205–55.

JORQUERA, B. and PUGIN, E. (1971). Sur le comportement du mésoderme et de l'ectoderme du bourgeon de membre dans les éschanges entre le poulet et le rat. *C.R. hebd. Séanc. Acad. Sci. Paris.* D **272**, 1522–5.

JURAND, A. (1965). Ultrastructural aspects of early development of the forelimb buds in the chick and mouse. *Proc. R. Soc. Lond.* B **162**, 387–405.

KAMRIN, A. A. and SINGER, M. (1959). The growth influence of spinal ganglia implanted into the denervated fore limb regenerate of the newt *Triturus*. *J. Morph.* **104**, 415–32.

KARCZMAR, G. A. (1946). The role of amputation and nerve resection in the regressing limbs of urodele larvae. *J. Exp. Zool.* **103**, 401–27.

KAUFFMAN, S. A., SHYMKO, R. M., and TRABERT, K. (1978). Control of sequential compartment formation in *Drosophila*. *Science, N.Y.* **199**, 259–70.

KELLEY, R. O. (1970). An electron microscopic study of mesenchyme during development of interdigital spaces in man. *Anat. Rec.* **168**, 43–54.

—— and FALLON, J. F. (1976). Ultrastructural analysis of the apical ectodermal ridge during vertebrate limb morphogenesis. I. The human forelimb with special reference to gap junctions. *Devl. Biol.* **51**, 241–56.

KERR, J. F. R., WYLLIE, A. H., and CURRIE, A. R. (1972). Apoptosis: a basic biological phenomenon with wide ranging implications in tissue kinetics. *Br. J. Cancer.* **26**, 239–57.

KIENY, M. (1960). Role inducteur du mésoderme dans la differentiation précoce du bourgeon de membre chez l'embryon de Poulet. *J. Embryol. exp. Morph.* **8**, 457–67.

—— (1964*a*). Régulation des excédents et des deficiences du bourgeon d'aile de l'embryon de poulet. *Arch. Anat. Morph. exp.* **53**, 29–44.

—— (1964*b*). Étude du mécanisme de la régulation dans de développement du bourgeon de membre de l'embryon de Poulet. I Régulation des excédents. *Devl. Biol.* **9**, 197–229.

—— (1964*c*). Étude du mécanisme de la régulation dans le developpement du bourgeon de membre de l'embryon de poulet. II. Régulation des deficiences dans les chimèras 'aile-patte' et 'patte-aile'. *J. Embryol. exp. Morph.* **12**, 357–71.

—— (1968). Variation de la capacité inductrice du mésoderme et de la competence de l'ectoderme au cours de l'induction primaire du bourgeon de membre, chez l'embryon de poulet. *Arch. Anat. microsc. Morph. exp.* **57**, 401–18.

—— (1969). Sur les relations entre le mésoderme somitique et le mésoderme somatopleural avant et au cours de l'induction primaire des membres de l'embryon du Poulet. *C.r. hebd. Séanc. Acad. Sci. Paris D* **268**, 3183–6.

—— (1971). Les phases d'activité morphogène du mésoderme somatopleurale pendant le développement précoce de membre chez l'embryon de poulet *Ann Embryol. Morphog.* **4**, 281–98.

—— and ABBOTT, U. K. (1962). Contribution a l'étude de la diplopodie liée au sexe et de l'achondroplasie Creeper chez l'embryon de poulet: culture *in vitro* des ébauches cartilagineuses du tibio-tarse et du péroné. *Devl. Biol.* **4**, 473–88.

—— and PAUTOU, M. P. (1976). Régulation des excédents dans le développement du bourgeon de membre de l'embryon d'oiseau. Analyse expérimentale de combinaisons xenoplastiques caille/poulet. *Wilhelm Roux Arch. Entw-Mech. Org.* **179**, 327–38.

—— —— and SENGEL, P. (1976). Limb morphogenesis as studied by Janus green B and vinblastine-induced malformations. In *Tests of teratogenicity in vitro*, pp. 389–415. North Holland, Amsterdam.

—— and SENGEL, P. (1974). La nécrose morphogène interditale chez l'embryon de poulet: effet de la cytochalasine B. *Ann. Biol* **13** 57–68.

KONIECZNA-MARCZYNSKA, B. and SKOWRON-CENDRZAK, A. (1958). The effect of an augmented nerve supply on regeneration in postmetamorphic *Xenopus laevis. Folia Biol. Warsaw* **6**, 37–46.

LACROIX, P. (1961). Bone and cartilage. In *The cell* (eds. J. Brachet and A. E. Mirski), Vol 5, pp. 219–66. Academic Press, New York.

LANDAUER, W. (1927). Untersuchungen über Chondrodystrophie I Allgemeine Erscheinungen und Skelett chondrodystrophischer Hühnerembryonen. *Wilhelm Roux Arch. EntwMech. Org.* **110**, 195–278.

—— (1931). Untersuchungen über das Krüperhuhn II Morphologie und Histologie des Skelets, insbesondere des Skelets der langen Extremitäten-Knochen. *Z. mikrosk.-anat. Forsch.* **25**, 115–80.

—— (1932). Studies on the Creeper fowl III. The early development and lethal expression of homozygous Creeper embryos. *J. Genetics.* **25**, 367–94.

—— (1933). Untersuchungen über das Kruperhuhn IV. Die Missbildungen homozygoter Krüperembryonen auf spateren Entwicklungsstadien (Phokomelie und Chondrodystrophie). *Z. mikrosk.-anat. Forsch.* **32**, 359–412.

—— (1934). Studies on the Creeper fowl. VI. Skeletal growth of Creeper chickens. *Storrs Agr. Exp. Station Bull.* **193**.

—— (1959*a*). A second diplopod mutation of the fowl. *J. Hered.* **47**, 57–63.

—— (1956*b*). Rudimentation and duplication of the radius in the duplicate mutant form of the fowl. *J. Genet.* **54**, 199–218.

—— (1965). Nanomelia, a lethal mutation of the fowl. *J. Hered.* **56**, 131–8.

LANDE, R. (1978). Evolutionary mechanisms of limb loss in tetrapods. *Evolution, Lancaster, Pa.* **32**, 73–92.

LASSILA, V. (1928). Beiträge zur Kenntnis der Entwicklung und Verknöcherung des soyenannen Fungenknorpels. *Annales Acad. Scien. fennicae Ser. A.* **31**, 1–220.

LAUTHIER, M. (1977). Étude ultrastructurale des stades précoces du développement du membre posterieur de *Pleurodeles watlii Michah.* (Amphibien, Urodèle). *J. Embryol. exp. Morph.* **38**, 1–18.

LAWSON, D. A. (1975). Pterosaur from the latest Cretaceous of West Texas: discovery of the largest flying creature. *Science, N.Y.* **187**, 947–8.

LE DOUARIN, N. (1971). Caracteristiques ultrastructurales du noyau interphasique chez la caille et chez le poulet et utilization de cellules de caille comme 'marqueurs biologique' en embryologie expérimentale. *Ann. Embyrol. Morphog.* **4**, 125–35.

LEOVY, S. (1913). Über die Entwickelung der Ranvier'schen zellen. *Anat. Anz.* **45**, 238–49.

LESSMOLLMANN, U., NEUBERT, D., and MERKER, H. J. (1975). Mammalian limb buds differentiating *in vitro* as a test system for the evolution of embryotoxic effects. In *New approaches to the evaluation of abnormal development* (eds. D. Neubert and H. J. Meiker), pp. 99–113. G. Thieme, Stuttgart.

LEWIS, J. H. (1975). Fate maps and the pattern of cell division: a calculation for the chick wing bud. *J. Embryol. exp. Morph.* **33**, 419–34.

—— (1977). Growth and determination in the developing limb. In *Vertebrate limb and somite morphogenesis* (eds. D. A. Ede, J. R. Hinchliffe, and M. Balls), pp. 215–28. Cambridge University Press.

—— SMITH, A., CRAWLEY, A., and WOLPERT, L. (1974). A quantitative study of blastemal growth and bone regression during limb regeneration in *Triturus cristatus. J. Embryol. exp. Morph.* **32**, 375–90.

—— and WOLPERT, L. (1976). The principle of non-equivalence in development. *J. theor. Biol.* **62**, 479–90.

LIOSNER, L. D. and WORONZOWA, M. A. (1936). Regeneration des Organs mit transplantierten ortsfremden Muskeln. *Q. Mitteilungen Zool. Anz.* **115**, 55–8.

LOCKSHIN, R. A. and BEAULATON, J. (1974). Programmed cell death. *Life Sciences.* **15**, 1549–65.

LOVEJOY, A. O. (1959). The argument for organic evolution before the Origin of Species. In *Forerunners of Darwin* (eds. B. Glass, O. Temkin, and W. L. Strauss), pp. 356–414. Johns Hopkins, Baltimore.

LUTZ, H. (1942). Beitrage zur Stammesgeschichte der Ratiten. *Revue suisse Zool.* **49**, 299–399.

McALPINE, R. J. (1956). Alkaline glycerophosphatases in the limb buds of the rat embryo. *Anat. Rec.* **126**, 82-96.

MacCABE, A. B., GASSELING, M. T., and SAUNDERS, J. W. Jr. (1973). Spatiotemporal distribution of mechanisms that control outgrowth and antero-posterior polarization of the limb bud in the chick embryo. *Mechanisms of ageing and development*, **2**, 1–12.

MacCABE, J. A. (1969). Morphogenetic pattern determination in normal and mutant chick limbs. Ph.D. thesis. University of California, Davis, USA.

—— and ABBOTT, U. K. (1974). Polarizing and maintenance activities in two polydactylous mutants of the fowl: diplopodia-1 and talpid-2. *J. Embryol. exp. Morph.* **31**, 735–46.

—— CALANDRA, A. J., and PARKER, B. W. (1977). In vitro analysis of the distribution and nature of a morphogenetic factor in the developing chick wing. In *Vertebrate limb and somite morphogenesis* (eds. D. A. Ede, J. R. Hinchliffe, and M. Balls), pp. 25–39. Cambridge University Press.

—— ERRICK, J., and SAUNDERS, J. W. Jr. (1974). Ectodermal control of the dorsoventral axis of the leg bud of the chick embryo. *Devl. Biol.* **39**, 69–82.

—— MacCABE, A. B., ABBOTT, U. K., and McCARRY, J. R. (1975). Limb development in diplopodia: a polydactylous mutation in the chicken. *J. exp. Zool.* **191**, 383–93.

—— and PARKER, B. W. (1976a). Polarizing activity in the developing limb of the Syrian hamster. *J. exp. Zool.* **195**, 311-17.

—— —— (1976b). Evidence for a gradient of a morphogenetic factor in the developing chick wing. *Devl. Biol.* **54**, 297–303.

—— SAUNDERS, J. W. Jr, and PICKETT, M. (1973). The control of the antero-posterior and dorsoventral axes in embryonic chick limbs constructed of dissociated and reaggregated limb-bud mesoderm. *Devl. Biol.* **31**, 323-35.

McKAY, D. G., ADAMS, E. C., HERTIG, A. T., and DANZIGER, S. (1956). Histochemical horizons in human embryos II. *Anat. Rec.* **126**, 433-64.

McLAREN, A. (1976). *Mammalian chimaeras.* Cambridge University Press.

MADEN, M. (1976). Blastemal kinetics and pattern formation during amphibian limb regeneration. *J. Embryol. exp. Morph.* **36**, 561-74.

—— and TURNER, R. N. (1978). Supernumerary limbs in the axolotl. *Nature, London.* **73**, 232-5.

—— and WALLACE, H. (1975). The origin of limb regenerates from cartilage grafts. *Actae Embryologicae Experimentalis* **2**, 77-86.

MADERSON, P. (1975). Embryonic tissue interactions as the basis for morphological change in evolution. *Am. Zool.* **15**, 315-28.

MATHUR, J. K. and GOEL, S. C. (1976). Patterns of chondrogenesis and calcification in the developing limb of the lizard *Calotes versicolor. J. Morph.* **149**, 401-20.

MAYNARD-SMITH, J. (1960). Continuous, quantised and modal variation. *Proc. R. Soc. B.* **152**, 397-409.

MEDOFF, J. (1967). Enzymatic events during cartilage differentiation in the chick embryonic limb bud. *Devl. Biol.* **16**, 118-43.

—— and ZWILLING, E. (1972). Appearance of myosin the the chick limb. *Devl. Biol.* **28**, 138-41.

MENDELL, L. M. and HOLLYDAY, M. (1976). Spinal reflexes with altered periphery. In *Frog neurobiology* (eds. R. Llinas and W. Precht), pp. 793-810. Springer, New York.

MENKES, B. and DELEANU, M. (1964). Leg differentiation and experimental syndactyly in chick embryo. *Rev. Romaine. Embryol. Cytol.* **1**, 69-77.

—— —— and ILIES, A. (1965). Comparative study of some areas of physiological necrosis of the embryo of man, laboratory mammalians and fowl. *Rev. Romaine Embryol. Cytol.* **2**, 161-72.

—— SANDOR, S., and ILIES, A. (1970). Cell death in teratogenesis. In *Advances in teratology* (ed. D. H. M. Woollam), pp. 189-215. Logos Press, London.

METTETAL, C. (1939). La régénération des membres chez la Salamandra et le Triton. Histologie et détermination *Arch. Anat. Histol. Emrbyol.* **28**, 1-214.

MILAIRE, J. (1956). Contribution a l'étude morphologique et cytochimique des bourgeons de membres chez le rat. *Archs. Biol. Liège* **67**, 297-391.

—— (1957). Contribution a la connaissance morphologique et cytochimique des bourgeons de membres chez quelques reptiles. *Archs. Biol. Liege* **68**, 429-572.

—— (1962). Histochemical aspects of limb morphogenesis in vertebrates. *Adv. Morphog.* **2**, 183-209.

—— (1963). Étude morphologique et cytochimique du développement des membres chez la souris et chez la taupe. *Arch. Biol. Liège* **74**, 129-317.

—— (1965). Aspects of limb morphogenesis in mammals. In *Organogenesis* (eds. R. L. DeHaan and H. Ursprung), pp. 283-300. Holt, Rhinehart and Winston, New York.

—— (1967*a*). Histochemical observations on the developing foot of normal oligosyndactylous (*Os/+*) and syndactylous (*sm/sm*) mouse embryos. *Archs. Biol. Liège* **78**, 223-88.

—— (1967*b*). Evolution des processus dégénératifs dans le cape apicale au cours du développement des membres chez le rat et la souris. *C. r. hebd. Seanc. Acad. Sci. Paris D* **265**, 137-40.

—— (1971). Evolution et déterminisme des dégenerescences cellulaires au cours de la morphogenèse des membres et leurs modifications teratologiques. In *Malformations congènitales des mammifères* (ed. H. Tuchmann-Duplessis), pp. 131–49. Colloques Pfizer, Amboise.

—— (1973). Indices d'une participation morphogène de l'épiblaste au cours du développement des membres chez les mammifères. *Arch. Biol. Bruxelles* **84**, 87–114.

—— (1974). Histochemical aspects of organogenesis in vertebrates. *Handbuch der Histochemie* **8**, 1–135.

—— (1975). Prodromes de la genèse du membre postérieur chez l'embryon de souris. Étude morphologique et histochemique. *Arch. Biol. Liège* **86**, 177–221.

—— (1976). Contribution cellulaire de somites à la genèse des bourgeons de membres postérieurs chez la souris. *Arch. Biol. Bruxelles* **87**, 315–43.

—— (1977a). Histochemical expression of morphogenetic gradients during limb morphogenesis (with particular reference to mammalian embryos). *Birth Defects* **13**, 37–67.

—— (1977b). Rudimentation digitale au cours du développement normale de l'autopode chez les mammifères. In *Mécanismes de la rudimentation des organes chez les embryons de vertébrés*, pp. 221–33. Editions du CNRS. **266**, Paris.

MINOR, R. (1973). Somite chondrogenesis. A structural analysis. *J. Cell Biol* **56**, 27–50.

MITROVIC, D. R. (1971). La nécrose physiologique dans le mésenchyme articulaire des embryons de Rat et de Poulet. *C.r. hebd. Seanc. Sci. Paris D* **273**, 642–5.

—— (1972). Presence de cellules degenerées dans la cavité articularie en développement chez l'embryon de Poulet. *C.r. hebd. Séanc. Sci. Paris D* **275**, 2941–4.

—— (1977). Development of the metatarsalphalangeal joint of the chick embryo: morphological, ultrastructural and histochemical studies. *Am. J. Anat.* **150**, 333–48.

MIZELL, M. (1968). Limb regeneration: induction in the new born opossum. *Science, N.Y.* **161**, 283–6.

MOHAMMED, M. B. H. (1978). Cell division of normal and mutant chick embryos. Ph.D. thesis, University of Glasgow.

MONTAGNA, W. (1945). A re-investigation of the development of the wing in the fowl. *J. Morph.* **76**, 87–113.

MOORE, W. J. and MINTZ, B. (1972). Clonal model of vertebral column and skull development derived from genetically mosaic skeletons in allophenic mice. *Devl. Biol.* **27**, 55–70.

MORATA, G. and LAWRENCE, P. A. (1977). Homoeotic genes, compartments and cell determination in *Drosophila. Nature, Lond.* **265**, 211–16.

MORGAN, T. H. (1906). The extent and limitations of the power to regenerate in man and other vertebrates. *The Harvey lectures* pp. 219–29. Lippincott, Philadelphia.

MOSCONA, A. A. (1960). Patterns and mechanisms of tissue reconstruction from dissociated cells. In *Developing cell systems and their control* (ed. D. Rudnick), pp. 45–70. Ronald Press, New York.

MOY-THOMAS, J. A. and MILES, R. S. (1971). *Palaeozoic Fishes* (2nd edn). Chapman and Hall, London.

MUNRO, W. M. and CRICK, F. H. C. (1971). The time needed to set up a gradient: detailed calculations. In *Control mechanisms of growth and differentiation. Society for Experimental Biology Symposium* **25**, pp. 439–54. Cambridge University Press.

86References

MURRAY, P. D. F. (1926). An experimental study of the development of the limbs of the chick. *Proc. Linn. Soc. N.S.W.* **51**, 187–263.

—— and HUXLEY, J. S. (1925). Self differentiation in the grafted limb-bud of the chick. *J. Anat.* **59**, 379–84.

NAPIER, J. (1967). The antiquity of human walking. *Scient. Am.* **216**, 55–66.

NEEDHAM, A. E. (1941). Some experimental biological uses of the element beryllium. *Proc. Zool. Soc. London. A* **111**, 59–85.

NEW, D. A. T. (1966). *The culture of vertebrate embryos.* Academic Press, London.

NEWMAN, S. (1977). Lineage and pattern in the developing wing bud. In *Vertebrate limb and somite morphogenesis* (eds. D. A. Ede, J. R. Hinchliffe, and M. Balls), pp. 181–97. Cambridge University Press.

NIEWKOOP, P. D. and FABER, J. (1956). *Normal table of Xenopus laevis (Daudin).* A systematical and chronological survey of the development from the fertilised egg till the end of metamorphosis. North Holland Amsterdam.

NOPSCA, Baron J. (1907). Ideas on the origin of flight. *Proc. Zool. Soc. Lond.* 223–36.

OLSON, E. C. (1971). *Vertebrate paleozoology.* Interscience, New York.

OPPENHEIMER, J. (1959). An embryological enigma in the *Origin of Species*. In *Forerunners of Darwin* (eds. B. Glass, O. Temkin, and W. L. Straus), pp. 292–322. Johns Hopkins, Baltimore.

OSTROM, J. H. (1969). Osteology of *Deinonychus antirrhopus*, an unusual theropod from the lower Cretaceous of Montana. *Bull. Peabody Mus. Nat. Hist. Yale Univ.* **30**, 1–165.

—— (1974). *Archaeopteryx* and the origin of flight. *Q. Rev. Biol.* **49**, 27–47.

—— (1976). *Archaeopteryx* and the origin of birds. *Biological Journal of the Linnean Society.* **8**, 91–182.

OWEN, R. (1843). *On the invertebrate aniamls.* London.

—— (1849). *On the nature of limbs.* London.

PANKRATZ, D. S. (1939). Motion pictures of foetal movements in the rabbit. *Anat. Rec. suppl.* **73**, 72.

PARKER, T. J. and HASWELL, W. A. (1940). *A text book of zoology* Vol. II. Macmillan, London.

PARKER, W. K. (1888). On the structure and development of the wing in the common fowl. *Phil. Trans. R. Soc. B* **179**, 385–98.

PAUTOU, M. P. (1968). Rôle déterminante du mésoderme dans la differentiation spécifique de la patte de l'oiseau. *Arch. Anat. micr. Morph. exp.* **48**, 311–28.

—— (1973). Analyse de la morphogenèse du pied des Oiseaux à l'aide de mélanges cellulaires inter-spécifiques. I. Étude morphologique. *J. Embryol. exp. Morph.* **29**, 175–96.

—— (1974). Evolution comparée de la nécrose morphogène interdigitale dans le pied de l'ambryon de poulet et de canard. *C.r. hebd. Séanc. Acad. Sci. Paris D* **278**, 2209–12.

—— (1975). Morphogenèse de l'autopode chez l'embryon de poulet. *J. Embryol. exp. Morph.* **34**, 511–29.

—— (1976). La morphogenèse du pied de l'embryon de poulet étudiée a l'aide de malformations provoquées par le vert Janus. *J. Embryol. exp. Morph.* **35**, 649–65.

—— (1977). Dorso-ventral axis determination of chick limb bud development. In *Vertebrate limb and somite morphogenesis* (eds. D. A. Ede, J. R. Hinchliffe, and M. Balls), pp. 257–66. Cambridge University Press.

—— and KIENY, M. (1973). Interaction ecto-mésodermique dans l'établissement de la polarité dorso-ventrale du pied de l'embryon de poulet. *C.r. hebd. Séanc. Acad. Sci. Paris.* **227**, 1225–8.

PEADON, A. M. and SINGER, M. (1965). A quantitative study of forelimb innervation in relation to regenerative capacity in the larval land stage, and adult forms of *Triturus viridescens. J. exp. Zool.* **159**, 337–46.

PIETSCH, P. (1961). Differentiation in regeneration I. The development of muscle and cartilage following deplantation of regenerating limb blastema of Ambystoma larvae. *Devl. Biol.* **3**, 255–64.

PINOT, M. (1969). Mise en évidence d'un rôle du mésenchyme axial sur la morphogènese précoce des membres de l'embryon de Poulet. *C.r. hebd. Séanc. Acad. Sci. Paris D.* **269**, 201–4.

—— (1970*a*). Le rôle du mésoderme somitique dans le morphogènese précoce des membres de l'embryon de Poulet. *J. Embryol. exp. Morph.* **23**, 109–51.

—— (1970*b*). Relations entre le mésenchyme somitique et la plaque laterale dans l'organogenèse précoce des membres, chez le Poulet. *Année Biologique.* **9**, 277–84.

POLEZAJEW, L. N. (1936). Die Rolle des Epithels bei der Regeneration und in der normalen Ontogenese der Extremitaten bei Amphibien. *Zool. Zhur.* **15**, 277–91.

POLLAK, R. D. and FALLON, J. F. (1974). Autoradiographic analysis of macromolecular synthesis in propectively necrotic cells of the chick limb bud I. Protein Synthesis. *Expl. Cell Res.* **86**, 9–14.

—— —— (1976). Autoradiographic analysis of a macromolecular synthesis in prospectively necrotic cells of the chick limb bud II. Nucleic acids. *Expl. Cell Res.* **100**, 15–22.

PRESTIGE, M. C. (1967). The control of cell number in the lumber ventral horns during the development of *Xenopus laevis* tadpoles. *J. Embryol. exp. Morph.* **18**, 359–87.

RAHMANI, T. M. Z. (1974). Morphogenesis of the rudimentary hind limb of the grass snake (*Ophisaurus apodus Pallas*). *J. Embryol. exp. Morph.* **32**, 431–43.

RAYNAUD, A. (1969). On the factors involved in the arrest of development of the limb buds in the lizard, *Anguis fragilis. Indian J. Zootomy* **10**, 47–53.

—— (1972*a*). Embryologie des membres rudimentaires des Reptiles. *C.r. hebd. Séanc. Acad. Sci. Paris* **4**, 241–7.

—— (1972*b*). Morphogenèse des membres rudimentaires chez les reptiles: un problème d'embryologie et d'évolution. *Bull. Soc. Zool. Fr.* **97**, 469–85.

—— (1974). Données embryologiques sur la rudimentation des membres chez les reptiles. *Bull. Soc. Hist. Nat. Toulouse.* **110**, 26–40.

—— (1976). Les modalités de la rudimentation des membres chez les embryons de reptiles serpentiformes. In *Mécanismes de la rudimentation des organes chez les embryons de Vertébrés.* pp. 201–19, Éditions CNRS **266**, Paris.

—— (1977). Somites and early morphogenesis of reptile limbs. In *Vertebrate limb and somite morphogenesis* (eds. D. A. Ede, J. R. Hinchliffe, and M. Balls), pp. 373–85. Cambridge University Press.

—— and ADRIAN, M. (1975). Caractéristiques ultrastructurales des divers constituants des ébauches des membres, chez les embryons d'Orvet (*Anguis fragilis L*) et de Lézard vert (*Lacerta viridis Laur*). *C.r. hebd. Séanc. Acad. Sci. Paris.* **280**, 2591–4.

—— —— and KOUPRACH, S. (1973). Étude ultrastructurale du mésoblaste de l'ebauche des membres de l'embryon d'Orvet (*Anguis fragilis L*) au cours de la periode de régression de la crête apicale. *C.r. hebd. Séanc. Acad. Sci. Paris D* **277**, 1671–2.

—— and VASSE, J. (1968). Les relations entre les somites et les ébauches des membres anterieurs, chez l'embryon d'Orvet (*Anguis fragilis*). *Arch. anat. micr. Morph. exp.* **57**, 227–54.

—— (1972). Les principales étapes du développement de l'ébauche du membre anterieur de l'Orvet (*Anguis fragilis L*) étudiées au moyen de l'autoradiographie. *C.r. hebd. Séanc. Acad. Sci. Paris D* **274**, 1938–41.

REIG, O. (1970). The Proterosuchia and the early evolution of the Archosaurs; an essay about the origin of a major taxon. *Bull. Mus. Comp. Zool., Harvard.* **139**, 229–92.

RENOUS, S., RAYNAUD, A., GASC, J. P., and PIEAU, C. (1976). Caractères rudimentaires, anatomiques et embryologiques, de la ceinture pelvienne et des appendices postérieurs du Python réticulé (*Python reticulatus* Schneider 1801). *Bull. Mus. Natn. Hist. Nat. Paris* (3e.sér.) **379**, 547–84.

REUSS, C. and SAUNDERS, J. W. Jr. (1965). Inductive and axial properties of prospective limb mesoderm in the early chick embryo. *Am. Zool.* **5**, 214.

RICHARDSON, D. (1945). Thyroid pituitary hormones in relation to regeneration II. Regeneration of the hind limb of the newt, *Triturus viridescens*, with different contributions of thyroid and pituitary hormones. *J. exp. Zool.* **100**, 417–29.

RIDDIFORD, L. M. (1960). Autoradiographic studies of tritiated thymidine infused into the blastema of the early regenerate in the adult newt, *Triturus. J. exp. Zool.* **144**, 25–31.

ROMANES, G. J. (1941). The development and significance of the cell columns in the ventral horn of the cervical and upper thoracic spinal cord of the rabbit. *J. Anat.* **76**, 117–30.

ROMANOFF, A. L. (1960). *The avian embryo.* Macmillan, New York.

ROMER, A. S. (1922). The locomotor apparatus of certain primitive mammal-like reptiles. *Bull. Am. Mus. Nat. Hist.* **46**, 517–606.

—— (1927). The development of the thigh musculature of the chick. *Journal of Morphology and Physiology* **43**, 347–85.

—— (1942). The development of the tetrapod limb musculature – the thigh of *Lacerta. J. Morph.* **71**, 251–95.

—— (1944). The development of tetrapod limb musculature – the shoulder region of *Lacerta. J. Morph.* **74**, 1–41.

—— (1949). *The vertebrate body.* Saunders, Philadelphia.

—— (1966). *Vertebrate paleontology* (3rd edn). Chicago University Press.

—— (1971). The Chañares (Argentina) Triassic reptile fauna. X. Two new but incompletely known long-limbed pseudosuchians. *Breviora* **378**, 1–10.

ROOZE, M. A. (1977). The effect of the Dh. gene on limb morphogenesis in the mouse. *Birth Defects.* **13**, 69–95.

ROSE, F. C. and ROSE, S. M. (1965). The role of normal epidermis in recovery of regenerative ability in x-rayed limbs of *Triturus. Growth* **29**, 361–93.

ROSE, S. M. (1944). Methods of initiating limb regeneration in adult anura. *J. exp. Zool.* **95**, 149–70.

—— (1971). *Regeneration.* Appleton Centry Crofts, New York.

—— (1974). *Regeneration.* Addison-Wesley Module 12. Reading, Mass.

ROSENBERG, E. (1875). Entwickl. der Wirbelsäule. *Morph. Jahrb.* **1**,

RUBEN, L. N. (1960). An immunobiological model of implant induced urodele supernumerary limb formation. *Am. Naturalist.* **94**, 427–34.

—— and FROTHINGHAM, M. L. (1958). The importance of innervation and superficial wounding in urodele accessory limb formation. *J. Morph.* **102**, 91–113.

RUBIN, L. and SAUNDERS, J. W. Jr. (1972). Ectodermal–mesodermal interactions in the growth of limb buds in the chick embryo: constancy and temporal limits of the ectodermal induction. *Devl. Biol.* **28**, 94–112.

SAUNDERS, J. W. Jr. (1948). The proximo-distal sequence of the origin of the parts of the chick wing and the role of the ectoderm. *J. exp. Zool.* **108**, 363–404.

—— (1966). Death in embryonic systems. *Science N.Y.* **154**, 604–12.

—— (1969). The interplay of morphogenetic factors. In *Limb development and deformity* (ed. C. A. Swinyard), pp. 84–100. Chas. C. Thomas, Illinois.

—— (1972). Developmental control of three-dimensional polarity in the avian limb. *Ann. N.Y. Acad. Sci.* **193**, 29–42.

—— (1977). The experimental analysis of chick limb bud development. In *Vertebrate limb and somite morphogenesis* (eds. D. A. Ede, J. R. Hinchliffe, and M. Balls), pp. 1–24. Cambridge University Press.

—— and FALLON, J. F. (1967). Cell death in morphogenesis. In *Major problems in developmental biology* (ed. M. Locke), pp. 289–314. Academic Press, New York and London.

—— and GASSELING, M. T. (1963). Trans-filter propagation of apical ectoderm maintenance factor in the chick embryo wing bud. *Devl. Biol.* **7**, 64–78.

—— and GASSELING, M. T. (1968). Ectodermal-mesenchymal interactions in the origin of limb symmetry. In *Epithelial–Mesenchymal Interactions* (eds R. Fleischmajer and R. F. Billingham), pp. 78–97. Williams and Wilkins, Baltimore.

—— —— and CAIRNS, J. M. (1959). The differentiation of prospective thigh mesoderm grafted beneath the apical ectodermal ridge of the wing bud in the chick embryo. *Devl. Biol.* **1**, 281–301.

—— —— and ERRICK, J. (1976). Inductive activity and enduring cellular constitution of a supernumerary apical ectodermal ridge grafted to the limb bud of the chick embryo. *Devl. Biol.* **50**, 16–25.

—— —— and GFELLER, Sr. M. D. (1958). Interactions of ectoderm and mesoderm in the origin of axial relationships in the wing of the fowl. *J. exp. Zool.* **137**, 39–74.

—— —— and SAUNDERS, L. C. (1962). Cellular death in morphogenesis of the avian wing. *Devl. Biol.* **5**, 147–78.

—— and REUSS, C. (1974). Inductive and axial properties of prospective wing-bud mesoderm in the chick embryo. *Devl. Biol.* **38**, 41–50.

SCHMIDT, A. J. (1958*a*). Forelimb regeneration of thyroidectomized adult newts. I Morphology. *J. exp. Zool.* **137**, 197–226.

—— (1958*b*). Forelimb regeneration of thyroidectomized adult newts. II Histology. *J. exp. Zool.* **139**, 95–127.

—— (1968). *Cellular biology of vertebrate regeneration and repair.* Chicago University Press.

SCHOTTÉ, O. E. (1961). Systemic factors in initiation of regenerative processes in limbs of larval and adult Amphibia. In *Synthesis of molecular and cellular structure* (ed. D. Rudnick), p. 161. Ronald Press, New York.

—— and BUTLER, E. G. (1944). Phases in regeneration of the urodele limb and their dependence upon the nervous system. *J. exp. Zool.* **97**, 95–121.

SCOTT, J. P. (1937). The embryology of the guinea pig. III. The development of the polydactylous monster. A case of growth accelerated at a particular period by a semi-dominant lethal gene. *J. exp. Zool.* **77**, 123–57.

—— (1938). The embryology of the guinea pig. II. The polydactylous monster. A new teras produced by the genes PxPx. *J. Morph.* **62**, 299–321.

SEARLE, A. G. (1963). The genetics and morphology of two 'luxoid' mutants in the house mouse. *Genet. Res.* **5**, 171–97.

SEARLS, R. L. (1965). An autoradiographic study of the uptake of S-35-sulphate during the differentiation of limb bud cartilage. *Devl. Biol.* **11**, 155–68.

—— (1967). The role of cell migration in the development of the embryonic chick limb buds. *J. exp. Zool.* **116**, 39–50.

—— (1968). Development of the embryonic chick limb bud in avascular culture. *J. Embryol. exp. Morph.* **17**, 382–99.

—— (1972). Cellular segregation: a 'late' differentiative charcteristic of chick limb bud cartilage cells. *Expl. Cell. Res.* **73**, 57–64.

—— (1973). Newer knowledge of chondrogenesis. *Clinical Orthopaedics* **96**, 327–44.

—— (1976). Effect of dorsal and ventral limb ectoderm on the development of the limb of the embryo chick. *J. Embryol. exp. Morph.* **35**, 367–81.

—— HILFER, S. R., and MIROW, S. M. (1972). An ultrastructural study of early chondrogenesis in the chick wing bud. *Devl. Biol.* **28**, 123–37.

—— and JANNERS, M. Y. (1969). The stabilisation of cartilage properties in the cartilage-forming mesenchyme of the embryonic chick limb. *J. exp. Zool.* **170**, 365–76.

—— and JANNERS, M. Y. (1971). The initiation of limb bud outgrowth in the embryonic chick. *Devl. Biol.* **24**, 198–213.

SEEGMILLER, R., FRASER, F. C., and SHELDON, H. (1971). A new chondro-dystrophic mutant in mice. *J. Cell. Biol.* **48**, 580–93.

SEELEY, H. G. (1901). *Dragons of the air.* Dover Books. (Reprint, 1967.)

SENGEL, P. (1971). The organogenesis and arrangement of cutaneous append-ages in birds. *Adv. Morphogen.* **9**, 181–230.

—— (1975). Discussion. In *Cell patterning.* Ciba Foundation Symposium 29 new series, pp. 119–21. Associated Scientific Publishers.

SEWERTZOFF, A. N. (1924). Development of the pelvic fins of *Acipenser ruthenus.* New data for the theory of the paired fins of fishes. *J. Morph. & Phys.* **41**, 547–79.

SHAROV, A. G. (1971). New flying reptiles from the mesozoic deposits of Kazakhstan and Kirgizia. *Trudy Pol. Inst. AN SSSR.* **130**, 104–13.

SHELLSWELL, G. B. and WOLPERT, L. (1977). The pattern of muscle and tendon development in the chick wing. In *Vertebrate limb and somite mor-phogenesis* (eds. D. A. Ede, J. R. Hinchliffe, and M. Balls), pp. 71–86. Cambridge University Press.

SHUMWAY, W. (1942). Stages in the normal development of *Rana pipiens* II. Identification of the stages from sectioned material. *Anat. Rec.* **83**, 309–13.

SINGER, M. (1954). Induction of regeneration of the forelimb of the post-metamorphic frog by augmentation of the nerve supply. *J. exp. Zool.* **126**, 419–72.

—— (1960). Nervous mechanisms in the regeneration of body parts in verte-brates. In *Developing cell systems and their control.* (ed. D. Rudnick), pp. 115–33. Ronald Press, New York.

—— (1965). A theory of the trophic nervous control of amphibian limb re-generation, including a re-evaluation of quantitative nerve requirements. In *Proc. Regen in Animals* (eds. V. Kiortsis and H. A. L. Trampusch), pp. 20–32. North Holland, Amsterdam.

—— (1973). *Limb regeneration in vertebrates.* Addison-Wesley Module 6, Reading, Mass.

—— and CRAVEN, L. (1948). The growth and morphogenesis of the re-generating forelimb of adult Triturus following denervation at various stages of development. *J. exp. Zool.* **108**, 279–308.

———— and MUTTERPERL, E. (1963). Nerve fiber requirements for regeneration in forelimb transplants of the newt *Triturus*. *Devl. Biol.* **7**, 180–91.

———— and SALPETER, M. M. (1961). Regeneration in vertebrates: the role of the wound epithelium. In *Growth and living systems* (ed. M. Y. Zarov), pp. 227–311. Basic Books, New York.

SKOWRON, S. and WALKNOWSKA, J. (1963). The development of regeneration buds after transplantation. *Folia Biol. (Warsaw)* **11**, 421–42.

SLACK, J. M. W. 91976). Determination of polarity in the amphibian limb. *Nature, Lond.* **261**, 44–6.

———— (1977*a*). Control of anteroposterior pattern in the axolotl forelimb by a smoothly graded signal. *J. Embryol. exp. Morph.* **39**, 169–82.

———— (1977*b*). Determination of anteroposterior polarity in the axolotl forelimb by an interaction between limb and flank rudiments. *J. Embryol. exp. Morph.* **39**, 151–68.

SLACK, J. M. W. and SAVAGE, S. (1978). Regeneration of reduplicated limbs in contravention of the complete circle rule. *Nature, Lond.* **271**, 760–1.

STARK, R. J. and SEARLS, R. L. (1973). A description of chick wing bud development and a model of limb morphogenesis. *Devl. Biol.* **33**, 138–53.

———— ———— (1974). The establishment of the cartilage pattern in the embryonic chick wing and evidence for a role of the dorsal and ventral ectoderm in normal wing development. *Devl. Biol.* **38**, 51–63.

STEEN, T. P. (1968). Stability of chondrocyte differentiation and contribution of muscle to cartilage during limb regeneration in the axolotl (*Siredon mexicanum*). *J. exp. Zool.* **167**, 49–78.

———— (1970). Origin and differentiative capacities of cells in the blastema of the regenerating salamander limb. *Am. Zool.* **10**, 119–32.

STEINER, H. (1922). Die ontogenetische und phylogenetische Entwicklung des Vogelflugel-skelettes. *Acta Zool., Stockh.* **3**, 307–60.

STERN, C. (1968). *'Genetic Mosaics'* and other essays. Harvard University Press, Cambridge, Mass.

STEVENS, J., RUBEN, L. N., LOCKWOOD, P., and ROSE, H. (1965). Implant-induced accessory limbs in urodeles: fresh, frozen and boiled tissues. *J. Morph.* **117**, 213–28.

STIRLING, R. V. and SUMMERBELL, D. (1977). The development of functional innervation in the chick wing bud following truncations and deletions of the proximo-distal axis. *J. Embryol. exp. Morph.* **41**, 189–207.

STOCUM, D. L. (1968). The urodele limb regeneration blastema: a self organising system. II. Morphogenesis and differentiation of autografted whole and fractional blastemas. *Devl. Biol.* **18**, 457–80.

———— (1975*a*). Regulation after proximal or distal transposition of limb regeneration blastemas and determination of the proximal boundary of the regenerate. *Devl. Biol.* **45**, 112–36.

———— (1975*b*). Outgrowth and pattern formation during limb ontogeny and regeneration. *Differentiation* **3**, 167–82.

———— and DEARLOVE, G. E. (1972). Epidermal–mesodermal interaction during morphogenesis of the limb regeneration blastema in larval salamanders. *J. exp. Zool.* **181**, 49–62.

STRAUS, W. H. (1946). The concept of nerve-muscle specificity. *Biol. Rev.* **21**, 75–91.

STRAZNICKY, K. (1963). Function of heterotopic spinal cord segments investigated in the chick. *Acta Biol. Hung.* **14**, 145–55.

STREETER, G. L. (1948). Developmental horizons in human embryos. Description of age groups XV, XVI, XVII, and XVIII. *Contr. Embryol. Carnegie. Inst.* **32**, 133–203.

—— (1951). Developmental horizons in human embryos. Description of age groups XIX, XX, XXI, XXII, and XXIII. *Contr. Embryol. Carnegie. Inst.* **34**, 165–96.

STRONG, L. C. (1961). The Springville mouse, further observations on a new 'luxoid' mouse. *J. Hered.* **52**, 122–4.

SULLIVAN, G. E. (1962). Anatomy and embryology of the wing musculature of the domestic fowl (*Gallus*). *Aust. J. Zool.* **10**, 458–518.

SUMMERBELL, D. (1974*a*). Interaction between the proximo-distal and antero-posterior co-ordinates of positional value during the specification of positional information in the early development of the chick limb bud. *J. Embryol. exp. Morph.* **32**, 227–37.

—— (1974*b*). A quantitative analysis of the effect of the excision of the AER from the chick limb-bud. *J. Embryol. exp. Morph.* **32**, 651–60. ,

—— (1975). Personal communication to Wolpert L. In Wolpert, L., Lewis, J., and Summerbell, D. (1975).

—— (1976). A descriptive study of the rate of elongation and differentiation of the skeleton of the developing chick wing. *J. Embryol. exp. Morph.* **35**, 241–60.

—— (1977*a*). Regulation of deficiences along the proximo-distal axis of the chick wing-bud: a quantitative analysis. *J. Embryol. exp. Morph.* **41**, 137–59.

—— (1977*b*). Reduction of the rate of growth, cell density and cell division following removal of the apical ectodermal ridge of the chick limb bud. *J. Embryol. exp. Morph.* **40**, 1–21.

—— (1979). The zone of polarising activity: evidence for a role in normal chick morphogenesis. *J. Embryol. exp. Morph* **50**, 217–33.

—— and LEWIS, J. H. (1975). Time, place and positional value in the chick limb bud. *J. Embryol. exp. Morph.* **33**, 621–43.

—— —— and WOLPERT, L. (1973). Positional information in chick limb morphogenesis. *Nature, Lond.* **224**, 492–6.

—— and TICKLE, C. (1977). Pattern formation along the antero-posterior axis of the chick limb bud. In *Vertebrate limb and somite morphogenesis,* (eds. D. A. Ede, J. R. Hinchliffe, and M. Balls), pp. 41–57. Cambridge University Press.

—— and WOLPERT, L. (1972). Cell density and cell division in the early morphogenesis of the chick wing. *Nature New Biol.* **238**, 24–6.

SWETT, F. H. (1927). Differentiation in the amphibian limb. *J. exp. Zool.* **47**, 385–432.

TABAN, C. (1955). Quelques problèmes de regénération chez les urodèles. *Rev. Suisse. Zool.* **62**, 387–468.

TARIN, D. and STURDEE, A. P. (1971). Early limb development of *Xenopus laevis. J. Embryol. exp. Morph.* **26**, 169–79.

—— —— (1973). Histochemical features of hind limb development of *Xenopus laevis. J. Anat.* **114**, 101–7.

THOMPSON, D'A. W. (1917). *On growth and form* (ed. J. T. Bonner, 1961). Cambridge University Press.

THOMSON, K. S. (1968). A critical view of the diphyletic theory of rhipidistian-amphibian relationships. In *Current problems of lower vertebrate phylogeny* (ed. T. Ørvig), pp. 285–305. Almqvist and Wiksell, Stockholm.

—— (1973). Observations on a near rhipidistian fish from the upper Devonian of Australia. *Palaeontographica,* **143**, 209–20.

THORNTON, C. S. (1942). Studies on the origin of the regenerating blastema in *Triturus viridescens. J. exp. Zool.* **89**, 375–89.

—— (1956). The relation of epidermal innervations to the regeneration of limb deplants in *Amblystoma* larvae. *J. exp. Zool.* **133**, 281–300.

—— (1957). The effect of apical cap removal on limb regeneration in *Amblystoma* larvae. *J. exp. Zool.* **134**, 357–81.

—— (1958). The inhibition of limb regeneration in urodele larvae by localised irradiation with ultraviolet light. *J. exp. Zool.* **137**, 153–75.

—— (1959). *Regeneration in vertebrates.* Chicago University Press.

—— (1968). Amphibian limb regeneration. *Adv. Morphog.* **7**, 205–49.

—— and STEEN, T. P. (1962). Eccentric blastema formation in aneurogenic limbs of *Amblystoma* larvae following epidermal cap deviation. *Devl. Biol.* **5**, 328–43.

THOROGOOD, P. V. (1972). Patterns of chondrogenesis and myogenesis in the limb buds of normal and *talpid*³ chick embryos. Ph.D. thesis. University College of Wales, Aberystwyth.

—— (1973). The appearance of muscle protein and myofibrils within the embryonic chick limb bud. *J. Embryol. exp. Morph.* **30**, 673–9.

—— and HINCHLIFFE, J. R. (1975). An analysis of the condensation process during chondrogenesis in the embryonic chick hind limb. *J. Embryol. exp. Morph.* **33**, 581–606.

TICKLE, C., SHELLSWELL, G., CRAWLEY, A., and WOLPERT, L. (1976). Positional signalling by mouse limb polarizing region in the chick wing-bud. *Nature, Lond.* **259**, 396–7.

—— SUMMERBELL, D., and WOLPERT, L. (1975). Positional signalling and specification of digits in chick limb morphogenesis. *Nature, Lond.* **254**, 199–202.

TOOLE, B. P. (1972). Hyaluronate turnover during chondrogenesis in the developing chick limb and axial skeleton. *Devl. Biol.* **29**, 321–9.

TSCHUMI, P. A. (1954). Konkurrenzbedingte Rückbildungen der Hinderextremität von *Xenopus* nach Behandlung mit einem Chloraethylamin. *Rev. suisse Zool.* **61**, 177–270.

—— (1957). The growth of the hind limb bud of *Xenopus laevis* and its dependence on the epidermis. *J. Anat.* **9**, 149–73.

TURING, A. M. (1952). The chemical basis of morphogenesis. *Phil. Trans. R. Soc. B* **237**, 37–72.

UMANSKI, E. (1937). Untersuchung des Regenerations vorganges bei Amphibien mittels Ausschaltung der einzelnen Gewebe durch Röntgenbestrahlung. (German summary.) *Biol. Zhurn. URSS* **6**, 757–8.

UNDERWOOD, G. (1976). Simplification and degeneration in the course of evolution of squamate reptiles. In *Mécanismes de la rudimentation des organes chez les embryons de vertébres*, pp. 341–52. Éditions du CNRS **266**, Paris.

VAN STONE, J. M. (1964). The relationship of nerve number to regenerative capacity in the developing hind limb of *Rana sylvatica. J. exp. Zool.*, **155**, 293–302.

VON BAER, K. E. (1828). *Über Entwichlungsgeschichte der Thiere. Beobachtung und Reflexion. I.* Gebrüder Bornträger, Königsberg.

VON JHERING, H. (1878). *Das peripherische Nervensystem der Wirbelthiere.* Leipzig.

WADDINGTON, C. H. (1962) *New patterns in genetics and development.* Columbia University Press.

WALKER, W. J. (1947). The development of the shoulder region of the turtle *Chrysemys picta marginata* with special reference to the primary musculature. *J. Morph.* 80, 195–249.

WALLACE, H., MADEN, M., and WALLACE, B. M. (1974). Participation of cartilage grafts in amphibian limb regeneration. *J. Embryol. exp. Morph.* 32, 391–404.

WARKANY, J. (1971). *Congenital malformations.* Year Book Medical Publications, Chicago.

WARWICK, R. (1973). *Gray's anatomy* (35th edn). Longman, London.

WEISS, P. (1925). Unabhängigkeit der Extremitätenregeneration von Skelett (bei *Triton cristatus*). *Wilhelm Roux. Arch. EntwMech. Org.* 104, 359–94.

—— (1927). Die Herkunft der Haut im Extremitaten-regenerat. *Wilhelm Roux Arch. EntwMech. Org.* 109, 584–610.

WELKER, H. (1878). Bau u. Entwickl. der Wirbelsäule. *Zool Anz.* 1, 291–5.

WILBY, O. K. and EDE, D. A. (1975). A model generating the pattern of cartilage skeletal elements in the embryonic chick limb. *J. theor. biol.* 52, 199–217.

—— —— (1976). Computer simulation of vertebrate limb development. In *Automata, languages, development* (eds. A. Lindenmayer, and G. Rozenberg). North Holland, Amsterdam.

WILLIAMS, J. P. G. and HUGHES, P. C. R. (1977). Hormonal regulation of post-natal limb growth in mammals. In *Vertebrate limb and somite morphogenesis,* (eds. D. A. Ede, J. R. Hinchliffe, and M. Balls), pp. 281–92. Cambridge University Press.

WITSCHI, E. (1956). *The development of vertebrates.* Saunders, Philadelphia.

WOLFF, E. (1958). Le principe de compétition. *Bull. Soc. Zool. Fr.* 83, 13–25.

—— and KAHN, J. (1947). Le régulation de l'ébauche des membres chez les oiseaux. *C.r. Séanc. Soc. Biol.* 141, 915.

—— and KIENY, M. (1962). Mise en évidence par l'irradiation aux rayons X d'un phénomène de compétition entre les ébauches du tibia et du péroné chez l'embryon de poulet. *Devl. Biol.* 4, 197–213.

WOLPERT, L. (1969). Positional information and the spatial pattern of cellular differentiation. *J. theor. Biol.* 25, 1–47.

—— (1971). Positional information and pattern formation. *Devl. Biol.* 6, 183–224.

—— (1976). Mechanisms of limb development and malformation. *Br. med. J.* 32, 65–70.

—— LEWIS, J., and SUMMERBELL, D. (1975). Morphogenesis of the vertebrate limb. In *Cell patterning.* Ciba Foundation Symposium 29, new series, pp. 95–119. Associated Scientific Publishers, Amsterdam.

WORTHAM, R. A. (1948). The development of the muscles and tendons in the lower leg and foot of chick embryos. *J. Morph.* 83, 103–48.

WRIGHT, SEWALL (1935). A mutation of the guinea pig, tending to restore the pentadactyl foot when heterozygous, producing a monstrosity when homozygous. *Genetics* 20, 84–107.

YABLOKOV, A. V. (1974). *Variability of mammals.* Amerind Publishing Co., New Delhi.

YASUDA, M. (1975). Pathogenesis of preaxial polydactyly of the hand of human embryos. *J. Embryol. exp. Morph.* 33, 745–56.

YNTEMA, C. L. (1959). Regeneration in sparsely innervated and aneurogenic fore limbs of *Amblystoma* larvae. *J. exp. Zool.* 140, 101–23.

YOUNG, J. Z. (1962). *The life of vertebrates.* Clarendon Press, Oxford.

ZWILLING, E. (1949). Role of the epithelial components in origin of wingless syndrome of chick embryos. *J. exp. Zool.* **111**, 175–87.

—— (1955). Ectoderm–mesoderm relationship in the development of the chick embryo limb bud. *J. exp. Zool.* **128**, 423–41.

—— (1956a). Interaction between limb bud ectoderm and mesoderm in the chick embryo. I. Axis establishment. *J. exp. Zool.* **132**, 157–72.

—— (1956b). Genetic mechanism in limb development. *Cold Spring Harb Symp. quant. Biol.* **21**, 349–54.

—— (1956c). Interaction between limb bud ectoderm and mesoderm in the chick embryo. IV. Experiments with a wingless mutant. *J. exp. Zool.* **132**, 241–53.

—— (1956d). Interaction between ectoderm and mesoderm in the chick embryo II. Experimental limb duplication. *J. exp. Zool.* **132**, 173–87.

—— (1959). Interaction between ectoderm and mesoderm in duck–chicken limb bud chimaeras. *J. exp. Zool.* **142**, 521–32.

—— (1961). Limb morphogenesis. *Adv. Morphog.* **1**, 301–30.

—— (1964a). Controlled degeneration during development. In *Cellular injury* (eds. A. V. S. de Reuck and J. Knight). Ciba Foundation Symposium, pp. 352–62. Churchill, London.

—— (1964b). Development of fragmented and of dissociated limb bud mesoderm. *Devl. Biol.* **9**, 20–37.

—— (1966). Cartilage formation from so called myogenic tissue of chick embryo limb buds. *Ann. Med. Exp. Biol. Fenniae.* **44**, 134–9.

—— (1968). Morphogenetic phases in development. *Devl. Biol. Suppl.* **2**, 184–207.

—— (1972). Limb morphogenesis. *Devl. Biol.* **28**, 12–17.

—— (1974). Effects of contact between mutant (wingless) limb buds and those of genetically normal chick embryos: conformation of a hypothesis. *Devl. Biol.* **39**, 37–48.

—— and AMES, J. F. (1958). Polydactyly, related effects and axial shifts – a critique. *Am. Nat.* **92**, 257–66.

—— and HANSBOROUGH, L. A. (1956). Interaction between limb bud ectoderm and mesoderm in the chick embryo. III. Experiments with polydactylous limbs. *J. exp. Zool.* **132**, 219–39.

Author index

Subject index

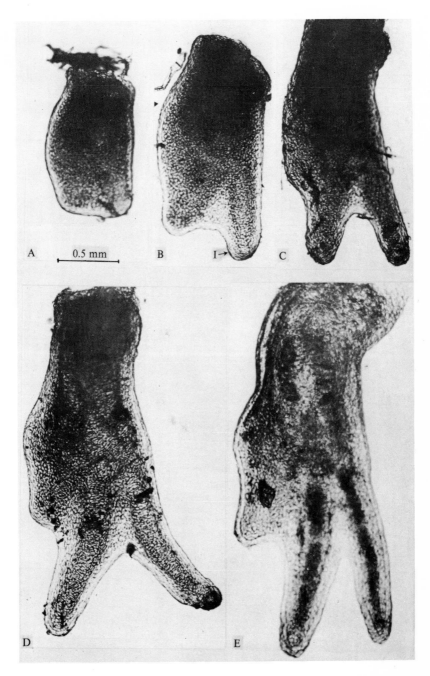

PLATE 1. Forelimb development in the axolotl. Note that the digits, unlike those of amniotes, are formed in sequence, starting with the first (digit 1). Eventually, four digits are formed. Stages are equivalent to those described by Hamburger for *Ambystoma punctatum*. A, stage 40; B, 41/2; C, 43; D, 44; E, 45.

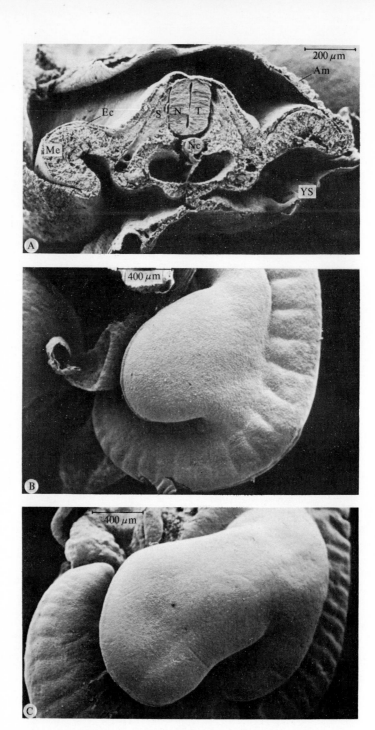

PLATE 2. Scanning electron micrographs showing the morphology of the chick limb bud. A, transverse section through a stage 18 embryo at wing bud level; B, stage 22 hindlimb bud; C, stage 25 hindlimb bud: note that the digital plate is demarcated and is wider than the zeugopod. There is a groove between digits 3 and 4. Am = amnion; Ec = ectoderm; Me = mesoderm; Nc = notochord; NT = neural tube; S = somites; YS = yolk sac splanchnopleure. (Courtesy of J. Hurle.)

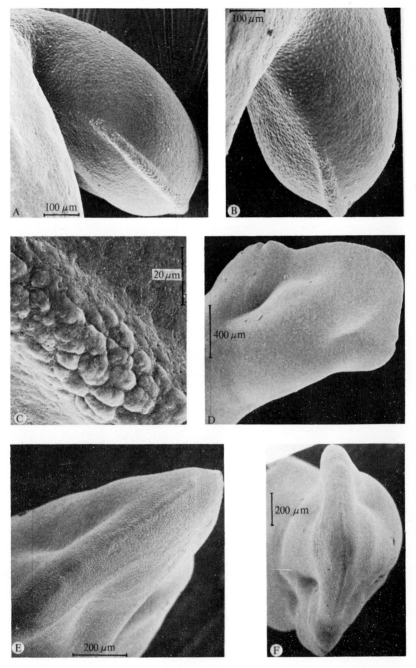

PLATE 3. Scanning electron micrographs illustrating chick forelimb development. A and B, stage 23, anterior and posterior views. The prominent AER is
shown in more detail in C. D–F, stage 30; D, dorsal view, E, posterior aspect,
and F, end on view. The AER is now restricted to the apex of the central (third)
digit.

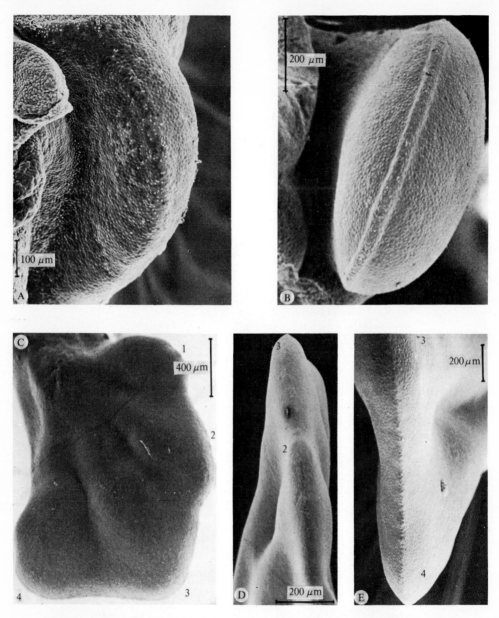

PLATE 4. Scanning electron micrographs illustrating chick hindlimb development. The pre-axial side of the bud is towards the top of the figure. A, first
appearance of the ridge in a stage 19 leg bud; B, stage 24 leg bud viewed end on
at the time of maximum elevation of the ridge; C–E, stage 31 leg, with digits
1–4. C, ventral view; D, digits 2 and 3 over which the ridge has regressed. The
ridge is still prominent over digit 4 (E).

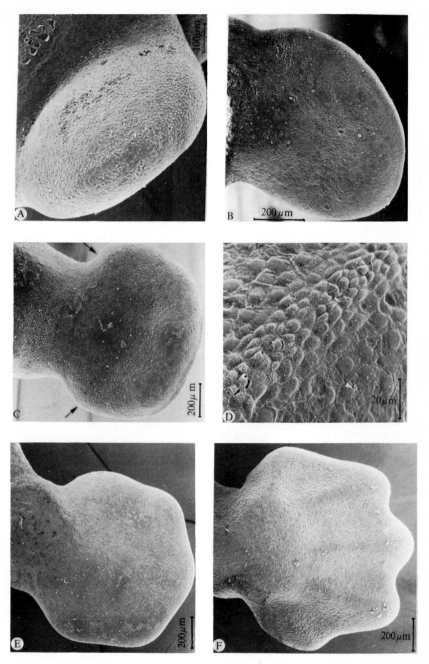

PLATE 5. Scanning electron micrographs illustrating mouse forelimb development. The pre-axial side of the bud is towards the top of the plate. All views are ventral. The AER is less prominent than in the chick. A, 10.5 days, B, 11.5 days, C, 12.5 days, with detail of AER (D). Note the ridge (between arrows) is much longer than in the chick. E, 12.75 days, F, 13.5 days. The five digital rays are now clearly defined (courtesy of D. S. Dawd).

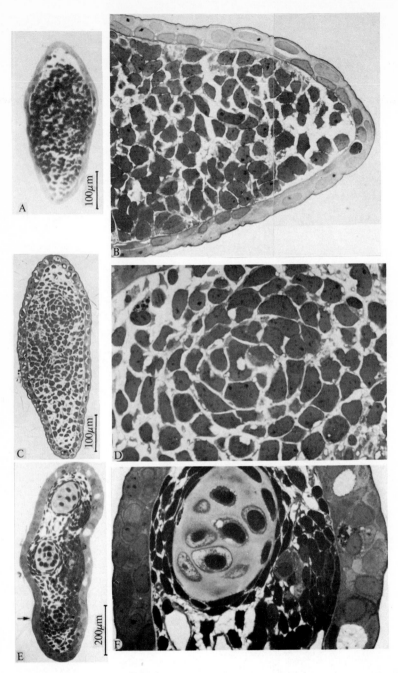

PLATE 6. Chondrogenesis in Axolotl forelimb as seen in transverse semi-thin sections stained with toluidine blue. A and B, Hamburger, stage 40: the prospective digit is filled with a loose network of mesenchyme. C and D, stage 41: the condensation phase. Note the closely packed central cells, surrounded by cells whose long axis is tangential. E and F, stage 45: the digit 1 cartilage 'model' is composed of chondrocytes surrounded by matrix; and is itself surrounded by perichondrial cells. Digit 3 (arrow) is condensing.

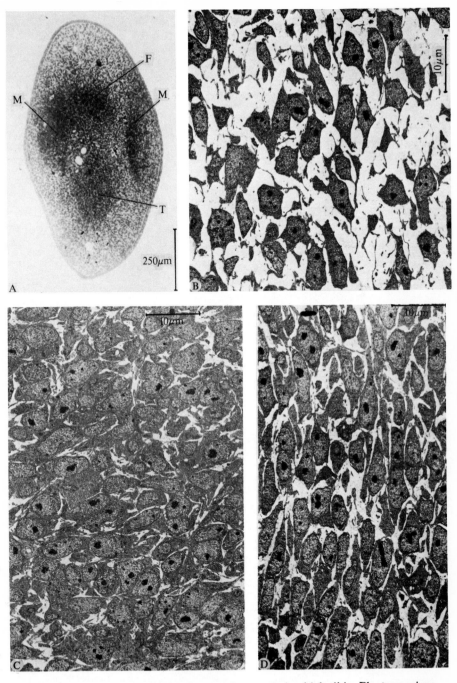

PLATE 7. The process of chondrogenesis as seen in chick tibia. Electron micrographs were prepared using double fixation (the glutaraldehyde–osmium tetroxide method: Thorogood and Hinchliffe 1975). A, transverse light microscope section of stage 26 hindlimb showing arrangement of skeletal condensations (F = fibula, T = tibia) and muscle blocks (= M). B, electron micrograph of undifferentiated mesenchyme. C. electron micrograph of the area of condensation (distal). D, longitudinal section through the more advanced (central) region of the stage 26 tibia showing the characteristic cell orientation at right angles to the long axis of the skeletal rudiment.

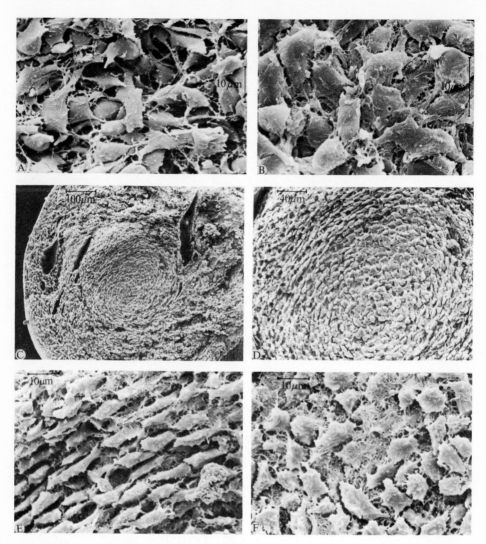

PLATE 8. Scanning electron micrographs illustrating the process of chondro-genesis in the chick limb. A, undifferentiated limb bud mesenchyme from the distal part of a stage 18 wing bud. Note long filopodia and extensive intercellular spaces. B, pre-cartilaginous condensation phase of a stage 24 tibia. The cells show extensive contacts and there is little intercellular space. C–F, transverse section of a stage 24 humerus in an early stage of chondrogenesis. C, low power; D, detail of the transected humerus. Note the 'whorling' of the peripheral cells shown in more detail in E. Centrally, the flattened chondroblasts with scalloped edges are already separated by the accumulating meshwork of intercellular material (F).

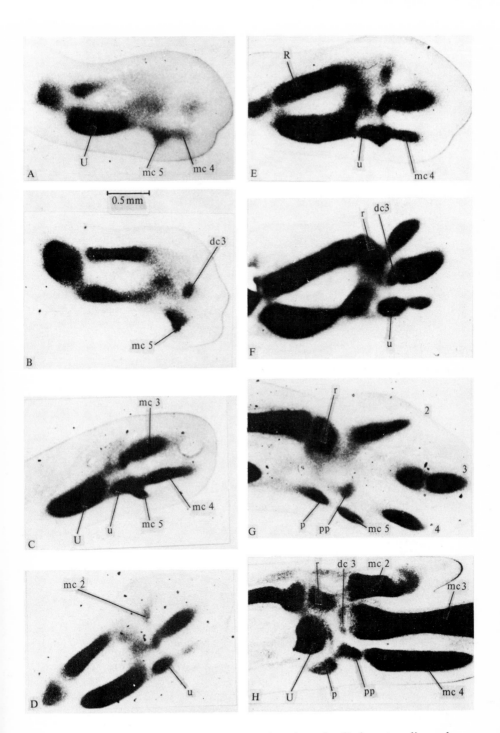

PLATE 9. The chondrogenic pattern in chick embryo forelimb: autoradiographs of $^{35}SO_4^{2-}$ uptake into chondroitin sulphate. Note that in the earlier pre-chondrogenic stages there is precisely the same number of condensations as in later chondrogenic 'models'. A, stage 27; B, stage 27/8; C and D, stage 28; E, stage 28/9; F, stage 29/30; G, ventral aspect of stage 30; H, stage 34. dc = distal carpal 3; mc = metacarpals; p = pisiform; pp = pisiform process; R = radius; r = radiale; U = ulna; u = ulnare.

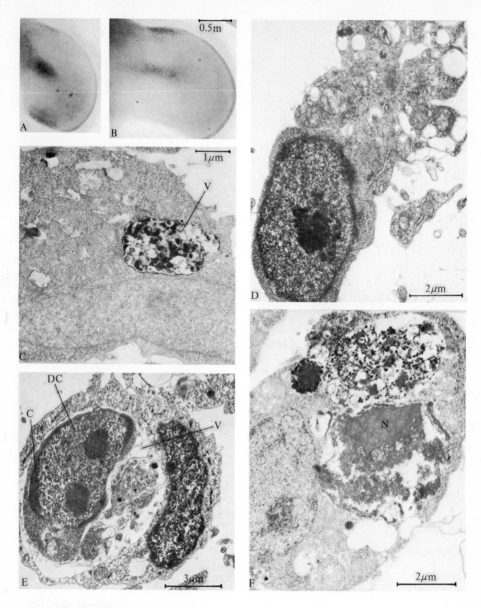

PLATE 10. Cell death in the chick wing bud. A and B, vitally stained wing buds at stages 23/4 and 25. C–F, electron micrographs of cell death in the wing bud PNZ. In C, the cell contains an autophagic vacuole (V), positive for acid phosphatase (black). This is the first sign of deterioration of an otherwise unchanged, apparently viable cell. D, dying cell; note nucleus surrounded by relatively unchanged cytoplasm, while vacuolated cytoplasm is in process of being shed. E, a dead cell (DC) is phagocytosed by a viable neighbour which has formed a vacuole (V) and would normally transform into a macrophage; note the chromatin condensation (C) of the dead cell nucleus. F, mature macrophage, containing several heterophagic vacuoles, one of which is strongly acid phosphatase positive (black), and nuclear material from a dead cell (N).

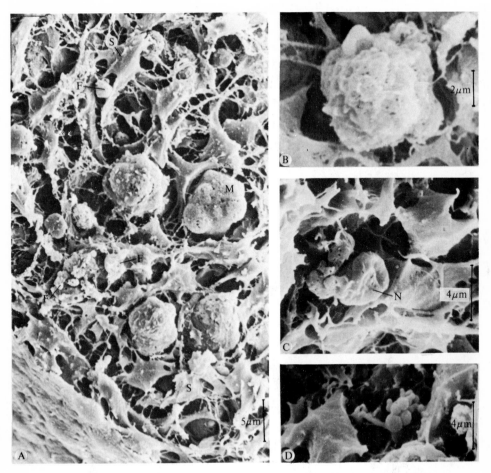

PLATE 11. Scanning electron micrograph survey of the chick wing bud PNZ. A, panoramic view of PNZ; note stellate mesenchymal cells (S), dead cell fragments (F), and macrophages (M). B, macrophage; C and D, fragmenting cells. Note the presence of a large rounded protrusion, probably the nuclear fragment (N), and some smaller pieces with holes in the surface in C.

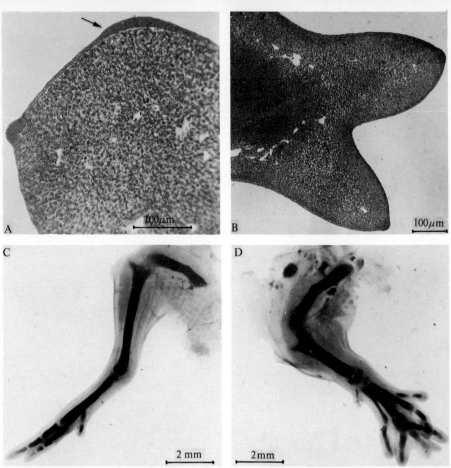

PLATE 12. In the *eudiplopodia* mutant of the chick two AERs form two rows of digits. A, section of a stage 24 mutant hindlimb bud. The arrow indicates the second AER. B, section of a stage 27 mutant hindlimb bud. Note the two axes of mesodermal outgrowth, each capped by an AER. C, normal and D, mutant 9.5-day embryonic hindlimbs. (Courtesy of P. Goetinck.)

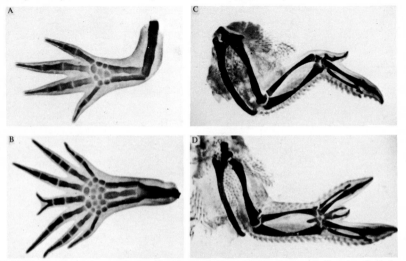

PLATE 13. Experimental duplication of the chick wing and the Axolotl fore-limb. Duplication has been achieved by grafting a flank region anterior to the prospective axolotl limb (Slack) or by grafting a ZPA into the pre-axial margin of a chick wing bud. A, normal and B, duplicated axolotl limbs; C, normal and D, duplicated chick wing. See text for further details. (Courtesy of J. Slack and C. Tickle.)